VIOLENCE

WORK

MICOL SEIGEL

VIOLENCE

WORK

STATE POWER *and the* LIMITS OF POLICE

DUKE UNIVERSITY PRESS | *Durham & London* | 2018

© 2018 Duke University Press
Printed in the United States of America on acid-free paper ∞
Designed by Matthew Tauch
Typeset in Minion Pro by Westchester Publishing Services

Library of Congress Cataloging-in-Publication Data
Names: Seigel, Micol, [date] author.
Title: Violence work : state power and the limits of police /
Micol Seigel.
Description: Durham : Duke University Press, 2018. |
Includes bibliographical references and index.
Identifiers: LCCN 2018002260 (print) |
LCCN 2018008083 (ebook)
ISBN 9781478002024 (ebook)
ISBN 9781478000020 (hardcover : alk. paper)
ISBN 9781478000174 (pbk. : alk. paper)
Subjects: LCSH: United States. Agency for International
Development. Office of Public Safety. | Police brutality—
United States. | Police training—United States. |
State-sponsored terrorism—United States.
Classification: LCC HV8141 (ebook) | LCC HV8141 .S386
2018 (print) | DDC 363.2/20973—dc23
LC record available at https://lccn.loc.gov/2018002260

Cover art: Koen Lybaert, *Deep blue I [Abstract N°2143]*.
Courtesy of the artist and Esther Santoyo Gallery.

CONTENTS

ACKNOWLEDGMENTS

Thank you, world, for the incredible privilege of writing this book, and all the conversations and relationships that seeded it and that it enabled.

For those vital engagements, thanks to so many brilliant friends and colleagues. First Stuart Schrader, who shared critical resources early on and generative insights all along the way, and whose forthcoming book will be the field-anchoring account of the transnational circulation of US policing in the early Cold War period. Next Martha Huggins, whose scrupulous *Political Policing* was indispensable, and who received me in her New Orleans home, guiding me at a crucial early moment; A. Naomi Paik, whose thorough and challenging review made this a vastly better book; and Gisela Fosado, Lydia Rose Rappoport-Hankins, and Maryam Arain at Duke University Press for wonderfully supportive shepherding through the publication process. Thanks also to the two anonymous press reviewers, and to the friends and colleagues who read sections or the entire object and offered invaluable feedback: Shana Agid, Ethan Blue, Melissa Burch, Alex Chambers, Giselle Cunanan, Keith Feldman, Ilana Gershon, Craig Gilmore, Kelly Lytle Hernandez, Nzingha Kendall, Dana Logan, Stephanie Kane, Courtney Mitchel, Margaret Power, Caitlin Reynolds, Jayn Rosenfeld (my mom), Peter Winn, Marilyn Young, Sarah Zanti, and Elana Zilberg.

To friends and colleagues in Indiana, my everyday lifelines, who heard chapters, read pieces, critiqued, and generously worked through knots: Marlon Bailey, Purnima Bose, Claudia Breger, Stephanie DeBoer, David Fisher, Lessie Jo Frazier, Walter Gantz, Ross Gay, Ilana Gershon,

Jeff Gould, Mary Gray, Shane Greene, Rae Greiner, Karen Inouye, Danny James, Colin Johnson, Eileen Julien, LaMonda Horton-Stallings, Kelsey Kauffman, Rebecca Lave, Susan Lepselter, Alex Lichtenstein, Ed Linenthal, Eden Medina, Marissa Moorman, Michelle Moyd, Khalil Muhammad, Maritza Quiñones, Ben Robinson, Susan Seizer, and Shane Vogel. To the IU American Studies community, especially my most enduring and satisfying intellectual interlocutors, graduate standouts Alex Chambers, Giselle Cunanan, Nzingha Kendall, Dana Logan, Courtney Mitchel, Rudo Mudiwa and Caitlin Reynolds, and former Inside-Out students Jarrod Wall, Michelle Jones and Anastasia Schmid. To the undergraduate students who have accompanied the Inside-Out Prison Exchange Program, inside and out, too many to list by name, I treasure you; you push my thinking about police and punishment in unexpected directions. To my fellow local organizers, indispensable to sustaining my energy and faith in the possibility of change, especially stalwarts Chris Abert, Bob Arnove, Mia Beach, Lindsey Badger, Ryan Conway, Hugh Farrell, Nick Greven, Sam Harrell, Megan Hutchison, James Kilgore, Erin Marshall, Bryce Martin, Bill Mullen, Willy Palomo, Lauren Taylor, and Judah Schept.

To my colleagues in the Critical Prison Studies caucus of the ASA, source of my most relevant and insistent academic engagements over the last half-dozen years: Shana Agid, Dan Berger, Lisa Bhungalia, Ethan Blue, Melissa Burch, Jordan Camp, Dan Chard, Simone Davis, Keith Feldman, Craig Gilmore, Ruthie Gilmore, Alan Eladio Gómez, Sarah Haley, Michael Hames-Garcia, Zoe Hammer, Christina Hanhardt, Gillian Harkins, Christina Heatherton, Rebecca Hill, David Hernández, Kelly Lytle Hernández, Kerwin Kaye, Marisol LeBron, Sonia Lee, Laura Liu, Jenna Loyd, Erica Meiners, Anoop Mirpuri, Naomi Murakawa, Jack Norton, Sujani Reddy, Dylan Rodriguez, Judah Schept, Rob Scott, Stuart Schrader, Rashad Shabazz, Dean Spade, Tamara Spira, Eric Stanley, David Stein, Brett Story, Heather Thompson, Emily Thuma, Lucia Trimbur, Elissa Underwood, and Tryon Woods.

To the participants in the always-provocative Tepoztlán Institute for the Transnational History of the Americas, especially those who engaged me on the subject of this book in 2011 and 2014: Marisa Belausteguigoitia, Devyn Benson, Ben Cowan, Reiko Hillyer, Bethany Moreton, Tore Olssen, Osmundo Pinho, Alexandra Puerto, William Robinson, Christy Thornton, Sarah Townsend, Pam Voeckel, Karl Swinehart, Dillon Vrana, Adam Warren, and Elliott Young.

To friends and colleagues who sent along sources or leads: Lindsey Badger, Melissa Burch, Beth Baker-Cristales, Purnima Bose, Michelle Brown, Rosie Bsheer, Jordan Camp, Brooke Campbell, Amy Chazkel, Julia Foulkes, Lessie Jo Frazier, Craig Gilmore, Ruthie Gilmore, Adam Goodman, Nick Greven, Matthew Guterl, Paul Kramer, Alex Lichtenstein, Jenna Loyd, Matthew Mitchelson, Tore Olssen, A. Naomi Paik, Tonia Poteat, Alexandra Puerto, Rosenilda Sant'anna, Judah Schept, Stuart Schraeder, Giovanna Shay, and Shane White. To scholars whose work has guided me in particularly useful directions: Lisa Marie Cacho, Angela Davis, Colin Dayan, Edward Escobar, Denise Ferreira da Silva, Ruthie Gilmore, Avery Gordon, Joy James, Julilly Kohler-Hausmann, Paul Kramer, Jeremy Kuzmarov, Alfred McCoy, Fred Moten, A. Naomi Paik, Lorna Rhodes, Dylan Rodriguez, Stuart Schrader, Bryan Wagner, Brackette Williams, Clyde Woods, Marilyn Young, and Elana Zilberg. To James Woodard, who suggested I consider OPS (at an AHA cocktail party, of course), to David Sartorius for housing me in DC during an early moment of research and to Shana Agid, whose reaction to my title made me realize that it was the right one. To Andrew Friedman for generous consultation and reflection on the question of anonymity and consent; to Paul Amar for guidance on Saudi Arabia; to Marilyn Young for challenging me to rethink oral histories, with sorrow at her passing; to Ashley Hunt for making art about disaster. To my fellow writers who made a pair of week-long summer retreats not just productive but completely fun: Claudia Breger, Myrna Garcia, Rae Greiner, A. Naomi Paik, Lucinda Ramberg, Susan Seizer, and Felicia Y. Thomas.

To organizers and respondents at a series of much-appreciated talks and conferences: Rosie Bsheer and Charlotte Kiechel at the Yale International History Workshop, October 2017; Elizabeth Hinton, Lisa McGirr, and my fellow fellows at the Warren Center seminar in fall of 2017; Michelle Brown, Tony Platt, and Judah Schept at *New Directions in Critical Criminology*, University of Tennessee, Knoxville, 2016; Josh Lund, Anne Garland Mahler, and Brackette Williams at *Men with Guns: Cultures of Paramilitarism and the Modern Americas*, University of Arizona, 2015; Nick Greven at *Drug War Capitalism*, Indiana University, 2015; Rhys Machold, Brendan McQuade, and Mark Neocleous at *Police Science for the Twenty-First Century*, Carleton University, Ottowa, 2015; Majed Akhter, Ishan Ashotush, Hamid Ekbia, Mark Neocleous, and Tyler Wall at *Reconfiguring Global Space: The Geography, Politics, and Ethics of Drone War*, Indiana University, Bloomington, 2015; Bree Carlton and Sharon Pickering at the Criminology Seminar Series, Monash

University, Melbourne, 2014; David Charles Goodman at the School of Historical and Philosophical Studies, University of Melbourne, 2014; Ethan Blue at the Perth USAsia Studies Centre's *Security Across Colonial Spheres: Policing Indigeneity, Citizenship, Alienage, and Criminality*, University of Western Australia, Perth, 2014; Thomas Jessen Adams, Frances Clarke, Miranda Johnson, Brendon O'Connor, Rebecca Sheehan, and Shane White at the *History on Mondays* seminar series, Department of History, University of Sydney, 2014; Gillian Cowlishaw and Luis Angosto Ferrandez at the Anthropology Seminar Series, University of Sydney, 2014; Lisa Guenther, Melissa Burch, Laura McTighe, Mercy Romero, Judah Schept, and Brett Story at *Rethinking Prisons*, Vanderbilt University, Nashville, 2013; Chris Garces and Lucinda Ramberg at the Latin American Studies Program Spring lecture series, Cornell University, Ithaca, 2013; Kathleen Belew at *Histories of Violence*, Northwestern University, Evanston, 2013; Suvir Kaul and David Kazanjian at *Transnationalism: A Useful Category of Analysis?*, University of Pennsylvania, Philadelphia, 2012; Judit Bodnar and Tatiana Matejskova at *Competing and Complementary Visions of the Social: History, Sociology, Anthropology*, Central European University, Budapest, 2011; and Alexander Dawson and Timo Schaefer at the UBC-CIPO (Consejo Indigena Popular de Oaxaca) roundtable "Democracy at Gunpoint: Violence and Politics in Contemporary Latin America," University of British Columbia, Vancouver, 2011.

For material support, thanks to the Charles Warren Center for Studies in American History at Harvard; the United States Studies Center at the University of Sydney; the American Council of Learned Societies; the IU Bloomington College Arts and Humanities Institute for supporting a workshop (and my co-organizers in that effort, Michelle Brown, Khalil Muhammad, and Judah Schept); the New Frontiers in the Arts and Humanities program of the IUB Office of the Vice Provost for Research; the IUB Office of the Vice Provost for International Affairs; and IU's Center for Latin American and Caribbean Studies.

To all the dedicated and skilled librarians and archivists who helped me get a handle on this unwieldy subject: Kate Doyle and Jesse Franzblau of the National Security Archive; Michele Welsing and Yusef Omowale of the Southern California Library; staff at NARA including Michael F. Knight, Head of Research, Joseph Schwarz, Civil Reference, David A. Langbart, Textual Records Division, and Amy Reytar, Reference Archives II Branch. To Jay Jones, city archivist, Los Angeles City Archives; Todd Gaydowski, records management officer, Los Angeles City Clerk's Office; Amanda DeFlorio, San Antonio City Archives; Donna Guerra, city archivist, San Antonio; Matt De Waelsche, archivist, Texana/Genealogy Department, San Antonio Public Library; Julia Goldberg, editor, the *Santa Fe Reporter*; Monica Blank, archivist, Rockefeller Archive Center; lieutenant Troy S. McElfresh, assistant section commander, Indiana State Police Public Information Office; Greg Mobley, archives specialist, IUPUI University Archives, Ruth Lilly Special Collections and Archive; and Ashley Ames Ahlbrand, educational technology and reference librarian, Indiana University Maurer School of Law. At Indiana University's Wells Library, gratitude to Linda Kelsey, reference and collections associate, government information; Lou Malcomb, documents librarian; Carrie Schwier, assistant archivist, Office of University Archives and Records Management; and the librarians at IUB responsible for receiving the *Newsletters*: Angela Courtney, Celestina Savonius-Wroth, and Nazareth Pantaloni III.

To the former members of the Office of Public Safety who yearn so deeply for their story to be told, with apologies reiterated once again that this is not that story; particular gratitude to those who were willing to recollect and muse with me in interviews: "Ned Antonik" (a pseudonym), Andrew Best, Jr., Richard Burton, Jan Carnahan, "Midge Good" (pseudonym), Morris Grodsky, Michael Harpold, and Al Turner; to those who granted permission to use images from their collection: Mike Harpold, Michael Truong, Charlie Vann, and John Weiss; and to those who sent me materials, particularly Andy Best, S. A. Bordenkircher on behalf of D. E. Bordenkircher, Mike Harpold, and Walter Kreutzer, who sent me his near-complete cache of *Newsletters*. Mr. Kreutzer's files will be the basis of the collection housed in Indiana University's research library system.

To Seth Fein, Julia Foulkes, Tonia Poteat, and Claudia, Jenna, Lucy, M'liss, M'riss, Steph, and the Susans for fierce and constant friendship and because I can't fit you into nearly enough other categories. To my parents for their inspiring curiosity as they push into new reaches of life, and a blessedly dependable soft landing. To my sister for braving challenges that would flatten a mere mortal. Finally, to Sarah Zanti, for pushing me to smooth my presence in the world while still believing unabashedly in my ability to change it.

Policing and State Power

... not all that is policing lies in the police.

—ROBERT REINER, *The Politics of the Police* (1984)

The controversy that has erupted since the police shooting of Michael Brown in Ferguson, Missouri, in 2014, bringing forth the Movement for Black Lives, marks ours as one of those moments unusually resonant with the past. The strikingly visible racial violence, great protest against it, and the gathering storm clouds of reaction recall not only the passage from Reconstruction to Redemption in the US South after the Civil War but also the 1960s and 1970s with their all-too-similar pattern of racist state violence rising to public view, protest and hopefulness about reform, and visceral, reactionary retrenchment.

The devastating lessons of those two periods are particularly important to remember. In the 1870s and 1880s, Redemption fed an early expansion of the US prison system, infinitesimal prior to the Civil War. The labor systems of convict leasing and the chain gang were developed to fit the country's agricultural and industrial economy, anchoring formal racial segregation along with state-sanctioned terror in the form of lynching. The 1960s and 1970s expanded that long historical undercurrent into the scaffolding of the current criminal justice system, that brutally sturdy cornerstone of Black and brown people's differential vulnerability to premature death, this time organized to warehouse and to idle a workforce no longer needed in the globalized service economy.[1] If we let history repeat itself again, these are the prospects we face.

The early period may be too different from our own to provide guidance for policy, but the 1960s and 1970s are starkly relevant. Police violence was especially important in the 1960s as catalyst to the urban uprisings that spread across the nation between 1964 and 1967. It was often an incident of police abuse of an African American city dweller that sparked the fires.[2] The ways people framed the problems and the solutions they devised echo eerily through contemporary debates about police racism, excessive use of force, brutality, militarization, and community relations.

Protestors in the 1960s and 1970s decried racist police and their brutal treatment of citizens. They denounced the dramatic rise they saw in Black civilian deaths at the hands of police and the great disparity of police-caused Black death—a rate consistently nine times greater than for whites.[3] They picketed the meetings of the International Association of Chiefs of Police, with "its displays of military hardware," insisting that there could be "no answers for crime when justice on the street comes in the form of beatings, harassment, arrests and murder."[4] They pointed out what they called even then the "militarization" of police, charging that in black areas, cops "view each person on the streets as a potential criminal or enemy, and all too often that attitude is reciprocated."[5] Black police officers got involved, calling for communication among black police executives, increasing the number of black police, sensitizing police to the problems of the black community, and confronting racism in criminal justice.[6] They argued for community policing, police-community approximation, police sensitivity trainings, modern technology to remove the opportunity for bias, officer accountability, citizen review boards, and greater police education.[7] Others indicted the "'bad apple' theory of police misconduct," urging instead a structural analysis of state violence overall in relation to political economy.[8] Many protestors today believe that their protests or reform ideas are new; we must remind each other that they are not.[9]

Civil rights–era activists got some of what they wanted. Government bodies, compelled to focus on police, "in part by widespread community outrage over police practices in the ghettos and barrios," sat up, took note, and made changes. Alas, as we now know with hindsight's perfect vision, the "reforms" they adopted were worse than inadequate. Public outrage was channeled into the narrowest options, "transformed into technocratic concerns about organizational structure and administrative policies" that would not touch the root causes of police racism.[10] These were in many cases the same police reform proposals offered fifty years prior to *that*: professionalize, remove political influence, raise standards, apply modern management techniques.[11] Hopes for "community policing" were particularly high, and therefore crashed especially hard.[12] Policing is at least as lethal as it has ever been, markedly in tandem with the prison system it justifies and feeds.[13]

Given the staggering, historically unprecedented numbers of Americans in prison, there should be no place to go but up. We should be at rock bottom. Yet there is something unique about our moment that augurs even worse. In both of the historical periods that ours evokes, reaction followed the abolition of a great evil: slavery first, and, a century later, Jim Crow segregation. This time we are perched on the edge of reaction without having abolished anything. Mainstream politicians were only just beginning even to *talk* about confronting mass incarceration prior to the 2016 presidential election, and even if such talk continues, existing proposals for shrinking it are tiny, partial, or end up actually feeding the system—"thinning the mesh and widening the net," as Stan Cohen already understood back in 1979.[14]

This kind of reform is not an improvement. But that is what most current proposals for police reform are. Calls for police diversity training, the hiring of officers of color, police body cameras, oversight, accountability, community policing, police-community approximation, police education, and so on all sound an uncanny echo. Like their 1970s predecessors, they will expand and relegitimate the police, and could justify another exponential increase of the number of people under state surveillance and control. It is clearly time to do something different.

A growing number of people think that policing cannot be reformed but only diminished—that the best way to decrease police abuse is to give police the smallest possible role in social life. Calls to defund, disarm, shrink, and even abolish the police are increasingly common.[15] More and more people are realizing that the problem is not individual bad apples or incidental racism or violence, but police, period. As Bryan Wagner has put it, "It's not racial profiling, or police brutality; it's that there is 'police' power functioning in this encounter" at all.[16]

Part of what prevents a critical mass from coming to embrace this position involves a failure to understand what policing actually is and why people grant it such latitude. What is police power? What are police? Why does it so fundamentally appeal? "Police" is one of the least theorized, most neglected concepts in the lexicon of reformers and activists today. Historians haven't helped.

Historians of the US police have mostly focused on uniformed local police departments. A wave of police history inspired by 1960s and 1970s urban unrest and activism was followed by a turn away, as the conditions that fostered interest in the police also contained the seeds of approaches that would lead historians elsewhere.[17] Social, labor, and ethnic historians, for example, found police less compelling as historical subjects than the people they policed, while for Foucauldians, police were less the point than the laws they applied. Many scholars therefore shifted over to pursue the history of crime rather than police, or of subgroups of police, or of policed populations.[18]

History as a field has also been distracted from the police power by its relative disinterest in theorizing the state. Even friendly observers charge the discipline with "not writing about the state at all," making it "invisible," engaging with it in practice but not approaching it conceptually, and generally evincing reluctance to theorize macrolevel concepts.[19] This reluctance was enhanced in the 1980s by a humanities-wide turn from states to nations and nationalism, and due to some of the same factors pulling historians away from the police: ongoing interest in writing "history from below" and Foucault's injunction to follow capillary power, which inspired wonderfully sophisticated analyses but led historians away from the formal channels of administrative power.[20]

With historians of the police otherwise occupied, much more work on police is produced in the social science fields related to criminal justice, which have been prolific in considering the question. This research is often applied and explicitly reformist, produced in close collaboration with current police officers and contemptuous of scholars removed from the spheres of police action. There the concept is defined as narrowly as possible. Police scholars' "'obsessive preoccupation with the study of public police personnel' . . . insists on identifying contemporary policing with 'the police,'" writes one critic; the field excludes "a vast area of policing . . . from the ambit of 'police studies,'" notes another.[21] The concept of police has been "relegated to the backwater of 'police studies,'" stuck in criminology where no one tries to make sense of the concept itself, "having encouraged the view that policing, like the criminal law of which it is supposedly part, is no more and no less than a set of instruments to manage something called crime."[22]

Against this body of scholarship, an alternative thrives. It is anchored by the indispensable *Policing the Crisis: Mugging, the State, and Law and Order* (1978). In this groundbreaking book, Stuart Hall, Chas Critcher, Tony Jefferson, John Clarke, and Brian Roberts analyzed the moral panic over "mugging" in Britain in the 1970s, refusing the common sense linking police to safety and pointing out not only that police do not protect all people but that they function to structure and amplify violence, as in the affirmative groundwork they lay to create crime waves and feed "law and order" panics.[23] In the conversation *Policing the Crisis* defines, scholars refute the branches or bases of the popular narrative based on the partiality of the police, their colonial, not metropolitan roots, including the importance of the US slave South in developing the patrol model, the erasure of racism from this rosy-tinted history, the absence of relationship between policing and crime reduction, and more.[24] Today a burgeoning body of tremendously powerful work on policing is emergent.[25] It is in dialogue with and in debt to the range of insightful work now being elaborated in the interdisciplinary field of critical prison studies (a subfield or cofield of critical ethnic studies), where *Violence Work* hopes to belong.[26]

These radical traditions, however, have not made much headway against the densely woven skeins of mainstream scholarship about policing. The dominant narrative of police history is still profoundly conservative and quiescent. It is an apology, produced by pro-police narrators, a tale of noble origins and ever-improving professionalization. It hearkens back to Sir Robert Peel's London Metropolitan Police, corps of the benevolent "Bobby" of 1829. Cities such as Boston, Philadelphia, and New York created these London-style police departments, or so goes the tale, driven by the pressures of crime due to immigration and urbanization, drawing on working-class ethnics and with an emphasis on social service provision. Overpoliticization prevented these forces from implementing best practices in the nineteenth century, unfortunately, but fortunately anticorruption measures and management reforms followed in the Progressive Era. Community policing and other innovations arrived in the 1960s and through the 1980s.[27]

This simplistic narrative leaves us with few analytic tools to challenge the idea of police. Even people who decry police abuses rarely interrogate the idea of police itself, allowing the image of the blue-clad officer of the peace to serve as definitional end point. A "common sense" prevails in the way Gramsci understood it, producing a deep fog.[28] "When people are called upon to explain on what terms and to what ends the police service is furnished they are unable to go beyond the most superficial and misleading commonplace."[29]

Perhaps this explains why such enthusiasm met Foucault's invitation to treat "police" as a verb and to analyze the ways in which policing suffuses the flesh of the collective, with many people taking on parts of the task of enforcing social norms. While astute in its understanding of the process of building hegemony, that kind of thinking turns away from the actual police. It proffers a slippery slope in which everyone along the famous "disciplinary continuum," on out to the local kindergarten teacher, would be included. This dilemma of definition casts the would-be student of police back and forth between unhelpful extremes: between the most limited definition of uniformed public police and the most expansive Foucauldian one, between the most restricted conceptualization of police work as crime fighting and the broadest as the keeping of public order. It leaves us disputing only superficial aspects of police practice, never taking up our assumptions about what police are or what they do, foreclosing challenge to the legitimacy of the police in a democracy.

Such a challenge is daunting, for the myths that legitimize police in a democracy are myriad. There are those that rely on a dichotomy between good and bad police (police are independent of the market except when corrupt, police are benign when behaving themselves), and others that back the populace into postures of grateful deference (police are public servants; their work is terribly dangerous). These self-evident alibis for superficial reform are fairly easily dismissed. The former are individualizing denials; the latter are savior fantasies. As for the nobility conferred by a willing assumption of risk, well, in the eye of the beholder, risk tends to loom. Federal occupational health statistics show police work to be relatively safe, nowhere near the top three fatality-prone occupations: agriculture, transportation, and mining. Police aren't even the occupation most at risk of violent death. That honor falls to "first-line supervisors of retail sales workers."[30]

Other myths, more potent because more complex, revolve around concepts of safety or security (police keep us "safe" or are anchors of public "security"), or take the concepts of legality and its inverse, criminality, as transparent (police uphold the law, police fight crime). Refuting these, activists challenge people to explore "what really makes you feel safe?" and political theorists deconstruct the notion of "security."[31] Criminologists point out that law and crime are deeply contingent, reflecting the biases of the time and the need to maintain social control, and challenge the unthinking equation of "harm" and "crime" by pointing out the intense harm done by actions never designated "crime" such as war, pollution, or systemic medical neglect.[32] These dual challenges render "crime" conceptually incoherent. It certainly survives as a category of experience for participants or police, but critical thinkers cannot maintain it as a category of analysis.

Crime is probably the most important myth legitimizing the police, so it is worth noting that even as a category of experience, police actually spend quite a small amount of their time dealing with what they call crime. As researchers and practitioners alike acknowledge, crime-related tasks are a tiny portion of a police officer's daily labor. "One of the earliest findings of sociological research on policing, replicated time and time again over the last fifty years, is that—contrary to popular images—most police work does not involve crime or at any rate law enforcement."[33] Instead "the overwhelming majority of calls for police assistance are service rather than crime related."[34] There is a mass of research showing that

> criminal law enforcement is something that most police officers do with the frequency located somewhere between virtually never and very rarely. . . . That less than a third of time spent on duty is on crime-related work; that approximately eight out of ten incidents handled by patrols by a range of different police departments are regarded by the police themselves as non-criminal matters; that the percentage of police effort devoted to traditional criminal law matters probably does not exceed 10 per cent; that as little as 6 per cent of a patrol officer's time is spent on incidents finally defined as "criminal."[35]

The things police do that do not have to do with "crime" could—and should—be done by other bodies: social workers, EMTs, fire fighters, traffic directors, garbage collectors, counselors, neighborhood associations, friends, and so on. That, not so incidentally, is the core of a practical, stepwise process of police abolition: begin to give to nonviolent agencies, piece by piece, the tasks currently allocated to men and women in blue.

Many people understand that police do lots of things that seem beyond their core role. These days it's not uncommon to hear people complain that police have taken on too much; they have assumed tasks that were never imagined as their purview.[36] It is certainly true that the United States in the last forty years has defunded every conceivable social program from health care to education to housing and shunted the money into the dismal nonsolution of the criminal justice system.[37] Yet to say that *anything* falls outside police purview is to get policing wrong in principle. The reason police do so much extraneous *stuff* is that police power is fundamentally malleable, open in both theory and practice. This is strikingly evident in the juridical traditions of law and political philosophy, where the police power is formulated as an empty vessel.

As a juridical principle, the police power is a vast blank, organized by historical-cultural norms, structured by institutional forms, and made more plastic by a great degree of individual officer discretion. The elaboration of the legal concept of the police power dates back to the Greeks in a lengthy political-philosophical thread. It is focused not on crime—it could not be, as the notion that the state should be responsible for crime developed no earlier than the late nineteenth century—but on abstractions: order, or the "public good," a "most expansive, and most amorphous" power.[38] Contrasting it with law, Walter Benjamin notes, "a consideration of the police institution encounters nothing essential at all. Its power is formless, like its nowhere-tangible, all-pervasive, ghostly presence in the life of civilized states."[39] Giorgio Agamben puts it this way: "In the juridical theory, the police is a kind of black hole."[40] Reflecting on a series of early theorists, Michel Foucault conveys their sense that police jurisdiction is essentially infinite. "The police includes everything," he observes. "'The police's true object is man.'"[41] Contemporary theorists agree. The police's responsibility for order gave it "an incredibly broad compass," "both inevitable and limitless"; "by its very nature, incapable of exact definition or limitation."[42] *Police* (in the singular, as in the legal principle) "is not disposed to definition . . ."; it is the remainder, "everything else," laid out in interminable lists that can never be exhaustive.[43] The absence of either generalizable definitions or limits means that the police power is "unstable across time."[44] It can be anything, and so is whatever its age requires.

In the United States, founding conceptions of the police power drew heavily from Blackstone's *Commentaries on the Laws of England* (1769), a text very much in the juridical tradition of wide leeway granted to police. Blackstone understood the police power broadly, judging it impossible to give a comprehensive list of the "very miscellaneous" and numerous offenses belonging under its wing. The United States assigned these powers to the fifty states, enshrining the principle of federalism in law, though not, as we shall see, in practice.[45]

Responses to charges of police brutality that defend the police on the grounds that their activities have expanded to include issues too far beyond their proper jurisdiction, then, are true only in a radical sense, for in juridical tradition, nothing lies outside that essentially limitless scope. Policing can be as much of a swollen behemoth as we let it be.

What, then, is the core of police power? Is there some essence of police work that could not be taken on by other agents? If "crime" doesn't hold up as a category of analysis, what does constitute its inalienable core? One answer, I think, lies in a classic formulation from field-defining police scholar Egon Bittner, who observed in 1970 that it is the potential use of force that constitutes the quotidian power of policing, the actual application of which is in most cases unnecessary.[46] That is the distinction between work that must be done by police and work that police could pass on to others: work that relies upon violence or the threat thereof. Violence work.

VIOLENCE WORK

The violence meted out by police is sometimes hard to see, and many people understand it as exceptional. They think police use violence only in extreme cases or when cops go bad, as in the wrongful use of force. That point of view misses the *potential* violence that is the essence of their power. Yes, the violence of the police is often latent or withheld, but it is functional precisely because it is suspended. It often need not be made manifest, because people fear it and grant it legitimacy, in direct extension of the legitimacy they grant to state violence, broadly—and indeed, granting legitimacy to police is one of the most important ways people legitimize the state itself.

Police legitimacy fortifies and rests upon state legitimacy because the two are rough expressions of each other. *Police* and *state* are differentiated by degree: police are the human-scale expression of the state. Scholars of politics and police have phrased this relation in compelling ways. Adam Smith understood police as "the science of government in a broad sense."[47] Agamben pulls out the tautology marvelously: "Police is the relationship of a state with itself."[48] Other thinkers offer helpful images: "Every police agent embodies a minute replica of the state ... the police are the state's most condensed governing organ."[49] State and state capacity are "phenomena of *police*"; "discourses of governance ... are quintessentially discourses of police."[50] "As a core component of the state's monopoly on the legitimate means of coercion, police practices epitomize sovereignty in action"; or, simply, regardless of some exceptional status we might like to delineate with the notion of "corruption," police are "fundamentally political."[51]

This is the reason the police power varies so widely: because it carries out the functions of governance. *Police* does what the state (and market—but hold off on that relation for a moment) needs to do, and that is potentially infinite. In some of the US Supreme Court's more conservative traditions (crucially the dissent in *Lochner v. New York*, 1905, now the prevailing consensus), the court essentially decided that any action identified as a police action is inherently legitimate. As Marcus Dirk Dubber explains, Lochner concluded that "*all* governmental power was police power. And it made no more sense to explore in case after case just where the limits of that power were to be drawn. For the power to police was in fact unlimited. To identify a state action as an exercise of the police power was to affirm its constitutionality. That was all there was to it."[52] The power to govern *is* the police power; the police refract the power of the state.

Violence is fundamental to police, then, because it also lies at the heart of the state. Max Weber's famous dictum regarding the monopoly on the legitimate use of physical force identifies violence as the defining quality of the state. Violence is also the core of pre-Weberian, Marxist, and Foucauldian as well as other poststructuralist conceptualizations of the state, absent only in some liberal accounts. Charles Tilly notes that political theorists since Machiavelli and Hobbes have "recognized that, whatever else they do, governments organize and, wherever possible, monopolize violence." By any measure, "governments stand out from other organisations by their tendency to monopolize the concentrated means of violence," whether legitimate or illegitimate.[53] Althusser recognized that the power of state violence is *constitutive*, the fuel that makes the state machine-apparatus run.[54] Ruthie Gilmore articulates the process through which violence becomes power: "The application of *violence*—the cause of premature deaths—*produces* political power in a vicious cycle."[55] The police actualize this essence of state power, as Egon Bittner recognized with his classic definition of the police as "a mechanism for the distribution of situationally justified force in society," invoking the Weberian definition and locating the police at its crux.[56]

Police realize—they *make real*—the core of the power of the state. That is what I mean to convey by calling police "violence workers." It is not intended to indict police officers as bad people, vicious in personality or in their daily routines. It is simply about what their labor rests upon and therefore conveys into the material world. This is a slightly different use of the term than that intended by its coiners, Martha Huggins, Mika Haritos-Fatouros, and Philip Zimbardo.[57] They use it to indicate either "direct perpetrators" or "atrocity facilitators," proximate to the application of state brutality. In grateful debt to Huggins and her coauthors, I borrow the term, crossing it with the insights of scholars of sex work who prefer that term to "prostitution" to correct the denial of the activity *as labor*. It takes work to represent and distribute state violence.

One necessarily confusing aspect of such a usage is the ambiguity of the very idea of "violence." Violence exists in a great continuum from the most immediate *thunk* of an impact to the most attenuated inflictions of discursive, epistemic, symbolic, psychic, and economic injury, as a great many theorists have pondered.[58] What kind of violence is it that is inflicted by violence workers? Certainly some of it is exacted neither by gun nor nightstick but by the absence of nutritious food to eat or conditions of labor that destroy the body. Some theorists call this "structural" violence, a concept useful in calling attention to the consequences of injustice and to seeing violence as constitutive of power, rather than inflicted and *then* judged legitimate or not depending on its agent, as a static reading of Weber might suggest.[59] The problem with this concept is that structural violence can suggest an amorphous problem, unconnected to historical institutions, too intractable to combat. This sort of violence comes to function in specific institutions with histories and futures, and it has real people behind it. To exercise its power requires work—again, violence work.

The gamut of violence is best grasped expansively, as Ruthie Gilmore does in her incisive designation, "the cause of premature deaths."[60] This capacious definition includes all the forms of violence beyond physical coercive force inasmuch as they constrict and immiserate, leading people to an early grave. It corresponds beautifully with Gilmore's well-known definition of racism, "the state-sanctioned or extralegal production and exploitation of group-differentiated vulnerability to premature death," and indeed, racism is the highly logical framework in which to understand the toil of violence workers, as we will discuss shortly.[61] In the most expansive reading of this definition, a wide range of people might be engaged in violence work, down to that legendary local kindergarten teacher. Mostly, I narrow my focus in this book to people whose labors are enabled by the fact that at some point they are entitled to bring out the handcuffs. Yet this potential openness remains, as in the scientists and other academics engaged in weapons development and related tasks whom we meet in chapter 5.

Even if we limit the discussion to the narrowest subset, people whose work is undergirded by the premise and the promise of violence, police are far from the only ones inhabiting the category. The term requires us to broaden our vision to include the great range of workers whose activity depends upon the threat or potential for violence, because their authority relies on that threat. Indeed, the term "violence work" is useful precisely because it requires this broadening. There are quite a few other sorts of work that it designates, including that done by people in any branch of the military, prisons or detention centers, high-level agencies such as marshals or customs officials, private security companies or corporate security forces, and perhaps even civilians whose violence is yoked to state purpose in gated communities, poor neighborhoods, or prisons.[62]

The essence of police work extends, therefore, beyond the patrol or the service call and far beyond the uniformed, public police to the much larger category of people who do violence work. People authorized to inflict violence might be ratified by a nonstate agent such as a private company, or be part of a mob enjoying effective social sanction, as with the KKK or other lynch mobs. Either way, such people are also channels for violence condoned by the state.[63]

"Violence workers" is a more disturbing term than euphemisms such as "law enforcement" or "security workers," and we should be disturbed. It is more accurately broad than the misleadingly governmental "police." It effectively conveys the full panoply of people whose work rests on a promise of violence, thereby displacing some of the weight of the assumption that policing is only or even primarily a state project or that the state is a watertight container or boundary for "the police," or even that police in the United States operate solely in US territory. "Violence workers" highlights the enormous range of activities such people do and the wide parameters of the ambits within which they do them.

"Violence workers" as a term therefore points to the paradox of the relationship between police and police work. Police both overflow and fail to fill their container. Police do things that do not need to be violence work—so much more—and violence work is done by more people than the uniformed public police—so very many more. How can this be, if police are expressing the essence of state power? How can people employed by private-sector entities, for example, be expressing the violence of the state?

This paradox is profoundly productive. Truly, "the history of police is the history of state power"; "all roads lead to the state in the concept of police"; police are "an appropriate mirror to reach the state's heart."[64] A shadow more tangible than its source, an expression in flesh and blood of a concept impossible to pin down, policing shows us something much more abstract and harder to see: the nature of the state. Our opening paradox—that violence work is performed by more than police and that much work performed by police doesn't have to be violence work—is itself a reflection of the state's nonconfinement to its supposed borders.

All objects are defined by borders. We figure out what a thing is in good part by noting what it is not. We place ourselves in relation to others, and things in relation to the rest of the world of things. *Police* and *state* are no different.

What are those boundaries? This book is devoted to discerning them, by following people who work to shore them up rhetorically and institutionally. In the chapters that follow, I tell a story of violence workers crossing the conceptual borders of police. The tale is a particular historical one, pursued in order to make a broader point about the myths that legitimate state violence. It involves a small group of unusual police who are introduced in the first chapter. They worked for a State Department agency, the Office of Public Safety, which ended abruptly, allowing us to trail them during the agency's tenure and after its termination as they switched back and forth between military and civilian spheres, left government employ for the private security industry or vice-versa, and promiscuously leapt borders of nations and of scale in a sort of a high-stakes shell game.

Violence Work draws from a recent chapter in the history of the US police to show police constantly and frequently crossing the borders supposed to contain them. It shows that these borders are myths—claims that present as natural but are actually deeply ideological, as Roland Barthes instructed.[65] For police regularly cross whatever lines we think separate civilian from military spheres, doggedly protect private interests or work for market employers, travel abroad, and operate at all levels of government up to the federal scale. Police legitimacy rests on a tripartite fiction. You could even say it rests on a lie.

In other words, a trio of mythic ideas characterizes a general understanding of police. First myth: police are civilian, not military. Second: they are public, not private, that is, state rather than market agents. Third: they are local; they don't work for government bodies any higher than municipal or state levels in scale, and they certainly don't leave US national territory.

Two of these myths are carefully tended: one, the notion that police are civilian, and two, that they are public. These borders are prescriptive and normative; people believe that police *should be* public and civilian. Charges of police militarization or privatization can be serious political challenges. Notably, such challenges recognize that in many cases they actually *are* private and/or military, but they see this merely as an aberration, albeit a dangerous one. Less controversial is the myth about police geography (small scale and domestic location), often taken for granted, as in the virtually unquestioned notion that police are fundamentally local.[66] When they do travel, they ruffle few feathers (it doesn't tend to register in mass media or other arenas of public concern), but nor do they trouble the notion of policing's minor scale and geographic ambit. These three borders, together, comprise the idea of police as legitimate wielders of power. Police authority is justified when these three borders are assumed to hold, and allowed to function invisibly.

These borders are conceptual, not absolute. As the chapters of this book narrate, police actually cross them regularly in practice, denying those crossings vehemently in all sorts of ways. The borders of policing are like national borders, which, as the field of border studies has so beautifully affirmed, still exert tremendous force even as all sorts of crossings and mixtures show them to be far more fluid than traditional political definitions assume. To look squarely at our ideas about the borders of policing can reveal how the popular notion of police achieves coherence and legitimacy—and lends the same to the idea of the state—by contrasting itself to concepts defined as outside it.

Following these crossings requires us to rethink much of what we assume about police, and since police are the translation of state violence into human form, to rethink a great deal of what we assume about the state as well. Tracking police back to the source of their power illuminates that power's disregard of borders that don't contain it either—even as it starkly contains the people who live or would live in its land with much more concrete kinds of borders. For the state, too, is discursively bounded by this same trio of distinctions: public/private, military/civilian, and territoriality at the national scale.[67] A democratic state is separate from the market, or so the story goes; it uses military action only beyond its borders, treating its citizens to gentler civilian strictures; and it acts independently from other states and primarily within its own territory and in relation to its populace so that the sovereign corresponds to a bounded imagined community—a nation-state in which there is coherence between state and nation.

As with the borders of the idea of police, the state is constrained by these borders only conceptually. The fiction of territoriality is belied by the foreign operation of state agents in collaborative arrangements of multiple states and market bodies intermixed so deeply that no national affiliation can be discerned. Such entities abound; some of them are the characters of this book. They are, for example, the members and then former members of the Office of Public Safety, a US federal agency established during the early Cold War to help professionalize allied nations' police. The Office of Public Safety was a State Department unit in operation from 1962 to 1974. Its goal was to spread modern police tactics so as to preserve order for democratic politics and economic progress. Trainers for the Office of Public Safety crossed US borders and transcended "normal" police scale by working for a federal body rather than a municipal or state police force. Chapter 1 introduces this odd agency that lifted US police up several rungs of scale and sent them over national borders to train foreign police. Placing its founding, operation, and demise in global and national contexts, the chapter narrates how the transnational currents of the Cold War sparked and shaped foreign police assistance and then brought it home, changing US policing significantly.

Another body mixing multiple market and state players was the security force organized in the mid-1970s by the oil giant Aramco to stand guard at its trade talks worldwide. That force included former US police officers, was headed by a former FBI agent, and trained at the expense of the Saudi government at the US International Police Academy (IPA), the school launched and run for twelve years by the Office of Public Safety (OPS), which had advised the Saudi government to form such a body. We meet this group of violence workers, which conjoined two governments at multiple scales and the massive corporate oil industry, in chapter 4. In another illustrative example, when local police in Vietnam, Laos, and Cambodia who had worked for the Office of Public Safety came to the United States after 1975 as refugees, they were warmly welcomed by former OPS. The two groups of ex-cops often identified more closely with each other than with their fellow citizens, and expressed strong patriotism alongside a sense of having been wronged by their state(s). Their patterns of nationalism and state affiliation confound notions of the proper alignment of those categories, as chapter 6 describes.

We follow OPS, furthermore, to see the state cross military-civilian borders through the activities of its violence workers, most directly in chapter 2.

OPS was founded when global conditions forced the United States to shift its foreign policy tactics from military to police actions in the name of civilian and humanitarian aid. The change was incomplete, for the priority was to counter insurgency, not to fight crime. OPS grew and operated in military realms, creating thoroughly mixed-sphere tactics, strategies, and goals. An intense effort was expended to present it, nonetheless, as civilian, revealing the stakes of appearing to cross this Rubicon.

The third border, that between state and market, is also on display in the OPS story. In chapter 3, we follow former OPS employees to Alaska where they animated a thoroughly miscegenated oil security apparatus, including state troopers, municipal cops, prison employees, and private businesses' security personnel; US federal government, state, and municipal bodies; and foreign national powers. In chapter 5, the fiction of state/market distinction is on display in the work of universities and think tanks that joined the explosion of police education, to which ex-OPS contributed generously. Institutes and centers deftly switched their ostensible public or private status to evade public criticism or benefit from federal largesse and private philanthropy.

If at one point all the human characters in this book worked for a minor federal agency, in other parts of their lives they served as municipal police and state troopers, or were employed by the federal government in both civilian and military posts, or were paid by private corporations in the fields then coming to be called "security." Some of these violence workers sometimes fit the category of police; other times they did not, and so they and their allies deployed discursive limits to the notion of policing to admit or exclude them, tracing for viewers in retrospect the boundaries of the concept of policing—and the police-anchored boundaries that project the state's constituent outsides—in the United States during a central decade of the Cold War.

Following OPS suggests that the crossing of one of these police/state borders invites the crossing of another. As the crossings accumulate and overlap, spaces dazzlingly hybrid in composition proliferate. These objects are well described by the Deleuzian concept of "assemblage," which admits any number of constitutive pieces, all of different character and scale.[68] "Assemblage" aptly describes the actual formations in which violence workers ply their trades, such as the hybrid security company Wackenhut, ostensibly private but built on government contracts at federal and state scales and nourished, as we will see in chapter 3, by the security needs of the Alaska oil pipeline, itself a product of transnational government and private-sector pieces. Political discourse is clarified through the concept of assemblage, which permits the juxtaposition of elements unlike in nature, scale, and degree of magnitude. The infamous rallying cry for "law and order," for example, integrated transnational, global-scale "tough on communism" fears and tactics. As chapter 1 narrates, the United States' imperial engagements abroad are a part of the language and logic of this notorious, prison-feeding, discursive-legislative assemblage. An equally critical element is the denial of mixture, as violence workers and their champions proclaim and perform the sanctity of each of these borders in plays for the deniability of the nature of their work. In those labors of border defense, laden with strategic misdirection, lie clues to the deadly "magic of the state."[69]

The border between public and private spheres, that is, the myth of the autonomy of state and market, is particularly vehemently defended, for it is the cornerstone of liberal capitalism, and all the more so of neoliberal capitalism. Classical liberal economists such as Adam Smith imagined public and private as cleanly distinct. Smith posited *homo economicus* as age-old and markets as naturally evolving long before states sprung up within them. Historian Karl Polanyi's *The Great Transformation: The Political and Economic Origins of Our Time* (1944) disputed this speculation. Markets need states, Polanyi showed; never has there been an independently operating, truly self-regulating market. Market economies grew not naturally but due to "highly artificial stimulants administered to the body social" and would destroy themselves and society if left to their own devices.[70] In the 1970s, political economist Nicos Poulantzas extended this line of thinking, roundly rejecting the notion that the political could be autonomous from the economic. Even more emphatically than Polanyi, he called the relation "inherent and theoretically unbreakable."[71] Poulantzas did not see the state as symptom (epiphenomenon) of the more "real" economic realm even as he maintained the core of the Marxist insight that the state serves the interests of capital.[72]

The notion that state and market are distinct, Marxist scholars recognize, is "an illusion, a trick, to fool the powerless into thinking that the state is neutral and above and beyond such sordid transactions."[73] In the second half of the twentieth century, such scholars developed this thread, asking, "Does the state exist?" relentlessly.[74] An influential contribution was Philip Abrams's argument in 1977 that the state was a social fiction, an implication, reified in practice. He called on historical sociologists to distinguish between a state-system and a state-idea, and to demystify the state by "attending to the senses in which the state does not exist rather than to those in which it does."[75]

Foucauldian-influenced thinkers have taken up the challenge of theorizing an abstraction with great sophistication. Departing from the agreement that the state is "not a thing," Wendy Brown describes an "unbounded terrain of powers and techniques, an ensemble of discourses, rules, and practices." Although Gilmore and Gilmore see it more concretely as a "territorially bounded set of relatively specialized institutions," they ultimately also posit its openness as a set of "ideological and institutional capacities," consonant with James Ferguson's subtle articulation, "the name of a way of tying together, multiplying, and coordinating power relations, a kind of knotting or congealing of power."[76]

Among the most unremittingly thoughtful of the Foucauldians is Timothy Mitchell, who has offered marvelous ways to think *around* the "imaginary coherence" of the state. Recognizing that what we call "'the state' arises from techniques that enable mundane material practices to take on the appearance of an abstract, nonmaterial form," Mitchell proposes that scholars seek to historicize the production of "state effects." Indeed, he insists, there are no states, only these "state effects."[77]

The state-effect has a function, Mitchell expands: it limits claims for equality and justice by carving up discursive and material space. It does so, he writes, "by acknowledging certain areas as matters of public concern subject to popular decision while establishing other fields to be administered under alternative methods of control. For example, governmental practice can demarcate a private sphere governed by rules of property, a natural world governed by laws of nature, or markets governed by principles of economics. Democratic struggles become a battle over the distribution of issues."[78] Note that this is essentially Poulantzas's understanding of the way capitalism projects an arena of the political into which no market activities are supposed to intrude.

Mitchell suggests that the mid-twentieth century saw an expansion of the supposed laws of "the market" as an "alternative technology of rule," effectively excluding more of the world from democratic contestation.[79] One name for this expansion is neoliberalism, the economic philosophy emergent since the 1970s that posits the separability of political from economic realms, and coaches its followers to assume *and desire* a radical autonomy of state from market. The paladins of neoliberalism prefer the freedom of capital and of corporations to that of the nearly eight million people in the United States now under some form of correctional control.[80]

The rise of mass incarceration under neoliberalism is no coincidence. A critical aspect of the market as "alternative technology of rule" is race, that central engine of postwar prison expansion. Race is a crucial technic for neoliberalism's exclusions, operating as it does to separate, define, and control populations—as Foucault put it, to "fragment[] the field of the biological that power controls."[81] In inextricable relation, the idea of the state operates to fragment a related field, producing the distinctions between the state and its others that Mitchell tags as a critical aspect of the exercise of power.[82]

Violence Work embraces Mitchell's charge to take seriously the elusive boundary between the state and its constitutive others. It works to reveal some of the internal boundaries—particularly those secured by ideas about the way police do their work—that feed the umbrella category "the state" in relation to the market, for in that nexus lie the most important aspects of modern power. There lie, as Abrams might say, the "actualities of social subordination."[83] To get at that intimacy, I use the simple term "state-market," as both adjective (as in "state-market power" or "state-market violence") and noun. Because the state is nonetheless a category that has purchase as an idea, I still also use "state" by itself, when talking about the state-idea that denies a connection to the market, for example, or the state-effect that people experience, or when exploring other theorists' consideration of the state. If this wavering of terms is confusing, all the better to underscore the elusive, ever-receding nature of the idea of the state.

The compound term "state-market" helps focus the structuring matrix capitalism provides for the state, and vice-versa. I mean to point out that the relationship is something of chicken and egg. As Poulantzas understood, neither came first: the state was "capitalist from the start, and not . . . an institution inserted into 'capitalist society.'"[84] Gilmore and Gilmore start from the other end, pointing out that capitalism had the state from the start: "There has never been a minute in the history of capitalism lacking the organized, centralized, and reproducible capacities of the state."[85] While the socialist and communist regimes in modern history dreamed of autonomy, they too worked to distinguish the state rhetorically from the realm of the market and thereby engaged in the dynamic under critique here. They could have done no less, moreover, operating within and subsiding back into the overarching framework of global capitalism as they did. In an important sense, the capitalist state is the only state we've known, though maybe not the only one we can imagine.

Just as old or older, just as inescapably essential, and thoroughly interwoven in this history is the idea of race. Race has been fundamental to capitalism from the first, scholars of this history have shown, exploring "the racial roots of capitalism," noting the way capitalism, from its emergence, made race "its epistemology, its ordering principle, its organizing structure, its moral authority, its economy of justice, commerce, and power."[86] The concept of "racial capitalism," redundant but helpful, points us to this inextricability. Robin Kelley expands:

> [Capitalism] emerged within the feudal order and flowered in the cultural soil of a Western civilization already thoroughly infused with racialism. Capitalism and racism, in other words, did not break from the old order but rather evolved from it to produce a modern world system of "racial capitalism" dependent on slavery, violence, imperialism, and genocide. Capitalism was "racial" not because of some conspiracy to divide workers or justify slavery and dispossession, but because racialism had already permeated Western feudal society. The first European proletarians were racial subjects (Irish, Jews, Roma or Gypsies, Slavs, etc.) and they were victims of dispossession (enclosure), colonialism, and slavery within Europe.[87]

Capitalism, Chris Chen points out, has always required "the systematic racialisation of [unfree] labour through the creation of an array of effectively nonsovereign raced and gendered subjects." *Race* is both a necessary engine and a product of capitalism: "'Race' is not extrinsic to capitalism or simply the product of specific historical formations such as South African Apartheid or Jim Crow America. Likewise, capitalism does not simply incorporate racial domination as an incidental part of its operations, but from its origins systematically begins producing and reproducing 'race' as global surplus humanity."[88]

Given racial capitalism's roots in feudalism, it is no wonder that even older notions of the state, such as that which arose in Renaissance Europe, tightly tied to the person of the prince, are racialized in concept.[89] Meanwhile the modern version was born in and of the dynamics of colonialism and differentiation of the human from affectable others described by Denise Ferreira da Silva, Sylvia Wynter, Nikhil Singh, and others.[90]

This is a necessary starting point in thinking about police in relation to the state. Many people agree that race is relevant to the activities of police, but they see this relevance as incidental or correctible through police sensitivity training or better regulation. The link is deeper and different. Police function to produce race, a category essential to the workings of the state-market under racial capitalism. Any analysis of US policing must consider its constitutive relationship to the racialization of Black and brown subjects, not only theoretically but also in history, with the US police's structural formation as an antiblack force.[91] In the United States, Saidiya Hartman has written, the police power as laid out by the Supreme Court is "little more than the benevolent articulation of state racism in the name of the public good."[92] This is an essential undergirding to discussions that may not always explicitly address race. For whoever says "state," "police," and "violence" in discussing the last three hundred years, says "race."[93]

One of the ultimate implications of this line of argument is an indictment of the state form. At the very least, it leaves us with little reason to invest hope in the state form under capitalism. Further, embracing the concept of assemblage to understand state power entails a distinct loss of coherence, since an object with the properties of assemblage is existentially untenable. This will appeal to people who lean toward skepticism in relation to the state, from prison abolitionists to anarchists of varying stripes. It will resonate with the notice in anthropology of groups who live together ably without states, and indeed, understand *state* as the source of violence rather than its solution.[94] This thoroughgoing critique of the state will be difficult, however, for many readers to swallow.

The urgency of the problem of state-market violence makes it incumbent to wonder why the ultimate implications of this argument are so difficult to accept—even for people who will accompany most of the steps. The affective investment in the idea of the state, and the corresponding investment in the notion that a human-scale branch of state power could live up to its ideals and genuinely "keep us safe," go very deep. While I do think that many people misunderstand the nature of police, policing, and the state, it is not the kind of misunderstanding that can be corrected with information. This isn't an ignorance that knowledge can simply displace. No clear-cut misunderstanding underlies the inability to follow the trail of violence work but a barrier beyond argument, nestled in the realm of dreams. The idea of a benign protector, the state, looking after us all via its proxy, police, is devastatingly seductive.

To begin to dismantle this investment, the structures of privilege and marginalization that make some people desire state violence will have to be dislodged. State violence that might hurt others more than oneself (or seems as though it might) is actually a reasonable choice for subjects formed in the crucible of the carceral state, even if it consigns their lives to misery as well.[95] This is true not only for the apocryphal white Trump voter, but for people of color who are regularly recruited to the defense of racial capitalism, given a system of rights and law in which "recuperating social value *requires* rejecting the other Other."[96] We must work to realign desire for Big Brother given that racialized populations are rendered criminal, terrorist, or alien as an *effect* of the operation of law.[97] Appeals to the state cannot save us from the state.

What could alter the investment in the notions of police and state, then, is that age-old bottom line: the redistribution of resources with equity in mind.[98] Not, this time, by the state-market. The best attempts of the energetic and capable activists in the state-focused movements of the 1930s to the 1960s have been countered, in the last fifty years, with a process of redistribution *up*, robbing from the poor to give to the rich. Violence work was key in this, as rising inequality was both facilitated and answered by expanded violence. As this book's conclusion will take up again, after the chapters have had a chance to tell their story, the explosion of prisons and policing in the United States—the carceral boom—is both product and engine of the state-market refusal to share the mid-century's wealth through just distribution of resources.[99] Getting people to accept this divisive, destructive, brutally constrictive situation was hard work. Yet again: violence work.

The concept of violence work is "good for thinking" for scholar-activists, in ways this book does not exhaust. It allows us to traverse police history to revisit the workings of power, focusing the forms the state-market wields to shield the fragments of its assemblage from scrutiny and challenge. The state cannot serve as focus directly; it is too big, too amorphous, too ghostly— there really is no there, there, after all. One can only approach the concept glancingly. *Violence Work* asks "police" to provide that guiding role.

Thus guided, we will see aspects of our world that are otherwise buried under the weight of assumption about public safety, the state, the private sector, citizen and stranger, place and scale. Lifting that weight, we contextualize police in the ideological landscape that contains and legitimates state-market violence. We interrupt the arguments that contain public criticism of the police at home and of the US military in its wars abroad, and that recirculate tragic conceptions of the varying value of human lives.

Violence Work's idiosyncratic angle of approach to understanding police identifies the projected boundaries of the state idea and tells stories of people transgressing them in practice while reinforcing them in discursive realms. This process built both pieces of the state-market's "legitimate violence"—the legitimacy *and* the violence—turning the global helm toward the ruinous lethality of the late Cold War.

The Office of Public Safety, the LEAA,
and US Police

In September of 1967, Otto Kerner brought an important witness to testify to the presidential commission he chaired, the US National Advisory Commission on Civil Disorders. The witness was Byron Engle, then director of the Office of Public Safety, a federal agency established in the early 1960s to provide allied foreign nations with training for their police. "Mr. Engle," Kerner explained to his colleagues, "will talk about the lessons learned from civil disorders in both this country and abroad, and the fundamental basic principles which apply internationally."[1] Kerner and his commission were charged with understanding the causes of the terrible urban disturbances of the mid-1960s, and preventing their recurrence. Crucial to their conceptualization of both the problem and the solution was, as Kerner signaled, a convergence of foreign and domestic spheres, with the hinge provided by a border-breaching body of police.

There is a great deal worth drawing out from this snapshot of a US national policy discussion around violence work. There is the glimpse of global conditions mattering to domestic policymaking. There is the notice of a federal agency that sent US police across international borders, flouting a fairly widespread sense that US police are local in the scope of their activity. Behind it, there is the racist state-market violence that provoked the riots the Kerner Commission was organized to consider, and ahead, the policies that emerged from this process, which precipitated the stunning expansion of the US criminal justice system that people today invoke with the shorthand "mass incarceration." Most importantly, there is the suggestion of the equivalence of domestic and foreign conflict and police response, which Kerner clearly found important. Engle didn't come up with this idea, but he and the agency he directed were active in its amplification.

In calling the work of the Office of Public Safety (OPS) to the attention of the influential Kerner Commission, Engle reveals a key facet of the legacy of that agency, which this chapter will shortly introduce in full. This important aspect of OPS's impact is underexplored. OPS has had its historians, both critical and laudatory, but they have focused on the agency's work abroad. Even OPS's most vehement critics have thus accepted the parameters of the autobiography its protagonists would write for it and for themselves. None have placed it in domestic context, much less in the fully transnational landscapes of police and state activity in which it emerged, operated, ended, and was reborn in various forms.

This chapter opens by telling the OPS story as an account of global and local currents swirling together, with OPS and its agents among the instruments doing the stirring. Thus reframed, the OPS story elucidates phenomena of far greater importance than the details of a minor federal government body. Moving along multiple levels of scale from the broadest ideological contours of the day to institutional formation to the microlevel of the individual, it shows the transnational history of the federal legislative acts of the late 1960s that poured federal dollars into policing, prisons, and other aspects of the US criminal justice system, primarily the Law Enforcement Assistance Administration, or LEAA, that dominant player in US criminal justice policy throughout the 1970s. To see the LEAA and its policy contemporaries as part of the legacy of OPS is a radical revision of both the histories of domestic policy and of foreign police assistance. Telling the story in this way reveals the geographic, public-private, and civilian-military border crossing involved in the expansion of violence work and its rising lethality in the period in which it was deployed to suppress domestic dissent in US antiwar and racial justice movements.

DEVELOPMENT, COUNTERINSURGENCY, AND THE OFFICE OF PUBLIC SAFETY

The grounds on which violence work in the United States and abroad would shift and grow in the 1970s depended on the ascent of the notion of economic development. As salve for global inequality, development theorists in the United States and Western Europe prescribed a regimen of modernization and economic growth. They claimed a progressive mantle of cultural relativism by rejecting colonial conceptualizations of the world as divided into civilized and barbaric peoples, though their views preserved much of the hierarchies of earlier generations. Against the political and economic claims of the anti-imperialist formation coming to call itself the "Third World," development discourse defined "Third World" spatially and specified it economically as "poor."[2] By the 1950s, the notion that the Third World required "development" in order to progress was powerful common sense, with Walt W. Rostow's *Stages of Economic Growth* (1960) articulating widespread consensus.[3]

With "development" as the cornerstone of hopes for victory over communism, policing moved to a privileged position in US foreign policy. Extending the logic of the postwar Marshall Plan for Europe to the rest of the globe, American officials crafted foreign aid to promote development and therefore faith in capitalism and in the United States. In this framing, assistance to foreign police had a number of attractions. It would (its champions thought) help maintain the order required for economic increase, and the ostensibly gentler approach of police seemed more promising than brute force in the famed Cold War struggle for "hearts and minds." Police assistance could be portrayed as technical and civilian; using it to replace military aid was more politic in a world in which military matériel was subject to critique as neo-imperial or interventionist. Finally, police were closer to the people, and therefore better poised for the gathering of intelligence.

This developmentalist, police- and order-focused, intelligence-centered approach comprised *counterinsurgency*, the series of fighting techniques developed to respond to guerrilla tactics and implemented by US military and police together as early as the Greek civil war of 1944–49.[4] While the term reached a general public sphere only in the early 1960s (still new enough in 1962 for the *Washington Post* to call it "the latest gobbledygook for finding and killing guerillas"), it had already emerged as the United

States' premier military priority globally at that point, its theoretical precepts elaborated in a "sprawling" literature by the early 1960s.[5]

Counterinsurgency entered diplomatic policy under Eisenhower, who inaugurated a police assistance program in 1954. Building on the US police role in occupied Japan and postwar hotspots including Korea, Greece (figure 1.1), and Iran (figure 1.2), and incorporating academic, private-sector, and government elements, this program was organized under the auspices of the International Cooperation Administration (ICA), relied for training facilities on US universities and the International Association of Chiefs of Police (a domestic organization despite its name), and was substantially supported by the CIA, whose eventual involvement with OPS would be constant and often acknowledged.[6]

Kennedy was also concerned to avoid the perception of imperialist positions, hopeful about humanitarian aid, and, more to the point, avid about counterinsurgency. His foreign policy was increasingly concerned not with actual attacks on the United States or its allies but with subversion from within, or "internal security," as the Cold Warriors called it. Police were closer to the people, and lived among them, which was key for tracking insurgency, and the service work police performed helped portray democratic governance as benevolent. So in 1961 when Kennedy replaced the ICA with the Agency for International Development (USAID) to oversee foreign aid, he gathered there the police programs he inherited, under the aegis of a new agency, the Office of Public Safety, or OPS.

Retaining many ICA personnel and offices, OPS expanded its operations dramatically, eventually reaching nearly fifty countries in Europe, Asia, Africa, and the Americas.[7] It opened the Inter-American Police Academy in the Panama Canal Zone in 1963, moving it to Washington in 1964 after protests by Panamanians over sovereignty became violent clashes; there it was renamed the International Police Academy.

Over the course of its dozen years of life, OPS distributed $200 million in arms and equipment to police forces in forty-seven countries, trained over 7,500 senior officers at its academy and other US schools, and sent nearly 1,500 advisors overseas to train over one million rank-and-file policemen. Its champions tout accomplishments in professionalizing and modernizing corrupt and haphazard police, and continue to praise its legacy even today.[8]

The agency also had many critics. The Office of Public Safety was dogged by allegations that it did not improve democratic police. It was accused of teaching torture and practicing political policing, and a number of

FIG 1.1 "Athens 1958." Future OPS members in a photograph shared in the *Newsletter* in 2010, showing both the continuity of personnel and the institutional continuity ex-OPS posited, far after the agency's demise, between pre-OPS police assistance and OPS itself.
SOURCE: *PSN* 156 (JAN. 2010), 1.

FIG 1.2 "Advisory team to the General Police Administration of Iran." A photograph shared in the *Newsletter* in 2005, again suggesting personal and institutional continuity with OPS predecessors. SOURCE: *PSN* 141 (DEC. 2005), 5.

scandals rocked its tenure at State. One such scandal involved the dictatorship in Brazil, whose abuses were increasingly evident in the United States in the early 1970s, casting less than favorable light on the branches of the US foreign policy apparatus that had supported the 1964 coup and continued to shore up the military government. Another focused on a prison in Vietnam that OPS advisors helped run. Named for its location on Con Son Island, the prison featured tiny, dank cells denounced as "tiger cages" by critics in 1970, and a delegation of antiwar activists including US congressmen visited and condemned the site. Just as this crisis was hitting the airwaves, the kidnapping and murder of OPS advisor Dan Mitrione by Tupamaro guerrillas in Uruguay brought stark publicity to the accusations concerning torture, particularly when the incident became the subject of a popular movie, *State of Siege*, released in 1973 by Greek filmmaker Constantin Costa-Gavras.

As the 1970s dawned, OPS employees were already nervous about their agency's future, and many began to seek new positions. Those who thought they saw the writing on the wall were correct. Congress held hearings in 1973 and 1974, ending by prohibiting police assistance through an amendment to the Foreign Assistance Act. With this, lawmakers terminated OPS, instructing its offices to wrap up their affairs within the calendar year.[9]

Yet the end of OPS was not the end of police assistance. Congress had allowed several exemptions, including one for narcotics policing, and another for programs paid for by the receiving countries. By the end of the decade, Congress had added exceptions for police assistance to countries where it seemed indispensable, and others on a temporary basis that proved to be quite durable, and so on, until police assistance was once again a quotidian part of US foreign policy as it is nowadays. Former OPS agents continued in that line of work throughout; when ICITAP, the International Criminal Investigative Training Assistance Program, which represents the reestablishment of officially recognized police assistance, was founded in 1986, ex-OPS were still around to join up.[10]

Unable to predict this vindication, OPS employees were stricken by Congress's 1973 decision.[11] They testified, lobbied, protested, and strategized about how to save their sinking ship. Solidarity, fed by frustration, led these workers to stay in touch, finding each other at conferences, in social visits, and working together again in new positions they often helped each other secure. Their desire to communicate led them to produce a circular, the *Public Safety Newsletter*, initiated soon after OPS's formal termination.

At the time we were completing the preparation of this issue of the NEWSLETTER we received several letters and phone calls from former colleagues who expressed concern with and over the Vietnam refugee situation. As a result considerable news and information has been exchanged which should be of general interest to our professional group. Consequently this issue has been expanded to include this additional news.

As originally planned this issue also includes the master mailing list of about 500 names. At this time we don't know the new addresses of those who were evacuated from S. Vietnam; consequently, we have retained their old addresses in this list. Please advise us if you know their new addresses.

P.O. Box 186, SANTEE, CA 92071 is a mail drop for several people who are cooperating in preparing the Public Safety NEWSLETTER. Please send Bio and activity information to this address, but so as not to confuse the Post Office please don't address envelopes to any specific individual when using it. Contributions will be forwarded to PHIL BATSON.

BIO-ACTIVITIES FORM: If you have not done so, please send in your completed Bio-Activities Form so we may include you in the BIO LIST to be printed in a future issue.

CURRENT ACTIVITIES: Please send in your current activities--that is what will make this a more interesting newsletter. This also includes people still with AID and other Government agencies.

SUGGESTIONS: Please send in any suggestions that will make this a more interesting NEWSLETTER.

CHANGE OF ADDRESS: If you have moved and the Post Office is forwarding your mail from your old address, please send us your new address. Also, if you plan to move soon, send in your new address if you know it.

If you do not wish your name listed, please advise and it will be deleted from future lists.

YOUR LETTERS: In most cases we assume that the news and comments you include in your letters to us are for general information and may be reprinted in the NEWSLETTER. In some cases we have written to be sure our correspondents have no second thoughts. However, if when you write, you include comments you don't want printed--please so indicate.

Please recognize that portions of the NEWSLETTER are typed up at the time news and information are received in your letters to us. As a result some of the contents is "dated" and has been overtaken by the "course of events." This is particularly true of this issue which covers the months of March, April and most of May.

CONTRIBUTIONS: This NEWSLETTER is an informal effort and we do not wish to get involved with a formal subscription process to support it. Instead we solicit contributions from interested people. The responses for financial assistance have been timely and are appreciated. Anyone wishing to contribute to the expense of future issues may send a check payable to PHILIP BATSON (our Treasurer) at his home. Philip Batson, 5847 Monte Verde Drive, Santa Rosa, Calif. 95405.

PHIL reports that as of May 14, $810.81 has been received from 86 contributors. Expenses up to that date had been $226.37. It is expected that the expenses related to this issue #4 will exceed $250.00. To the best of our knowledge these contributions are not tax deductible.

BOB DAVENPORT provided the following information concerning the Saudi Arabia survey. "The team of experts were sent to SA to perform a survey of the Ministry of Interior and its dependencies in the Kingdom of Saudi Arabia. HERB HARDIN was the team chief and there were eighteen team members plus a secretary, LORETTA ROMERO from OPS, Washington, D.C. Actually, HERB and I were the only OPS members but two former OPS Advisors came aboard as "contract" people. DONALD BORDENKIRCHER covered Penology and ROY HATEM handled "Patrol." The other team members were from various federal, state, city and private organizations and covered Civil Defense, Fire Fighting, Passports, Immigration, Highway Patrol, Records and Identification, Criminalistics, Communications, Manpower and Training, Computers, Special Security Forces, Coast Guard and Frontier Forces. We were based at Rijadh and took field trips to various cities to acquire information for the survey. Received excellent cooperation and re-newed old friendships with graduates of IPA. My assignment was urban traffic. I was appointed Acting Chief of the team when we left the States. HERB arrived a week later but was med-evacuated to Beirut a day later. JACK GOIN was then appointed Chief and he arrived a week later. JACK will be the last to leave on April 25."

JOHN WIESS has provided the following information concerning the VN refugee situation as it applies to former OPS'ers. If someone wishes to sponsor a former VN National Policeman but do not know the name they should write to: John A. Wiess, Admin. Officer, IATF, Dept. of State, Washington, D.C. 20253. If you write JOHN be sure to include your telephone number so he can call back.

NORM ROSNER and JOE JENKINS are with JOHN in Wash. D.C. BOB GOLLING is at Ft. Chaffee and JOHN KESSLER is at Eglan AF Base.

1

FIG 1.3 Front page of first numbered issue of the *Public Safety Newsletter*, May 1975.

⌐THE PUBLIC SAFETY NEWSLETTER

DECEMBER 1988	THE PUBLIC SAFETY NEWSLETTER	EDITOR: A. T. STALEY
ISSUE #64	A NON-PROFIT JOURNAL SERVING	OVERSEAS EDITOR: JULIA SENSIBA
14th YEAR OF PUBLICATION	FORMER PUBLIC SAFETY ADVISORS	WEST COAST EDITOR: NICK YANTSIN
	P. O. BOX 1372	
	FAIRFAX, VIRGINIA 22030-1372	

OPS.DVG

SEASONS GREETINGS!
NEWSLETTER STILL ALIVE!

FIG 1.4 *Newsletter* masthead in 1988 showing the OPS insignia and surprised pleasure at the survival of the *Newsletter.* SOURCE: *PSN* 64 (DEC. 1988).

Never distributed far outside its original audience, the PSN survived on the labor of dedicated volunteers, editors passing the baton to others when they tired of the task. From the early garage mimeograph operation featuring tiny-print pages dense with addresses and news of career moves and personal lives (figure 1.3), it evolved in sophistication, surprising even its editors with its staying power (figure 1.4). It is still published regularly in 2017, now in online, full-color digital editions, these days featuring many memorials as this generation of civil servants passes on.

The *Public Safety Newsletter* is a bedrock of this project. I found it when I began to communicate with former OPS agents, after my research led me to one person's presence on Facebook. After lengthy conversations with him and others to whom he kindly introduced me, I was granted the opportunity to solicit copies of the PSN in its own pages. With hunger for their story to be told, ex-OPS responded generously. One former agent sent me his near-full set of back issues; others sent smaller caches. While I have not told the story of vindication that many ex-OPS yearned to read—and despite my protestations that I would not, I'm afraid some still held out hope—this project makes other stories possible: the PSN will be archived in the Indiana University libraries for public consultation in perpetuity.

The *Public Safety Newsletter* allowed ex-OPS to follow and support each other's progress, and it allows the historian to see something of their lives and thoughts. It has been invaluable in my attempt to understand the phenomena of which OPS and its former agents were a part. The project of professionalizing and modernizing police, it helps to reveal, was consequential at home as well as abroad.

LESSONS FROM FOREIGN POLICE ASSISTANCE

In the 1940s and 1950s, most US development theorists paid little attention to domestic events, assuming underdevelopment to be a foreign malady. In the 1960s, however, they found a domestic application, when riots rocked US cities from Watts to Harlem. The urban disturbances that began in 1964 and extended to some three hundred cities before the end of the summer of 1967 felt to many Americans like waves of threatening chaos, particularly amid the assassinations of JFK in 1963 and of Robert Kennedy and Martin Luther King in 1968; widespread violence following King's assassination; unrest at the Democratic National Convention that same year; other civil rights and antiwar protests; and the 1968 archipelago of protest and violent state repression worldwide.[12]

The protests were stunning to observers who had thought the United States immune. Many people had been convinced of the difference between the United States and the "less developed and newly emerging Free World countries" with their "emotional imbalance," as OPS founders had put it in 1962.[13] Their profound confidence in the superiority of US law enforcement and national character turned out to be, in retrospect, uncannily predictive: "It is not hard to visualize what civil disturbances and riots our own country might experience if we lacked the respected and efficient and well established Federal law enforcement investigative mechanism for preventing such Communist-inspired activity and insuring internal security, and did not possess the economic, social and political maturity we have evolved since emerging as a free nation."[14] Contemplating the assumptions required to pen such a passage makes it easier to imagine the shock and confusion evoked when the protests began.

The 1960s protests allowed development theorists to bring their favored framework home.[15] Observers were attracted to the notion that downtrodden domestic sites required development, as (they thought) Third World locations did. Rather than suggesting any structural interdependence between immiserated inner cities and wealthier areas, or finding racism in housing, health, education, or employment conditions, this interpretation displaces the source of the ill entirely onto the problem zone—just as development

THE OFFICE OF PUBLIC SAFETY | 33

theory at the global scale denies the relations of capital that distribute wealth unevenly around the globe.[16] In this they echoed OPS founders who in 1962 explained that Third World nations' unrest owed fully to "reasons rooted in *their own* political, social, cultural, and economic histories."[17]

After the riots began, politicians, city authorities, and police officials began to compare the Third World to US cities, with Vietnam the illustration always closest to hand. As Tracy Tullis documents, "The Vietnam war haunted the domestic scene: in the escalating war in the cities, it served as tutor and warning, model and metaphor."[18] During the rebellions in Watts, Los Angeles, in 1965, LAPD chief William Parker compared his situation to "fighting the Viet Cong"; Daryl Gates, then serving as a field commander for Parker, agreed that "the streets of America had become a foreign territory."[19] Gates and fellow officers began reading up on Vietnam, consulting with marines at the nearby Chavez Ravine facility to prep themselves on counterinsurgency and guerrilla warfare.[20] At the National League of Cities in 1966, Detroit mayor Jerome Cavenagh compared the guerrilla warfare on US city streets to the Mekong Delta.[21] After the Detroit uprisings in 1967, Lyndon Johnson framed his administration's response in ways that echoed the US stance in the war in Vietnam. As Rostow, then Johnson's national security advisor, pointed out to him, this was a powerful claim to stake, as it would resonate with the American public.[22] Objects of this policing used the comparison too, accusing the United States of levying its Cold War fighting power against its own citizens, as when the Chicano paper *Inside Eastside* declared police were "waging a 'cold war in East L.A,'" or in activists who saw echoes of themselves in anti-imperialist resistance fighters such as the Viet Cong.[23] The comparison became bedrock common sense. In the 1980s, Reagan's attorney general would justify Justice Department law enforcement spending with the effective argument that the DOJ was "the internal arm of the nation's defense."[24]

The communications channels that allowed people to make this comparison are myriad and capillary; only some are visible in retrospect. News reporting outlets were surely some of the most important, in their reporting on overseas policing. Other conduits were actual people involved in policing in Vietnam and other Third World locations, and here OPS returns to our tale. From the field, OPS employees communicated with US audiences in a range of ways. The paths of their transmissions to US venues were obvious and overt in the early years of OPS operations, the period in which these comparisons began to be made. In later years, the agency came under public scrutiny and began to conceal its work, and some of the means through which it influenced US police practice closed or were hidden, but plenty of others remained open and in full view.

The Office of Public Safety opened many portals for exchange between US and foreign police work. The simplest was the hiring of regular municipal police for short periods; when they were done, they went home, taking their overseas experiences with them. Many police officers were posted to these short-term tours of duty ("TDY" in the lingo), though some of the details are blurry, with uneven attempts at secrecy.[25] Such quick trips were simple entry points for OPS experience to inform police work in the United States. In 1962, the agency's very first year, the Los Angeles Board of Police Commissioners approved the detailing of sergeant J. Mejia and officer H. J. Guevara to the State Department for USAID work. The commissioners later extended their forty-five-day detail by several months and then issued permits for the two to be employed full-time by USAID.[26] In 1963, chief of Los Angeles Police William Parker was asked by no less than Robert Kennedy, a strong OPS supporter and key to the founding of the Inter-American Police Academy, to lend personnel to the Department of State for police assistance abroad. The LA commissioners sent sergeants Robert Hernandez and Abel Armas to Caracas for ninety days. Later comments show that the commissioners knew the receiving agency was the USAID "Public Safety Program" and did not consider that information sensitive, and, further, were not entirely happy about sending LAPD into what they considered dangerous situations.[27] Perhaps aware of such ambivalence, the USAID's chief administrator sent a thank-you note to Chief Parker in December of that year praising the sergeants by name for service that "strengthened Venezuelan police performance considerably and was an important factor in thwarting an intensive terroristic campaign by which communist elements hoped to prevent the Presidential election there on December 1." The letter sparked a lively debate in the commission meeting, the minutes state, without further detail.[28]

While the policy was clearly controversial, it did not end. The LA county sheriff lent Miguel Gutierrez and Paul Gutierrez to teach police administration in the Panama Canal Zone in 1963, where they joined Albuquerque detectives Eddie Chavez, Felipe Sandoval, and Mel Holguin. Four LAPD detectives joined three from San Antonio in training Caracas police for OPS in 1963 and 1964; several LAPD also served in the Dominican Republic, perhaps around 1967.[29] In 1964, the commission approved the detailing of

Chief Parker himself to India for USAID work with police there.[30] These trips across territorial borders were complemented by travels into military arenas: soon the Board of Police Commissioners would approve LAPD personnel to attend sniper training at the Marine Corps Base in Quantico, training demonstrations held by the Department of Defense in Washington, DC, and SWAT training at the Marine Corps' Camp Pendleton.[31]

The general public, including the officers' colleagues and communities, could watch this exchange in the media. While USAID records today strain to conceal this information, police departments at the time did not. The LAPD, probably the most secretive force in the nation, was unconcerned to keep this contract work under wraps. In 1962, the Los Angeles Board of Police Commissioners issued a press release discussing the leaves of Mejia and Guevara.[32] They publicized the work of several LAPD officers who retired to work for the State Department advising police in Vietnam in 1966, and allowed the media to cover the event when several commissioners accompanied deputy chief Thad Brown to Mexico City that same year for municipally contracted collaboration (not OPS) to prepare for the 1968 Olympic Games.[33]

A *Los Angeles Times* article on OPS, printed in 1963, filled in details. Reporter Robert Thompson celebrated the agency's work, noting among other aspects the hybrid roles it encountered in foreign police forces. Outside the United States, Thompson wrote, "the police are far more powerful than they are here. In a real sense, they possess the manifold authority and responsibilities that in the United States are divided among local police and sheriffs' offices, the FBI, the Border Patrol, the Immigration Service, the Secret Service, the Coast Guard, and narcotics, counterfeiting and tax collecting agents."[34] In contrast, the article implied, US police were well contained, roles divided in the system of checks and balances that should make Americans proud to vest their trust in the agents of their state. Ironically, of course, the article showed precisely the opposite, detailing a case of US police working readily on all these tasks. No wonder the journalist labored rhetorically to reestablish the clean borders of US police work, borrowing steam from the international comparison of modern democracy in the United States to chaotic miscegenation abroad, a time-tested element in apologia for US imperialism.[35]

Longer terms of duty with OPS opened further opportunities for exchanges of ideas, tactics, and philosophies with US police. A pair of OPS emissaries to Caracas in 1964 is suggestive. Gregory Luna and Richard Martinez, born six months apart, were both San Antonio PD, both enrolled at the same college, and both had been in military service in the mid-1950s, Martinez overseas to Korea, and Luna in exotic Pittsburgh. The two spent just over three months together in Caracas as OPS police trainers.[36] Martinez returned to Venezuela as a full-time public safety advisor for OPS. He went on to postings in Uruguay, El Salvador, and Mexico, remaining abroad until at least 1977 with the narcotics units that survived the end of OPS.[37] Luna returned from Venezuela to finish his law degree, quit the PD, and become prosecutor for the City of San Antonio. He is fascinating in the very opposite direction he then moved. In 1968, Luna opened a private law practice and helped to found MALDEF, the Mexican American Legal Defense and Education Fund, whose board he chaired for four terms. He was elected to the Texas House in 1984 and the Senate in 1993, where he served until just before his death in 1999.[38] If these friends stayed in touch, which their long association prior to 1964 suggests, how was Luna affected by the awareness of his friend's work? How did his own experience abroad and his friend's ongoing counterinsurgency work in Latin America color his assumptions?

Luna's story is worth detailing for its exceptional qualities, but it points to a wider dynamic. Just as prisons during the Gulf Wars put up photograph corkboards in staff rooms to laud coworkers away on temporary assignments to Iraq and Afghanistan, police departments that sent clusters of officers abroad surely kept abreast of their activities in collegial support.

The Office of Public Safety was far from the only importer of the lessons of US police work overseas. Guided to this question by OPS, we begin to see it everywhere. Virtually any point at which one touches down in the historical record, Cold War counterinsurgency experts with experience abroad trace more channels into US police work. Before OPS, people such as British SIS (Secret Intelligence Service, also known as MI5) agent Rolf Larson came to the United States after serving in Brazil and Bolivia, assigned to Arizona to do FBI anti-Communist work.[39] On the cusp of OPS in 1962, general William P. Yarborough reviewed counterinsurgency in Colombia for JFK and later oversaw US Army illegal surveillance of US citizens in civil rights and antiwar movements.[40] Well after OPS, the dynamic continues with the infamous Vietnam vet Jon Burge, who applied the techniques he learned torturing people in Vietnam to his Chicago suspects, or Richard Zuley, who interrupted his Chicago police work for a stint with prisoners at Guantánamo and was accused of torturous interrogation techniques in both places.[41]

Let us conclude this section with one particularly telling border-crossing Cold War cop. In his cautionary autobiography, *Bad Cop—No Doughnut*, former OPS-Costa Rica agent Andy Best recounts a run-in with someone who introduced himself as the director of the Drug Enforcement Agency stationed at the US Embassy in Mexico City, a brash young man named Joe Arpaio.[42] Excelling in border-crossing police work in Mexico and Central America, Arpaio advanced to become the head of the DEA's Arizona branch. He was with that agency for a twenty-five-year stretch, precisely the period in which Arizona led the national turn toward law-and-order, tough-on-crime detention practices. Arpaio would later be infamous as "Sheriff Joe" of Maricopa County, Arizona, who pitched his "Tent City" of Korean War–issue army tents in 1993, made "green bologna" sandwiches for inmates, and reintroduced the chain gang, including, in 1996, the first female chain gang.[43]

COMPARISON AND ITS CONSEQUENCES

This comparison between rural Third World locales and US cities, their problems, and those problems' solutions—strengthened by the exchange OPS facilitated between regular municipal police and violence workers overseas—would connect military strategy to urban policy throughout the rest of the 1960s and the 1970s, and not just in policing. In communications, mapping, data mining, labor management, and emergency preparedness, urban planners and policymakers suffused in the comparison's reigning common sense engaged in diverse conversations and collaborations with other defense intellectuals, transforming their fields of operations.[44]

Police were important to this dynamic not only in the transnational current they sparked but also in building ideological consensus for the US application of counterinsurgency tactics, thanks to their supposed focus on crime. As the notion of foreign-domestic equivalence became hegemonic, anticommunism fed the position coming to be called "tough on crime."[45] Both allowed for the radical distancing of self from a demonized, threatening Other, racialized to block the analysis of interconnection. Vietnam in particular could evoke this racialized menace, both in the figure of the guerrilla Viet Cong and the disorderly antiwar protestor spreading drugs and chaos on the home front. As public fear increasingly linked political protest to riots, and both of those to crime, a tough stance for democracy seemed a logical complement to a similar hard line against crime. Los Angeles police chief Thomas Reddin's fears were prototypical: "The present Negro movement is just as subversive as the past Communist movement or just as dangerous as the organized crime movement."[46] This is precisely the principle OPS developed and applied in its work abroad.

That the nascent rallying cry for "law and order" comprised both "tough on communism" and "tough on crime" adds a crucial transnational dimension to the work of scholars who have traced the ways US policymakers used criminal justice systems to contain the threats posed by urban unrest and civil rights activism.[47] Policymakers and citizens could make arguments about the need for law and order in response to unrest because US imperial engagements abroad gave them language and logic. The deeply racialized foundation of both doctrines could also build on each other quietly, implicitly.

Ideologically, Cold War foreign police experience (as in but not limited to OPS) was hot-burning fuel to the punishment paradigm. Counterinsurgency doctrine considered declared war to be barely different from low-intensity conflict, held dissent in contempt (even seeing political dissent and common crime as the same), and cultivated rock-solid confidence in the justice of its ends over means that struck others as inhumanly harsh. The sense that it was appropriate to transfer techniques between foreign and domestic settings nourished the emergent tough-on-crime consensus, supplying authority and expertise to lawmakers bent on enlarging the US criminal justice system. It was in this atmosphere that the policies and programs that would determine the course of policing and a great deal more of the domestic criminal justice system over the next quarter-century were designed.[48]

This was the atmosphere, for example, within which the presidential fact-finding commissions organized to respond to the urban distress of 1964–67 would do their work, particularly president Lyndon B. Johnson's Commission on Law Enforcement and the Administration of Justice of 1965–67, and his National Advisory Commission on Civil Disorders, 1967–68, respectively nicknamed the Katzenbach and Kerner Commissions after the figures at their helms.[49] The Katzenbach and Kerner Commissions were direct responses to the riots of the 1960s, charged with understanding their causes and preventing their recurrence. Both reflected the prevailing wisdom regarding the relevance of military expertise for their domestic purposes, soliciting testimony for their domestic problem-solving mission from authorities with overseas military experience. They even each heard from OPS specifically, the Katzenbach Commission receiving information on technologies such as police radio transceivers used by OPS in Vietnam, while Kerner et al. appreciated the services of two former Public Safety Agents as consultants, and a featured presentation from director Byron Engle, who appeared to explain the paramount role of law and order in securing the conditions for progress, as we encountered in this chapter's opening anecdote. The Kerner Commission incorporated into its widely read final report all of Engle's proposals for intelligence, public service, community-relations programs, emergency police units, and communications coordination.[50]

Such instances of influence reinforced the atmosphere into which they were received, which already posited a perfect convergence between foreign and domestic spheres. As noted above, Kerner introduced Engle with the promise that he would confirm that convergence. Engle's testimony was received by listeners possessed of a robust faith in the applicability of counterinsurgency theory to US conditions. In this they reflected wide consensus.

Upon this scaffolding, the Kerner and Katzenbach commissions built prescriptions for police expansion. Nicholas Katzenbach, attorney general and then undersecretary of state under Johnson, had lobbied for and then implemented the Law Enforcement Assistance Act of 1965, which authorized him as attorney general to distribute grants to fortify law enforcement (*while* chairing his commission). His commission's report, *The Challenge of Crime in a Free Society*, along with the publications of its multiple task forces, advocated expanded programs in a wide range of law enforcement subfields. The Kerner Commission's report also offered plenty of support for policing, Engle's recommendations among them.[51] The upshot was the Omnibus Crime Control and Safe Streets Act of 1968, expanding the smaller law from 1965 that had already begun to strengthen police lobbying power, inflate concern over crime, promote technical efficiency, and legitimize the idea of federal support for local and state law enforcement. The 1968 act, dubbed a "master plan" for federal crime policy, set up the Law Enforcement Assistance Administration, which would translate the tenets of counterinsurgency into domestic practice through sheer, cold cash, a stunning redistribution of national resources to police and other violence work.[52]

THE LAW ENFORCEMENT ASSISTANCE ADMINISTRATION: OPS FOR US POLICE?

The Law Enforcement Assistance Administration, or LEAA, as it is known, was the financial mechanism for the translation of counterinsurgency expertise into US domestic policing. Its mandate was to move money, using block grants, to encourage the fifty states and private entities to develop public-safety-related programs of all types, including prisons, courts, victims' services, and related areas such as alternate dispute resolution and treatment for addiction. Yet police departments, directly or indirectly, received the lion's share of its resources—and it was a pretty big lion.[53] From a sixty-million-dollar budget in its launching year of 1968–69, LEAA appropriations more than quadrupled to $268 million in 1970, still doubling to $529 in 1971, growing 27-fold to $1.75 billion between 1968 and 1972. Between 1972 and 1979 the agency's budget traced an arc with a high point of $1,013,000,000 (over one billion). When Reagan phased the program out in 1982, it had spent eight billion dollars on state and local crime control, "a mammoth institution" that had funded and created eighty thousand state and local projects.[54] This astonishing move by the federal government to underwrite the apparatus of punishment is an underappreciated part of the US state's carceral turn.

Scholars of the LEAA note that its core purpose was to professionalize the police.[55] This is an eerie echo of OPS. Indeed, the LEAA and OPS shared everything that followed from professionalization: expansion, counterinsurgency tactics, intelligence, updated technology, and more. No one at the time made the connection, perhaps in part due to the logic of comparison, which forbids equivalence (comparisons require distinction; not this *is* that, but this is *like* that), but mostly, I think, due to the US ethnocentrism that minimizes the relevance of the world to our domestic affairs.

The LEAA-OPS convergence emerges in one former agent's tale of job seeking after the demise of OPS. The "criminalist" Morris Grodsky secured a part-time consultancy for a computer firm, to write grants to the LEAA. "I wrote up a prospectus," he explained to me, for funds to support an innovative study:

> I was going to get a group of Public Safety people—people who were out in the world, I would get them together, people who had some expertise, who had worked in Latin America, . . . And what I would do is a study of terrorism or subversive actions in those countries [in Latin America] where we would contact the police to get their point of view. We would contact the various elements of these groups—the FALN, FARC, and so on, who were in jail, and get their point of view. We would survey the police notifications that came out in periodicals during the time of their activity. We would get the newspapermen's point of view,

the police point of view, the terrorist point of view, and maybe the public point of view, and write it up, and publish this as a paper that would be diffused among the American police forces.

Grodsky explained to the LEAA "that this would be useful to American police in terms of understanding subversive activity in Latin America." The LEAA denied the grant, but then later tried to hire Grodsky directly to perform precisely the project he had proposed. Already employed elsewhere, Grodsky declined, but in retrospect, he agreed that the LEAA and OPS shared a common core. "Probably it would read the same except that one was for foreign police, the other for American police," he reasoned.[56] Grodsky's anecdote offers yet another illustration of the two agencies' shared reliance on the analogy between foreign and US urban hot spots, on notions of development and perfectibility, and on an assumed similarity between dissent and crime, as well as the sense reigning in the United States at the time that foreign police practice was highly relevant to its domestic counterpart. The LEAA extended all these assumptions, fueled by overseas police assistance and counterinsurgency doctrine, into US policing policy and practice.

The LEAA came into existence in the world seeded by the logic of overseas police assistance, including OPS and its predecessors. But its star rose as OPS fell: the years of the LEAA's first great impact, the early 1970s, were the years of OPS scandal and termination. The great irony of this timing is that the LEAA did at home what Congress had just decided should not be allowed to continue abroad. It was a domestic application—even a massive expansion—of a policy that had just been deemed a failure. This will not surprise anyone familiar with the constant rhythm of criminal justice reform, in which failing practices are simultaneously bemoaned and expanded.

That the LEAA was seeded by the logic of overseas police assistance also meant that when those police assistants came home after OPS closed its doors in 1974, the LEAA would offer ample opportunity for employment. Their experience was abundantly relevant. The raft of LEAA employees among ex-OPS included Joe Mulvey, who worked as a regional administrator for the LEAA in Denver, and then an area director in its Audit and Program Review Office in Sacramento; Dave Powell, who became area director for the Office of Criminal Justice Assistance for the New England area LEAA, later switching to an address in Virginia; and Robert C. Lowe, who worked on LEAA affairs for the Seminole County Sheriff's Office.[57]

In addition to those who worked directly for the LEAA, many more ex-OPS worked for LEAA-funded projects. As a senior coordinator in the Law Enforcement Division of the California Governor's Office of Emergency Services, Francis L. Barnett worked on various LEAA-funded projects, most notably a training film designed for police at all levels.[58] Thomas Finn was offered a job on a five-year LEAA-funded program to develop standards and an accreditation process for law enforcement agencies, he noted proudly.[59] James L. McMahon secured "a job as director of an LEAA funded project with the National Sheriffs' Association concerned with Courtroom Security."[60] Frank L. Miller served as "a Criminal Investigative Consultant operating under a grant from the LEAA studying the involvement of organized crime" in North Carolina.[61] Roy Hatem was "directing a project, under an LEAA/Bureau of Indian Affairs contract with the Miccosukee tribe, to develop a viable law enforcement system," he told his former colleagues.[62] Robert Reynolds was grant manager for the Michigan State Office of Criminal Justice Programs, indicating LEAA employment or engagement.[63] John Moxley worked in a position in Topeka that required "a considerable amount of skill in Federal grantsmanship," he wrote.[64] The grants were surely requested from the LEAA, I conclude, not only because the LEAA is the body that would have received such proposals in that moment but also because Moxley soon after moved to Washington "to accept an LEAA staff job," the *Newsletter* reported, "working in the Training Division" and with LEAA-sponsored training centers around the country.[65]

The LEAA also created opportunities for ex-OPS to return to regular police work, a growth field thanks to LEAA-funded expansion. "Almost everybody" who couldn't retire got jobs with law enforcement, Grodsky remembered.[66] Indeed, more demobilized OPS agents seem to have taken up positions in US policing than in any other field. Of the 432 employees I have tracked through the *Newsletter* in the first seven years after the agency's closure, there are details of employment for 333 (twenty-five offer no information, and seventy-four simply retired). Of these, I count ninety-nine in some form of police work, including employment by regular municipal or state PDs, Public Safety Divisions, vice squads, sheriffs' offices, district attorneys, and the International Association of Chiefs of Police (IACP). To give a sampling, these included Frank Jessup with the Indiana State Police; Joe Jones in Salt Lake City; Ronald Holko in Farmington Hills, Michigan; Harvey Howell in Pima County, Arizona; Bob Galli in Washoe County, Nevada; Robert Cavenaugh in Cook County, Chicago; David De la Torre in Los Angeles County; Andy Best in Maricopa County, Arizona; and Robert Angrissani with the IACP.[67] These new positions were sites in which the lessons of their work abroad could continue to ramify, whether they concerned the equivalence of foreign and domestic venues, the applicability of counterinsurgency tactics at home, or the racist suppression of dissent.

OPS agents importing overseas techniques in particularly influential ways included people such as Doug McCollum, who became senior criminal intelligence analyst for the Investigative Service Division of the Washington, DC, Metropolitan Police Department; Lee Echols and David Phillips, who returned to found the Association of Former Intelligence Officers and to lobby Congress and the public to support intelligence work; and William W. Herrmann, a researcher for the Systems Development Corporation after his labor as a police advisor in Thailand and southern Vietnam, who introduced the concept of "controlled response" to urban disorders.[68]

These Cold War cops also came home to key roles in US prisons, just then beginning the growth that would take off in the 1980s. Ex-OPS agents returning to posts in prisons or jails numbered a good baker's dozen, in my count. The Florida Correctional Department hired Donald Olive, while the Wackenhut Security Corporation paid the bills for Donald Marion and Kenneth Burns.[69] Charlie Huff went back to Leavenworth; Joe Oaks was supervisor of the Pasadena Jail; Phil Severson directed the Maricopa County Jail; and Donald Bordenkircher was warden of the West Virginia Penitentiary and then the Kentucky State Prison at Eddyville.[70] Added to the ninety-nine returning to policing, this means that 112 out of 333—one-third—returned to work in policing or prisons. This count must be multiplied by the factor of all those who went on to work for private security companies, industrial safety consultancies, urban planning, prosecutorial and detective work, law enforcement training academies, and other visible or influential violence work domestically.

EVALUATING THE LEAA

With ex-OPS among its animating agents and the logic of counterinsurgency as wind in its sails, the LEAA changed the landscape of the US criminal justice system profoundly. It expanded it quantitatively, centralized and federalized it, and made it many times more lethal by distributing deadly technology. What it did not do is diminish crime. From that vantage point it was widely decried as a failure. Crime as measured by the FBI's annual *Uniform Crime Report* (UCR) continued to rise along with public fear of crime.[71]

Yet in terms of its impact on policing, the LEAA's effect is undeniable. The UCR traces a rise in police employees from 269,271 in 1963, just prior to the LEAA's predecessor OLEA, to 657,833 in 1980, a period in which the US population rose from 154,736,000 to 281,138,000. This represents a rise in the ratio of police to population from 1.9 to 2.5 police per 1,000 people.[72] This does not include people employed in other sectors of criminal justice. The Department of Justice calculated that in the 1970s, federal spending on criminal justice rose 62 percent, and on police specifically, 52 percent.[73] Some estimates of police growth are even higher.[74] Quantitatively, the LEAA grew US public safety employment rolls—the most visible part of the violence work sector—substantially.

The LEAA was also enormously important in shifting landscapes of public safety and policing qualitatively. It was the "first significant federal assistance to Criminal Justice," ushering in a new paradigm of law enforcement by bringing police forces that were scattered, fragmented, and uncoordinated, under federal management and measurement.[75] Here is another way in which the LEAA echoed OPS: in the federalization of criminal justice, the LEAA tugged US policing toward the centralized and often explicitly military models often operative in nations receiving OPS assistance.

Beyond numerical growth or federalization, the LEAA's most striking alteration of US policing involved new technology, some of it developed for overseas wars. Prior to the 1960s, there had been only minor technological updates since the big revolution of the police radio and patrol car of the 1930s.[76] New technology seemed a quick and easy way to change US policing, at least on the surface, and so the LEAA leaned into weapons transfers abundantly, to the point of complaints of overemphasis on hardware.[77] The timing of the Vietnam War was essential in this capacity, as aerospace and electronics industries then energetically developing weapons thrilled at the chance to sell them at home as well. To boost innovation even further, the LEAA and its predecessor, OLEA, funded three National Symposia on Law Enforcement Science and Technology in 1967, 1968, and 1970.[78] Military research and development and manufacturing firms proposed batteries of new armaments for use in US cities, some then used abroad, others being developed for such use, such as tear gas, dye gas (to identify rioters later), infrared surveillance, slippery confetti, stink bombs, electrified water stun guns, and so on. The experience of overseas police was spotlit in this process, as in the case of an OPS police consultant who testified to a symposium on mob control technologies held in Chicago in 1967.[79]

New technology was marketed to police all the more as it seemed likely that US participation in the Vietnam War would end. The LEAA assisted manufacturers, who feared drying demand, to address a domestic market, placing advertisements in industry journals such as *Police Chief, Law and Order, Law Enforcement Community*, and *Industrial Security*. Together, the federal agency and private companies easily "convinced domestic law enforcement agencies that they needed such things as helicopters, short take-off and landing aircraft, night vision instruments, and other such big-ticket items heretofore sold only to the Pentagon"—and then provided the gadgetry for free.[80] If in philosophical realms the paradigm of counterinsurgency was framing US policymakers' and city officials' approaches to their tasks, the LEAA opened the spigot for the technologies of counterinsurgency to come to their disposition.

Of the various technologies featured, tear gas and helicopters in particular quickly gained favored status in domestic arsenals. Tear gas was adopted widely, helped out by the prominence the journal *Police Chief* awarded advertisements for the product.[81] Choppers appeared as dedicated police vehicles first in Los Angeles in 1966, thanks to a grant to the LAPD for that purpose from the LEAA's predecessor, the OLEA. By 1972, at least 150 police departments around the country had taken to the air, and two years later, over three hundred could boast of at least one flying patrol. The LEAA was generous in funds for helicopters, especially if they were intended for riot control, a task it disproportionately favored with funding.[82]

MILITARIZATION OR EXCHANGE?

Many people think of these technological advances as "militarization." They certainly reveal police and military sidling up to each other, too close for comfort for those who would defend the borders of police. Yet while the technologies were borrowed from war, they were developed specifically for counterinsurgency, a doctrine that thoroughly integrated police, as we have seen, and as the next chapter will lay out in more detail. Helicopters were used in war prior to policing not because helicopters are somehow fundamentally military but because the military boasts greater resources for research and development. Tear gas clearly demonstrates the shared use of lethal technology by police and military forces, and the constancy of exchange between them. It did not simply travel once, from overseas battlegrounds to the home front. It was developed over a century ago for police suppression of domestic dissent, by French chemists put to the task. By the First World War tear gas had become military technology, embraced again by police to combat protest immediately following the end of hostilities; since then, it has been used in uneasy streets and fields of war alike.[83]

Even the SWAT team, that notorious LEAA-funded counterinsurgency project, reflects military-police exchange rather than police militarization. The notorious LAPD SWAT team formed in 1968, complete with snipers. Other similar units soon began to follow, such as the San Diego SWAT team organized thanks to a $140,000 LEAA grant. The SWAT team did have origins in war: most of its members were Korea or Vietnam vets, and they trained at the Camp Pendleton military base. The FBI invited local police to Quantico to train in SWAT and "Sniper Suppression"; SWAT team members could also learn tactics at the Fort Belvoir US Army Research Institute.[84] But SWAT team tactics are quintessential counterinsurgency, not at all appropriate for the classic battlefield model of war. They are transnational rather than military, funded when lawmakers came to read domestic landscapes in the light of foreign engagements.

The centrality of technological change to the transformation of US domestic policing in the era of the LEAA is nowhere more clear than in communications and data analysis. Police in the United States in the late 1960s and 1970s acquired, mostly for the first time, complex communications systems, computer-assisted mapping, and planning tools.[85] These were specifically recommended by the *Task Force Report: Science and Technology* (1967), prepared by the Institute for Defense Analyses at the request of the Katzenbach Commission.[86] This report proposed a National Inquiry System, pieces of which began to be set up nationwide.[87] The intelligence system SEARCH (System for Electronic Analysis and Retrieval of Criminal Histories) was set up in July 1968, fingerprint identification systems were established in New York and expanded elsewhere, and the FBI planned a National Crime Information Center with centralized computerized files and terminals in all major cities.[88]

Intelligence was a fundamental piece of the growth in US police data gathering and analysis in this period. It also shows exchange rather than "militarization" given its basis in counterinsurgency. Intelligence was a vital component of counterinsurgency and the reason police, who can live among and be of the population, were thought superior to soldiers for its pursuit. The LEAA's founding Katzenbach Commission, in its *Challenge of Crime in a Free Society*, recommended prioritizing police intelligence units to fight organized crime. The Kerner Commission agreed. The LEAA therefore funded several multistate regional intelligence entities, which helped regular police forces exchange information all while claiming to be nongovernmental. Dedicated intel crews also began to appear in local police forces.[89]

The LEAA thus "quickened" what Frank Donner calls the police intelligence "surge" with a "statutory mandate" to focus on organized crime and "riots and other violent civil disorders." "This entire movement for intelligence solutions to unrest," Donner details, "produced an extraordinary proliferation of new police units and an equally extraordinary expansion of established ones."[90] "Truly," a reviewer commented in 1976, "it appears that we brought the intelligence operations from Indo-China home to the United States and substituted 'criminals' for 'the enemy.'"[91]

Note that organized crime was a part of the rationale for intelligence for Kerner, Katzenbach, and the LEAA. The commissions' shared emphasis on organized crime points to one of the key alibis for the federal government's entrance into the war on crime. Proscriptions against federal policing kept crime policy at the level of the fifty states until the 1960s. Organized crime was the exception, the one area in which the federal government was legally permitted to be involved.[92] By painting organized crime as a behemoth spreading far over state lines and terrifyingly deadly, federal law enforcement champions could propose to fund criminal justice without appearing to step on state toes.

Perhaps it would be useful to remember here that in the United States, the principle of federalism insists that the exercise of police power is assigned to the fifty states, while to the federal government is reserved the right to regulate interstate commerce. Indeed, the ostensible federal-state division grants something close to immunity for laws or actions that respect this distinction: any state statute judged to be an exercise of police power enjoys "a trump of constitutionality." Yet the federal government has long exercised police power in practice, preserving through judicial rulings and legislation the legal fiction of its remove from that realm.[93]

The scale-busting shifts in law enforcement in this period relied on carefully constructed fear of organized crime. This threat had been spotlit by the televised Kefauver Committee hearings in the early 1950s, teaching a wide public to support the extension of crime control to the federal level.[94] It extended well beyond Katzenbach and Kerner to such figures as Nelson Rockefeller, who emphasized organized crime along with juvenile delinquency in his successful campaign for governor of New York, where his actions would seed the end of prison reform and the beginning of the hypercarceral war on drugs.[95] Organized crime was the public justification for the notorious Association of Law Enforcement Intelligence Units, or LEIU, the organization that pulled together the secretive network of police organizations that had gathered intelligence on political activists beginning with early twentieth-century red squads. The LEIU claimed that its founding purpose in 1956 was to combat organized crime, insisting when confronted with illegal activities by its members that it focused only on organized crime, and tracked only organized crime figures within its database. The LEIU automated its file systems thanks to funding from the LEAA in 1971 and upgraded them with another LEAA grant in 1978.[96]

Organized crime is useful in justifying transgressions of scale because it constructs a worthy rival for the state-market. In place of the puny Davids punished for trivial offenses, it conjures a Goliath whose threat justifies extensive and lethal reaction. Indeed, it displaces, onto the figure of the "criminal," the mutability and fluidity of the violence wielded so lethally by the state-market. The adversary it conjures deserves a counterstructure national in scope. No wonder the "war on crime began in the 1960s in large part as a war on organized crime."[97] No wonder the LEAA was so generous with the LEIU, and to other police intelligence projects that could also be framed as fighting organized crime.

In the 1970s, open discussion of police intelligence work became less common as the practice came under attack for civil liberties violations, and as the abuses of COINTELPRO came to light. The practice did not end but went underground or took cover as "community relations" programs, becoming a permanent part of regular police practice.[98] Its magnitude in the era of the NSA is the direct legacy of these innovations.

CONCLUSION: CONSEQUENCES

Ultimately, then, the LEAA, aided by OPS ideologically and occasionally directly, grew the criminal justice system consequentially. Police forces and their budgets swelled, and the harm they did correspondingly intensified.

"The growth of the police and their military capacity, pumped by LEAA funding, has understandably made them more deadly," charged Sidney Harring, Tony Platt, Richard Speiglman, and Paul Takagi in 1977.[99] As Lennox Hinds, past director of the National Conference of Black Lawyers, complained in 1979, "The patterns and practices of police abuse have been exacerbated by the creation and development of LEAA national resources which have increased the 'kill power' in large and small departments by financing developments in weaponry, communications systems, surveillance techniques, and intelligence operations."[100] The LEAA amplified the lethality of violence work by funneling government largesse aimed at pacifying foreign and domestic hotspots into policing and security.

Neither the champions nor the critics of foreign police assistance think of this as the legacy of OPS. They do not identify the LEAA, much less mass incarceration, as following from the logics OPS also followed and fed. The champions mostly remember congressional termination and are furious at the naiveté and ignorance, as they see it, of "the liberals" whose actions closed their doors. The critics, meanwhile, denounce the continuity of foreign police assistance as a mockery of congressional intent. To narrow OPS's legacy to foreign police assistance and place OPS's champions and critics in simple opposition is not helpful. Like the liberal and conservative positions on crime and security Naomi Murakawa has shown to be so close, these are basically the same version of the OPS story.[101] To see the agency's most sobering legacy requires placing it against its ideological backdrop and connecting it to the transnational history of domestic policing, as this chapter has done. This tale of interwoven local and global currents expands the narration of the rise and fall of OPS into a drama unfolding on domestic as well as overseas stages.

In the 1970s, policing crossed international borders, following and feeding powerful transnational currents. Conditions changed in this decade. Not because police began to cross from civilian to military modes in this period, however; not because Vietnam brought military technology to the police for the first time. The changes represent the iterations, in their day, of the constant crossings and exchanges that define police and state power in the modern world.[102]

Changing conditions reflected the effects of technological innovation, creating ever more deadly weaponry used not only by uniformed police but also in the swelling prison system and elsewhere along the extended spectrum of violence work. The other factor in this equation was the virulent social and economic inequality manifest visibly beginning in the 1970s. As this book's conclusion will explore, inequality intensifies violence in obvious and immediate as well as structural and deniable modes. Together inequality and technological change, *Violence Work* eventually argues, compounded the lethality of violence work.

Understanding the growing lethality of police as a product of inequality plus deadly technology helps resist the popular assumption that the 1970s saw the militarization of the properly civilian police. In fact, OPS demonstrates something completely different, as the next chapter will detail. Its actual operation features not the pollution of one category by another—military inroads into a cleanly civilian process—but overlap, a thorough coincidence of military and civilian. OPS agents straddled the military-civilian divide at every moment of the agency's life and afterlives. The agency had wrestled with the difficulty of defining military and civilian spheres from the moment of its foundation, or even before: OPS was in part a *product* of the need to distinguish, rhetorically, what are in practice deeply overlapping fields. Chapter 2 delves into this "border" protecting the legitimacy of violence work: the line dividing civilian police from the military.

OPS will continue to serve as guide through the rest of this book. Following people who worked for OPS during and after its tenure reveals policing functions jumping the barricades set up to contain it conceptually. It reveals police crossing geographic borders and leaping levels of scale, shows military and civilian to be at best artificially distinct, and conveys the profound intermixture of public and private police work as state and market ventures mix in tangled skeins of profit and violence.

Civilian or Military?

Distinction by Design

In 1964, in a jubilant assessment of a course he had recently offered to police in Brazil, a USAID worker named Stanford C. Smith offered a wartime
memory: "I always recall getting on the radio to tell the gun crews what
they hit while doing forward direction or observing during World War II.
It was a boost to their morale and made them feel a sense of accomplishment. The local courses here in Brazil are analogous."[1] Despite the fact that
Smith was involved in training Brazilian *police*, he found in his *military*
service a more relevant point of comparison than anything in his twenty-
four years as a state police officer.[2] As this chapter will explore, the State
Department's Office of Public Safety, which employed Smith, belied the
notion of a military-civilian divide, disregarding it in practice while labor-
ing to sustain an image of clean distinction.

   The distinction, as we will see, is a vanishing horizon. Definitions of "military" and "civilian" tend simply to accept that military means associated
with war while civilian is everything else.[3] The Geneva Convention section
on the protection of civilians, for example, doesn't define *civilian* in the
abstract, and gives a simple definition of civilian*s* as noncombatants. War

and peace researchers note simply the lack of definitions of these terms, or "the negative definition of 'civilian': any person who does not belong to a long list of combatants."[4] Criminal justice scholars of police tend simply to presume their object to be civilian. Such scholars "have been quite comfortable with the military/police dichotomy. . . . Most assume that studying the police and military is a mutually exclusive undertaking."[5] This is largely also true for scholars of the military, who tend to accept the integrity of these distinctions as given.[6] Popular definitions presume mission differentiation such as attack versus protect, or geographic scope as in abroad versus home, distinctions that do not survive even a cursory examination. Historically, the borders between military and police are blurry at best. Civil-military distinctions in the United States have never been absolute, with "overlapping police and military tasks" routine since the early republic, military models the basis of police organization throughout US history, and municipal police regularly consulting, training, or being trained by military personnel as a matter of course.[7]

Twinned vehicles of state violence, police and military rub up against each other constantly in history and theory. "Speculating that the police could be anything but paramilitary," posit prominent police scholars Peter Kraska and Victor Kappeler, "denies the existence of the inherent bond—historically, politically, and sociologically—between the police and military."[8] Thus is the military-civilian distinction vague, "flimsy," "rarely clearcut" and "usually full of tension," even to the point of no distinction under certain regimes, as Anthony Giddens has reasoned.[9]

The ostensible political neutrality of the police, a subset of the military-civilian split, is equally untenable. Military action, famously "the continuation of politics by other means," has explicitly political goals, while civilian policing is supposedly focused on nonpartisan challenges (namely "crime," as discussed in the introduction). Critical scholars of the police power recognize instead that policing is invariably political. In her keystone account of foreign police assistance, including OPS, Martha Huggins calls it "fundamentally political" in principle, and establishes indisputably that US police assistance in the Americas was political in practice, despite its self-presentation as a "nonpolitical and legal-rational instrument" for democratization. Public pronouncements notwithstanding, Huggins wrote, "the covert plans and programs of US internal security specialists have been expressly aimed at making foreign police into a political extension and servant of US military and CIA internal security concerns."[10]

Huggins's recognition that police are "fundamentally political" is not (only) an accusation of corruption that calls for reform but an observation about form itself: policing is the materialization of state-market power. As the introduction explored, police and state are both defined by the violence they dispose, a violence that the military also wields (free of the accompanying disavowal). Military-civilian blurriness indexes this common ground between military and police in relation to the state. Kraska concludes, "The foundation of military and police power is the same—the state sanctioned capacity to use physical force."[11]

The military-civilian split is not a surgical analytic device but a common sense, that powerful hegemonic field.[12] Preserving distance between the avowedly political project of the military and the purportedly neutral one of police allows some state violence to be claimed as apolitical, inevitable, even deserved. The military-civilian split also works to reassure a populace that state violence is mild within its own territory, the truly lethal tactics reserved for others beyond the pale. The split implies that the state disposes two radically different kinds of violence, one for foreigners and the other for members of the imagined community, encouraging blindness to the lethality inflicted on the nation's internal others while rationalizing the infliction of unlimited havoc in liberal war.[13] In all, the military-civilian split projects police as relatively gentle and politically neutral in comparison and contrast to the military, sustaining the legitimacy of police *and* war, and with that, the integrity of the state-market project.

The military-civilian split transcends its conceptual vacuity to survive as conceptual border only because people work hard to make it do so. The constant disclosure of indistinction sends the defenders of this regulatory idea scrambling to protect it. The dedicated ideological labor required to shore up the bounds of the civilian-military distinction is serious violence work.

This chapter follows that labor, tracing the fine blue-green lines that circumscribe "civilian" and "military" violence work. It narrates the birth and operation abroad of the Office of Public Safety and the career paths of some of its demobilized agents after its termination, particularly military or hybrid military-civilian careers. Noting the active labor OPS personnel devoted to differentiating civilian and military spheres alongside their constant erosion of that distinction in the course of their work, it spotlights this basic technic of state-market power.

The Office of Public Safety well illustrates the contradictions entailed in producing the categories of "civilian" and "military" as separate ideas when their arenas are so broadly overlapping. Its architects encountered this paradox from the founding moments of the agency's creation as an ostensibly civilian body in a military realm.

International relations changed dramatically after World War II, forcing US policymakers to reimagine their approach. The postwar anticolonial revolutions that signaled the resounding end of formal European imperialism haunted US military and diplomatic strategy in the early Cold War, shaping political possibilities and limits from the late 1950s on.[14] Under these conditions, military aid could be counterproductive; police assistance seemed to offer a safer route.

Proclamations of deference to smaller nations' sovereignty suffused the political landscape that produced OPS. In a speech introducing the Alliance for Progress to Latin American diplomats in 1961, President Kennedy positioned the United States, the hemisphere's neocolonial superpower, as anticolonial ally: "Our nations are the product of a common struggle— the revolt from colonial rule."[15] The text of that speech was tucked into a folder of "background" for OPS policy guidelines, along with the testimony of assistant secretary of state for inter-American affairs Edwin M. Martin assuring a congressional subcommittee that the "nineteen independent, sovereign nations [of the Americas], as properly jealous of their independence as we are," were "firmly committed in inter-American treaties to the principle of non-intervention in each other's internal affairs."[16] Kennedy's speech and Martin's testimony, examples of rhetoric ubiquitous at the time, rang in the ears of the agency's founders.

Within this political conjuncture, policymakers repackaged intervention as humanitarian aid, addressing the moral economy emergent in the wake of Nazi genocide.[17] Humanitarian aid had long worked to manage anticolonial resistance in the interests of capital and empire, and during the Cold War it boasted the additional advantage of appearing to respect the sovereignty of smaller nations and to raise standards of living, proving the superiority of democracy and capitalism.[18] Embraced in official rhetoric and written everywhere into policy, this logic powered the vast expenditures and bureaucracies of the Marshall Plan, the Alliance for Progress, and USAID. It also quite literally justified the creation of OPS: background for the agency's general policy guidelines included congressional testimony from the head of USAID in 1962 explaining that while the aid policies of the mid-1950s had been mostly military, during his term economic assistance had been increasing, used more and more "for humanitarian and development ends." The nation's "humanitarian ideal" had become the standard measure for aid provision, he promised.[19] The strategists who created OPS carried this testimony in their collective briefcase.

The framework of humanitarianism meant that the practical work of founding OPS would consist of moving existing programs from military to civilian institutions. This absolutely explicit process was often a clear and open one-to-one conversion: "The President desires that careful consideration be given to intensifying *civil police* programs in lieu of military assistance where such action will yield more fruitful results in terms of our primary internal security objectives," explained a 1962 NSA memorandum, a cabinet-level policy statement drafted to promote the creation of OPS.[20] Another high-level drafting document explained that the military's focus on securing borders was being redirected to "internal security," the euphemism for the suppression of dissent via counterinsurgency: "All Military Assistance Programs throughout Latin America either have been or are in the process of being redirected to the problem of Internal Security throughout the Western Hemisphere."[21] This document promoted OPS by noting that the new agency would build on solid ground: previous programs of Department of Defense support for foreign police. In the new climate, however, the DOD could no longer be the home for such support, and so OPS was placed in the Department of State.

The discussions of previous police assistance programs suggest that DOD involvement in policing had become inconvenient just prior to OPS's founding. Proponents of police assistance were still keen to justify it on the basis of its venerable history, but suddenly they also had to deny the military-civilian intimacy implied by that history. This produced some quite awkward positions, as the policy paper quoted above demonstrates: "The Department of Defense does not support 'police' forces in the common definition of the term. Using the term 'police,' however, in its generic sense, to include paramilitary forces such as Gendarmeries, Constabularies, and Civil Guards which perform a police-type function and have as their primary mission the maintenance of internal security, the Department of Defense supports police-type organizations in 6 countries—Panama, Nicaragua, Costa Rica, Iran, the Philippines and South Vietnam."[22]

Within the admission of DOD policing is a denial, an audible attempt to ward off any implication of illegitimacy by insisting that the nation's premier military authority did not *really* include police. These were merely "police-type organizations." The tautology is tight: "in the common definition of the term" police are civilian and therefore *could not* exist in the ministry devoted to war. Officials practically recognized that the "common definition" is empty of substance while fervently defending it as ideology.

Not only did officials acknowledge that previous police assistance had fallen under the jurisdiction of the DOD, but many would have preferred to leave it there, fretting that State lacked the chops to oversee it. Ultimately, however, the formal status of the agency trumped the question of competence. The decision came down from on high: "The Committee [on Police Assistance] believes that this management should be civilian in character."[23]

To convey this "character," OPS officials often emphasized the technical aspects of their agency. The word "technical," with its suggestion of specialized expertise, effectively wards off scrutiny from critics who are not themselves police. Its assurance of the detachment of violence workers offers the state as neutral administrative entity, never acting in fleshly passion but simply applying, objectively, the best practices of a mature discipline. Its model of politics fits a nineteenth-century Weberian bureaucracy but with neoliberal distance from the embarrassingly intimate work of a classic colonialism. OPS champions found frequent occasions to employ the term, from the founding Committee on Police Assistance that called itself "technical" in its longest self-description, to the ubiquitous packaging of OPS work as "technical assistance," to the location of on-the-ground functions in a "Technical Services Division."[24]

Officials designing OPS well understood that their mandate was to present as civic assistance. From the outset of Kennedy's involvement, policy advisors guided the government to "preserve the civilian character of the program, rather than associating it with either our military assistance or our clandestine effort."[25] Note the advisors' effort to preserve OPS free from potential association with the CIA, a target of critique for its questionable tactics but also an obviously political entity—not a productive affiliation for an agency that needed to appear devoted to apolitical tasks.

The Office of Public Safety was a creature of its political circumstance. Its design was not motivated by a disinterested altruism aimed at allied nations' civilian sectors, nor did anyone pretend it had anything to do with a desire to diminish "crime." It was created because of the image police assistance could project, which fit the formally postcolonial early Cold War period's need to respect national sovereignty and humanitarian ideals.

"IMAGE OF A CIVIL ORGANIZATION"

While some Cold Warriors hoped their efforts would genuinely improve people's lot, all cared deeply about appearances. Police looked better. Police were "more acceptable than the army as keepers of order over long periods of time," noted the Committee on Police Assistance, the prestigious interagency committee convened in 1962 to propose and plan what would eventually become OPS.[26] Police were "more acceptable to the people as a normal regulating force," an AID (US Agency for International Development) official echoed to the House Foreign Affairs Committee in 1963. Even on occasions when force was required, he elaborated, if police inflict it, "damage to life and property is held to a minimum," and in the all-important context of the Cold War, "communist attempts to characterize the application of force by governments as brutality is minimized."[27] Police assistance would even help the image of the *military*, an official explained in May 1962: in order to assist in "creating a more favorable image for military forces," the United States planned in 1963–1967 to decrease military assistance in favor of "increased emphasis on *civic action* programs."[28]

In these calculations, the perception of police was as important as their service. An airgram from AID's Washington bureau admonished its employees to remember that police should labor equally to serve their constituencies and to recast perceptions of that service, reminding its branches to pay "particular attention to promotion of the concept that the police should be and should be known as the servants rather than the oppressors of the people."[29] (Why the latter would be necessary if the former were true was not explained.) A draft of "Overseas Internal Defense Policy Guidelines," a key launching document for OPS, admitted that the US government was not "against violence or revolution, *per se*, as historic agents of change." People could die, the policy guidelines offered with stunning cynicism, as long as their deaths did not appear to come from Yankee hands: "In countering insurgency, the major effort must be indigenous. . . . In internal war it is always better for one national to kill another than for a foreigner—especially one with a different skin coloration to do so."[30] Explicit in their emphasis on image, these guidelines hoped to train local forces for the anticommunist crusade not out of any respect for cultural competency or the value of long-standing relations but simply because locals looked better. "The active participation of non-indigenous forces in counter-insurgency operations can be counterproductive," they continued; "it (a) dilutes the nationalist appeal, and hence the acceptability, of the local government, (b) makes the United States a target for anticolonialism and (c) permits the communists to associate themselves with the forces of nationalism and anti-Westernism."[31] This is a fascinating acknowledgment of anticolonial critique rendered essentially in the terms of that critique. In addition, it used a proxy to fight decolonial resistance: foreign police, it hoped, would serve as prosthetic materializations of global capitalism's state-market violence.[32]

This policy paper, part of the shaping of OPS, was simply, if brutally, pragmatic. No democratic ideal or principle would stand in the way of US political priorities, certainly not trivial academic distinctions between military and civilian spheres. Given the nature of "internal warfare," it reasoned, "deterrence and suppression requires a blend of military and non-military countermeasures and corrective actions."[33] Pragmatism meant choosing the right tool from the toolkit without regard for sphere.

Along with this pragmatism regarding appearances, US policymakers were sanguine about cost. Some of the time, the focus was simply on the bottom line. The Committee on Police Assistance Programs weighed police versus military assistance for the president in July of 1962: "The cost per man is much lower than for the military because police live among the people and do not require the extensive staff and logistic support needed by military units," the committee explained to Kennedy's receptive ears.[34] Such calculations were candid. The chairman of the Joint Chiefs of Staff, encouraging more funding for OPS, advised the Special Group for Counterinsurgency (Kennedy's important executive-level policy coordination body) in 1965, "The United States could repeatedly incur high political and national costs by being forced to redress by military force insurgencies that could have been dealt with more effectively in their earliest form by adequate police capabilities achieved through comparatively small US expenditures."[35] In this vision of task transfer from military to civilian bodies, no mission distinction intruded, no sense of military and civilian police action as qualitatively different. Police rather than military force was a simple question of expediency: military force was expensive, so civilian intervention would replace it. This was a conception not of police as crime-focused versus the military as bellicose but of civilian police as prevention and military action as cure, making an ounce of the former amply cost-effective.

Early on, strategists of police assistance regularly acknowledged that civilian and military bodies coincided in practice. The Committee on Police Assistance specified in 1962 that police paramilitary units were an integrated part of police work, and not only made no objection to such integration but found it extra reason to support police: "In many cases, police forces supplement the army's counter-guerrilla capability with their own paramilitary units."[36] These forces, the recipients of US aid, the committee recognized, were often thoroughly mixed: "'paramilitary' in organization, 'military' in equipment, and 'police' in mission."[37] Initial guidelines for OPS often acknowledged the variability of definitions of police work, such as the airgram to country teams passing along language readers may recognize as an echo of one of OPS's founding documents: "'Police' is used generically to include the regular police as well as paramilitary units within civil police organizations and paramilitary forces such as gendarmerie, constabularies, and civil guard which perform police functions and have as their primary mission maintaining internal security."[38]

In addition to noting the hybrid character of foreign police and military forces, US policymakers recognized that their own nation had long mixed police into its military body. The Committee on Police Assistance acknowledged that there had been civilian-military mixture in pre-OPS police assistance, sketching a continuum of violence work: the Defense training assistance program "involves the full spectrum necessary to produce military preparedness and may include 'police training' despite the fact that DOD does not support police forces in the common definition of the term."[39] Note the denial that once again follows the confession, barely rephrased from the Department of Defense report—Defense "does not support police forces in the common definition of the term." This reiterated protest underlines both the overlap and the unease it subtended.

These machinations confirm that OPS was no impartial initiative launched to contain common crime, but a key player in "internal warfare," a fully political project. Every observer, friend or foe, grasped that what gave the Public Safety program life and justified its continued existence was its formal nonmilitary status. While scholars of OPS have paid attention to the ways its employees attempted to circumvent the congressional prohibition that ended their agency's work, they have pointed less to the political shell game that governed its start.

The point is not that OPS was "really" military aid but that any attempt to characterize OPS as either primarily military or essentially civilian oversimplifies—in a particular ideological way. The placement of OPS in the Department of State rather than Defense should not be understood as civilian rather than military but as political above all.

As important as its location in State were the material bases on which OPS was founded. These were, quite literally, military bases, namely Fort Davis in the Panama Canal Zone, where the Inter-American Police Academy was initially sited. This proximity and cooperation, organizers hoped, would help to transfer policing functions cleanly over to OPS. Yet a neat reassignment would be tricky, given the lack of clean distinction to maintain in the first place. The hybrid character of state-market violence, confounding the borders of civilian and military spheres, becomes ever more clear when we turn to the actualities of OPS practice in the field.

MIXED IN PRACTICE

The Office of Public Safety mixed military and civilian elements from the very start, in the people it selected to populate its ranks. Officials made a pointed attempt to recruit domestic police to bolster OPS's civilian status. They advertised for new hires in *Police Chief* magazine, a publication of the International Association of Chiefs of Police, and recruited through personal contacts in the IACP as well as municipal and state forces in Los Angeles, Indiana, New York, and elsewhere.[40] Unfortunately, the attempt to recruit state and municipal police proved difficult. Many local police were unwilling to move abroad, so recruitment was slow, plus federal agents often questioned the capacities of local cops. An early report, after assuring its audience that it had no "intention of minimizing the professional competence of US police personnel," argued that domestic police work did "not give personnel the knowledge of foreign police administration required to assist the police of the underdeveloped, newly emerging nations."[41] The recruitment effort thus expanded to include military police, retired military personnel, police assistance agents from OPS's predecessor, CIA officers with police assistance or paramilitary experience, and employees of the FBI, the US Border Patrol, the Treasury Police, and the Secret Service.[42]

Still, most OPS employees had some police experience. But not *only* police experience. Those who were state, county, or city police had often entered that service from stints in the military, serving in World War II or Korea. In fact, many of them had ridden wartime experience right over the military-civilian divide into a career in law enforcement, judging military skill sets good preparation for civilian policing.[43] Further, civilian posts were far from the only ones they had held after youthful service; many also had private or further military experience. An early memo assured the Special Group for Counterinsurgency that OPS recruits featured "an average of 16 years of job-related experience in civil law enforcement, military service or private industry."[44]

OPS was thus a body made up of diverse pieces, or, more exactly, of pieces diverse unto themselves, and its agents piled on further layers of diverse experience as they performed their duties. They crisscrossed national borders, agency loyalties, and civilian and military lines. The first director of OPS, Byron Engle, is a good example; he had been director of personnel and training for the Kansas City, Missouri, police department, and then police advisor in Japan after World War II, as well as an agent for the CIA, an affiliation he never clearly abandoned.[45] Many OPS officers had trained in postwar Japan; many were CIA; many also cycled through wartime and postwar Korea, Vietnam, Laos, and Cambodia on their way to Latin America or elsewhere.

OPS took these already-complex subjects and deepened the texture of their experiences even further. It placed them in theaters of war governed by military authorities, exposed them to military training, and set them the inherently hybrid tasks of counterinsurgency. Counterinsurgency was a particularly important context, as discussed in the previous chapter. Developed and implemented by military and police together in the earliest moments of the Cold War, counterinsurgency was at a peak in the period of OPS's operation, a key reason for its establishment, and a crucial element in its civilian-military hybridity.

Counterinsurgency casts military forces in "police-like" roles and brings police to adopt military characteristics, confusing the traditional police/military distinction of "citizens at home / enemy abroad" by teaching security forces to target the enemy within.[46] Valuing police work because police could constitute an "intimate point of contact between government and citizen," it emphasized in particular intelligence and paramilitary operations, facets of policing usually considered the military end of police work at best.[47] A former member of the Joint Chiefs' staff who was intimately involved in the implementation of counterinsurgency observed that this practice "broke down the flimsy partition separating civilian and military authority."[48] As OPS's quintessential, overarching method, counterinsurgency ushered OPS personnel across political borders police are not supposed to cross and instilled martial principles that are not supposed to guide them. OPS personnel were responsible for the "functional integration of all indigenous police, paramilitary, and military forces into a unified counterinsurgency effort," observed Michael Klare.[49] Klare meant this as critique, but OPS agents were often proud of the coordination they facilitated, though they began to discuss it differently as their agency came under fire.

OPS centered this formal mixing at the heart of its operations, the Inter-American Police Academy (IAPA). This was OPS's main training facility, set up in the Panama Canal Zone, home to the command center for all western hemisphere military operations. There the police academy was a short five miles from the School of the Americas (SOA), the infamous college for Latin American military officers. Organization and curriculum for the IAPA were designed under the supervision of military officers and in conversation with SOA instructors, a situation that pulled the question of the respective roles of military and civilian forces to the surface. Then director Byron Engle reassured Congress in 1963 that OPS nevertheless retained its civilian essence. Though the officer in charge of the academy in the Canal Zone was "in close contact" with SOUTHCOM commander in chief General O'Meara, Engle admitted, he assured the committee that OPS assistance "was classified as technical rather than military."[50] Note the function of this use of "technical," serving in Engle's phrase as a synonym for "civilian," with all the implications of detached objectivity and unimpeachable expertise.

A decade later, Engle presented a different take to Thomas Lobe, who studied OPS just before it was dismantled. As opposition to OPS mounted in Congress, Engle asserted that he had been uncomfortable with the police academy's location in an army installation. "It made it difficult to convey to police trainees a sense of the separation between police and military," Engle told Lobe, even claiming that he had moved the academy to Washington to facilitate the teaching of that key distinction.[51] With this revision Engle erased the agency of Panamanians who manifested their sovereignty in the Canal Zone, forcing the academy's relocation. He also bypassed his own earlier protestations. Engle rolled with the punches, granting earlier concerns as justified in order to insist they had been resolved, spinning to maintain the military-civilian distinction needed to portray his agency as legit.

The IAPA was a crucible for mixture even as it strived to instruct its agents in the value of separation. Academy instructors were far from uniformly civilian, including CIA, FBI, Border Patrol, and various armed forces vets, and they faced classrooms that mixed "military and police officers with ranks that ranged from sergeant to colonel."[52] An internal debate showed their ongoing negotiation of the civilian-military relation. SOA instructors thought civil police incapable of dealing with crises, leading to an argument over the respective abilities and prerogatives of military versus civilian forces. One IAPA instructor's reflection on this debate reveals that the conditions of OPS's foundation brought its officers to face tenets of law enforcement philosophy that might have remained tacit otherwise. To address the issue of whether police or military forces were better equipped to handle crises, SOA and OPS instructors produced a film, a process that pushed Fort Davis personnel in both institutional positions to grapple with the question. Titled *The First Line of Defense*, the film explained that the police "have primary responsibility for maintaining internal security with the military in a supporting role." When completed, it served as a training tool for OPS.[53] While clarifying the primacy of police for counterinsurgency, this elucidation did not dismiss the military. It simply set a basis for initial organization, understanding that police-military relations would be worked out on the ground.

What OPS officers found on that ground was even more complicated again. They often worked alongside military comrades, as a photograph of a Public Safety "conference" in Vietnam in 1970 well illustrates (figure 2.1). Former OPS hand Adolf Saenz remembered several active duty military police and Green Berets by name in his autobiography.[54] OPS agents were often assigned to train paramilitary organizations such as SWAT-type commando teams.[55] Most importantly, training foreign police forces brought OPS personnel into contact with police forces organized along military and paramilitary models. Asian, Latin American, and African police forces are often centralized and even federal, and some specifically military. These mixed models of civil and military structure in assisted countries' police forces varied widely, reflecting diverse histories of formation in colonial and national contexts.

OPS officers encountered these hybrid models with varying reactions. Saenz recalled his surprise at the diversity of police systems he encountered in the American republics where he was assigned. Civil police organizations under military control in El Salvador, Panama, and elsewhere, he

FIG 2.1 Photo of an OPS conference in Vietnam in 1970, showing PSD (Public Safety Division) employees mixed seamlessly together with MR-4 (Military Region 4) personnel
SOURCE: *PSN* 173 (FEB. 2017), 1. PHOTOGRAPH COURTESY OF JOHN WEISS.

explained, were "considered traditional, legal, and moral."[56] In contrast, Morris Grodsky proclaimed himself "not at all surprised" to discover that police in Latin America were part of the military or thought of themselves as military, "because in most cases police were actually a part of the army." He cited Nicaragua as exemplary. There, he explained, "police rode around in jeeps, dressed in military uniforms, carried machine guns. They didn't patrol. They were a repressive force; still part of the National Guard." For Grodsky, the task for OPS was precisely the demilitarization of such forces. He recognized, however, that the transformations they effected were sometimes shallow. After OPS assistance, "in many places, police had different uniforms, drove regular cars, and carried .38's like US police. But in many cases they were only cosmetically different."[57]

The high-level government body that founded OPS understood these differences, from afar, in the condescending moral framework of development. "Newly emerging countries" often had "primitive notions of police science and service," wrote the Committee on Police Assistance in its report in 1962.[58] "The police concept to which we have become accustomed in the mature democratic environment of the United States is different from that existing in the less developed and newly emerging Free World countries," a contemporary account put it. "For reasons rooted in their own political, social, cultural, and economic histories—coupled with the natural confusion and emotional imbalance incident to new-born independence—their concepts of the roles and functions of police are sometimes vague, non-existent, or viewed with public fear and distrust."[59]

Agents in the field did not all dispense this smug evolutionism. Some were able to see the traces of colonial histories and the logic of other methods of organization. In Brazil, OPS rural advisor Glen Hill encountered a paramilitary policing unit on a 1965 tour of São Paulo, noting its reflection of Brazil's Francophilic past and France's colonial power:

> A . . . problem continues to exist within the innate character and tradition of the Forca [sic] Publica. From 1909 until 1930, French Army Staffs served as advisors to the Forca. This heritage has traditionally influenced the Forca and knowingly or unknowingly, directed it towards the conformation of a "Gendarmarie" type organization. As is commonly known, the French Gendarmarie is an elite unit that recruits from the French Army, and only those who have achieved NCO rank or have served at least 3 years. With this brief background, it is more understandable to find a very large para-military unit in São Paulo performing civil police functions, while being operationally oriented along military lines.[60]

This uncensored observation, interesting in its insight into the knitting together of European and American imperialisms, shows agent Hill's clear sense that policing should be civilian.

Hill characterized the Força Pública's militarism as a "problem," but his colleague George Miller, who had concluded a field visit to São Paulo three months prior, had a slightly different take. Miller (a former police officer from Pennsylvania) reported that the Força Pública was "a well disciplined and seemingly well equipped para-military organization" of about 25,000, including 6,000 "Shock-troops." He observed their discrepancy in function: "Despite the police responsibilities assigned to this force, the orientation seems to be completely military." Yet Miller ultimately did not judge the Força's mission compromised. He praised their "awareness of police problems" and "sophistication of operations." His praise of a commander who "did display a clear concept of the police versus the military mission and of the need to develop a public service image of police" suggests that the problem with confusing civilian and military lay not in itself but in the difficulties it posed for projecting a positive public impression.[61] OPS's intense concern over image only grew as the agency faced mounting public censure.

As this suggests, the need to project an image of distinct civilian and military spheres was felt well beyond the leadership and into the ranks of Public Safety advisors. Lower-level officials also amply realized that haziness regarding these categories threatened their agency's survival, and often seemed to value image independently of the substance they might have argued it reflected. In US congressional hearings, OPS officer T. Brown revealed that OPS officers assigned to Brazil disregarded the civil-military distinction, particularly in relation to the 1964 coup, which they supported. Yet Brown proudly insisted that US aid had improved the Brazilian police's "image as a civil, as opposed to military organization." Hastening to belittle any substantive mixings, Brown tripped over his own awkward assertion: "The fact that military officers are assigned to head the various organizations is really aside from that."[62]

The concern OPS officials voiced when they encountered a compromised civil-military distinction may at times have been cynical, given how much they did to erode it. When expedient, OPS advisors actively overrode civilian-military divisions, as when those divisions caused conflict or competition among policing bodies within a single nation. In Brazil, where the civil guard, military police, and Força Pública competed with each other for resources, respect, and authority, OPS officials often felt it their duty to improve interpolice relations, effectively crossing and blurring group boundaries in pursuit of the greater goal of coordination.[63] In trainings there, OPS deliberately mixed military and civilian police in the student body, echoing its practice at the IAPA. In 1965, Dan Mitrione gave a course on patrol techniques in Niteroi, across the bay from Rio de Janeiro. That course included both civil and military police. For them, he reported, it was a novelty to be together, and they exhibited "much fellowship," to his eye.[64] His OPS division facilitated the acquisition of materials, including patrol vehicles, which were distributed to both civil and military police, including "Shock Force" troops in both.[65] A training in Salvador, Bahia, in 1966 also grouped military police and *delegados* from the Department of Public Safety, with fine results, the trainer judged.[66] When George Miller went to advise Guatemalan police about industrial safety in June of 1965, he convened a meeting with the heads of police and military intelligence, interpreting it "optimistically as possible door-opening into development of coordinated intelligence services for the country."[67]

Despite its extensive intelligence focus, OPS was often embarrassed by revelations of its involvement with this ostensibly military and political arena. McClintock contrasts this attitude with the 1980s, when police assistance embraced the emphasis it "unashamedly placed on political investigation and intelligence" as well as special operations.[68] During OPS, nevertheless, its champions denied charges of political policing, stipulating an ideal neutrality. Defending the Guatemala program from stateside critics, one writer acknowledged that OPS was countering political dissent, but he justified its presence with the classic police alibi: common crime had also been widespread, causing "at least as much misery and loss as the insurgency."[69] Joining political activity and crime as the proper object of police, this writer fed the conflation of crime and dissent at the heart of domestic crime policy. In straining to project an impossible political neutrality he also suggested, inadvertently, that OPS had exacerbated the problems it hoped to solve, or at least been powerless to relieve them.

AFTER OPS: MILITARY CAREERS
FOR POLICE TRAINERS

The ease with which Public Safety agents moved over to formal military realms when their program was cancelled shows they had indeed been well prepared for work on the far side of the civilian-military line. Several simply joined the armed forces. Paul Lococo, for example, served in the army after his time with PSD Vietnam.[70] James A. MacGregor worked for the Army's STRATCOM (Strategic Communications Command) after his OPS service.[71] Verman Claudio served an OPS telecom unit in the middle of a thirty-year career in the army from which he retired as a colonel in 1969.[72] Frank Cohen described himself as one of the early military details to the

IPA, the International Police Academy (the new name for the IAPA after its move to Washington, DC), meaning he was a military man assigned to teach there. He went on to serve as provost marshal, an armed forces position in charge of the military police for the military district of Washington, one of the US Army's major commands.[73] (The hybridity of both a military police and a military district based in the District of Columbia is noteworthy, along the way.) Some ex-OPS agents moved to other hybrid bodies such as the Border Patrol, which hired David Morgan, Gerald Brown, and F. J. Danforth.[74]

Quite a few ex–Public Safety officers negotiated positions in Defense attaché offices, intelligence-gathering military sections of ambassadorial missions, since 1965 located institutionally within the Defense Intelligence Agency.[75] The intelligence-gathering priority of counterinsurgency made this a logical move for ex-OPS officers including Samuel McKinney, Edward Burke, Paul Sabol, Paul Vukovich, and John Rodriguez, who all served DAOs after leaving OPS employ. McKinney joined the DAO's Operations and Plans Division; in 1975 the *Newsletter* reported that he was on his second tour with DAO Saigon, though anticipating a reduction in force and so looking for police or security work back home.[76] Burke served the same mission.[77] Sabol became DAO liaison to the Republic of Vietnam Armed Forces, where he stayed until some point in 1976.[78] Vukovich worked for an unspecified branch of the DAO Saigon, extending his military engagement with a short tour of duty at the Vienna Air Force Base in Ohio upon his return.[79] Vukovich interestingly went on to work for a military body belonging to a foreign country, the Saudi Arabian National Guard, though as an advisor on the payroll of a private security firm, the Vinnell Corporation (we will meet him again in chapter 4).[80] Rodriguez worked briefly for the DAO Saigon in logistics and administration before returning to the United States (with his Vietnamese wife, a phenomenon explored in chapter 6) to take up posts with civilian bodies: the Department of Commerce and later the IRS.[81]

Merging police and military work in the field of intelligence was Lee Echols, who declined to say exactly who his employer was beyond "one of the many U.S. intelligence services."[82] (His colleague Adolf Saenz identified him as CIA, which his absence from the *Biographical Register* would seem to confirm.)[83] Echols had a heterogeneous background, including work for the Border Patrol and US Customs as well as serving as a sheriff in Arizona prior to his work overseas.[84] After retiring from OPS, Echols lectured at military colleges including the Counter Insurgency School at North Island, Eglin Air Force Base, and the Air Force Command and Staff College in Montgomery, Alabama. In the face of what he feared was diminished congressional support for intelligence agencies, Echols, with OPS colleague David Phillips, founded the Association of Former Intelligence Officers and toured the nation, lecturing to students of all sorts to support fledgling chapters of his AFIO.[85]

Many of the ex–Public Safety agents who returned to regular domestic police work also continued to cross over into military realms in the course of their regular professional lives. They completed military-led training programs such as those conducted for sniper or SWAT teams or received military technology such as helicopters and advanced weapons technology to integrate into their departments' operations, as noted in chapter 1.

CONCLUSION: COLD WAR CONFLATIONS

OPS easily, constantly stepped out of the ostensibly civilian realm into the world of politics and war. Its allocation to US allies, its focus on industrial security, and above all, its assignment of counterinsurgency meant that it could do no less. Counterinsurgency is unquestionably political policing, for it criminalizes dissent. With counterinsurgency as priority, OPS would maintain its founding close relationship with the CIA and the clearly political work performed by that agency. Eventually, charges of "political policing" would be a part of the agency's undoing.

The friends of foreign police assistance thus went to great lengths to deny any such boundary blurring on the part of OPS agents. An OPS official in Bahia in 1970, for example, scoffed at accusations that death squads were eliminating opponents of the military government. "It is significant that to date all so-called victims of the 'Death Squad' were individuals with records of activity only in common crimes. As far as is known there have been no political assassinations attributed to the 'Death Squad,'" he explained, following with a rejection of claims (since proven beyond a doubt) that the Brazilian government tortured and killed political prisoners.[86]

While there may have been cynicism in this or other similar denials, many OPS champions were true believers in the proximity (if not identity) of common and political crime, a belief encouraged by the ideological frame of counterinsurgency and related to and nourished by the criminal-

ization of the civil rights movement then under way in the US.[87] This conflation, part of the late twentieth century's choking of effective resistance
to injustice, points to the exclusion inherent within a liberal rights framework.[88] Alas, the very logics of liberal freedom underpin the oppression they
purport to overcome.

A course on "Common Crimes and Terrorist Crimes" proposed for
the IPA promised to discuss "ordinary crimes of violent extremists" and
to "emphasize that the crimes committed are in a legal sense no different
than the so-called common crimes." Class discussion, the proposal expected,
would lead "toward the conclusion that the act is a crime and the perpetrator
is a criminal regardless of his political motivation."[89] This is the thinking
that undergirds the phenomenon Jonathan Simon documents, of framing
crime in terms of war.[90] Simon and other critics of "militarization" might
be interested to learn that this framing is not new but characterizes US
policing at all moments of its history.[91]

As the civil rights movement gained momentum and as criticism
mounted of US-supported coups, military dictatorships, death squads, and
cross-national collaborations such as Operation Condor, OPS officers felt
more beleaguered, more aware of the importance of denying the practices
their soft and naive critics (as they characterized them) misunderstood
as illegitimate. While early on, OPS champions such as the Committee on
Police Assistance were matter-of-fact about including military and paramilitary forces in OPS's jurisdiction, by the early 1970s they were unwilling
to admit any such mixtures. In telling language, officials denied that OPS
ever worked outside civil arenas. Engle's successor as OPS director, Lauren
Goin, in a memo to the AID administrator in 1974, rebutted all allegations
of torture, political policing, and CIA cover. He insisted in reference to
South Vietnam prisons, for example, that OPS work was "totally in the area
of humanitarian aid," an allegation he was ultimately unable to sustain to
Congress.[92] Even in the twenty-first century, he was still insisting that OPS
had been civilian. In a 2002 elegy written to laud Public Safety, Goin used
the term "civil" to modify "police" eight times in seven paragraphs.[93] Goin
clearly protests too much, but his excess is helpfully diagnostic. So is that
of other former OPS officials who also persevere in contending, even into
the new millennium, that their role was to *de*militarize foreign police.[94]
Precisely because OPS was a site of such fertile exchange between those
bodies designated police and military, respectively, Goin and others had to
insist so vehemently on its confinement to one side.

Even the archives reveal these labors of denial. Recall Stanford Smith's wartime memory, which opens this chapter. Smith's jolly anecdote seems to have struck his superiors as benign, for they left it accessible, despite the noteworthy conflation of military and civilian action (not to mention the disturbing suggestion that OPS training gave Brazilian police the satisfaction of having destroyed a target). Yet evidence of assistance to military or paramilitary organizations was clearly removed from public view. Within the unclassified—that is, uncensored—portion of USAID records at the US National Archives (by far the smaller portion of the voluminous paper cache) are folders for "paramilitary" and "military police," each containing a single sheet of paper.[95] If at one point OPS bureaucrats found enough material under such categories to justify separate folders, they later apparently deemed such records unfit for public review. An unexpected task of revision faced OPS apologists after congressional investigations convinced many observers that the program had violated standards of democracy and decency.

Goin's protestations in 2002 probably reflected his hopes around US aid via police assistance after 9/11 and before the launch of the US assault on Iraq in early 2003, and they remind us of the relevance of OPS's legacy as US police programs abroad continue. Goin's assertions cannot displace the evidence showing that OPS was a decidedly ambiguous body, a site for the blurring of military-civilian roles instructive to everyone who encountered it.

OPS ended for several reasons, but most simply, its termination marked its champions' failure to convince the US Congress that police assistance was the straightforward civilian, technical mission it claimed to be. That it failed to live up to its self-styling was not only the fault of its individual agents but also a consequence of the window it opened—and opens for us still— onto the emptiness of that venerable fiction, the military-civilian divide.

THREE

"Industrial Security" in Alaska

The Great Public-Private Divide

">. . . a developing service industry no different in
principle from any other service industry."

—RAND Corporation characterization of
private security, 1972

PUBLIC POLICE?

This chapter and the next focus on the public-private distinction, the notion that business and trade take place on a plane separate from governance. This absolutely critical dividing line is what makes it possible to
think and act as if there even *were* such a thing as a state (or a market), a
public versus a private sphere, so it's worth looking at closely.[1] Common
parlance often suggests that the state is tautologically public, *the* public entity par excellence, "public" then escaping the status of adjective modifying
"state" and rising to the level of synonym, as if a brick-level defining quality. As an actualization of state *as* power, police shares in this definitional

circularity, hovering between "is" and "must be" public, the existential and the imperative circling each other without resolving.

This is why challenging the public status of the police can convey such a devastating critique of the state. Luckily for those who would like to craft such a challenge, a genuine accounting beyond a charge of shallow or reparable police "privatization," it is actually quite easy to see how hollow are "police" claims to be public, whether because so much violence work is done by people in private employ whose work is identical to the work done by uniformed public police and who themselves are or have also been uniformed public police, or because the entities that employ violence workers are such swirling assemblages of state and market structures.

I am not the first to note the bonds between these chain-linked concepts. People who think about police in critical ways seem to come to see them fairly quickly. Observers of police have contemplated the "complex, ambiguous ways" public and private relate to each other. Stuart Hall points out that mixed or hybrid public-private forms abound, and that the boundaries of public and private are always shifting, "not natural divisions, but socially and historically constructed."[2] Historians of uniformed urban police in the US and Britain often note that private policing preceded the public version, founded to support colonial ventures—Europe's classic colonizing companies (the British South African Company, the Royal Nigerian Company, the Imperial British East Africa Company, and the East India Company) all had their own proprietary police—and have extensively diagrammed the ways public police work breaches the public-private divide, keeping the "dangerous classes" in place, protecting financial interests, and preserving social order.[3] Les Johnston notes that public-private divisions in policing are "taken as natural and self-evident distinctions. But in fact, the extent of their overlap makes simple opposition between them (and related oppositions between the state and the market, the formal and the informal) impossible to sustain."[4]

The *formally* private police must also be approached free of the presentist assumption that they are recent and with a clear vision of their complex intertwinings with public police. That is, not only have public police long labored in the service of capital, but private police do the work of the state—or rather, in an application that truly shows the utility of this concept, the state-market. Private police predated the public police of the 1830s (Peel's Bobbies), and the two have coexisted at all points since. The for-profit William J. Burns International Detective Agency and the Pinkerton National Detective Agency, for example, composed the only national police force prior to the creation of the Federal Bureau of Investigation in 1909, paid by the state indirectly via federal government contracts. Those agencies were less displaced than absorbed into the FBI, which built on their records systems and drew personnel from their ranks. The growth of private policing during the Cold War was as dependent on public support as it had been during the era of Burns and Pinkerton. The familiar contract form was supplemented by innovative ways to direct resources to private police, such as mandating security for federally funded research and development, and government forces took all sorts of measures that created a broad climate of support. Recently observers have been visibly outraged at private security companies' *military* service to the state-market, as Michael Kempa observes, another instance of police border crossings' summoning each other.[5]

This book, most intensively in this chapter, tries to draw out one implication of these insights: that state and market are so deeply intertwined as to be in practice and in essence inextricable. While there may be fragments that appear to belong to one side or another, the wholes exist only in their join.

Might a critical mass be ready to act on these insights? If not quite yet, perhaps it might help bring that possibility closer to consider the dizzying array of public-private crossings and hybrid forms that the OPS story reveals, both in its operation and its aftermath. This chapter treats mostly the latter; chapter 4 encompasses both. Chapter 3 comes first not chronologically but just logically, because it analyzes a relatively simpler situation. The border crossings of violence workers guarding oil in Alaska, an ostensibly domestic location, are one layer less convoluted than those of their counterparts in the Middle East.

Following former OPS employees to Alaska, this chapter explores the second of three conceptual borders of policing. Chapter 2 discussed the boundaries between military and civilian spheres. Here the focus moves to the arenas of public and private. The move is cumulative rather than a clean switch, for we continue to notice transgressions of the military-civilian divide in Alaska. To them we add the profound intermixtures of public and private policing. Interestingly, the crossing of one border seems to invite a crossing of another; in their overlap, spaces bewilderingly hybrid in composition are constantly proliferating.

Two factors converged in the early 1970s to make Alaska a key site for exploring the nature of violence work. One involves the Trans Alaska Pipeline
System; the other, the Office of Public Safety. The OPS story, as this book
has narrated, involved Congress terminating the program, sending its employees scrambling for new positions, and adding layers of resentment and
feelings of betrayal to the Cold War furies already tormenting the former
G-men. The pipeline story threatened at first to be a similar tale of galling
defeat. After oil was discovered on Alaska's North Slope in 1968, producers
proposed a system to pipe precious crude from Prudhoe Bay to Valdez on
Prince William Sound and on to refineries and distributors in the lower
forty-eight. The proposal was launched to Congress in 1969, a particularly
inopportune moment: the 1960s environmental movement was strong and
widely supported, and it staunchly opposed the construction project. A
terrible oil spill in the Santa Barbara Channel in January 1969 had just
spotlit the oil industry's worst potential, making it the environmental
movement's premier bête noire.[6] The pipeline suffered further delay due to
Native American land claims and the review requirements of the National
Environmental Policy Act, giving the opposition time to organize locally
and nationally, file lawsuits, lobby legislators, and otherwise gather forces.[7]

Happily for pipeline constituents, an energy shortage in 1973 shifted the
balance. Oil was already tight by the summer of that year, but the shortage
became a crisis when the Organization of Petroleum Exporting Countries
imposed an oil embargo in retaliation for US support of Israel in the Yom
Kippur War.[8] From the embargo's debut in November 1973 until March 1974,
oil prices soared, doubling and then quadrupling the dollar price per barrel.
Americans saw a fourfold increase in gas prices, rationing, and memorably
long lines at the pump. The embargo threw the nation into economic and
political turmoil, forcing the Nixon administration to negotiate Middle East
policy and all Americans to examine their energy habits. Some observers
credit the embargo with inspiring the conservation measures of the later
1970s, such as fuel-efficient car designs, shifts in home heating to coal and
electric, and the manufacture of energy-efficient appliances. In the short
term, however, the effect was immediate and clear: Nixon called upon the
United States to stockpile oil, and pro-pipeline sources surged conclusively
ahead. Advocates for the pipeline gathered the votes needed, resolved the

legal challenges, and amassed concrete and steel. Congress approved the pipeline, and haul road construction began.

The Alyeska Pipeline Service Company, the consortium of seven oil producers responsible for the project, began calling for labor. Offering ten-hour days, time and a half on Friday and Saturday, and double on Sunday, pipeline work seemed to assure a small fortune, all the more attractive in the context of the embargo-produced recession. Construction workers flooded the state, creating boomtown conditions in cities and camps all along the proposed pathway. As the state swelled with workers, businesses multiplied to compete for workers' spending power, particularly in the entertainment sector. Bars proliferated; alcohol, sex work, crowding, and the huge population of single young men seeking to blow off steam led to rowdiness and fear of crime. Local police responded anemically, their numbers weakened by defectors who jumped ship to join the lucrative construction boom themselves.[9]

The security industry marched eagerly into the breach. In September 1974, the Wackenhut private security corporation announced that it had won a fifteen-million-dollar, three-year contract to provide security to the pipeline.[10] Wackenhut's stock immediately gained five-eighths of a point on the New York Stock Exchange, and the company's Alaska subsidiary began gathering its forces.[11] Just as OPS was releasing its employees to the job market, then, Wackenhut Alaska began calling for manpower to secure the pipeline. Little wonder that former OPS men were among the first to respond.

Ex-OPS agents in Alaska filled both government law enforcement positions and posts within the "free" market. Their movements, geographic and institutional, outline the contours of police work for our backward gazes. Because former OPS employees stepped easily over the state-market divide when their agency folded, tracking their career moves shows the deeply interpenetrated world of public and private policing, the astonishing growth of the field of private policing in this period, and the surge in the field people were calling "industrial security," a subset of the security industry.

The security industry was an assemblage of imperfectly coherent fragments of public and private spheres. It included Alaska state troopers, municipal cops, public safety employees, and other government police, on the one hand, and on the other, security personnel hired by businesses or contracted out to governments, including the US federal government, state and municipal bodies, and foreign national powers. A hydra-headed hybrid, it was animated by violence workers.[12]

Alaska is a particularly good place to see the concrete pieces of this formation under construction, literally—the infrastructure that would move labor, capital, and natural resources around to convert perilous surplus into flexible accumulation.[13] Alaska's tale includes individual career paths as well as the institutional webs cementing private security companies to government bodies at municipal, state, international, and intranational levels. It shows the relationship of industrial security to US imperial adventures abroad and domestic containment within. It highlights ongoing commitments to contain and colonize native people as a part of interlocking foreign-domestic endeavors. Most important, it narrates a case in which security as a project grew through the conflation of those several missions into an indistinct, menacing question that only it could claim to answer.

The Alaska case beautifully illustrates the importance of the fear that is the security industry's most basic building block. In a classic case of what sociologists call "moral panic," the US federal government helped foment this fear, supporting the nominally private security industry well beyond its essential financial contracts.[14] After examining ex-ops in Alaska, following individual Public Safety agents and the institutions offering them new employ, this chapter explores two related panics, one larger umbrella panic that encouraged the growth of industrial security overall, and one nested within that, organized specifically around the Alaska pipeline. It shows how the security industry fed on the production of a wave of fear manufactured in Cold War years—fear of crime, communism, subversion, moral dissolution, social collapse, and other Great Disruptions, not necessarily pinned to any concrete threats, in fact probably necessarily unhinged from actual material menace, though highly logical in the era of anticolonial revolts, armed socialist rebellions, civil rights and racial justice movements, and the like. This fear, even if we judge it justified, was unattached to its objects. It was pure, primal affect; distilled product of moral panic—fear as fuel, not as viscous as oil, but a key natural resource nonetheless.

CAREER MOVES: OPS LABOR MIGRATIONS

Many who headed to Alaska for pipeline work imagined they were following crusty trappers and lonesome pioneers. These mythic figures of frontier ideology, alibis for territorial expansion, were far from the norm. First,

FIG 3.1 Tom Staley, who would later join OPS, in Alaska during the Korean War. SOURCE: *PSN* 154 (APR. 2009), 6.

one-fifth to one-sixth of Alaska's population was Native.[15] Second, Alaska's demographic and economic growth prior to the mid-1970s was overwhelmingly the work of the US government. In ongoing waves of colonization, the federal government sent settlers to the land, the US military serving as its active arm. Alaska had actually been governed by the military for a time after the US purchase.[16] But it was World War II that truly transformed the state demographically. Alaska's strategic importance surged thanks to the Aleutian Islands' proximity to Japan, which captured two of them early in the conflict. From a handful of men at one military barracks and a total of 70,000 inhabitants in 1939, bases emerged like spring lupine, growing a population of 138,000 by 1950.[17] Former OPS agent Tom Staley shows us this dynamic still in motion in the 1950s: writing to his fellows in 2009, Staley included a picture of his much younger self near an Alaskan air base, explaining, "Korean War comes along, and we all moved up to Adak, Alaska, a foggy airfield en route to Korea" (figure 3.1).

By 1974 the numerical balance of the state's population was associated with the military. In the early Cold War years, the Department of Defense spent vast sums in Alaska, and DOD workers were more than half the Alaskan workforce. Given the multiplier effect of military personnel and their families' needs, about two-thirds of Alaska's "private business income was generated directly or indirectly by defense," concludes military historian

Laurel Hummel. "The defense industry was the biggest employer and biggest spender from 1940 to 1970"; it was only "overtaken by the oil industry when the North Slope fields started producing in 1977."[18]

Hummel calls the pipeline "the first major nonmilitary construction project ever in the state."[19] Yet as OPS labor will show, the pipeline had military personnel involved, military structures of organization and command, ties to military projects and priorities, and, given the strategic importance of oil, abundant military implications. Following the workers shows us these relationships up close.

A few OPS agents went to Alaska simply to put their shoulders to the wheel, in pipeline construction. Robert Craft wrote from Anchorage that he had moved up from Idaho in the expectation (soon fulfilled) of construction work.[20] Yet those who dug ditches were in the minority; most former OPS employees were involved instead in policing, in realms both public and private.

In the private sector, they were security workers such as Lee Worthen or Glenn Gray, both of whom relocated to Fairbanks for Alyeska Security.[21] Gray was a field security supervisor, responsible for monitoring and supervising two security service contractors, "providing security from Prudhoe Bay to Valdez, Alaska," he reported proudly.[22] Kenneth Burns, a former PSA (Public Safety Agent) in Saigon, took a position as area manager for Wackenhut in Arizona and New Mexico. When the pipeline call came, he was moved to Alaska and promoted to manager of operations, second in command for Wackenhut there.[23] In 1976, he moved over to Philips Petroleum Company (PPCO; now Conoco Phillips) in Fairbanks, as safety/security manager.[24] Burns had another former Saigon PSA for a colleague at Wackenhut, a fellow named Guy Gibson, and Gibson informed his colleagues that he was working with the son of another former OPS officer, Clyde Call.[25]

In July 1976, the OPS newsletter wrote that Gibson was "back with American Guard and Alert, a Wackenhut subsidiary, in Anchorage as Operations Manager with the rank of Major. Just prior to his present assignment, Guy was with the parent Wackenhut operation in Fairbanks and Valdez."[26] That "back" reveals three separate stints with Wackenhut: the subsidiary, the parent operation, and then back to the subsidiary. This was a moment of great mobility as people took advantage of the opportunities pipeline work conferred. Note also that this private security company borrowed military order: Gibson was assigned the "rank of Major" by American Guard and

Alert. This may have been flattery or vanity, but it also may simply have reflected the logics that structured these men's sense of how a "force" should be organized. As people traveled across the formal public-private divide, they drew pieces of the other systems along behind.

As the multiple notices of friend clusters and workmates evince, many of these men knew each other, and some helped others secure their new positions. Like labor migrations in other contexts, these were complex personal networks.[27] Gray spent social time with Burns; Burns asked for help locating a former colleague (Chuck Petry) so he could make him a job offer, and showed his desire for more such contact by lobbying his fellow former OPS officers for a reunion.[28] Both Gray and Gibson were friends with a Fairbanks police officer named Jan (known as "J. B.") Carnahan.[29]

Carnahan takes us over to the government side of the equation. He was one of the former OPS agents who went to Alaska to work not for the pipeline corporations directly but in the public part of what I will call, in this chapter, the "security world," for the holism that phrase implies. Indirectly, however, such workers owed their new jobs to Alyeska, as Carnahan well understood: "When we came back and I went to work, . . . there was nobody there. . . . Wackenhut had recruited them all, for at least twice the wage, sometimes as much as three [times], and all the policemen were gone."[30]

Carnahan was an outlier in Fairbanks; most ex-OPS in public service landed in Juneau, such as Gerald Williams, a district court judge there, or Richard Burton, a former state patrolman and trooper who was Juneau's chief of police until the end of 1974.[31] Burton gave up that post to accept appointment as commissioner of Alaska Public Safety, a position that allowed him to extend a helping hand to several more former OPS colleagues.[32] Burton's Department of Public Safety included Frank Gorham, a former sheriff, police sergeant, lieutenant, and captain prior to his OPS work in Saigon, Bangkok, and Chiang Mai. Gorham served as planning, research, and development supervisor.[33] Burton probably appointed former OPS-Vietnam agent Lowell Janson to be Alaska State organized crime prevention coordinator, since that post was based in Burton's office. Janson promised further collaboration with the ex-OPS network when he wrote to the *Newsletter* that he would be in touch with those in police-related work as he went about the business of fighting organized crime.[34] Finally, Charles Sothan, originally from Arizona, accepted the position of deputy director for the Alaska Division of Corrections, overseeing five hundred employees at eight facilities, plus rural outposts.[35] Sothan, too, had experience in a police department before OPS, which posted him to Saigon and Monrovia between 1967 and 1972.[36]

"Charlie [Sothan] states that he believes that Juneau, for it's [*sic*] size, has more OPS people than anywhere," the *Newsletter* reported in December 1976.[37] Sothan might have made a similar argument for the whole state of Alaska, given the Juneau crew, the Fairbanks chief, and the Alyeska/Wackenhut employees. Reporting these whereabouts by the end of 1976, this contingent of the OPS dispersal had reacted with alacrity to the pipeline's victory in Congress, and the doors it opened to public and private security work there.

INDUSTRIAL RELATIONS

The private security firms the OPS officers joined in this moment were a tangled array of relations. Alyeska, American Guard and Alert, and Wackenhut Alaska were all pieces of a single whole. Alyeska was the entity made up of seven oil concerns that constituted the "pipeline construction consortium," the umbrella under which the oil companies came together. Alyeska followed in the revered footsteps of earlier colonizing companies in Alaska. The California-based Alaska Commercial Company took over the seal rookeries from the Russian American Company, the "arm of the Russian government" that held monopoly rights over the seal fur industry from 1799 until the United States purchased Alaska in 1867. Both follow in the tradition of the archetypal European colonizing corporations, the British East India Company first among them as quintessential company-state (the Russian American Company was explicitly modeled on it), all leading unevenly into the sovereign state-market fusion we will meet in the oil fields of Saudi Arabia (Aramco) in the next chapter.[38]

Like the colonizing companies of European imperial ventures, Alyeska contracted its own security. When Wackenhut of Alaska, Incorporated, a subsidiary of the Wackenhut Corporation, was awarded the multimillion-dollar contract to provide security services for Alyeska, it did so both as American Guard and Alert and under Alyeska's name, allowing workers such as Glenn Gray and Worthen Lee to call their employer "Alyeska Security."[39]

Wackenhut is a key feeder company for this composite form. To readers today, Wackenhut is best known as a private prison corporation, although Wackenhut Alaska was not then in and never moved to that line of work. In the 1980s, some states began approving measures allowing the contracting out of prison systems; Alaska refused. Despite years of attempts by construction corporations and the politicians they fund, voters in Alaska consistently rejected the proposals.[40] There is an indirect relationship, however: Wackenhut Alaska's financial health in the pipeline period contributed to the overall strength of the corporation, allowing it to expand when the corrections field became fertile. This happened in 1984, when The Wackenhut Corporation (TWC) formed Wackenhut Corrections Corporation (WCC). This corrections-focused division became a wholly owned subsidiary of TWC in 1988 and was publically traded after an initial public offering in 1994. A Scandinavian group bought the parent company, but WCC stayed out of that deal.[41] As of 2003 it has gone by the name The GEO Group, Incorporated.[42]

Wackenhut, then, was a private *security* company, what used to be called a "detective agency" or "private investigator." When it formed in 1954, it quickly joined the ranks of the two security giants already in existence, the Pinkerton and Burns Detective Agencies. These private police bodies were large, active, and underappreciated pieces of US police history. They comprised, as noted above, the elements of the only national police force prior to the formation of the FBI in 1909, formed the first centralized criminal records system, and shaped US law and policing practice for cops in all manner of uniform.[43] These bodies did not shrink when government law enforcement began its obscene swelling in the 1970s. They grew, too. In fact, they grew more.

Private policing had been on a dramatic upward swing since the end of World War II. So startling was this rate of growth that observers have called it a "quiet revolution"—though a "rebirth" rather than a novelty.[44] The number of fee-for-service private police firm employees doubled in the 1960s, enjoying a growth rate of 7.4 percent annually, nearly twice the 4.2 percent growth rate of the public police in the same period—in itself a considerable rate of increase. Both private and public police were expanding, but private police more quickly. "By 1975 the ratio of public to private police (in-house and contract) was 0.9:1 in the United States," nearly one to one. A decade later, the ratio had grown to one to two. The private police outnumbered their public-sector colleagues two to one.[45] In dollar terms, by the mid-1970s, Americans were spending ten to fifteen billion dollars annually on private security services. In the course of daily life, the average

American had "more personal contact with and is under more scrutiny and control by the private security guard than by publicly supported police officers."[46] Private security "dwarfs public policing, by any measure of analysis," as Michael Kempa noted in 2001, adding that the growth has made distinguishing the two nearly impossible, substantively: "There are currently no functions performed by public policing agencies that are also not somewhere and sometimes performed by private security actors."[47] Shared growth has entwined police across the public-private divide.

In the early Cold War days, the industry was still dominated by the "big three" private security companies, Burns, Pinkerton, and Wackenhut. Their revenues "more than tripled between 1963 and 1969, rising from $93 million to $312 million," and then nearly doubled again in the first half of the 1970s.[48] Only the last of these was a Cold War body, a formation that well endowed it to thrive in its field. Its founder, former FBI special agent George R. Wackenhut, hired other former FBI and retired state and federal government agents to swell his company's ranks. They implemented a policy of hiring from "old-boy networks of retired federal agents . . . especially from among those in government service eying a lucrative retirement opportunity in corporate or private security."[49] Former OPS agents, with their carefully tended network, beautifully fit the bill.

OPS had something else in common with Wackenhut: both organizations had faced and overcome a legal barrier to the provision of security services. Wackenhut had creatively sidestepped a congressional prohibition of federal government contracts with private detective agencies. The prohibition dates back to the 1892 Homestead Strike, a bloody gunfight between agents of the Pinkerton Detective Agency and striking steelworkers in Homestead, Pennsylvania. In its wake, Congress prohibited the federal government from contracting with Pinkerton or similar detective services.[50] Wackenhut's legal counsel found a loophole around the Anti-Pinkerton Act by creating a subsidiary whose employees were not "detectives" but simply "guards."[51] This newspeak allowed for the survival and growth of Wackenhut, and the rest of the security industry along with it.

OPS agents had invented similarly creative ways to circumvent Congress's prohibition of foreign police assistance in 1974. Although they could not salvage the agency itself, by moving to other policing bodies they blithely circumvented Congress's directive to halt the work they had been doing for OPS. They moved to agencies within USAID, such as the Office of Narcotics Control, the Office of Country Financed Technical Services, or the Technical Services Bureau, or outside USAID in the Federal Aviation Authority, USOM (United States Operation Mission), or the State Department's Defense Attaché Office, and so on. They sustained the International Police Academy, and most baldly, they kept intact those programs authorized by the "Section 607" exception.[52] As one man who became a telecommunications specialist for AID wrote to his former colleagues, his new employ was "really the same kind of work we were doing for Public Safety. Only now we are looking after AID employees and contractors' safety."[53]

Wackenhut's transcendence of the congressional prohibition against federal contracts for private cops and the OPS agents' circumnavigation around the ban on US police assistance both helped to erode the strictures that might otherwise have kept policing inside its expected boundaries. These were some of the many instances in which the industrial security world was produced *as* a public-private, domestic-transnational, military-civilian hybrid—a violence worker assemblage.

OPS agents fit so well into these hybrid bodies because their organization had itself been a pronounced mix of public and private pieces. This is most clear in OPS's embrace of the project of "industrial security," a key part of its overall labor. OPS personnel in host countries ranging from Colombia to Saudi Arabia to Guatemala were dedicated to industrial security.[54] In a letter to the chief of AID's Industry and Private Enterprise Office in 1965, OPS's Brazil chief wrote of the importance of protecting "vital governmental installations and private owned industrial facilities." He concluded with the organization's overall belief in the importance of industrial security: "In view of the terrorist activities carried out in Viet Nam, Thailand, Colombia, Venezuela and other South American countries, the USAID believes that the protection of vital government installations and critical industrial facilities is necessary in the economic development of Brazil."[55]

The many employees who fled their sinking ship for positions in private security companies show that this work had prepared them well for the private sector. One former PSA was "an Industrial Security Specialist with PACEX in Hawaii" by 1975; another worked for Gallo Winery, providing industrial safety and security; a third set up security systems for Owens-Illinois, a glassmaking conglomerate with plants all over the world; and still another was a manager for a Bay Area industrial security specialist.[56] From Texas, one former agent announced he was associated "with the University of Houston's special Industrial Security program," showing academic involvement in this industry.[57] Another studious type performed surveys for a private security firm called LECAR (Law Enforcement Consulting and Research), contracted by both government and private bodies.[58] At the Miami Beach meeting of the American Society of Industrial Security in 1980, former PSAs met and reminisced.[59]

OPS officers looking for this kind of work benefited from the cachet government training imparted to violence workers. They enjoyed great credibility on the job market, while the fervent of the expanding security industry created opportunity after promotional opportunity, enhanced by private security companies' affirmative attempts to hire former and retired state and federal agents to fill out their growing ranks.[60]

The federal government was essential to the private security industry, both in terms of the funds Wackenhut lawyers' artful dodges helped keep flowing into its coffers, and in terms of personnel. Consider Alyeska. A migratory stream of G-men filled its ranks, just as they had for Wackenhut at its foundation. Alyeska's police-blue uniforms were donned by former federal government employees. The borderline between corps of public and private violence workers, and therefore between public and private *violence*, supposedly sacrosanct in a democratic nation, was the barest of legal fictions. Federal monies sustained the privates, and the people were the same. They merely switched their hats.

The hat switchers well understood this. J. B. Carnahan commented that his former colleagues in OPS who went to work for Wackenhut stayed in the same line of work, "whatever Wackenhut became and became and became." His point was that Wackenhut's various name-changes were only skindeep: "They were called several different things, [but] they were pretty much manned by the same people. . . . In government contracting, you get a new contractor coming in, let's say you get a native corporation, it comes in and gets the contract; it keeps the same people, except for their management, up on top, but yeah, the people don't hardly change at all."[61]

In addition to providing contracts and personnel, the federal government worked to help justify the growth of private security, and of hybrid public-private ventures, in the early Cold War years. Through neutral sounding "study," it sought to build consensus for private security. In the late 1960s, the Law Enforcement Assistance Administration (LEAA) funded the RAND Corporation to produce a report on private security. This document, published in five volumes in 1971, was boosterish and hortatory. It portrayed private policing not as a threat but as an asset, and as a helpful junior partner to the public police.[62]

RAND itself is a noteworthy public-private hybrid, a political body in market guise. While taking decidedly conservative positions on criminal justice questions and promilitary positions on foreign affairs, it claims to have no politics at all.[63] But its self-proclaimed neutrality is belied by its close relationship to government bodies, especially military ones.[64] RAND's neutrality is a cipher, index of the state's own attempts to dissemble its active corporate and military agenda; a more precise way to understand RAND is to see it as coextensive with the state.

The RAND reports did not just encourage the development of private security. They argued that it already existed anyway, and constituted "a developing service industry no different in principle from any other service industry."[65] Aligning private security with the massive tectonic shift from manufacturing to service under way in the US economy at the time, RAND portrayed the move as inescapable and irresistible. This is a remarkable admission of the coincidence of this industry's growth with neoliberalism's volcanic reshaping of the landscapes of labor.

Despite this straining to pretend a clean public-private divide remained— or perhaps because of it—many state representatives well understood the hybridity of violence work. They portrayed the private security industry as essentially their jurisdiction despite its legal status as private. In 1975, a Justice Department official working for the LEAA to develop statutes for regulating the industry explained why his office understood their relationship as intimate. "Studies have shown there is more money being spent annually on private security than on police," this official told the *New York Times*. "It's a major part of the crime prevention effort nationally and we can't afford to ignore it."[66] Note that even in this acknowledgment of collaboration and regulation, the unnamed official maintained a neat rhetorical border between private security and public police.[67]

Following up on the RAND report, in the mid-1980s the Department of Justice hired Hallcrest Systems to pen another installment of this argumentatively active project. The DOJ's mandate to Hallcrest was "to advance the reform agenda RAND had initiated." Hallcrest fully complied. The Hallcrest Report, published in 1985, called policing a "product" and private policing an "industry" involved in "servicing" "crime and fear of crime," and it defended the RAND report from what it portrayed as academic concerns about civil liberties.[68] It also observed that Americans were spending twenty billion dollars a year on private security, more than the government spent on all federal, state, and local law enforcement agencies combined.[69]

The project continues; the next follow-up report was prepared in 1990, and found similar rates of increase.[70]

The National Institute of Justice funded and guided these reports. It also supported the creation, in the early 1980s, of the Joint Council of Law Enforcement and Private Security Associations, an umbrella bringing together the International Association of Chiefs of Police, the National Sheriffs' Association, and the American Society for Industrial Security.[71] Its director embraced public-private collaboration, grateful that private security could "assume some of the burden now borne by overworked public law enforcement agencies, thereby freeing them to concentrate their efforts in areas where their involvement is essential."[72] The wheels of rationalization and institutionalization ground ahead, hard, together.

Government forces encouraged private companies, the general public, and colleague branches of government to purchase security and support the growth of the industry, not only through these institutional, legal, and ideological modes but also by seeking to instigate fears that private security could soothe. Private companies were often not interested in investing in their own security systems. It seemed a waste of money, or not really necessary. To convince corporate personnel to spend money on security services involved careful tutelage; they had to be taught to fear, and what to fear, and to crave the correct palliative.

Security world ambassadors had been hard at work manufacturing the fear their industry required since the leading edge of the Cold War. Under the Internal Security Act of 1950, the McCarthy-era law that established the Subversive Activities Control Board, for example, the US Armed Forces gave industrial defense trainings for business leaders, well-attended gatherings supplemented after 1968 by a series of seminars developed by the FBI in conjunction with the National Association of Manufacturers (NAM).[73] NAM taught its how-to's an average of once a month in cities across the nation, and published a booklet titled "Bomb Threats to Industry, Suggested Action to Protect Employees and Property," a collaborative project with the US Office of the Provost Marshal General. That office produced a manual titled "Industrial Defense against Civil Disturbances, Bombings, Sabotage," while the US Chamber of Commerce distributed "How to Counteract Violence."[74] Similar publications abounded.[75] In 1970, the director of the American Society for Industrial Security admonished the nation: "Any company with its head bolted on right has a bomb security program." In the odd event that some wayward ostrich had missed this critical proviso, that society's members, "security executives and manufacturers of electronic security systems," would be only too happy to set them up.[76]

The security world, across the private-public continuum, fed on institutional structures and individual elements, and in a more nebulous realm, on ideological production. It grew in direct proportion to the panics conjured around the various bogeymen of the Cold War period. The Trans-Alaska Pipeline offered a particularly combustible fuel for this fire of fear, on some levels more valuable to the security world than oil.

PIPELINE PANIC

The Trans-Alaska Pipeline provided the occasion for the circulation of massively overblown fears of terrorism and industrial sabotage, far out of proportion to the attacks the pipeline has actually suffered in its more than forty years of operation. Once exposed as rhetoric, pipeline fears reveal a great deal about the context of their articulation, the things people at the time truly feared, and the projects they were actually protecting.

Fears of deliberate destruction of the pipeline have been voiced throughout its operational life, a constant hum of worry even before the oil began flowing. "Middle East terrorists are considered the most likely candidates to launch an organized attack on the pipeline," the *LA Times* reported in 1975, "but in an era of growing radical terrorism, the list hardly stops there. 'That pipeline is the biggest target in the world for some nut,' said a top state official. 'We're talking about dedicated terrorists, not just disgruntled environmentalists.'"[77]

To agents of the security world, terrorist attacks were not lightning strikes, unlikely but still worth planning a response. They were certainties. "It will happen," declared Richard Burton, the former OPS agent then serving as chief of Alaska's Department of Public Safety; "I am as sure of that as I am sitting here." An editorialist for the *Milwaukee Sentinel* reproduced Burton's comment and the full panorama of fears:

> Burton warned of the danger of terrorist or blackmail bands virtually hijacking the pipeline by seizing hostages at the control station at pump station No. 1 and the one at the Valdez terminal.
>
> "They could go in and take the operators as hostages for a ransom attempt," warned Burton.

He's also concerned over policies of militants in the American Indian movement and by North Slope Eskimos who might take political action to stop the oil flow. They haven't accepted the Native Claims Settlement Act and they now continue to claim all of the North Slope for their own use.

But there are others who worry more about the tactics of the New World Liberation Front, the Red Guerrilla Family, the Peoples' Light Brigade and the Emiliano Zapata Unit. They are centered in the San Francisco Bay area. And, there is still the Weather Underground.[78]

This bizarre maelstrom jumbles together a surfeit of radical organizations to magnify their threat, locating them in a hippie HQ more fantastic than geographic. The mention of hostage-taking leans on the panic roused up around that phenomenon, loosely based on events such as the Attica prison rebellion and airplane hijackings but far out of proportion to their likelihood. It reveals the terrified Cold Warrior imagination around groups who were less of a threat to the state than the state was to them. Note the confusion of terrorist attack with the possibility that Native activists might "take political action." Legal, perhaps, but as terrifying to Burton as any midnight foray.

Major national newspapers circulated this scattershot excess, attributing it to important state agents and credible representatives of industry. "Pipeline Sabotage Worries CIA," observed columnists Jack Anderson and Les Whitten in the *Washington Post* in 1976.[79] The CIA was born to fear, but even the modest GAO (Government Accounting Office) feared pipeline sabotage, it admitted in 1979.[80] The consequences projected as the result of pipeline attacks were dire. Saboteurs "could send the United States into an economic tailspin overnight."[81] Visions of financial ruin and political breakdown danced in their heads.

The actual objects of this field of bad dreams spring into focus in one particularly revealing paranoid fantasy. In a piece in the *Chicago Tribune*, columnist Lowell Ponte called the pipeline the "biggest target in the world for terrorists." Sharing plans for upcoming exercises to test pipeline defense mechanisms, Ponte invited readers to "step briefly into [defense planners'] nightmares": "It is winter, 1978, in northern Alaska. Six weeks ago the sun stopped shining here. . . . Now in all directions the frozen tundra stretches white and flat. The dark line of the Alaska pipeline zig-zags across this ghostly landscape. Two figures approach, wearing snowshoes. Dressed in white, they are nearly invisible except for their faint shadows."[82] These stealthy, feral ghosts plant a crop of bombs, of course, and "monstrous explosions rupture the pipeline at a dozen places along a 100-mile stretch."[83]

That the *Tribune* would print this fiction in the first place points to the climate that made such incendiary hyperbole acceptable as news. But there is more to be gleaned from this piece. Its characters are not garden-variety terrorists, appropriately dressed for the weather. Fading into the brilliant background, they represent a classic case of the "blinding whiteness" haunting American "hearts and texts," as Toni Morrison so compellingly writes.[84] Into the Alaskan tundra, the nation's collective unconscious projected its "nightmares," making their mythic existence into concrete justification for the expansion of the security world.

This motley crew of potential threats to the pipeline imagined by the Milwaukee *Sentinel* op-ed writer, Richard Burton, the CIA, GAO, and Lowell Ponte of the *Chicago Tribune* all recall the vibrant activism of the period. It is no coincidence that it was in this moment that private security grew so large. It was a facet of the violence work organized to combat articulate and effective insurgency.[85] This is the context in which we must understand not only the rise of the prison system and the public police but also the private security industry.

Particularly resonant in this moment was the powerful challenge to the pipeline comprised by the quintessential repressed subjects of American empire. Native people throughout the northern land, including Inuit, Aleut, Dene, and other groups, pressed land claims throughout the 1960s in a movement related to civil rights challenges in the lower forty-eight. Pipeline constituents realized that they could not move forward without settling the land claims pending for decades, and a historic if distinctly unsatisfying settlement was reached in 1971.[86] Imperial anxiety surfaces as mirror image of its usual demon savages, in the white-swathed evildoers of Lowell Ponte's pipeline panic.

Native claims also further challenge the structures of assumption subtending postcolonial capitalism. Native sovereignties, oases of exception where US rule is rejected, open ulcerated little tears in the nation-state's assumed convergence of territory and identity. Native sovereignties in Alaska confuse the issue even more by bridging two nation-states, the United States and Canada.[87] Transnational models of sovereignty that reject the relegation of land to property challenge the capitalist nation-state on multiple levels. Their revelations of a multistate state—beyond federalism, beyond any consistency in the character of those states—remind us of the non-natural status of all these ideas, of their historical character. That which has not always been, can change.

The fear-based structure of feeling evident in 1970s discussions of the Trans-Alaska Pipeline is powerful and lasting, though it changes to adapt to shifting contexts. In 2003, looking back on thirty years of oil in Alaska, journalist Joe LaRocca reiterated a set of well-rehearsed talking points: "Imagine, if you can, what murderous outrages skillful, committed, well-trained and resourceful international terrorists with unlimited funds and high explosive devices could wreak upon the pipeline system," he invited. True, he admitted, in the past this had not been much of an issue, as "the pipeline has been the target of several domestic episodes of sabotage committed by inept crazies which had no serious or lasting consequences." But these episodes showed the pipeline's vulnerability. After the terrorist attacks in 2001, he contended, a "new role as a geopolitical defensive weapon has been thrust upon [the pipeline]."[88] LaRocca's worry hinges here on the threats that seem to have materialized in the post-9/11 world. This sense of novelty is very common, but it too has a critical ideological function. It hides continuity in the social force exerted by the threat of "terrorism." The Cold War was an "age of terror," too.

The pipeline was (is) the perfect occasion for such alarmist projections because it is, in fact, impossible to protect. It is simply too big, and its eight hundred miles traverse too forbidding a climate to allow for thorough policing. In the beginning, pipeline spokesmen appear to have understood the impossibility of protection. "The pipeline is indefensible," granted Alyeska president E. L. Patton in 1975. "There's no way of protecting this thing unless you've got unlimited manpower."[89] In 1976, a congressional expert told the *Washington Post* the same thing: "The pipeline is indefensible."[90]

In the end, the very vastness of the pipeline's frigid setting may have been its best defense. The worst-case scenarios of sabotage and ruin were never realized. The deliberate acts can be counted briefly. In 1977, a novice trapper tried to blow up some pipe just north of Fairbanks; another sabotage act in 1978 spilled eight thousand barrels.[91] Even these puny incidents (compare to the 257,000 barrels spilled by the *Exxon Valdez*), absurdly disproportionate to the vast technology and manpower rallied to the pipeline's defense, showed the ineffectiveness of the security systems in place.[92] The incident in 1977 was the work of a clumsy youngster who nonetheless had no trouble approaching his target, and Alyeska's security system didn't discover the damage for five days; in 1978, it was a private pilot who detected the leak.[93] In the estimation of former OPS agent, then Fairbanks police sergeant J. B. Carnahan, Wackenhut was "pretty much ineffective," though in his pragmatic view, it didn't much matter: "We've only had like one incident, really, on the pipeline when somebody shot a couple of times at it with a hunting rifle and put a hole in it. He went to jail pretty quick."[94]

The failure of the terrorist threat to materialize reveals the virtues of such pragmatic views, and shows the fearmongering to have been a textbook moral panic. Its function, in retrospect, has been to buttress the case for the expansion of the security world.[95] As such, it was a fortuitously timed piece of a massive and protracted process. It rested on the labors spent to convince business leaders that their endeavors were under attack, and to teach them how they should respond, and on the sustained support provided to the private security industry by federal government studies and contracts.

That oil production was the occasion for this episode of security world growth is also no coincidence. The perception that resource scarcity causes violence, and scarcity of oil in particular, is enormously common. As Matthew Huber, Timothy Mitchell, and other radical geographers have pointed out, the notion that oil production is ruled by scarcity is mistaken. In fact, it is surplus that has characterized—even plagued—oil production. Oil scarcity must be carefully socially produced, and a key ingredient in its production is violence. Any commodity must be (perceived as) scarce in order to trade; violence is essential to produce "the scarcity necessary for the operation of commodity relations."[96] Put simply, capital requires scarcity, and the violence workers to produce it.

In Alaska, not only the rhetoric of alarm that circulated in the public sphere but also the sheer material forces gathered to guard the construction site and then the working pipe helped further intensify the terror of scarcity and the sense of need for security, broadly. Within those material forces were many individuals such as the former OPS agents who were already integrated into the security world. They were veteran Cold War combatants who had embraced the abstract concept of the discourse of security, and were only too happy to plant it anew in the fertile soil of Alaska's oil industry panic. With old and new colleagues in Alaska they brought this experience to bear, not exactly back home, but in a space that transcended the domestic. A still-imperial space, Alaska was a perfect site for the mixing of foreign and domestic fears about security, and the infinitely vulnerable oil pipeline was the perfect object for such fears.

Fear is a terrifically productive affect. Its "rhetorical energy" structures human relationships to the world.[97] Fear pushes people to invest in things that impoverish their lives, and helps to obfuscate the broader structural contexts of such impoverishment by focusing on trivial individual instances. In the case of the Alaska pipeline, fears of sabotage or terrorist attack helped shroud the enormous risk present in its everyday operation, materialized in the *Exxon Valdez* spill as in the many lesser accidents it has suffered. Great harm has been inflicted by the regular operation of the pipeline, its construction pollution, and leaks and spills from accidents large and small.[98] The global oil trade confirms these risks with devastating regularity, as the intense, routine pollution associated with oil extraction doggedly poisons the planet.[99] Diverting attention from this terrible consequence, fear of pipeline attacks helped feed the security world, weaving the logics of security deftly and deeply into the matrix of the pipeline project.

Thus did the security world encounter a fertile occasion to cultivate the idea that the United States required *security*, was in need of protection from, well, we need not know what, exactly. All we truly need to know is that the world is a terrifying place, and we must have gates, walls, guns, prisons, big strong men, and the energy to fuel them all. In Alaska, a dizzying array of players—Alyeska, OPS and Wackenhut, state and local cops, OPEC, the US Army—came together around the pipeline, showing us what policing really is by executing, by constituting this dense assemblage that was both conflictual and contradictory. "Police," they reveal, means something so much messier, more dispersed, more devoted to capital, and so much less coherent or conspiratorial than our imaginations of Big Brother, or the beefy bloke on the beat, in blue.

BLURRING THE THIN BLUE LINE

Because the legitimacy of governance in a democracy hinges upon a clean line between market and state, the encroachment of private security into arenas perceived as the state's jurisdiction provoked its fair share of alarm. Many government agents raised their voices to oppose private violence workers' infringement upon public service work, or to resist the growth of private security provision even for business and industry. Many others spoke up to defend the superiority of government violence workers, military and police, over the privates. Whether these were genuine principled refusals or calls to arms in a turf war, these seeming challenges accepted the essential structure of state power and worked to reinforce its framework.

Audible denunciations of private security circulated in the public eye in 1975 and 1976 as the question of pipeline safety loomed. Military and federal government agents voiced doubts regarding the ability of private forces to address the pipeline's defense needs. As construction proceeded, they insisted that "the only source of manpower capable of limiting damage to the pipeline would be the federal government, ranging from National Guard foot patrols to the most sophisticated Defense Department surveillance techniques."[100] They evoked the common image of rent-a-cop buffoons to contrast it with alarmist depictions of the lethal threats they faced: "You can't expect a bunch of Loomis guards to protect the line against people with bazookas and recoilless rifles."[101]

Police officers added their denunciations of the incompetence of private guards, working another angle. Rather than extol the virtues of the overwhelming resources and centralized coordination of a military force, they invoked the valor of the individual lawman, dedicated to the principles of public order. Former OPS agent and Fairbanks police officer J. B. Carnahan dismissed Alyeska security's efforts as insincere and ineffective:

Q: *Do you think that the need for security for the pipeline was exaggerated?*

A: Yes, I do. Not only was exaggerated. We had drugs, prostitutes, up and down the pipeline camps: where the hell was security? It obviously was doing what Alyeska wanted it to do: nothing.[102]

Carnahan makes a sharp distinction between the kind of checkpoint shivering he understood as the bulk of Alyeska employees' labors and the "real" police work of fighting crime.

Carnahan loved police work; he actually chose to return to the beat after a stint in public relations, moving from that relatively cushy post back to chilly patrol.[103] Alaska must have been a particularly satisfying place to project oneself as a valiant strongman given its Wild West feel. As a news feature in 1977 promised, "Artic lore is full of stories about legendary lawmen who always got their man, who made strong men tremble and women sigh."[104] The cowboy machismo was explicit, with the Texas Rangers making their expected appearance as point of comparison. Against this romantic image of the frontier hero, the sallow security guard could hold no candle.

Carnahan's dismissal of private security work is sharply critical, and certainly genuine. From one angle, this is evidence that the pieces of the security world did not need to love each other; it is the incoherence Deleuze identifies as typical of the assemblage. In more conventional sociological terms one might simply ascribe it to the heterogeneity of the state.[105] Yet in at least one dimension, this critique actually fortified the whole. Those who spoke out, even with principled integrity, inadvertently fed the phenomenon they were attempting to protest: their vehement declarations of distinction between public and private defended the legitimacy of the state, helping to preserve the *idea* of government as distinct from the market even as vast government resources were devoted to the growth of private security and the public-private hybrids of the security world.

Because they launched their protests from within a paradigm in which state and market forces could and should be distinct, these dissenters granted the grounds of state validity and legality—even though the forms in question mocked the distinctions they claimed to honor in the first place. It would have been enormously difficult for these critics to avoid this paradox, for as violence workers they incarnated the essence of state power, actualized it in their everyday activities. The structure of the state was stamped into their habits, or habitus, to the point that it shaped their notions of the possible.[106]

Let us not abandon the seeds of possibility the assemblage invariably contains. Carnahan's critical viewpoint reveals unscaled vertices of possibility. In his late seventies when I interviewed him in 2012, Carnahan still lived in Fairbanks with Roberta, his wife of fifty-plus years. He spent most mornings entertaining commuters with an engrossing talk radio program. Listeners surely tuned in for his gentle demeanor and ready wit, which he also brought fearlessly to his analysis of state power and violence:

Q: *Do you think that the country is feeling threatened right now, because of the war on terror?*

A: I think the government feels threatened. I don't think the people have come to the point where they understand what that's all about. But the government feels threatened. And it's when the government feels threatened that silly things start to happen. I mean security, we have now intertwined police and security to the point that to do anything, to suggest anything that would lessen security almost becomes an anti-American move. You have to be conscious of that and always think about what you're doing. It's kind of interesting to me, and this is an aside, that all you have you have to do to get the American government to spend fifty million dollars, is to put four needles into a turkey sandwich. [laughter] But tell me, who wins in that deal?

Q: *Is what you're saying now part of the new outlook that you gained after retirement . . . ?*

A: I don't think it was after retirement. I've had this outlook for a long time, and part of the time that I was in Vietnam. You don't deal with the federal government very long before you realize that this isn't exactly the way it's supposed to be.

Q: *Would fellow OPS ex-employees agree with you about these things?*

A: No, I think a lot of them, they might be split, but I think a lot of them would go with the security part. Because you know, I was [in OPS] five years but a lot of those guys spent their whole careers working with the federal government, and I think they might think that it's justified. And a lot of security *is* justified. I just think that you have to continually evaluate what you're doing. When's the last time you heard of anybody being killed with a pair of nail clippers, for example? Somebody has got to have some common sense and go in there and say, okay, what are we doing here? Why do we do each one of these things? Every time you take a freedom away, that's a loosely used word, but every time you cause the citizens to do something that they don't want to do, you have to think to yourself, what am I doing? Who is in charge here? Are the people still in charge? And they are. But sometimes we do things without really giving a lot of thought. And usually when we feel threatened. Or we feel we can't stop something. That kind of, it's born out of frustration, I think, more than anything else.

Q: *I'd like to go back to the 1970s for a minute . . .*

A: So would I! [laughter] . . .[107]

In this analysis, Carnahan rejects the security measures that have become a war-on-terror common sense, mocking them as "silly." He notes the evolution of "security" into a keyword, a dense knot of signification so close to the national heart that its antithesis is also the antithesis of the national ("anything that would lessen security almost becomes anti-American"). Carnahan critiques US government practice not just in the war on terror but consistently ("You don't deal with the federal government very long before you realize that this isn't exactly the way it's supposed to be"). In contrast, he insists on the first principles of democracy, shaped as a question ("Are the people still in charge?"), which he answers in the affirmative ("And they are") but in a mode that I read as yearning rather than certain that that is indeed the case, since it is followed by another critique of the thoughtlessness of recent, pro-security policy ("we do things without really giving a lot of thought"). Carnahan's sharp analysis of such policy as fueled by fear ("when we feel threatened. Or we feel we can't stop something. That kind of, it's born out of frustration") reminds us that the nightmare fantasies of terrorists sabotaging the Alaska oil pipeline are with us still, if dressed for warmer climates.

Perhaps if consensus builds against the brutal neoliberal security market-state, worldviews such as Carnahan's would have the opportunity to evolve in one of the other directions they already contain. So we close with Carnahan's words of wisdom, and his playful wish to return to the 1970s. *Violence Work* argues that there is, indeed, a great deal to be learned there.

━━━━━━━━

While for some former OPS officers Alaska was a final destination, for others it was just another node on an ever-expanding global circuit. In early 1977, Glenn Gray reported that he was "processing for departure to Saudi Arabia to be Safety/Security Engineer for Holmes and Narver on their ARAMCO Project."[108] Alaska had provided him with a launching point into the oil security industry based in the Middle East, a boomerang leg of his jet-setting career. Alaska is a logical jumping-off point for imperial adventures because the state itself was—and continues to be—defined by an ongoing rhetoric of frontier and practice of colonialism, devoted to the production of modern empires' unctuous lifeblood (oil), and spatially as well as demographically a functional outpost of US empire. Gray's travels take us deeper into the coils of this transnational, imperial history of the security world, where state-market assemblages sprawled over national borders, entwining themselves into Leviathans of fearsome proportions.[109]

FOUR

Corporate States and Government Markets for Saudi Arabian Oil

In November of 1975, the *Washington Post* reported that Sanders Associates, a New England Defense Department contractor, was negotiating a deal for security technology with the Saudi Arabian Ministry of the Interior. The firm had "flourished on top-secret electronic warfare contracts," the *Post* elaborated, and amid the "post-Vietnam defense spending slump" now hoped to provide another country with over "$172 million worth of the sort of internal security technology that Congress decided the US government should stop providing other countries when it closed down the Agency for International Development's Office of Public Safety last July."[1]

The *Post* reporter was correct: this was precisely the sort of technology that the Office of Public Safety had provided. In fact, the link was even tighter than that, far tighter than a responsible journalist could speculate: it was OPS itself that had suggested the Saudis acquire the tech. The negotiations were pursuing the recommendations of a survey performed by OPS, one of its final acts as it wound down its formal activities—what one former agent called an "epilogue to OPS." In one of the earliest *Public Safety Newsletters*, he elaborated, "As a footnote to the last OPS activity, the government of the Kingdom of Saudi Arabia had requested the [US Government] to do a comprehensive survey of its Ministry of Interior. This is perhaps one of the most complex surveys undertaken by OPS, complicated further by the demise of the Office"—but not derailed by it.[2]

Despite this suggestion that the project survey ended OPS's story—an "epilogue," a "footnote to the last"—there is more to tell. For when the survey was completed, ex-OPS officers did not quite quit the scene. In a long and fruitful set of engagements, it would not be Sanders but demobilized AID employees who would implement their survey's recommendations.[3] All the way through the decade ex-OPS personnel were still in Saudi Arabia, as this chapter will detail, expanded into a range of security-focused capacities. They worked for private companies, US state bodies, and directly for the Saudi government. Under the auspices of both private and public entities and mixtures of the two, they provided services and technology that Congress had expressly prohibited.

The "technical" assistance Saudi Arabia would commission from former OPS agents and others would take forms that blithely transcend state or market boundaries. These entities show us the strain in their agents' claims regarding the accountability of democratic institutions to citizens and the independence of a market free from state manipulation, where all players meet on equal grounds. Instead we see the interlinked flows of state-market power in the moment of Cold War democratic capitalism, joining the first world's colossus and a monarchic nation that is at once an object of colonial intervention, a wealthy producer of the era's most ideologically charged and materially valuable energy source, and a powerful regional stronghold. Without suggesting that such complexity is unique to the period beginning in the late twentieth century, *Violence Work* explores these daunting cyborgs that trample the categories structuring prevailing ideas of government legitimacy, democracy, and justice. In this chapter, we follow a horde of these centauresque state-market assemblages as they emerged in the aftermath of the formal police assistance program in and related to Saudi Arabia.

SPECIAL RELATIONSHIPS

The twentieth century saw European, especially British control of the Mideast cede to that of the United States. In the interwar period, Britain maintained control of Kuwait, Bahrain, Oman, and the Trucial States (countries bound to Britain by truce). Thanks to its strategic location for the Second World War, the region began to loom in US policy horizons. The US was particularly keen to establish an airbase in Dhahran, and so the Roosevelt administration threw its support behind King Abdulaziz ibn Saud, becoming a critical political player in Saudi politics and replacing Britain as the primary imperial power there for the duration of the Cold War.[4] The so-called "special relationship" between Saudi Arabia and the United States grew from this root.

Like so many other places in the era of decolonization and anti-imperialist nationalism, Saudi Arabia boasted a vibrant political left. Activists organized to democratize and reject imperial control, in tune with and inspired by regional events, as Mosaddegh nationalized the British-owned Anglo-Iranian Oil Company in 1951, Nasser nationalized the Suez Canal in 1956, and other Gulf nations asserted themselves in relation to the "Seven Sisters" oil companies (Esso, Mobil, Standard of California, Gulf Oil, Texaco, British Petroleum, and Shell). Perhaps Saudi Arabia might have moved in similar directions. King Saud was not unwilling to consider the possibilities. Under his rule, for example, the Saudis broke with the US in 1954, rejecting a military agreement and terminating technical assistance programs, while a major labor strike in 1956 pressured Aramco to improve conditions for its workers. But the US was determined to crush socialist factions and popular unrest, and energetically supported politicians who would supress them, namely Crown Prince Faisal, who successfully displaced Saud (his brother) in 1962. Panicked over ongoing radicalism in the region including revolutions, defections, and coups, Faisal launched a brutal program of repression with US (and British and Israeli) support that lasted through the 1970s. Pressures to nationalize continued, forcing compromises such as the 1973 transfer of oil rights from the companies to the producing nations. In return the companies were promised that they could buy the oil back at a certain percentage of the posted price.[5] A special relationship, indeed.

OPS belongs in this calculus of US aid dedicated to the project of Cold War repression. OPS worked in Saudi Arabia from its earliest days as an organization in 1962—the very year Faisal succeeded in banishing his brother—through regularly renewed commitments all the way to 1975.[6] In exchange (for the range of assistance, not only for OPS), Saudi Arabia levied its influence within OPEC to ensure that oil would be priced in US dollars.[7] With oil denominated in American currency, the United States would be greatly favored in trade of the world's most important commodity. By

1967, US control of oil reserves was up from 10 to 60 percent, while British ownership dropped from 70-plus to about 30 percent.[8] In a self-reinforcing cycle, greater US political power gave Gulf states a greater interest in the US dollar and therefore in US financial power. Mideast nations, Saudi Arabia first among them, were "junior partners" to this order, deeply implicated and actively in support of the US-dominated global capitalism emerging in this period.[9]

We enter this swiftly moving narrative, then, during a set of "hinge years," as the global system of oil-based power faced tangible pressures for decolonization of international relations and democratization from within.[10] What we see in this period is the elasticity of a system responding to pressure by moving its material and rhetorical resources around.[11] Specifically, in the early 1970s, the Gulf states consolidated their national control of oil just as the economic policies of neoliberalism saw their first significant applications. Neoliberalism countered the nationalizations and other socialist hopes of the decolonizing world, levying economic-scientific authority to argue that states should step out of the way of the market. Yet as neoliberalism proclaimed deregulation its watchword, its agents acted to support strong, even activist, states and state policies. The economic arrangements made under the auspices of neoliberalism were neither deregulation nor some simple opposite such as state-market collaboration. Their relationship was more intimate than the formal collaboration of separate actors; these objects were complex assemblages, inextricably interfaced, confounding any genuine autonomy of state and market.

As these bodies formed, eroded, and recombined, neoliberalism's agents found ever more cunning ways to claim their formal autonomy. Little is more indicative of the hypocrisies of this paradigm than the solution Nixon and Kissinger found to Gulf state nationalism, the militarist "Nixon Doctrine" of arming client states through arms sales rather than aid, not only a boon to authoritarian regimes but a "bonanza for American defense contractors."[12] When critics, even other branches of the US government, opposed these provisions, as Congress did, for example, in prohibiting police assistance, that assistance simply flowed into ready private channels and other government bodies, straining credulity regarding the hard separation between government and private sector that is supposed to guarantee accountability for the former and open, equal access for all in the latter.

The continuities in the Saudi branch of OPS reflected the uniqueness of the US-Saudi special relationship, including the wealth it generated, as the Saudis paid for the aid they received. In technocratic lingo, OPS–Saudi Arabia was a "host-country-financed" program, and as such seemed possibly immune from the ban on foreign police assistance written into the Foreign Assistance Act, due to the exception defined in Section 607 of the revised act. As OPS management understood it, the Saudi Arabian program was a "Section 607 exemption," the only program in the world at the moment of Congress's decision that fit those terms.[13] For a short time it even seemed as though it would not actually end at all.

The director of OPS by the time of termination, Lauren "Jack" Goin, briefed his colleagues regarding counsel's interpretation of the terms of the termination as set out in the FAA for 1973. They had "up to eight months after the Act is signed under Section 617 to effect an orderly phase-out in each program," Goin advised, noting that "narcotics control assistance efforts, funded by A.I.D. under the authority of Section 481, may continue as can totally reimbursed (Section 607) programs."[14]

So as Public Safety agents around the globe prepared phase-out surveys of OPS programs, the Saudi Arabian program moved in the opposite direction. There OPS prepared not to wind down joint activities but ramp them up, embarking upon an ambitious technical survey.[15] The project would be a large-scale undertaking, as John Weiss detailed: "The survey is encompassing organization and management, civil defense, fire fighting, passport procedures, immigration, penology, highway patrol, records and identification, criminalistics, patrol traffic, communications, personnel administration/manpower and training, computer applications, special security forces, and coast guard activity. The final report of as much as 800 to 1000 pages must be translated into Arabic and presented to the Minister of the Interior."[16]

The survey leaned not only on the nine OPS agents already in place but also imported new people to Saudi. A team of "nineteen professionals, plus our front-office secretary, Loretta Romero, were assembled from federal and state governments, city agencies and the commercial sector," and set off in early 1975.[17] Herbert Hardin was team chief until illness sent him home, when Goin himself took his place.[18] Two former OPS advisors "came aboard as 'contract' people, Donald Bordenkircher to cover Penology and

Roy Hatem on 'Patrol.'" Other team members were gathered from federal, state, city, and private organizations.[19]

Administrators hoped Section 607 would allow OPS to implement the recommendations it set forth in the survey. Unfortunately, that was not to be. There was too much public outrage at the allegations of torture and political policing leveled at the agency; the congressional ban ended up terminating OPS in full, to the great frustration of those convinced of the need for its services.

Goin and fellow administrators were devastated at the prospect of losing the "unique assets" OPS had developed. Together they brainstormed about how best to safeguard their work.[20] Goin himself authored multiple drafts of strategy proposals in the period immediately following the congressional ban. His preference was to create a "successor organization to OPS" (one idea was an "Office of Criminal Justice Management") or, as he set out baldly in another document as outline letter "A": "Transfer the function to another agency or Department," such as Justice, Defense, or Treasury.[21]

Goin made these proposals despite a full understanding that Congress had expressly forbidden OPS from redirecting its work into other channels. As Goin reminded his sympathetic readers, "It is the intent of Congress that present programs being conducted by the Agency for International Development in foreign countries should not be transferred to some other agency of the government in order to avoid this prohibition."[22] Nevertheless, he planned to do precisely this. He had to plan carefully, Goin well knew, for any proposal that contained a hint of police assistance would have an "image problem with Congress"—it would face, he wrote whimsically, "rough sledding."[23]

Some heirs apparent did emerge, of course, narcotics police being the most infamous example.[24] Some assistance survived under other nebulous auspices, such as the program in Iran, which lasted until March 1976.[25] Other programs continued via the exemption for "reimbursable assistance," even though the Saudi program as a whole could not take this route. The Joint Commission on Economic Cooperation, an agency still within USAID, however, fit this description. John Ziegler, one of the nine Public Safety staff members employed at Saudi Arabia's Department of Technical Services as of 1971, was with the Joint Commission's US–Saudi Arabia version by January 1976. "John says it's a form of AID with the host government paying the bills and the program is managed by the Treasury Department," the *Newsletter* reported, adding that John was the first employee there, and had set up the office. "Many of the new staff were former AID personnel," it disclosed; Ziegler expected 100 to 150 US government employees by July. Some of these would come from the ranks of Public Safety; Ziegler wrote that he had crossed paths with many former OPS employees already.[26]

A sister or perhaps parent organization was USAID's Office of Country Financed Technical Services—another application of the useful concept of the "technical." Bob Brougham, an ex-OPS employee, worked for this body and wrote to his fellows about it. The Office of Country Financed Technical Services operated out of AID's Technical Assistance Bureau, Brougham explained; his work there involved "trying to generate host country financed services."[27] Brougham was based in Washington, but traveled; in 1978 he wrote that he was on his way to Lagos to "drum up business for A.I.D. under the law that provides for aid to countries that are able to pay for it (reimbursable assistance)," presumably a reference to Section 607 of the FAA.[28] So even without the umbrella of OPS, the agency's work continued uninterrupted.

Goin's other idea about how to continue OPS operations despite the congressional ban involved dispersing the employees to other capable agencies. "B," he lettered his second plan, would be to transfer officers individually "to LEAA, to DEA, Customs, or State Security to carry out assistance within confines of their specific authorization." While this option would not build police aid institutions, Goin judged it acceptable for some short-term goals. This, for example, was the solution for Abdel Alkassim, another of the nine Public Safety agents in Riyadh when OPS was terminated. Alkassim moved to a second (or was it third?) US government entity providing aid for a fee, the US Army Corps of Engineers, which had operated in Saudi Arabia at least since 1972.[29] By 1976 the corps had absorbed Alkassim, a Jordanian-born graduate of Kansas State with an engineering degree.[30] Around the world, this is what many OPS employees did, as other scholars of OPS have observed.

For previous scholars, the point of revealing OPS agents' questionably legal transfers to other bodies was to decry the circumvention of congressional will. The superlative scholarship of such researchers as Martha Huggins or Michael Klare did this compellingly. But when we expand the lens to see illegal transfers not only in the moment of OPS's retirement but also before that in its heyday and then well after its demise, it becomes clear that transgressions were not exceptional, not specific to this moment. Violence workers shuffled around the various branches of state and market regularly, fitting easily into many more spaces than the formal concept of "police" allows us to notice. Such shuffling was (and is) the quotidian, constitutive process of state-market formation as an unlimited set of fluid assemblages. To protest a single transfer misses the need to protest the underlying forces spurring the movement on, and preserves the legitimacy of the large-scale process by granting the most visible violations the status of exception.

Further, in following the money around violence work, it is myopic to limit the search to the public sector. Goin didn't. In strategizing about OPS's options in the face of congressional sanction, Goin allowed for the possibility of carrying out the same work in the private sector. He offered up, in the document cited above, a "Plan C":

> C. *Establish a Private Corporation.* As a non-profit corporation, with its objectives to provide overseas police assistance. The gap in the U.S. ability to help others in this area would be filled.
> · Manpower now in OPS would be offered jobs with the corporation.
> · The corporation would have to function to achieve U.S. foreign policy objectives.
> · Its activities would be in step with and assure the success of the IPA.
> · It would have to receive its funds from 607 types of funding arrangements, contributions from foundations, etc.[31]

This, ultimately, was exactly what Goin did when he left Saudi Arabia. In November 1975, the *Public Safety Newsletter* reported that Goin

> ha[d] established and is President and Chairman of the Board of Public Safety Service, Inc. The company is "designed especially to meet a management need of foreign countries desiring to procure U.S. resources in their development efforts. It is not designed to provide these resources itself, but to use professional knowledge and experience gained in the (AID) Office of Public Safety over nearly two decades in their acquisition for foreign governments who are clients." Jack [Goin] says that "being convinced that the Office of Public Safety job is not done and that our government is not apt to do much in helping our foreign friends develop their police, I've forged ahead on my own."

The editors congratulated Goin and noted that he invited former OPS personnel available for long or short-term work to write to him in Washington.[32]

It's hard to say what is more misleading, the promise to obey Congress while scheming every which way to undermine it, or the suggestion that private-sector police assistance would be "nonprofit."

DOING WELL BY DOING GOOD

Altruism is optional in the provision of foreign aid. Aid in general—OPS is no exception—breeds advantages aplenty for the donor. OPS-SA (Saudi Arabia) generated profit-making opportunities for US bodies across the public-private gamut. Most directly, profit came from the monies the Saudi government paid the US government for these "fully reimbursable" OPS services. OPS had created a "Department of Technical Services" within the Saudi Ministry of the Interior—OPS's patron for this survey and primary contact in general—in 1968. Between 1968 and 1973, one report assessed the value of the work in that Department at $1,974,348.88, including programs in riot control, telecommunications, criminalistics, investigations, records and identification, administration, and more, in addition to extensive technical advice and assistance to the Coast Guard and Frontier Force in administrative and logistical policies and procedures, navigation, search and rescue, channel markings, watercraft maintenance, patrol schedules, contraband and smuggler interception, logistics, and sea telecommunications capabilities.[33]

In addition, OPS facilitated contracts between the Saudi government and private corporations. An assessment in 1969 calculated that "the Saudi Arabian Government has procured $501,796 worth of US manufactured equipment" through OPS. "It is quite probable," the report pointed out, "that the sale of US manufactured products will increase significantly in future years."[34] Indeed, there is no indication that this sort of arrangement diminished in any way. In early 1973 when the Saudi Department of Technical Services planned a new crime lab, a commercial group from the Fisher Scientific Company of Pittsburgh visited Riyadh to inspect the site and prepare an offer, as did the British-American Abbott Laboratories, showing that a corporate body's national affiliation didn't concern the trainers.[35] A few months later the Public Safety agent responsible for the Saudi Coast Guard and Frontier Forces dedicated himself to support for AVCO, an aviation manufacturer. The agent visited Jiddah "to observe AVCO Corporation training and maintenance operations."[36]

This seeding of public and private profit was not limited to Saudi Arabia; it was the rule for OPS worldwide. As OPS was nearing the end of its operations in 1974, director Goin pointed out that over just the previous seven years, some nineteen countries had spent $39.3 million dollars on amenities provided by OPS's Technical Services Division.[37]

Well after OPS quit the scene, this galvanizing of profit for both private and public entities continued. In the post-OPS era, Bob Brougham and his Office of Country Financed Technical Services worked not only to generate demand for services provided by USAID, as noted above, but also by other US government organizations (such as the US Army Corps of Engineers, as we have seen) *and by private businesses*. As Brougham wrote to his former fellows, "We are trying to generate host country financed services, not only for AID or other USG (US government) entities, but for private industry as well."[38]

Why is this *aid*? Why does this exchange of services and products for money not count as trade? While economists may insist on semantic differentiation based on this or that technical detail, these are post facto rationalizations of a process that effectively sidesteps the checks and balances supposedly in place in market interactions. In these exchanges there is no competition. Prices are not set in relation to any other producers or consumers. The goods exchanged follow political alliance rather than deeper need. This phenomenon reminds us of the deep imbrication of states in profit making, and the equally profound reliance of markets on capitalist states. As Goin and his minions readily understood, foreign aid under capitalism generates profit for the providing country, well beyond "host country financed services" or "reimbursable assistance." Aid is highly self-interested profit seeking.[39] On the balance sheets of global debt, the profit United States and other First World entities derived from "aid" to Third World countries is missing.

MASTERS OF ALL THEY SURVEYED

Understanding the profits derived from police assistance helps to clarify that what we are tracing is a history of neoimperial exploitation.[40] It is "neo" because it is not simply a metropolitan nation directing the affairs and exploiting the resources of a colonized one but US and "junior partner" Saudi Arabian governmental and corporate elites working to exploit workers and natural resources together. This dynamic emerges even more clearly in the mechanism of the survey.

The OPS survey of 1975 was one in a long line of reiterated surveys. Throughout its operations OPS had plowed its labors with these studies.[41] Surveys stitched together government and corporate entities in ongoing rationalizations for their joint and several services. They helped make the case for facilities or capacities needed that could then be offered as aid or bid out to corporations. The mechanism of the survey in Saudi Arabia (as elsewhere, surely) helped create the complex web of public and private collaboration this chapter is gradually outlining.

Regularly reinitiated, these studies launched as if ever and still unprecedented. Surveys were repeated as if none had come before. The regularity of the survey form is telling. It secures the fiction of untouched ground, the frontier ever extending to the horizon, always unaltered by "Western" contact, always available for the first footprint. It encourages the hubris, secured by amnesia, that underpins US as well as other imperial interventions. The amnesia of US police aid is particularly impressive given its regular renewal. In 2006, I had the opportunity to interview then Los Angeles police chief William Bratton regarding his travels in Latin America. He was sure no American police officer had ever gone before.[42] The confidence of being the first to modernize and professionalize an isolated force, a classic sense of discovering virgin territory, is one of US police aid's most striking mechanisms of operation.

The survey initiated in Riyadh in 1975 as OPS wound down was as committed as any to the notion of its own novelty. Its agents betrayed no recognition that they would examine well-known programs, the products of long collaborations with the Ministry of the Interior, and of survey after survey after survey. Yet this disavowed labor would help them anyway—all the more so, actually. The surveys and contracts OPS had facilitated throughout its operations would now allow its employees to switch to the fulfillment side. As OPS disintegrated, some of its employees would follow the logic their work had organized, moving over to work for the corporations actualizing the recommendations of their surveys.

Saudi Arabia survey team members were scheduled to leave in April 1975.[43] When their work was done, "the survey team and the remaining office staff will be disbanded to go their separate ways. Thus ends the epilogue to OPS," Weiss predicted placidly.[44] Some OPS staff did go home.[45] But many found employers who were doing similar or adjacent work. The business created for US corporations by aid to Saudi Arabia, and OPS specifically, allowed significant numbers of former OPS employees to remain there after 1975, not with US government entities but with private concerns, or with hybrid corporate bodies made up of some of each. Even in the case of ostensibly private-sector businesses, the relation to government groundwork and contracts raises the question of whether they deserve to be called "private" at all.

QUACKS LIKE A PRIVATE

Former OPS personnel interested in remaining in Saudi Arabia after 1975 found plentiful opportunities in the nominally private sector, all dedicated to cultivating the ground OPS had tilled. Many of the companies they joined were busily carrying out the recommendations of one or another OPS survey.

In 1978, a group of ex-OPS reported to the *Newsletter* that they were together again in Saudi. A hearty crew provided services to the Morrison-Knudsen corporation, a civil engineering and construction company, working on a major construction project, the King Khalid Military City. Among the "former OPS & Vietnam hands working on this project in Saudi," wrote Jim Lewis, were Mike Dobrichan, Pete Bishonden, Dick Braaten, Gunther Wagner, Arthur Goodchild, and himself; Steve Mayfield and Tom Staley were also involved.[46] Mike Dobrichan described the work as "a 10 billion dollar project to construct a self-sustaining city for a population of 70,000." The project, he expected, would take seven to nine years and some 20,00 [*sic*] workers from the United States and other nations.[47]

This work was categorized, in the main, as "security." James Lewis was "Deputy Chief, Security (Investigations/Staff Services)," later promoted to manager of security or chief of security services.[48] Arthur Goodchild, a British agent who had worked with OPS, was "heading up the Security Training section" as the contract was winding down.[49] Dick Braaten called himself a "security officer" for Morrison-Knudsen; Pete Bishonden was "Chief, Security Services"; and Gunther Wagner, who started as "Senior Specialist (Investigations)," was deputy chief security administration by the time he left in 1980.[50]

There is a distinct absence of any mention of crime fighting in these work descriptions, so heavily tilted toward industrial security. Industrial security—guarding and keeping order for corporate installments, especially, of course, oil rigs—was the bulk of OPS labor in Saudi Arabia. In public arguments against terminating OPS, however, its champions focused on a more conventional definition of police work. The program in Saudi, explained one briefing document, aimed "to provide assistance in specialized fields of police organization and management, such as criminalistics, records and identification and otherwise to develop the police institution so that it has the capability of enforcing the laws of the country in a humane manner." (It also tried to tap into fears of communism by warning, ominously, that "the discontinuance of the program would provide an opportunity for other nations with other than western ideology to fill the gap.")[51] In the face of possible termination, OPS proponents worked hard to frame this labor as police work.

As OPS actualized industrial security, it was "police work" in another sense: its work force. Most of the men on the Ministry of Interior survey and the Morrison-Knudsen project were former police. Following World War II army service, Hardin had been a commander with the Albuquerque police department.[52] Goin had worked in crime labs after wartime navy service and before his postings abroad.[53] Hatem was a municipal police patrolman-lieutenant after his time in the army.[54] Braaten was both a municipal detective and a county sheriff who had also served in the marines.[55] Lewis was a deputy sheriff and police officer after coast guard experience, as well as a public safety officer for a university.[56] Ziegler had been a marine and then an Arizona police officer.[57] Jack Campbell had a thirteen-year career with the (parapolice) coast guard before signing up with OPS-Saigon.[58] Of the crew in Saudi for whom the State Department provided pre-OPS employment history, only one was without police experience.[59] Training for local, domestic policing, supplemented by federal paramilitary experience, was apparently excellent preparation for international private security work.

Arthur Goodchild chose an interesting metaphor to report that he was still working for Morrison Knudsen in September 1980; in this (formally) civilian, private post he was "soldiering on," he wrote.[60] The monarchic, martial elements of "King Khalid Military City" surely helped frame such reflections.

These workers helped secure still other pieces of the state-corporate network, which emerge in the career paths of their colleagues. Probably reflecting a recommendation of the survey, for example, in 1976, former OPS agents Paul Vukovich and Christy Moyers wrote that they had accepted posts "instructing the Saudi National Guard," essentially the same task they had performed for OPS.[61] They were doing so, though, "with Vinnell Corporation in Saudi Arabia," and lamented to their former colleagues that working for a contractor was a "long, sad cry from Public Safety and Vietnam."[62] They didn't explain the distance.

Walter Boyling worked for the private United Development Consultants as a field advisor and training instructor after his departure from Vietnam and Public Safety (in 1969, well before the termination) in Saudi Arabia as well as Iran, Africa (he didn't say where), and Madagascar.[63] Later Boyling joined the Arabian-American Oil Company, Aramco, at their Berri Jubail gas processing plant.[64] Glenn Gray, another former OPS agent in Saudi with Aramco, adds other corporate employers to the mix. Gray left the Alaska pipeline security company to accept a post as "Safety/Security Engineer for Holmes and Narver on their Aramco Project," he wrote.[65] On vacation in Bangkok in early 1978, he reported that he had completed one assignment in Saudi Arabia and would return to another, this time as "Project Security Supervisor for Bechtel Corporation on their port project," continuing his work in the "Near East" through the end of the decade.[66] In November 1980, the *Newsletter* printed a flier from "the HBH Company listing job opportunities in Naval Operations and Maintenance in Saudi Arabia, Arlington, Va. and Little Creek, Va."[67]

United States universities were a part of the mix as well. Gordon Young reported that he was on his way to Saudi Arabia with Aramco "in conjunction with the University of Houston's special Industrial Security program" in early 1978, staying until some point in 1979.[68] Jack Goin wrote in October 1979 that Sam Houston State College in Huntsville, Texas (seventy miles from and not affiliated with the school Young mentioned, the University of Houston), had an LEAA contract to train Saudi police officers in traffic law enforcement—was this too a recommendation of the survey?—and that they would be hiring six "faculty." He invited former PSAs to apply.[69] Houston's prominence here likely has something to do with the oil companies based there, already transnational in their holdings, rivalries, and histories.

Several more former OPS personnel were in the Saudi capitol, Riyadh. Two were with the King Faisal Specialist Hospital and Research Center there—Robert Phippen in 1976, and Wayne Lockhart, who went there to work in security in April, 1980, with his wife Mary Kay.[70] Also in Riyadh were Abdel Alkassim and John Ziegler, discussed above.

Ziegler was a popular guy. Several former Public Safety agents passed through Riyadh to visit him. Ed Merseth was one, the *Newsletter* reported in early 1976; at the end of that year it reported he was vice president of international activities for Public Management Services, in McLean, Virginia.[71] Jack Campbell was a consultant with Fargo International who also passed through Riyadh visiting Ziegler.[72] Campbell later relocated to Virginia with Hydrotronics of McLean as manager of their international programs.[73]

So Campbell and Merseth visited Ziegler and then returned to McLean, the site of CIA headquarters (the neighborhood of Langley is in McLean).[74] On the one hand there is nothing astonishing in this, as OPS's ties to the CIA are well documented and acknowledged, and probably continued for many ex-OPS CIA operatives who remained abroad. What is interesting is that Merseth and Campbell both worked for *private* companies headquartered in McLean. There is no necessary CIA connection—McLean is far from a one-company town—but if there were, it would simply add one more to the list of democracy-flaunting state-market amalgamations we are noting in case after case.

Former OPS agents worked not only in Saudi Arabia but throughout the oil industry. Whether their new jobs reflected transnational connections forged by OPS or by oil itself is hard to tell. Del Spier enjoyed quite a long career with Ashland Oil in Kentucky in their security department, directing "worldwide operations."[75] Spier hired Gunther Wagner as his assistant.[76] Glenn Walters wrote that he had "a two-hat position as Marine Manager and Special Projects Manager for a Marine Hydrographic Survey Company headquartered in Houston. Our principal clients, not surprisingly, are the major oil companies" as well as "various Sea-grant Universities and the U.S. Government."[77] Others were hired directly by foreign governments as if they had simply eliminated the US state middleman. Monroe Scott established himself as a freelance consultant to petroleum companies, which landed him a contract in Honduras as "advisor to the Ministry of Natural Resources for Logistics, budget and plans. He has his own staff and anticipates considerable travel through the country."[78] In 1979, the *Newsletter* considered that "old Djakarta hands may be interested to know that Dave and Nora Fowler, the contract pilot with the Air Police in the mid 1950's is now flying for Continental Oil Co. of Chad."[79]

Nor were former OPS workers in the Gulf restricted to oil. Fred Powell let his former colleagues know that he had become a public safety consultant for a "firm of consulting engineers (TAI, Inc.) in Tehran, Iran," and had secured a contract as manager on the multiyear "Iranian Police Project," which involved a nationwide microwave bearer network, seven engineers, and eleven administrative personnel.[80] Frank Walton performed a large-scale study of law enforcement in Kuwait for LECAR (Law Enforcement Consulting and Research), a private firm.[81] In December 1976, during his tenure with United Development Consultants, Walter Boyling gave a mailing address on Kharg Island, Iran, care of Stanwick International, a US-owned company formed to work in overseas markets, which contracted with the Imperial Iranian Navy in the 1970s.[82] From there he moved to the work we have noted he performed in Saudi Arabia for Aramco.[83]

KEEPING COMPANY

To review, the employers of former Office of Public Safety staff still in Saudi Arabia included Holmes and Narver, Aramco, Morrison-Knudsen, the Vinnell Corporation, HBH (a joint venture of Holmes and Narver, Bendix Field Engineering Corporation, and Hughes Aircraft), Bechtel, United Development Consultants, the University of Houston, Sam Houston State College, King Khalid Military City, Berri Jubail gas plant, King Faisal Specialist Hospital, the Saudi Ministry of the Interior, the Saudi National Guard, the Saudi police, the Saudi Navy, the US Navy, the US Army Corps of Engineers, the US–Saudi Arabia Joint Commission on Economic Cooperation, USAID, the CIA, and surely others. Ex-OPS personnel worked for multiple employers at once because their employers merged in crenulated collaborations that preserved corporate and state-market distinctions on paper only. In spirit they were overlapping government-corporate subjects, fusions of two nation-states and immeasurable markets, melding police and military expertise and bringing the compound to industrial sites. In this roiling mixture, the agents formed in OPS were occasionally training police, paramilitary, or military forces but much more often providing "security" for vast infrastructural projects, producing the international security industry emerging in this moment alongside the extraordinary US and Saudi prosperity of the 1970s.

This "complex morass of agencies" was composed of bodies whose "formal status and operating territories cut across the public-private divide" as well as bridging a range of other sorts of borders.[84] The ostensibly private companies employing ops alumni are instructive. Holmes and Narver is an engineering company with a complex corporate history, including some iffy business practices.[85] For our purposes, it is relevant primarily because of its relationship to its longtime collaborator, the Arabian-American Oil Company, Aramco, unquestionably first among peers in its tentacular reach and amazing biography. Founded in 1933 (as was Holmes and Narver) to manage a concession that Standard Oil of California had obtained with the government of Saudi Arabia, it added Texaco (now Chevron) in 1936; Standard Oil of New Jersey and Socony-Vacuum (both now ExxonMobil) bought in a dozen years later. The company renamed itself Aramco in 1944, growing powerfully over the years, especially in the 1970s.[86]

In the 1970s, a flourishing Aramco organized its own private security force. ops's hand is visible here. Its "Surveillance and Protection" survey in 1971 of "Saudi Arabian Oil Fields and Installations," performed for the Ministry of the Interior, had warned the ministry that Aramco should but did not have "a full-time industrial security professional." It advised the company to create a uniformed security force, noting that the company's previous failure to do so might have been related to "an effort to avoid allegations that the company has established an internal police force."[87] Dismissing this concern blithely in passing, the survey continued on, noting that several different bodies within the Saudi Arabian government had responsibility for oil security and recommending that a single authority be designated, such as the Ministry of the Interior. In conclusion, survey authors felt the need to explain the tangled webs of government and private ownership involved in Aramco, which at that moment was owned by foreign oil companies but paid 50 percent of its gross income, less operating expenses, to the Saudi government, and was made up of extraction, refining, pipeline, and shipping facilities situated throughout the kingdom and owned by complex government and corporate entities, including a US corporation, Tapline.[88]

In 1976, Aramco's new security force traveled to Florida to guard talks the company was holding there with the government of Saudi Arabia. Other observers have focused on the security force's travels, suggesting the force was mobilized to prevent a repeat of a hostage taking by pro-Palestine guerrillas in 1975 at an oil industry meeting at opec's headquarters in Vienna.[89] But this is a classic disaster alibi for a step people had long hoped to take in any event. In fact, the security force was a measure ops had recommended years before the Vienna incident, and its principal operating location was *in* Saudi Arabia. These travels highlight the startling transnational tangle this force comprised. It was an internationally mobile body made up of former US American cops, headed by former FBI agent George W. Ryan, and had been trained—at the expense of the Saudi government—at the US International Police Academy (IPA), the school launched and run for twelve years by OPS. Ryan himself contained all the ingredients of these mind-numbing cocktails: FBI experience, work for Aramco in Saudi Arabia, and (concurrently) the presidency of the American Society for Industrial Security—and even a familial relation to OPS: his brother was PSA Jack Ryan, killed in Saigon in the 1960s.[90] The Byzantine coils of the security industry wound around Aramco's multisited, miscegenated body, where the US government provided facilities to train a private security force on a foreign government's dime, conjoining two governments and the massive corporate oil industry under the umbrella of the security world.

In the late 1970s and 1980s, the Saudi government nationalized Aramco. Successfully foreclosing any genuine popular control of natural resource wealth, the monarchy took over from the private consortium gradually, like other OPEC states also then moving to manage their own natural resources in the era of pan-Arab nationalism that ended the region-wide "concessionary regime."[91] Saudi Arabia purchased 100 percent of the firm in 1980, and in 1988 replaced the company with a new national body via charter and royal decree. This moment of pure public status was, however, short-lived. As a government entity Aramco soon moved hungrily *back* toward the private sector, purchasing interests in Korean, Filipino, Chinese, European, and US companies, even expanding into "integrated chemical" production through collaboration with Dow Chemical in 2011.[92]

Because the US government did so much to help Aramco's profit margins, Aramco is the company cited by state theorist Timothy Mitchell in a 1991 statement of his ongoing argument that we should speak not of states but of "state effects."[93] In this as in so many similar cases, the edges where the state ends and the private company begins are indistinct. Watching individual workers move from federal agencies such as OPS and the CIA into Aramco's security force—where they performed essentially identical tasks—certainly strengthens this impression.

Morrison-Knudsen, a similarly impressive behemoth, offers further confirmation of this line of argument. Founded in 1912, it joined the consortium that built the Hoover Dam in 1931, eventually building 150 more dams worldwide. In its heyday it was a vast and diversified enterprise including mining, space-launch facilities, prison construction, and site prep-aration work for the Trans-Alaska Pipeline. After acquisition by a rival firm in 2007 it would help constitute one of the five largest providers of technical services to the US Department of Defense.[94]

The Vinnell Corporation, finally, has taken particularly visible steps across the public-private line, provoking fury at its profit-driven milita-rism. In 1995, its talents were recognized by bombers who targeted the Saudi National Guard and their American trainers. These trainers, just like Paul Vukovich and Christy Moyers back in 1976, were still, in 1995, employees of Vinnell. In an exposé on Vinnell in the *Progressive* in 1996, William Hartung quoted a retired American military officer on the bombing: "I don't think it was an accident that it was that office that got bombed. If you wanted to make a political statement about the Saudi regime, you'd single out the National Guard, and if you wanted to make a statement about American involvement, you'd pick the only American contractor involved in training the guard: Vinnell."[95]

The Saudi National Guard is the corps that protects the "Saudi monarchy from its own people," wrote Hartung in his critique of Vinnell.[96] An OPS surveyor found precisely this in 1969. At a civil disturbance in 1967 at Aramco headquarters in Dhahran, police had not only been unable to calm protes-tors but seemed to be "themselves actually directing or engaging in mob ac-tivities." Eventually it was the National Guard's batons that dispersed the crowd. The OPS survey author understood that the egregious working conditions Aramco inflicted on Saudi Arabian employees was the source of much dissatisfaction, as Robert Vitalis has documented exhaustively.[97] Despite the proclaimed humanitarian focus of USAID, Aramco's labor vio-lations did not concern him, nor was he unhappy about the government's "basically authoritarian bias." The Saudi government claimed to be able to "take care" of communists, he noted. Unruffled by this chilling phrasing, he simply confirmed, "The local American consensus is that this is essentially correct at this time."[98]

It makes sense that OPS would knit itself to the National Guard, a fit-ting object for violence workers devoted to the protection (and produc-tion) of the state—not only their particular state, Saudi Arabia, but also the *idea* of the state in the abstract. It also feels abundantly logical that OPS would contract primarily with the Saudi Ministry of the Interior, a body Steffen Hertog calls a "fiefdom" with "almost unlimited staying power";

a "a rule unto itself."[99] A state within a state, yet another deviation on state norms, reminds us of the internal heterogeneities of states in their infinite variations—another level on which the concept of the state is incoherent.

That the state is incoherent is a fact of great analytic importance.[100] The state's incoherence can function as a mechanism of power, particularly in moments in which government officials still think they need to cleave rhetorically to democratic principles. The state's incoherence can itself provide the resources with which to shield its relationship to the market from public view, for it allows for the endless shell games we see so abundantly in the history of police assistance in Saudi Arabia. As this chapter has narrated, police assistance programs were born from one of these shell games: when military aid fell into disfavor, the US National Security Council developed police assistance programs to accomplish the identical objectives. Nixon and Kissinger conceived another work-around, substituting arms sales to client states for aid. A third shuffle involved the tremendous oxymoron of "reimbursable assistance." In the face of public concern over the cost of foreign aid (a canard in the first place given the predatory nature of aid, but not one that could be discussed publicly), the United States simply asked for money in return, changing neither the profit-loss columns nor the distribution of resources to allies of questionable character.

When police assistance earned censure and then overt prohibition, its crafters dreamed up several circumvention plans, and lower-level actors fashioned still another, simply finding new jobs in which they could continue virtually the same tasks. In the structure of the oil industry we see a few more, such as the move by former colonial powers to release formal ownership of oil wells while retaining the rights to distribute and price petroleum and its products, in order to appear to respect national sovereignty. Another is the Gulf state governments' use of ostensible nationalizations to answer popular demands for the democratization of oil wealth, bolstering US political and economic power and basking in its reflected light and heat.

These shell games involve moving things over ostensible borders from military to civilian, public (state) to private (market), and across levels of scale from national to transnational. In the era of the welfare state, critics sometimes hoped they might be able to call upon the state to respect its own laws and cease this travel. Today, both hopefully and tragically, activists are much less likely to imagine such a strategy. They see that the grossly expanded criminal justice system has foreclosed 1960s hopes for real social justice, cemented ideologically and financially by the war on terror, and understand that the only state services that have grown are punitive ones. It is primarily, perhaps even only, the carceral capacity of the state that has expanded.[101] It is now widely clear that the state is an unlikely savior—that the solution to the state is not *more state*.

CODA

When four agents of Blackwater USA were killed in Fallujah in 2004 and their bodies displayed on a bridge over the Euphrates River, Americans expressed outrage. Newspapers called the deaths "slayings" and termed the hanging "an act of savagery . . . sheer bestial violence."[102] In addition to the predictably Orientalist outcry against the "barbarity" of the "terrorists," outrage was also directed at the private contractor Blackwater, echoing the outrage directed at Halliburton for its war profiteering in the rebuilding of occupied Iraq.[103] Well-developed strands of critique of private military companies now entwine collective memory of these events.

The public sense of wrongdoing about private military contracting, although abundantly justified, hinges on a well-fed amnesia regarding its history. A PBS Frontline documentary cited Peter Singer, author of *Corporate Warriors: The Rise of the Privatized Military Industry*: "You're talking about an industry that really didn't exist until the start of the 1990s," Singer claims. "And since then, it's grown in size, in monetary [and] geographic terms."[104]

This sense of an essentially new phenomenon harkens back nostalgically to an era when war was purely military, uncorrupted by private, for-profit operations. It shares much with the amnesia around the militarization of policing, highlighted in August 2014 in Ferguson, Missouri, where police in combat gear added insult to the injury of their murder of young Michael Brown. The coverage of this scandal placed Homeland Security and the War on Terror at the bases of the military excesses of domestic police. Experts decrying events in Ferguson called the problem at best "decades" old; one reporter cited a "17-year-old" exposé as proof of the ancient nature of the beast, preserving the sense of recent uptick: "The *security-über-alles* fixation of the 9/11 era is now the driving force."[105]

The projection of an era of purely civilian policing balances the imagination of a purely military war-fighting machine. These twinned delusions are historically inaccurate, and in their presentism they get the nature of the capitalist state dangerously wrong. Violence workers—those laborers whose tasks include the prerogative to levy violence, whether they are officially civilian, military, or private—have blurred military and civilian activity, mixed public and private spheres, and easily crossed territorial boundaries throughout US history. This category of laborers and the crossings their work entails reveal the inseparable nature of state and market in capitalist democracies; that is, they show the ostensibly democratic US state to be as deeply involved in markets as are socialist or fascist states. Their crossovers highlight the work state officials do to justify the violence required by capital by stabilizing the notion of the state: state agents' efforts to separate civil from military arenas, delineate public and private spheres, and draft images of police as local, domestic workers, are critical pieces of the legitimation of rule.

The denunciation of private companies for doing the government's dirty work, while certainly justified in many respects, upholds the idea of an autonomous market. It is a brick in its correlative creation. For to think of companies such as Aramco or Vinnell as separate from the government or the military—to understand them as private sector entities or civilian—is illogical. Such bodies function only and always in tandem with the US government, working alongside it or just out of sight where government agencies are not permitted to go. To think of government agencies as different because accountable is to refuse to admit that they place their functions into ostensibly private companies whenever they need to evade accountability. Such collaborations are regularly exposed as the antidemocratic unaccountable violent evil that they represent, and just as regularly continue to receive those lucrative government contracts. Vinnell, Aramco, and others are not the only problem here, and sanctioning them will alter no part of the arrangement they comprise. What must change is what allows the powers that claim legitimacy for their violence, structural and spectacular, to hide their workings with the fictions of the borders between the market and the state.

Professors for Police

The Growth of Criminal Justice Education

When he was recruited into OPS, J. B. Carnahan realized he was a novel kind of cop. He was young, he told me, "and in those days, you have to realize, we were considered the new breed. We were college going, we were deep into training." If previously, new police officers were simply apprenticed to a veteran for a few weeks and then sent out on their own, Carnahan had much more intense preparation. "When I came on board, . . . this was all pretty new stuff. I had to have a psychiatric examination, we had physical agilities, I had to stand before a board for about two hours, and talk to people who were in law enforcement in ranking positions. It was the 'new deal,' it was the new way things were done." This was what OPS sought for its ranks, Carnahan explained. "That's who they were looking for. . . . They went to [recruit in] different places where law enforcement was on the upswing education-wise."[1]

This chapter tells the story of that "upswing," the massive growth of US police training and education, including the rise of criminal justice as an academic field of study, in relation to the Office of Public Safety. As a small program, OPS has no causal claim to stake regarding the growth of US police education. Not only was it too modest to have leveraged real influence, but it existed alongside, not before, the explosion of police training domestically. In fact, OPS is arguably a *product* of the enthusiasm for police education that caught fire in the 1960s. OPS was certainly created in the context of changes in military strategy and foreign policy discussed earlier in this book. But it evolved as it did—as a training program—alongside new ideas then gaining purchase in the United States about education and police.

The relationship of police to education was shifting quite dramatically in this moment. The federal funding for the expansion of law enforcement discussed in previous chapters included generous allocations for training law enforcement personnel. That support had a dramatic impact on a system that had not previously emphasized education for police, and certainly not college. In addition to the sheer growth it encouraged, it drew police over the border between public and private employ as federal efforts led private think tanks and foundations into the funding game as both donors and recipients. It encouraged transnational exchange by generously funding projects designed to bring counterinsurgency tactics designed for war abroad to domestic arenas. Federal support for police education also siphoned police across levels of scale as it expanded the corps of federal police and centralized their training at a school substantially staffed by returning OPS police trainers. Overall, the expansion of police education entailed substantial police border crossing, though it was neither unique nor innovative in that respect, as police border crossing accompanies policing everywhere.

The Office of Public Safety guides us through this history because it was a part of every step. Its precursor was a Cold War project out of Michigan State University at East Lansing, which operated a training program in Vietnam as a part of its pioneering expansion of police education. OPS succeeded MSU in Vietnam, and many OPS operatives had MSU degrees. When OPS ended, many of its employees went into teaching, taking their overseas curricula with them to LEAA-funded programs nationwide, including the new centralized training center for federal police.

Revisiting the tale of US police education as related to its foreign complement reveals insights not usually encountered when the history of US police education is narrated as a purely national story. It focuses a spotlight on the continuity between police education in the United States and police assistance overseas, showing the constant connections between domestic and foreign policing. It traces violence workers crossing from public to private spheres with ease, sometimes to avoid accounting for actions public opinion might deem undemocratic. It follows people defending the legitimacy of the state-market by working to deny, justify, or obscure police border crossing, whether those are the borders of the United States when American police go abroad, the borders of scale when policing is organized at federal rather than the state or local levels, or the borders of public and private arenas. (This chapter does not so much touch on the third border of policing, the military-civilian distinction; the educational aspects of this border are visible in the discussion of the IAPA/IPA in chapter 2.)

The story of the rise of police education is also worth revisiting, finally, because the consequences of this mingling of violence and education have been so very deep and wide. The changes in law enforcement education helped grow policing enormously, arguably without improving it. The growth of police education created an enormous academic infrastructure devoted to and invested in the criminal justice system, linking the two in a police-education nexus that has eroded the progressive and liberatory potential of public education. Ultimately the end point of the changes this chapter narrates is the instrumental, neoliberal university, handmaid to mass incarceration.

A BRIEF HISTORY OF POLICE EDUCATION

By the late nineteenth century, US police recruits received at least some specialized training, though formal police academies did not emerge until 1916, when the first was established at the University of California at Berkeley. Berkeley's unique precedence was due to August Vollmer, the city's chief of police, widely considered a great innovator. In addition to implementing bike and car patrols and scientific crime detection, Vollmer was the first to appoint college graduates as patrolmen. He developed academic criminology, and students flocked to Berkeley to learn his methods. The program he set up was "by no means a chronicle of progressivism," recalled the editors of *Social Justice* upon its demise in 1976. It was "a program of good old-fashioned law and order" with "little patience even for the niceties of liberal social science."[2] This lament echoes through the history of postwar police education and criminal justice study, as this chapter will explain.

Vollmer is a notable predecessor in the field of police training for our purposes because his violence work began abroad, in and after military engagement, in the Philippines where he helped to police Manila after serving in the army during the American attack of 1898. Back in the United States as a police chief, Vollmer's international engagements continued, notably in Cuba and China.[3] Vollmer's trajectory reminds us that as far back as we cast our gaze, we encounter military-civilian mixing and connections between foreign (imperial, transnational) and domestic violence work.

With Berkeley grads as the exception, and despite modest growth in police academies as a result of the reforms of the 1930s, for the most part police pursued relatively short training courses of a few weeks at most, were not expected to hold college degrees, and did not continue their education throughout their careers.[4] It was only in the late 1960s and 1970s, thanks to federal government largesse, that US police went back to school en masse. Government programs funded individual police directly, supported police departments to train their personnel, and subsidized college degree programs. Crucial, again, was the Omnibus Crime Control and Safe Streets Act of 1968 and the organization it created, the Law Enforcement Assistance Administration, which funded educational endeavors indirectly and directly via its Law Enforcement Education Program (LEEP).

When President Johnson signed the Safe Streets Act, he extolled its educational influence, praising its "pioneering" loan forgiveness programs and tuition grants for law enforcement personnel. The act also greatly expanded training for state and local police officers at the FBI's national academy, enhanced by the National Defense Education Act, which added similar police education programs and loan forgiveness for students entering law enforcement.[5]

Splendid funds were devoted to the growth of police education and higher education programs in criminal justice. LEEP awarded more than fifty grants in its first three years to help establish college degree programs in law enforcement. In 1969, it spent nearly $7 million dollars on over 400 higher education programs. In 1970, that number was up to over 725, and in 1971 it gave over $20 million dollars to over 900 institutions. Overall, federal funds for crime research and statistics rose from $13.4 million in 1969 to over $110.2 million in 1976.[6]

Programs multiplied apace. In 1960, there were 26 full-time law enforcement programs; the IACP tallied 78 programs in 1964. In 1970, as counted by the LEAA, there were 608. In 1976, a National Criminal Justice Educational Consortium study found 867 institutions with at least one criminal justice program and another 95 planning to start one.[7] Writing specifically of LEEP, Richard Allinson counted 184 programs in 1966–67, just before

LEEP was created: "Then came LEEP and the field boomed." By 1979, there were "some 1,500 institutions offering crime-related programs in higher education," and they reached a great many people: "At its zenith in the mid-1970s, when its annual budget was about $40 million, LEEP supported as many as 100,000 students per year."[8]

LEAA funds were necessary fuel to the fire, so much so that when those funds dried up with the end of the LEAA in the 1980s, schools such as Kentucky experienced a program-threatening drop in enrollment. Police simply couldn't—wouldn't have been able to—afford to go to school without them.[9] As police historian Samuel Walker concluded, federal programs unequivocally revolutionized police studies.[10]

BORDER-CROSSING IN POLICE EDUCATION

Police education grew thanks to both federal and private support, violating the common sense that US policing is local and public. Funds flowed both to and from private and semiprivate think tanks, institutes, and research agencies, swelling private coffers as well as university endowments. Support came not only from the LEAA, its predecessor, and the National Institute of Law Enforcement and Criminal Justice (the LEAA's R&D arm), but other federal bodies such as Project Agile, the Pentagon's research program on counterinsurgency, or the Advanced Research Projects Agency, also a Pentagon body, as well as the FBI, DEA, the National Institute of Corrections and the Bureau of Prisons, the Federal Board of Parole, the Immigration and Naturalization Service, the Departments of Transportation and Treasury, and the National Science Foundation.[11] Private professional associations added their resources, including the American Bar Association, the American Correctional Association, and the IACP. The Ford Foundation was the largest private funder of crime research; it sponsored the Police Foundation, the American Justice Institution, the Vera Foundation, and the Institute of Judicial Administration, among others. Other private funders included the Russell Sage and Guggenheim Foundations.[12]

This wave of support also drew on and fed transnational exchange. Funds were particularly generously distributed to universities and think tanks willing to redirect the attention they had lavished on counterinsurgency abroad to the supposedly comparable needs at home. The Institute for Defense Analyses (IDA), a body that coordinated university researchers on military projects with the support of the Pentagon's Advanced Research Projects Agency, was one of the largest such bodies, operating out of a ten-story headquarters in Washington, handling hundreds of projects at a time.[13] The IDA's colleagues included the Defense Research Corporation of Santa Barbara, the Research Analysis Corporation, the Simulmatic Corporation of New York City, the Center for Research in Social Systems (formerly SORO) at American University in Washington, the federally appointed commissions that functioned like think tanks, and many university bodies.[14]

These groups mixed university and government function inextricably; they represented a "fusion of social science and statecraft," as Joy Rohde has shown. One particularly tight such relation was that of the Special Operations Research Office, or SORO, created in 1956 at American University in Washington, DC. Protests erupted over its university-government (especially CIA) ties; a name change in 1966 failed to mollify protestors, leading American to withdraw its participation in 1969. As this book has chronicled for many bodies straddling the public-private divide, the mixed nature of the group made it easy to reestablish on private footing: SORO was absorbed into a private, for-profit contract research agency, just as other university-based research institutes such as the IDA and the army's Human Resources Research Office were.[15]

One of the effects of the development of these research units in the political context of the 1960s was their divorce from academia, with serious consequences, in some views. Rohde explains that the protests that eventually derailed most academic engagement in Cold War anticommunism alienated progovernment and applied social scientists from academic communities. This development drove a "wedge between national security researchers and most academic social scientists," so that government scholars, "ensconced in private think tanks and contract research offices lining the Washington, D.C., Beltway" became less responsive to advances in academic scholarship. Rohde's devastating conclusion, ultimately, is that "the estrangement of academia from national security research left government work in the hands of second-rate scholars who implicitly supported the political status quo."[16]

Rohde's research is essential, but let us not limit it to this variation on the objection to privatized policing or private prisons based on their remove from the public eye, which supposedly confers accountability. For just as public policing and prisons do not necessarily open themselves and respond to public review, remaining within an academic environment is no guarantee of political independence (nor first-rate scholarship). Scholars still heed the will of their funders, and radical scholars are always less likely to win government support.

A better way to understand the problem with academics' moves from universities to private think tanks is to remember how close they were to violence workers. They were authorized to imagine tremendous violence and to invent ways to make that imagination reality, and their labors were informed by the awareness that the state they served would assert its prerogative to levy violence (wage war, for example), using the products of their research. While their sense of themselves as engaged in war or conflict may have been attenuated by their distance from killing fields and their wielding of pens instead of swords, defense and weapons researchers labor at the thinnest remove from the soldiers who end up plying the products of their design. Placing these scholars next to violence workers allows us to return to this book's principal point regarding the crossing of the conceptual borders of police and state. These workers, like violence workers sensu strict, crossed the public-private divide without a blink. They labored for agencies created at private universities but supported by public funds, or at public universities but easily transferred to the private sector when their campuses came to host significant opposition to their presence. These crossings often served to defend their work and, more broadly, the legitimacy of its violence.

POLICE EDUCATION AND FOREIGN
POLICE ASSISTANCE

As this makes clear, police education was by no means a purely domestic phenomenon. Its transnational roots are rarely acknowledged, but they were powerful and important. Vollmer's transnational experience and impact gesture to the global currents involved in early twentieth-century developments. During the Cold War, those currents involved universities' lending their expertise abroad, including in policing. One particular innovator was the Michigan State University branch in East Lansing, a direct predecessor to OPS and perfect illustration of the conjoined history of foreign police assistance and criminal justice education.

Michigan State University entered the arena of academic engagement in foreign policy during World War II, like many other universities offering their talents to the state. In that period, the federal government funded academic defense and weapons research and recruited scholars to serve as specialists and engineers. By the mid-1950s, John Ernst chronicles in his account of MSU in Vietnam, universities were the recipients of about $300 million a year from the Pentagon. "Schools such as the Massachusetts Institute of Technology and Stanford University became weapons laboratories," wrote Ernst, while other universities did things that sounded very much like OPS. "Among others, Michigan State and the University of Kentucky sent advisors to assist politically troubled developing countries threatened by communism."[17] Indiana University sent advisors to Iran; so did the University of Southern California (USC), which also contracted to teach at OPS's International Police Academy. Georgia Tech worked in Paraguay.[18] But MSU was the biggest and most consequential of the US universities involved in foreign police assistance. Its program operated all over the world, training police in Germany, Indonesia, Korea, Thailand, and, with particular import, Vietnam. MSU was internationally famous, Ernst confirms by recalling writer John Le Carré's reference to it in one of his famous spy-fiction novels.[19]

MSU's work in Vietnam grew from a friendship between political science professor Wesley R. Fishel and rising Vietnamese politician Ngo Dinh Diem. In 1953, approximating Saigon and East Lansing, Fishel brought Diem to the university as a consultant to the Governmental Research Bureau, where Diem drafted a reform program. After the Geneva Accords, then Prime Minister Diem requested US aid, so the US Foreign Operations Administration (FOA), an AID predecessor, sent a trio of MSU faculty on a fact-finding mission to evaluate a possible technology assistance program. Their report recommended that MSU, in collaboration with South Vietnam and the FOA, implement the reforms Diem had drafted in Michigan. The MSUG, or Michigan State University Group, evolved from those recommendations into its eventual consequential, controversial, full-fledged political advisory capacity.[20]

Within a few years, amid the burgeoning antiwar movement, MSU "students and faculty alike increasingly denounced United States intervention in Vietnam and argued that institutions of higher education should not serve as adjuncts to the federal government in other countries." As Ernst explains, the story of the MSUG faithfully traces the arc of academia's complex involvement in the Cold War.[21]

Diem was angered by the protests and in 1962 declined to renew the MSUG's contract. During its three periods of service provision over seven years, however, the Group was involved in critical projects in police and civil service training and administrative institution building.[22]

The MSUG was ideological and material predecessor to OPS. Most treatments of OPS simply identify the MSUG as its institutional precursor as well.[23] While continuity in spirit abounds, there was actually a separate Public Safety program organized by the United States Operations Missions (USOM) in Saigon in July 1959 when the MSUG was still going strong. Relations became strained; the two programs felt themselves to be in competition to recruit staff and stepped irritatingly on each other's toes. Frank Walton, chief of USOM's Public Safety Department in Saigon, was notably antagonistic to the MSUG, and MSUG campus police consultant Arthur Brandstatter publically returned the favor. It was the USOM Public Safety program that most directly birthed OPS.[24]

Still, there was real continuity between the MSUG and OPS in other forms. MSU materials show up in OPS archives, showing that OPS borrowed them wholesale.[25] More importantly, there was continuity in personnel, as we see so often with OPS: quite a few OPS officers had been MSUG, or had gone to Michigan State as students. The *Newsletter* named some of the MSU staff that had later joined Public Safety: Tommy Adkins, Charlie Sloane, Bob Gollings, Paul Shields.[26] The editors nostalgically asked Sloane for help in locating "some of the MSU types" so that they could offer to share the *Newsletter* with them, showing the importance they lent their shared origins.[27] In the wake of their respective expulsions, it seems that any remaining bad blood between the MSUG and OPS's parent organization was forgiven.

Other OPS officers had MSU degrees. Bob Weatherwax earned a BS from MSU in 1956.[28] David Greig graduated with the same degree in the previous year.[29] Jim McMahon got his in 1951.[30] Robert Reynolds did a BA in political science at MSU with a minor in police administration.[31] Norman Colter served in Korea and worked as a sheriff, prison guard, and policeman before going back to school in his thirties. He earned a BA and MA from MSU and then taught criminal justice at Merrimack Community College in Saint Louis for twenty-two years. While at Merrimack, Colter took a three-year leave of absence to work for OPS in Saigon, teaching at the police academy there.[32] Al Turner, who had gone to MSU's School of Police Administration after he left the navy, unambiguously called the MSU effort the "precursor of the AID program to Vietnam."[33]

OPS officers had MSU degrees largely because MSU degrees were the ones to have. The MSU School of Police Administration, now called the School of Criminal Justice, had been among the first of its kind. When it was established in 1935, MSU was the only program in the United States to offer a bachelor's in police administration, and for a while shared the field only with Berkeley. By the 1950s it was considered the best such program in the country, consistently awarded the highest rankings and accorded great esteem in the field. Its graduates anchored the growth of other programs that began to be established in the 1960s.[34] Among these, we should count OPS.

Overseas police assistance rode the fervor for police education gathering momentum in the 1950s. As the opening anecdote to this chapter recounted, J. B. Carnahan remembered the recruitment effort as sharply focused on his generation because of its emphasis on training. He regarded himself as one of the "new breed" of educated cops, unlike "in the old days [when] they just hired some guy off the street and he became a policeman. And that was it." Carnahan attended the first Concord Northern California Police Academy, calling it "a brand new thing, the Police Academy. Before that, you hired some guy, and you said ok, you ride around with him for a week, then you go out and do it yourself." OPS clearly wanted educated recruits. As Carnahan continued, "That's who they were looking for. They went to Northwestern, for example, for their traffic people. They went to different places where law enforcement was on the upswing education-wise."[35]

OPS both drew on and contributed to this movement. The 1965 Memorandum to the Special Group on Counterinsurgency fueling OPS's growth touted OPS educational facilities centrally. "The Training Division is developing a multi-language library of police and related texts and a film library for police training. Arrangements were completed in October 1964 with Georgetown University to provide English language instruction to non-English-speaking IPA students from Latin America as a supplement to the Academy program." Congratulating OPS on the number of students graduated and currently enrolled, the memorandum justified its recommendation to expand.[36] Clearly the "Special Group (CI)" agreed.

The emphasis on education was central to OPS operations in the field; its bread and butter was police training, obviously. But even beyond that, OPS was fully focused on education abroad, not limited to practical training. Its archives are full of educational materials in folders and boxes labeled "Higher Education," "Professional Education," "Secondary," "University of Wisconsin," "Vocational Training," "Edu. General," "Elementary," and so on.[37] The education focus of the OPS police program was evident to the public as well—and not always in a positive light. In Maceio, Brazil, students protested OPS with signs denouncing "the agreement between the [Brazilian] Ministry of Education and USAID," among other placards.[38]

When termination loomed, some OPS champions hoped its educational projects might save it—or at least be exempt from congressional prohibition. They established a "worldwide Public Safety Training fund" for the 1975 fiscal year for police officers from Third World countries, promising also to consider students from wealthier nations who might have independent funding.[39] The projection of this fund into the year *after* the crucial modification of the Foreign Assistance Act shows the hubris and hope we have seen before in OPS attempts to circumvent congressional prohibition. Education, they calculated, would be too popular to cut. Attempting to buttress this possibility, the organization released laudatory reports of its IPA successes, including the degrees possessed by its professional staff.[40]

Education would not save OPS, but OPS did more than its fair share for police education. A great many of its demobilized personnel went to work in the educational arena, seeding criminal justice and police education programs in universities across the country with their transnational experience. They moved into government-run domestic police training as well, including one striking instance of the federalization of police education, the Federal Law Enforcement Training Center, which they substantially animated. The rest of this chapter moves from analyzing and describing the trends toward police education that buoyed OPS along in their wake, to the currents of this same stream that OPS itself fed.

FROM THE SHORES OF MONTEZUMA TO THE HALLS OF ACADEME

Quite a few OPS employees came home and went back to school, offering a fascinatingly fine-grained picture of the expansion of police education. Individual OPS officers who joined the academic endeavor upon their return to US territory pursued degrees such as the JD, an MA in educational communications, or a PhD in political science. They worked on undergraduate degrees in law, water technology, anthropology, and business.[41] The students were mostly not in fields of police education or criminal justice. That picture changes drastically when we look at teachers instead.

Former OPS employees at the podium included just a few at East Coast schools. There was the director of security and safety at Brandeis University, the provost marshal for the Military District of Washington who eventually joined the staff of the University of Maryland, and a faculty member at Norwich University, a private military college in Vermont, who later taught law enforcement while serving as that state's police commissioner.[42] The scant representation of OPS retirees in this region may reflect the resistance of more elite institutions to police education, often seen as substantially vocational.

Many more were to be found in the Southeast. Two became professors at Dekalb Community College in Roswell, a suburb of Atlanta, where another ex-OPS officer was among their students.[43] One of the early MSUG members professed at Marshall University in West Virginia. He was involved with the Marshall Council for International Education and ran an exchange program taking criminal justice students to Sweden.[44] Donald Bordenkircher, author of *Tiger Cage* and a West Virginia and Kentucky prison warden, was a member of the boards of two criminal justice departments, one also at Marshall University.[45] Another ex-OPS was police chief in Blacksburg, Virginia; he taught at the local police academy and was part-time faculty in the criminal justice program at New River Community College.[46] Still another taught law enforcement at Northern Virginia Community College in Alexandria.[47]

In the Southwest, several former OPS found positions at the New Mexico Law Enforcement Academy in Santa Fe, including the director, assistant director, and two instructors.[48] Just a few ex-OPS taught in Texas. Sam Houston State College in Huntsville invited former OPS employees to apply for their positions training Saudi police officers in traffic law enforcement, we recall from chapter 4, and the University of Houston's "special Industrial Security program" also sent at least one ex-OPS to Saudi.[49]

California had a significant contingent. One person taught hunter safety and various rifle range courses at Claremont Junior College.[50] Another taught administration of justice at City College while working on his MA, later teaching at Sacramento City College.[51] A third taught part-time in the Criminal Justice Department of Palomar College.[52] An ex-OPS agent who was chief of security for Modesto Junior College also taught courses in the administration of justice there, all while pursuing graduate work at USF.[53] John Kenney taught public administration at USC for thirteen years (with ex-OPS among his pupils), and then criminology at Cal State Long Beach for twenty-three. Linking several eras of police training, in 1987, Kenney founded August Vollmer University, a small BA-, MA-, and PhD-granting criminology school invoking the former Berkeley police chief.[54]

In the Midwest, one returning OPS employee found a position with the Traffic Institute at Northwestern University.[55] Another became a safety education director with the Chicago Police, teaching in the Chicago Police Department as well as working with municipal courts "conducting classes for Traffic Violators."[56] A third earned a PhD from a distance-learning program and returned to a chieftancy in Oklahoma while holding teaching positions at colleges there, in West Virginia, and in Canada.[57]

Within the Midwest, Indiana distinguishes itself. Perhaps I noticed this because I live in Indiana now, but the Hoosier state was something of an epicenter for ex-OPS involved in education, and well illustrates the kinds of projects and people the flows of federal dollars sustained. Michael Mc-Cann was "an Assistant Professor of 'Police Administration' at Indiana University's School of Arts and Science" when he was recruited to train the Iranian National Police at their college in Tehran. From there he went to OPS, eventually rejoining the faculty of Indiana University on a criminal justice project.[58] Jim Lewis had been at Purdue University prior to OPS. He married a woman he met while on duty in Greece and thereafter split his time between Greece and Indiana, teaching in extension programs on the US air base near Athens, one for the University of Maryland and another for Hartford Community College, and working as "an administrator for Public Safety at Purdue."[59] Stanley Guth was at Indiana University with the Organized Crime Prevention Program, remaining active in Indiana State Police affairs while there.[60] In addition to the Indiana University faculty, J. Russel Prior was the director of police and safety at Vincennes University, a junior college, where he taught in the Law Enforcement Associates Degree Program. Meanwhile, he lived in Bloomington, site of IU's flagship campus.[61]

It is not as surprising as one might think to find so many returned OPS agents in Indiana, for the state had provided a disproportionate number of Public Safety employees in the first place. Frank Jessup, Walter Whalen, and David Laughlin had all been Indiana state cops. Robert Bush called Indiana "home," and Jim Lewis's family was from Evansville.[62] John Herczeg was police chief in Garrett.[63] Joseph Lingo had been director of Public Safety for the state.[64] John Clark went (home?) to Indiana after OPS, living in Fort

Harrison.[65] The Hoosiers even claim Dan Mitrione, the Richmond, Indiana, police officer whose abduction and death at the hands of Tupamaro guerrillas in Uruguay was the occasion for Greek filmmaker Constantin Costa-Gavras's anti-OPS movie, *State of Siege*.

Of the returnees, Lewis was probably a hands-on administrator for campus police, and Prior may have been purely a classroom teacher, but the others were all involved in research, reflecting Indiana University's active criminal justice research and public service profile. IU had stepped fully into the revenue stream generated by the LEAA for applied law enforcement education. It received a grant to train the Richmond Police Department regarding its Merit Commission, for example, and another to apply networks and systems analysis to juvenile justice.[66] IU's School of Public and Environmental Affairs (SPEA) was founded in 1972 with a "mission to provide specialized assistance for units of state and local government."[67] That very year SPEA came together with the Indiana Organized Crime Prevention Council and Indiana Criminal Justice Planning Agency, the state's LEAA oversight body, in a project funded by the LEAA to detect and deter organized crime. A funding route sheet emphasized this project's intent to coordinate state and local bodies.[68] Throughout the decade IU was awarded funds for this work with the Organized Crime Prevention Council.[69]

This project reminds us of how easily federal funding was awarded based on the claim to combat "organized crime" (as discussed in chapter 1). The specter of this statelike object worked to justify the dual and connected expansions of the criminal justice system and criminal justice as a field of study. Indiana highlights the university-state nexus sparked by such legitimizing myths, built up through federal funding, and staffed by people with overseas training experience.

Crossing the conceptual borders of policing is a messy affair; police work usually straddles all of the borders identified in this book and probably a handful of others. In the case of police education, we see not only the public-private crossings of funding and the transnational travels of university and individual trainers but also the violation of the borders of scale from local to federal contexts. The quintessential example of this move is the establishment of the Federal Law Enforcement Training Center, or FLETC, which ex-OPS substantially animated in a striking instance of the federalization of police work alongside the denial thereof.

Among the OPS employees who returned to work training future police, a notable contingent went to work at a school organized by the Treasury Department to train the police of the myriad federal agencies that host security forces. This may itself be a surprising observation for those who haven't considered how many federal agencies actually contain their own autonomous internal police. Our guide to this story is Al Turner, MSU graduate and veteran of OPS in Vietnam, who tenders his life course with deliciously deadpan wit.

Turner's story runs through all the aspects of the history narrated in this chapter. It begins at MSU, where he studied, and which provided him with contacts vital to the later shape of his career. Turner's tale highlights the fecundity of the academic root—the MSUG—while detailing one of a series of training-focused branches. After MSU, Turner completed an unsatisfying stint in the NYPD, then moved to the Treasury's Bureau of Alcohol, Tobacco, and Firearms thanks to the recommendation of a fellow MSU graduate. "It turned out to be one of the biggest mistakes of my life," Turner quipped. "It was deadly boring. Not at all like the movies." But it led him to OPS, and beyond. "One night on night duty, leafing through *Police* magazine, I saw an ad for OPS," Turner recounted. He recalled that the guest speaker at his Treasury Academy graduation had been OPS director Byron Engle. The ad "talked about the opportunities in foreign countries to train police officers, travel, the benefits of foreign service. A real snow job." Turner sent in the application, and arrived in Vietnam in early 1966.

Turner wasn't keen on the program. He called it quits when his contract was up, he told me, "because they were only operating in Vietnam and it was only a matter of time before I either became a complete alcoholic, or lost my family to divorce, or got myself killed."[70] He went back to school, receiving an MA from John Jay in public safety in 1970, and then returned to Treasury. There he became an instructor with the Treasury Law Enforcement Training School, a program to train officers from ATF and several other federal agencies. He attributes his hiring there, and internal promotion, to OPS, or rather, to the hiring officer's assumption that OPS had provided much better training than Turner believed it had: "My selection was based on the training in antiterrorism I had supposedly received in Vietnam. Which was a joke. Hey, you know that joke, how can you tell the terrorist? He's the guy with the carrot in his ear. I got promoted to Grade 13, the

higher levels of chiefdom in Treasury." Turner wanted to go back to policing, but instead moved with the school when his superiors needed to quash
a labor dispute. In his own marvelous voice:

> My time was coming short and I wanted to go back into the field. They
> told me I could go back into the field in New York, but I would have to
> drop a grade. I said bullshit. A friend interceded for me—a lawyer I knew.
> It turned out just then they consolidated the LETC, built around Trea-
> sury. Also they decided they needed a police training center and needed
> a director. They interviewed all over the country. And they hired me.

> Q: *Wow, they offered you the position to absorb and neutralize your protest?*

> A: Yeah, and it worked. I became the director.[71]

Turner explained that the Treasury training program was expanding, and
pointed out the relationship to the growth of law enforcement broadly:
"TLOTS [Treasury Law Enforcement Officer Training Center] had been in
existence for many years. At first it was just bringing in the instructors
into a conference room and constructing the training. Up until Kennedy,
Treasury law enforcement was a very small operation. But when Kennedy
came in, the whole law enforcement totally exploded. They wanted to go
after organized crime, wanted to get into internal revenue. So overnight the
thing exploded." Even the spark provided by "organized crime," however,
wasn't quite enough. As the planners labored to convince fellow agencies
to join the consolidation, they gained credibility and urgency from a dramatic series of skyjacking attempts.[72] Turner understood this fully: "Then
what happens? Airline hijacking. So they get Customs, FAA, etc., together
and they decided they needed Air Marshalls trained by FAA. . . . We had
an assistant secretary for Treasury, Eugene Rossides, who wanted to move
the Treasury school into the consolidated one. Its first training focus: Sky
Marshalls." Taking advantage of the skyjacking panic to boost momentum
for a change whose ground they had carefully prepared, Treasury officials
accelerated the consolidation of federal police training programs and finally secured a space that could accommodate it, a recently closed Naval
base in Glynco, Georgia.

In Glynco, the Federal Law Enforcement Training Center, or FLETC, set
itself up. FLETC is important in the history of police training. Its champions give it credit for professionalizing its students, a claim that must always
be taken with a grain of salt, as it is a constant in the history of police train-

ing at home and abroad. I think FLETC's consolidation of federal police training was noteworthy because it gave violence workers from the various agencies a sense of identity *as police*, expanding the kind of training they received, bringing their collective practice into line, and facilitating lateral movement across the various federal bodies employing police.

In this innovative venture of consolidated training for federal police, OPS had a central role. Turner drew on his OPS connections to staff the new center: "We started from scratch. And I needed staff. This was 1974–75. Public Safety was going down the tubes. So I picked up Morris Grodsky, and Rogers, and a whole bunch of 'em. I was probably the biggest employer of ex–Public Safety types. I gave them an opportunity for a second career. None of them disappointed me."[73]

Grodsky became "Supervisor, Criminalistics Branch," alongside "Richard Rogers, Supervisor, Communications Skills Branch," as well as "Glen Boyce, Senior Instructor; Chester Jew, Senior Instructor; Tori Groshong, former secretary at IPA," who became secretary to the director of the Police School, "Jack Larrimore, Supervisor, Legal Branch," and Bob Davenport, who counted seven former OPS members on staff.[74] As Turner admonished me, "If you want to put down anything that the [former OPS] AID advisors did, they put FLETC on the map and it's a big operation."[75]

Turner served "under Art Branstetter [*sic*]," as the *Newsletter* editors reminded their readers, "the ex-Michigan State School of Police Administration Director."[76] Brandstatter had been one of the fact-finding team whose report in 1954 had recommended the creation of the MSUG, and was an ongoing consultant to the MSUG while it existed; he also served the MSU School of Criminal Justice as dean.[77] His selection comprised yet another thread stitching together MSU, OPS, and FLETC.

The FLETC crew had seeded other instructional landscapes with their OPS experience before moving to Glynco. Grodsky had a stint with a private consultant and a part-time professorial appointment at American University.[78] Rogers was course director for FLETC's predecessor in Treasury when it was still in Washington.[79] Davenport, who had been an IPA instructor for three years while at OPS, patrolled for customs and then returned to the repurposed IPA as a customs officer trainer.[80]

Grodsky's teaching reveals the strong continuity between OPS teaching and FLETC training. Assigned to Brazil for OPS, Grodsky had "helped set up their National Institute of Criminalistics, which is like the FBI," he told me. For instructional materials, Grodsky created his own, adapted from resources available in the United States at the time. After four years, he was reassigned to the United States to teach at the IPA in Washington. After OPS was terminated and Grodsky moved to FLETC, he took his Brazilian curricula with him. In Glynco, he explained, "I used materials I had developed in Latin America; I used those same materials in Georgia. Slides, fingerprinting, firearms identification, question documents. All disciplines in forensic science, I used them there."[81]

Beyond FLETC, other OPS also recycled curricular materials for US instruction. Phil Ogden, teaching at Modesto Junior College while studying at USF, wrote to his former colleagues asking whether anyone could share with him the syllabus from the Vietnam CORDS Training, the Civil Operations and Revolutionary (later Rural) Development Support program implemented in Vietnam in 1967 to win hearts and minds.[82] Whether he wanted the syllabus in order to request transfer credits or to be reminded of its contents, the request clearly shows the continuity between his instructional work in Vietnam and his teaching and learning in California.

Grodsky had no hesitation in recounting his recycling of educational materials. His candid exposition opens a rare lens on the transnational circulations involved in police training: Grodsky took materials readily available in the United States, cycled them through a Brazilian filter, and reapplied them to US federal police training. Brazil's police force was not centralized like many in Latin America, but was "state by state," Grodsky remembered, with a military police force also under the governor, and a newly created federal police.[83] Despite whatever surface differences separated US and Brazilian police forces, Grodsky found US ingredients good raw material for his courses in Brazil, and then his Brazilian materials perfectly appropriate for instruction of American police.

Perhaps Grodsky's openness reflected the mellowness of age. He was into his eighties when I interviewed him, wonderfully reflective and kind. Perhaps Grodsky had simply always been this way. His self-published autobiography details his youth in an orphanage in Denver and his choice of criminalistics as a career because government support for his education (the GI Bill) wouldn't last long enough for medical school.[84] In any case, Grodsky is an exception in his frank discussion of his border crossing. The officials who organized and ran FLETC, in contrast, strained to deny any suggestion of police out of place. They were particularly wary of implications that the United States was training a national police force, something of a third rail for people who believe that federalism guarantees democracy. "Ever careful to avoid anything that might lead to a national police force," insisted Frederick Calhoun in *The Trainers*, the elegiac history of the institution he wrote in 1996 for its silver anniversary, "those who oversaw the professionalization of federal law enforcement searched for some happy medium to exploit the common foundation uniting tax investigators, prison guards, park rangers, land managers, [and] court police."[85]

The related but distinct possibility that the US federal government has its own police also makes patriots such as Calhoun distinctly nervous. *The Trainers* strains to portray the officers trained at FLETC as united in their duty to law but "separated by distinct spheres within that system of laws. Like planets around the sun, they made up a well-defined universe of distinct rotations."[86] Calhoun enlisted a scalar metaphor to dispatch FLETC's problem of scale. In discussing Arthur Brandstatter and MSU, Calhoun baldly disavowed police transgressions of territorial borders. "Both Brandstatter and the Michigan State program focused on state and local issues, the policeman on the beat," he wrote. "Michigan State graduates tended to fill the ranks of the state and city police forces."[87] The amnesia regarding the MSUG's well-known work in Vietnam is complete. Calhoun explains that Brandstatter left FLETC in 1982 for "the newly created National Center for State and Local Law Enforcement Training."[88] Note, in this center's title, yet another scale-busting oxymoron.

When the jumble of the various levels of scale on which US police actually operate comes to light, as when local and state police are educated at a federal facility or, worse, recruited into the federal agencies whose work includes policing—when police so clearly and obviously transgress the spirit of the principle of federalism—repair to the ramparts is rapidly organized. Calhoun's paeans to FLETC in *The Trainers* are this genre of repair. The balance of his damage control is pure, unadulterated adulation. FLETC "transformed society. . . . By professionalizing its police, the United States enhanced its democracy."[89] Such reverence, banal as it is, exemplifies the exaggerated self-congratulations conferred in this moment upon the "professionalization" of police, reproducing for US domestic police training all the claims that had been made and rejected regarding police training abroad.

The claims made for FLETC echo those being made for the contemporaneous expansion of police education generally. They direct us to turn to those claims, to consider the consequences of this period's tectonic shift in the relationship of education and police.

The changes in police education were certainly dramatic in number and description. In New York City, for example, a grant in 1968 created the nation's largest municipal training academy and grew the NYPD to over 31,000 sworn personnel, up from an authorized strength of 18,800 in 1949. The new curriculum included "intensification and humanization of the educational experience," with new counselors, criminalistics, dramatization, and "civilian professional personnel, teaching behavioral and social science units as well as units in law."[90] These sorts of listings were typical in the new curricula, and the claims made for them sounded wonderful: greater professionalism and courtesy, better communications skills, less use of force, greater awareness of and support for civil rights, greater tolerance for difference and sensitivity to racial tension, less attraction to military organizational models, more openness to outside reformers and ideas, less anxiety, and more feelings of preparedness on the job.[91]

Yet critics were unsure whether positive developments actually came of all this effort. Did education—especially college—really improve policing? Unevenly, concluded Samuel Walker; only in careful relationship to practice, found Gerald Griffin.[92] In an early study in Saint Louis, Dennis Smith and Elinor Ostrom found that not only did training not make better police but, on the contrary, left police feeling less prepared, more likely to use force, and more interested in military discipline.[93] The scholarly rigor of the new education in criminal justice was also challenged. A Police Foundation report in 1979 charged that it was "intellectually shallow, conceptually narrow, and provided by a faculty that is far from scholarly."[94]

Part of the problem was that police were tightly circumscribed in the classroom. The activist members of NARMIC (National Action/Research on the Military-Industrial Complex) pointed out that police were not simply supported to learn whatever they pleased. Courses were carefully monitored, with a supervisor's permission or approval required for each course. Financing was set up to penalize those who did not go to work for the criminal justice system afterward or who left the police or were fired. Even courses in topics already taught on many college campuses, such as business administration, government, economics, or sociology, were usually "special sections taught by police officials, FBI and Bureau of Narcotics agents, and retired military officers," segregating and limiting police students' educational experience.[95]

Police education was not that open-ended, curiosity-inducing expander of horizons so fondly projected by liberal hopes for the project of public education. Its focus was far more limited, as visible most clearly in the discipline it subtended. From the consequences of police education for police work *in* the field, now we turn to its effect *on* the field—the academic fields of study its growth allowed.

The ambiguous conclusions about the effect of federal funding on police education echo in evaluations of criminal justice or criminology (and here I take the two as synonymous) as a field of study. Quantitatively, the growth of the field is undeniable. Yet its qualitative effect is unclear. Did it come to offer a platform for superior scholarship? Did it improve the administration of the criminal justice system, police, and prisons? These questions are vibrant, unresolved debates among practitioners.

Most reviews of criminology as a discipline note its roots in nineteenth-century Italian anthropology, most famously Cesare Lombroso. They chart its move to sociology in the 1920s with the Chicago School, its academic specialization in the middle of the twentieth century, and huge growth in the 1960s and 1970s. College programs added graduate degrees, and needed people with those advanced degrees to fill the ranks of their faculty. An IACP count in 1975 tallied 121 MA programs and 21 granting the PhD.[96] Membership in the American Society of Criminology grew from 7 people at its founding in 1941 to 2,970 members in 1999.[97]

Criminology in that period seethed, becoming well populated and ever more diverse in focus. Dae Chang and Jerome McKean call criminal justice not a field but "a complex of sub-disciplines" containing a little bit of everything—all the intellectual currents from Marxism to feminism to cultural studies, write David Garland and Richard Sparks—including a good-sized radical wing.[98] Still, criminal justice is generally a conservative field, largely located, as Garland and Sparks also point out, "within the institutions of the criminal justice state."[99] The field is politically rather timid, as even a president of the American Society of Criminology admitted in an inaugural address.[100]

The period of social fervent in which the discipline grew explains this bifurcated field. On one end were Marxist and other radicals, inspired by protest. On the other, far more populated end were scholars funded vigorously by the federal government, devoted to controlling unrest. Just as sociology emerged to manage mid-nineteenth-century conflict, William Arnold explains, criminal justice developed from "the turmoil of the 1960s in the United States and elsewhere" and was devoted to its containment, thanks in good part to its state funding, as Arnold continues: "Since the funds for the discipline and its attendant research came primarily from the federal government, the discipline and research have been strongly oriented to reforming the criminal justice system, i.e., making it more effective without threatening too much either our civil rights or our stratified economic order. Necessarily, then, research has been powerfully influenced by politics, especially the vicissitudes of funding and shifting concerns of governmental agencies. It has been, as sociology was in its earlier years, melioristic."[101] Arnold summarizes some of the more frequent critiques that characterize the field as descriptive rather than prescriptive, overly interested in "evaluation," focused on law and political science, and minimally theoretical, with some exceptions. They criticize it for being "the handmaiden of the establishment" and academically weak.[102]

Criminology is therefore rarely of use to policy except as apology. Illustratively, its policy relevance was greatest in its most unfortunate episode, the misuse of Robert Martinson's suggestion in 1974 that in the field of prison rehabilitation, "nothing works." The cynical political exploitation of that work—unruffled by Martinson's retraction—was immeasurable, destroying rehabilitation programs and greatly expanding "tough on crime."[103]

In a self-selecting process, therefore, it was scholars interested mostly in applied study of the criminal justice system who gravitated to the new or reorganized departments of Administration of Justice, Criminal Justice, Policy Science, and so on. These were the departments that swelled over the decade of the 1970s from 209 to over 1,200 programs in 664 institutions, including more than twenty doctoral programs. Meanwhile, the current of radical Marxist criminology generally remained within older departments such as sociology, widening the gaps between the two.[104] Sociologists charged that universities shifted funds from their field to criminology to cash in on educational tracks that most directly fed students into ready jobs. Critical thinking was threatening to employers in the criminal justice system, creating a glassy, anti-intellectual curriculum. Sociology suffered decreasing enrollments, while numbers grew in what Farrell and Thomas come right out and call the practitioner-oriented and racist field of criminal justice.[105]

Because criminology often treats racism as secondary or incidental to the operation of the criminal justice system, it fails to analyze the deep and sinuous ways race operates in that system. As Naomi Murakawa and Katherine Beckett have detailed, the dominant definition of racism in criminology not only constricts its own insights but also makes racism worse. They call this prevailing mode of analysis the "penology of racial innocence: the study of punishment that obscures the operation of racial power in penal practices and institutions," exacerbating racist effects by forcing complainants to prove impossible standards of intent and causation, insisting that the individual bear the full brunt of systemic effects.[106]

Critics from within offer some of the most biting autocritiques. The condescending, positivist, obsessively quantitative "criminological imagination," Jock Young laments, is unmindful of history and has abandoned the discipline's early hope for transformative politics.[107] The dominant standard for research in criminology is "extraordinarily conservative," charged Todd Clear in his presidential address to the American Society of Criminology in 2009, and the prevailing "what works" model of policy evaluation "a kind of slavery to the present," preventing the devising of actual solutions to the problem of mass incarceration.[108] The disciplines of criminology and criminal justice help to create, staff, and legitimize the prison system, and the pipeline sending so many Americans into it, write Judah Schept, Tyler Wall, and Avi Brisman. Even "when criminology does call critical attention to the pipeline," they write, "its gaze remains decidedly reformist." Writing from one of the earliest and most important academic institutions in the field, Eastern Kentucky University's College of Safety and Justice, Schept and his colleagues note their employer's founding by the "security-carceral state" and despite many left-leaning colleagues, their discipline's complicity with ongoing carceral projects.[109]

CONSEQUENCES IN THE CLASSROOM

These critiques of what is now a massive scholarly endeavor turn us to the subject of the academy itself. As important to question as the effect of police education on policing is its effect on education. While it is beyond the scope of this book to do more than gesture to the changes in the US educational system that may be related to the police-education nexus, a few speculative observations are in order.

One enormous change in American higher education in the last forty years involves its soil-clod empiricism. The neoliberal university places tremendous emphasis on evaluation, "learning outcomes," and tight linkages between higher education, specific career paths, and immediate postcollege job acquisition. This pedagogical instrumentalism recalls police education and criminal justice in spirit. As a critic of police education noted in 1971, "One effect of such contracts is to encourage the tendency on American campuses to see social science as primarily a practical tool for social management and control."[110] He saw ahead to the turn away from belief in scholarship as itself of value—ephemeral, unpredictable, critical—to the insistence that academic study be a tool, necessarily practical or else unjustifiable, quantifiable for purposes of assessment, and bankrupt if not summarily "efficient." Here lies another register in which the carceral state has altered the landscape of historical and other academic research and teaching practice.

The growth of police education accompanied a rise of police on campus for other troublesome pursuits. NARMIC's Ann Flitcraft pointed out that the police flocking to campuses were not all students. Some were studying the campus, funded by the same bodies underwriting police education to carry on research on such topics as why students rebel, how to control drug use, and campus militancy. The prescriptions they proposed to control youth entailed "changes in the educational institutions themselves to reorient students' attitudes as well as their behavior," she wrote presciently.[111] Police were also on campus to police students directly. Documenting one notable instance, Flitcraft pointed to the LEAA's provision of $288,405 to the Mississippi State Commission in 1970 for "a specially created all-black arrest force" made up of police from across the state supplemented by deputized, armed janitors and cafeteria workers, to arrest students at the all-black Mississippi Valley State College. To break a strike, this force arrested 894 students—more than a third of the student body—making it the largest mass student arrest in US history.[112]

In a dramatic inverse relation, as police went back to school, the people they most brutally policed saw their educational opportunities increasingly constrained. The federal government ended the practice of busing that enforced *Brown v. Board of Education*, and the United States began a steady resegregation, confining Black, brown, and other poor students once again in underresourced, overdisciplined schools.[113] Legislatures began to defund higher education, and colleges complacently raised tuition, edging out the working and poor students who had begun to benefit from the nation's brief, shining moment of genuinely accessible public education, or edging them into suffocating debt.[114] Affirmative action programs came under attack, and university administrators clipped their wings with varying degrees of glee.[115] The "school-to-prison pipeline" was constructed.[116] Concurrently, education behind bars shriveled. Citing the notorious "nothing works" slogan from criminologists they did continue to fund, policymakers began defunding and disbanding prison education programs in the late 1970s just as prison populations began to climb.[117] The denial of Pell Grants to prisoners in 1994 was one more nail in that coffin.

The rise of police education has ultimately been devastating in both criminal justice and educational arenas. The "war on education" (as Eric Blumenson and Eva Nilsen term it) had its roots in the police-campus nexus of the 1970s.[118] Police education and criminal justice have approximated mass incarceration and academia by involving more university-based people in courts and prisons as "experts," investing universities in the growth of the system as a site for jobs for its graduates, and interweaving prison-industrial and academic-industrial complexes.

Not that this should be surprising. Schools, as Poulantzas, Althusser, Foucault, and their students have famously reminded us, are ideological institutions, part of the apparatus of state, or more appropriately (because messier), fragments of state-market assemblages. These brutal tangles of state-market violence call for skepticism about academe, whether for students hoping to enter violence work or diminish it, particularly when it presents itself in the form "public education" has come to take in our day.

The next chapter turns toward the personal, to bring us to another dimension of violence work. Having examined former OPS employees' professional trajectories through imperial state-market institutions, we step into the microrealm of the intimate and the affective to notice a crucial piece of the ways their history reveals the lived contradictions of violence work.

SIX

Exiles at Home

A Refugee Structure of Feeling

The year after OPS ended, the US lost the war in Vietnam. With the fall of Saigon in April 1975 and the evacuation of US personnel, Vietnamese associated with the defeated regime or its American supporters fled, joining others displaced by wartime violence. Fast on the heels of returning Public Safety personnel, then, were waves of Southeast Asian refugees.

Like explorations of prison phenomena, most discussions of Vietnamese refugees begin by doing the numbers. This many people left southern Vietnam in the month leading up to and just after the fall of Saigon. This many left over subsequent months. This much shipwreck, piracy, starvation. This many languished at sea, this many turned away from ports of call, this many made it to US shores. They then turn to biography or autobiography, filling in with anecdote the outlines laid down by the numbers.[1] I will forebear from rehearsing statistics, for the figures fulfill an ideological function. The quantitative portrait of refugee movement conveys gravity, anchoring the key elements of the liberal refugee narrative: people left because the communist regime established in the United States' wake was terrible; people came to the United States because it is the ever-benevolent, welcoming host.[2]

This is certainly what the former Public Safety agents felt. They were deeply concerned with the migrants' plight, rehearsed the refugee narrative extensively, and welcomed them proudly to America—and not at all from afar: ex-OPS involved themselves immediately and deeply in refugee assistance. They helped people who became refugees, sometimes by receiving whole families, sometimes as full-time refugee relief workers, sometimes just as volunteers. Some of their assistance flowed from relationships they had formed during their work abroad, including marriages, though they also acted out of the less intimate bonds of collegiality and friendship. They were particularly keen to help their former "counterparts" (the police or other officials with whom they worked most closely in the field), and some even found work for those people in local US police departments, completing an astonishing circle. The pages of the *Public Safety Newsletter* reveal, as we shall see, a broad spectrum of engagements, deep interest in the fate of the refugees, and pride in their success stories.

Like the Vietnamese who came to suburban Virginia introduced in Andrew Friedman's original survey of this dynamic, these "imperial intimates from abroad" stitched an unanticipated transnational social field anchored by a range of relationships: "Through sex, love, friendship, and longtime working partnerships developed by covert capital agents stationed in Vietnam for nearly two decades, agents and Vietnamese intimates created a mobile US shadowed transnationalism, underwritten by empire, that literally took place locally between South Vietnam and Northern Virginia in houses, offices, leisure landscapes, and other social spaces."[3] As other historians have agreed, the familiar and quotidian life of empire is a necessary part of its machinery.[4] The ramifications of imperial intimacies also unfold within the postcolonial metropole, as Friedman establishes and this chapter attempts to extend.

In our case, the fabric of OPS-refugee relationships illuminates the contours of imperial nationalism and the lived outlines of the concept of police. The identifications, alienation, nostalgia, and pain these relationships bring to light work to debride our expectations for the stability, territorial overlay, and coherence of the building-block concepts of nation, state, and police. They also point us to important facets of this period of US history, crystalized into something we might understand as what Raymond Williams called a "structure of feeling," a historically specific edifice of perceptions and principles, the unevenly shared hopes and fears of a social body.[5]

In the structure of feeling revealed by former OPS officers' engagement in refugee relief lies a critical aspect of violence work on which this book has not yet touched, a tension deep within. It is that violence workers are *workers*: people whose labor power is appropriated to produce surplus value. (You do not have to be an orthodox Marxist to grasp that no profit comes from a worker paid exactly the value their labor adds.) Not only is violence work *work*, but it is often poorly paid and, frankly, crappy work. This is, in fact, one of the sources of historians' inability to understand policing. Uniformed public police in US cities have overwhelmingly been working-class, allowing observers to delink their interests from those of elites. If "police" is accepted as no more and no less than the uniformed public police, and the state imagined as a coherent body of people involved in governing, this position can make sense.[6] If, instead, we bear in mind the ultimate source of police power, perhaps by using a concept such as "violence work," the relationship springs into focus.

Their exploitation as workers is easily overlooked in relation to (and by) violence workers. It can be hard to see exploitation for workers whose salaries satisfy them, because under capitalism the same entity, the employer, both exploits and pays.[7] It is even more difficult in the case of people who also derive a sense of self from that entity, moving us into the realm of affect. There we find violence workers' identification with the state-market, enhanced by nationalism, militarism, and attendant masculinities. These function psychically to compensate for the stresses of exploitation. They are analogs of the "wages of whiteness" noted by historians of slavery, of the "racial bribe" described by critical race legal theorists, ways the state-market heads off the frustration that can organize workers to act in solidarity against the wage.[8]

It is hard to see the exploitation of violence workers until something disrupts the cycles of identification. Here lies another reason OPS is an ideal object of analysis: its employees suffered precisely that disruption. Their affective investments in the state-market were jarred by Congress's termination of their agency and their subsequent experiences. The wounds they sustained through termination left them scarred by bitterness and resentment, alienated from the country they thought they had served. In the refugees, ex-OPS saw versions of themselves.

This mirroring is evident in the complaints OPS had and still have about their agency's termination and their treatment in its wake, in the intense refugee relief work ex-OPS performed, in the social field ex-OPS cultivated with the migrants, and in the stories they told about refugee flights to

America, in which OPS agents appeared both as saviors and as martyrs. These complaints reveal that their refugee tales were also autobiography. It seems that former OPS agents realized and articulated their own alienation and injuries through real and projected relations to Southeast Asian migrants. Their relationships involved not only objectification but also identification.[9] They had, after all, been ejected from the same countries, though they never quite put it that way.

Former OPS officers' active identifications with foreign nationals complicates our understanding of nation, and their self-descriptions as state agents who felt wronged by the state helps insist on the incoherence of the concept of the state. Here was a group of former US government workers, as a whole highly conservative and certainly nationalist. Against expectations, they were not anti-immigrant in the case of Southeast Asia. They were actively pro-immigrant, and moreover their identification with Southeast Asian migrants was easily greater than their sense of similarity to US Americans just then protesting the war or marching for racial justice. The social field ex-OPS and Southeast Asian refugees formed was tantamount to an imagined community, one that managed to overlook the absence of shared US citizenship and of whiteness.

This chapter aims to parse the evolving contours of US nationalism in this period, following the ways ex-OPS's identifications with refugees produced a kind of small-guy populism with interracial and transnational reaches. The rise of right-wing anti-big-government conservatism in the 1980s, disavowing overt racism while comfortably supporting racist structures such as prisons, makes another kind of sense in a world in which a refugee structure of feeling prevailed, iterated in one striking version by former US government police officers who sought out an array of unexpected relations with Southeast Asian migrants, from distant benefactors to sponsors to hosts to employers to colleagues to the most intimate of family ties.

"CASUALTIES OF THE COLD WAR"

The former employees of the Office of Public Safety felt deeply wounded by their agency's termination. They were bitter over accusations of political policing and torture, adamant that Congress had misconstrued conditions at Con Son Island prison in Vietnam, and outraged that the CIA didn't come more effectively to their defense. When they returned to the United

States, their experiences on the job market added insult to injury as they found themselves deprived of the welcome they felt they deserved and found their OPS experience denigrated by prospective employers, especially within other branches of government.

Former Public Safety agents were bereft when "the libs killed OPS," as Andy Best put it in 2007.[10] In 2012, he described the feeling to me as having been "cut off at the knees."[11] Morris Grodsky used a telling metaphor in describing the multiple fields in which he and his colleagues went to work after the termination: "There was a real diaspora," he told me (unprompted), using a word notable for its implications of expulsion and exile.[12]

Ex-OPS experienced tremendous culture shock when they came home. They moved from a context in which all of their contacts were vehement and committed anticommunists to one in which the war's very rationale was questioned. It pushed J. B. Carnahan to take his family far from California: "Well, first of all, I had at that point nonwhite children, which I'd never considered what that would be any kind of a problem, but I think the biggest problem was attitudes of the war, and how much misinformation that people had about the war, and the Vietnamese people, and the region. And even though they would fight to the death for their opinion, it wasn't based on any knowledge they had about anything, and I just felt uncomfortable, and so, we left."[13]

An awkward logic emerges here—wouldn't nonwhite children have been more comfortable in multiracial California than in militarized Alaska? Carnahan attempted to harness the diversity paradigm prevailing at the time of our 2012 interview to place his family on the higher moral ground. He laid the explanation of his differences with Californians at the time on "misinformation" and public opinion "not based on any knowledge."

Misinformation was also the explanation Ned Antonik settled upon in his attempt to convey the difficulties ex-OPS had faced. Reaching for that favorite bugaboo, "the media," he explained to me, "Yeah, you're trying to do a good job, and then they're saying, hey, you're oppressing the people. That's not my field, politics, but it's very clear how media can be mishandled."[14] Antonik's bewildered outrage reflected the dissonance between his confidently held worldview and the very different positions taken by many of his fellow Americans.

The other major arena of resentment for ex-OPS involved their treatment on the job market when they came home. Many law enforcement agencies rejected the former OPS officers when they returned from abroad. Several wrote in to the *Newsletter* about their difficulties finding new posts. Frank Jeffers wanted to return to police work, but, he complained, "everywhere I went I was either overqualified or didn't have enough recent experience," charging employers with failing to value his OPS work abroad.[15] An anonymous writer in the *Newsletter* made it clear that this was the result of the charges against OPS. After the termination, he wrote, "I found myself treated like an ex-felon in the D.C. government sectors up to and even being asked to leave the room during a job interview with LEAA. I will not dwell on the past, but it will suffice to say that I and my family suffered through 10 years of guilt and depression as a result of the terminal OPS experience." This writer was explicit that he considered *himself* "one of the casualties of the Cold War."[16]

Mike Harpold, the editor of the *Newsletter* in the period of my research, encountered similar barriers during his post-OPS job search. He told me this story about encountering not-so-subtle insult when he tried to return to his position with the Border Patrol:

> I had what was called reemployment rights. If I go over for two years, at the end I would be reinstated. But when I came back I . . . went over to the border patrol HQ and got in to see the chief and the deputy chief of the border patrol at that time, and they said, "Well, Harpold, glad to have you back," and I said, "Glad to be back, and I'm ready to go home to Bakersfield and go to work." And they said, "Oh, you can't go to Bakersfield, we don't have any vacancies—how about Yuma, Arizona?" And I said, "How would I get my family down there?" They said, "Why don't you ask the State Department, see if they'll send them down there."

That was the first offense, snide but utterly clear to Harpold. It became even more explicit as the conversation progressed:

> Well, there was no way in hell they were going to do that. So not only was I going to have to pay to move my family down there but I was going to have to wait a year for the general upgrade. There were several other benefits that I was not going to be eligible for, and I kind of protested a little bit, I said, "Look, I'm entitled to be reinstated." They both looked at me and said, "Good loyal Americans stayed right here in the United States." That from a head of a law enforcement administration.[17]

Harpold's fury had dimmed in retrospect by the long and honorable career he eventually completed for the Immigration and Naturalization Service, but at the time, he amply conveyed, he felt humiliated. Along with a useful reminder of the heterogeneity of state bodies, Harpold's experience brings us to feel the tension in violence workers' relationship to the entity that employs them.

For ex-ops, this tension extended even to their own organization. Individual psas chided their own agency—ops itself—for the elitism revealed in stories of their travels. Former trainers did not have the means to travel for fun or refugee support, Bill Kirker complained in response to news items relating some particularly globe-trotting exploits. Most of us, he wrote, "do not have unlimited resources to gad about the world. We don't expect to take the next plane to Kuala Lumpur or Bangkok or Chad in pursuit of some elusive phantasy [sic]; we don't expect to attend a wedding in Costa Rica or visit a friend in Guam. Most of us are retired or semiretired. We live in modest rural communities & we are regularly engaged in church or community affairs. . . . Inflation is rapidly consuming our reserve capital and our pensions are no longer adequate to provide the so-called good life."

Yet even while offering this critique, Kirker insisted on support for the refugees: "I'm deeply concerned about the refugees from Vietnam and Cambodia. I know that many psd members actively sponsored many such refugees for safe haven in the U.S.A. I'm proud of my association with this noteworthy christian [sic] endeavor. I follow the activities of the Catholic Relief Services and I financially support that function as my civic and spiritual duty." But, he insisted, his family's most immediate problem was how to stay warm that winter, and he challenged the *Newsletter*'s editors to take his interests into consideration: "If this description of our present life styles is not compatible with your ideals of adventure and comdradrie [sic] then by your standards feel free to drop me from your mailing list. But if you agree that the welfare of our comrades is our number 1 concern then I shall be content that I have written this letter."[18]

Kirker's antielitism hit a nerve. Margie and Morrie Looney wrote to agree. "Like Bill [Kirkus] [sic], our small church supports the Catholic Relief Organization as we are concerned about the refugees world wide and this organization tries to assist all refugees regardless of race or country of origin." The Looneys were content with their farming life, they explained, but worried about what they clearly intended to categorize as normal, humble things: inflation, "the hostages held by the Iranees," former coworkers abroad in "the hot spots of the world," and "our foreign police friends who due to circumstances in their countries can no longer wear with safety their ipa pins or practice procedures openly that were taught them by PSD advisors."[19] Chiding their former fellows for assuming all ex-OPS were people of means, these writers revealed that some *Newsletter* readers' resentment toward elites extended even to the upper echelons of OPS.

As time went on and public memory did not vindicate them, ex-OPS feelings of betrayal only mounted. In 1998, Donald Bordenkircher published a book-length refutation of accusations of improper treatment of prisoners in Vietnam, *Tiger Cage: An Untold Story*, coauthored with his wife, Shirley Bordenkircher. Several interviewees advised me to read *Tiger Cage* as the definitive account of Con Son Island, the controversial South Vietnamese prison run with the help of US advisors. Congress investigated purported abuses and conditions there, contributing to the eventual decision to terminate OPS. The tiger cage controversy, Bordenkircher wrote, "stands as one of the most successful operations ever undertaken by Hanoi's Department of Psychological Warfare."[20]

The tiger cage episode sparked resentment, not of Congress but of the CIA, OPS's closest collaborator, its covert arm, perhaps even its raison d'être. Many ex-OPS blamed the CIA for OPS's demise. In *Tiger Cage*, Bordenkircher accused ambassador William Colby, a CIA officer (publically acknowledged, including in Colby's own autobiography of 1978), of sacrificing OPS in an attempt to save the CIA's clandestine counterinsurgency program, Operation Phoenix. Colby was taking heat for Phoenix, Bordenkircher explained, and Colby's "damage control objective was to save the CIA before the Senate Foreign Relations Committee." He could have protected OPS, Bordenkircher charges; he had the capacity: "Colby had the power, authority, and political clout to save Public Safety." But, alas, "someone or something had to take blame for the Phoenix program and its purported excesses. He gave them Public Safety."[21] This is a fairly widely shared understanding. Even Michael McClintock, no friend to OPS, called the CIA the "worm" in the OPS "apple," in specific relation to Phoenix.[22]

How far the tide of public memory had turned against them was evident in 2005, thanks to an advertisement for a forthcoming summer seminar titled "Exorcising the Demons of the Past: Seizing New Opportunities to Promote Democratic Policing," organized by OPS's parent organization, the Agency for International Development (USAID) (figure 6.1). The "demons of the past," *Newsletter* readers realized in horror, were them. Michael McCann, furious, wrote several times to the director of AID to protest "the Agency's reference of my colleagues and me as 'demons' in the title of one

2005 Summer Seminar Series

EXORCISING DEMONS OF THE PAST: SEIZING NEW OPPORTUNITIES TO PROMOTE DEMOCRATIC POLICING

Session Organizers: Liz Hume, DCHA/CMM and Michael Miklaucic, DCHA/DG

JULY 7, 2005

FIG 6.1 Title slide for USAID's scheduled summer seminar, July 2005. SOURCE: PRIVATE COLLECTION OF *PSN* EDITOR MIKE HARPOLD.

of your Summer Seminar series."[23] McCann's complaints eventually coaxed an apology, Harpold told me, still sputtering about the seminar: "What it was, was, they were trying to disavow—this is the USAID today—our reputation during the Cold War. The reputation being that we were training foreign police to torture, and all sorts of stuff." Harpold was thrilled at McCann's success: "So Mike took 'em on. That had never been the truth. The fact that we had been libeled all these years. So they cancelled the seminar and we got a written apology from the director. So one teeny victory in all these years."[24]

Harpold's concern with public memory was widely shared, as evident in the production of an entire special issue of the *Newsletter* on the controversy (figure 6.2). Andy Best asked me whether I had seen the Wikipedia entry for OPS. "Do you know what's on there?" he asked. "Did you read it? Did you see that we tortured, and so on?" I said I had, and that it seemed the former PSAs were angry and frustrated with such public perceptions. "You got that right!" he exclaimed, laughing. Torture was also something Antonik was also anxious to clarify, thirty-five years after the fact: "I mean, if there was a Public Safety guy somewhere that irregular police work was

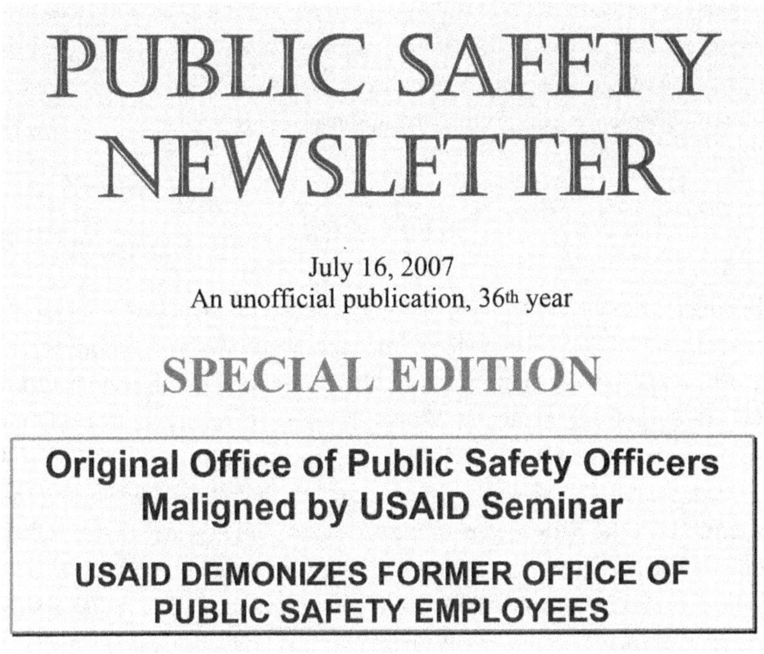

PUBLIC SAFETY NEWSLETTER

July 16, 2007
An unofficial publication, 36th year

SPECIAL EDITION

Original Office of Public Safety Officers Maligned by USAID Seminar

USAID DEMONIZES FORMER OFFICE OF PUBLIC SAFETY EMPLOYEES

FIG 6.2 Header for the special edition of the *Public Safety Newsletter* published to detail the USAID seminar and ex-OPS responses to it. SOURCE: *PSN* (JULY 16, 2007).

going on, he didn't go screaming to the authorities, hey, stop that immediately, because he would just be dismissed. He might slowly work on things that he finds quite unusual, but in order to do his job, he's got to observe for a long time."[25] This is the position Public Safety defenders took when their proximity to torture was proven; it is noteworthy that they still feel called upon to reiterate it.

Antonik's ongoing sensitivity to criticism of OPS shows the long life of these feelings. He worried that my research proposal, published in the *Newsletter* as part of my request for interview subjects, "seems to criticize people in the Public Safety program" and expressed concern about "some of the language. For example, we weren't doing police work. We were training foreign police, but they were the ones doing the police work in their countries. We just provided training, to help them professionalize, do their jobs better."[26] Antonik rose to defend OPS, along with the borders of policing itself. Conventional definitions of legitimate democratic policing require this labor of insisting not only that US police work is local—to travel would violate its strictures of scale—but that all policing is the work of locals, anywhere on the globe. In his vindication of OPS, Antonik struggled to fortify the categorical borders of policing, as this book has observed state-identified violence workers do, over and over again.

RELIEF WORK

Feeling frustrated, abandoned, and misunderstood, then, ex-OPS employees contemplated their homeland, including their nation's reactions to the growing cohort from Southeast Asia. One of the results of this conjuncture was an outpouring of support for the refugees, involving both paid and volunteer work, and the intimate labors of sponsorship.

Refugee relief work was a logical move bureaucratically, given OPS engagement in the nations generating the 1970s refugees and then USAID's official role in refugee work. Quite a few former OPS employees engaged in it, both as administrators of policy in Washington and as staff for the various camps. One man became deputy director for AID management and personnel, working from Washington to staff the Refugee Processing Centers.[27] Another was handling "the knotty administrative support functions" for AID after doing the same for the Interagency Task Force on Indochina. "Right on, JOE!!" lauded the eds.[28] Another was assigned to the AID Refugee Task Force, and a fourth worked both central administrative and camp posts for the refugee center in Guam, Camp Pendleton, and the Indiantown Gap refugee center.[29]

Others felt strongly enough to put their shoulders to the wheel for free. On their own dime, for example, two ex-OPS "attempted to contact a number of refugees who were with PSD or were PSD counterparts" in Guam, where they happened to be consulting for the Guam Department of Public Safety.[30] These men were already stationed where the refugee camp was located, but other volunteers traveled considerable distances to do this work. "Dudley Britton . . . visited Ft. Chaffee, Ark., refugee center and located a number of Vietnamese with whom he had worked and as can be expected, took a 'Dudley' interest in them." Showing the assumption that many readers would want to do the same, the editors offered Britton's aid: "If anyone needs help locating Vietnamese in Ft. Chaffee we are sure that Dudley will be pleased to assist."[31] Another person reported that in his retirement, he was spending "a great deal of my spare time and money trying to help the Lao refugees who escape to Nong Khai Refugee Camp in Thailand," and wrote of plans to do even more: "If my health permits, I plan to accompany my Thai housekeeper Kosoo[illeg] to Thailand in late Feb or early March [1980]."[32]

For people in the United States unable to contemplate extensive travel, individual refugee sponsorship was an appealing way to help. Sponsors would secure an apartment and pay rent for a few months, guide people through bureaucratic processes such as getting a driver's license, registering for English classes, or figuring out how to look for a job, and otherwise orient their charges to a new city and country. They pledged short-term support, hoping the person or family would be on their feet after that, able to sustain themselves. Much discussion of sponsorship in the pages of the *Newsletter* reveals that this was an attractive role for many ex-OPS agents, and the *Newsletter* further actively assisted these efforts by sharing information on how to go about becoming a sponsor. The editors devoted an entire page and a half of an early issue to instructions for sponsoring refugees, organizations helping process them, and local details.[33] It then detailed the efforts of its many contributors who followed its instructions. One man was "helping a VN refugee family"; another "had a group of 47 persons that he was sponsoring"; a third "had 13 Vietnamese which he says makes a full house. He and Caroline find it interesting and a lot of fun."[34] An anniversary party included "10 Vietnamese, most of whom were my proteges [sic] in entering the U.S.," the husband wrote.[35] Far from simply describing the efforts of its readership, the *Newsletter* was an active agent in the construction of consensus around the proper reception of the refugees.

Refugee relief work wielded a psychic wage. The resentment at OPS's cancellation and grief over the loss of the war were both addressed by the suggestions of refugee neediness and US benevolence tangibly reproduced in such labor. This narrative is spotlit in one amazing story detailing a nasty posttermination experience and eventual refugee relief work, conveyed by Michael Harpold in his generous, detailed interviews. Harpold's story shows the heartfelt affect ex-OPS refugee relief workers felt even as it also reveals the deep conservativism their work rested on and fed.

Harpold was and is a committed humanitarian whose significant and selfless service spotlights the paradox of ex-OPS refugee work: the inadvertent reproduction of the liberal underpinnings of US nationalism and empire; and the deep sense of cross-national, transstate identifications between refugees and North American benefactors.

Harpold was an active and effective worker on behalf of Southeast Asian refugees. His labors contributed directly to the passage of the field-changing Refugee Act of 1980. By 1978, having landed on his feet after his expulsion from the Border Patrol, Harpold had risen in the ranks of the Immigration and Naturalization Service. Feeling a connection to Southeast Asia, he asked to be allowed to travel to the region to gather data to inform INS policy. He remembered the journey in our 2011 interview:

> In 1978, Vietnamese were still coming out of Vietnam, three years after the end of the war. It wasn't supposed to be that way. The war was supposed to be over. The last thing anyone in this country wanted to deal with was Vietnamese refugees. I was working back in Washington, D.C. for our [i.e., INS] HQ, ... So I started reading these news reports about why Vietnamese were still coming out. The government didn't want them coming out so they were calling them economic refugees, . . . they were starting to pile up in refugee camps around Thailand, Singapore, and some even got to the Philippines. Those governments didn't want them. They started turning to the U.S. government, well, we didn't want them either. So at any rate I asked [INS director] Castillo, how about letting me go over and take a look. So he did. There was a little bill before Congress to admit 6000 of them. That was kind of as a sop to Thailand and Malaysia because they were piling up in these refugee camps by that time by the thousands. So I toured the refugee camps from Cambodia to the Singapore border. And I actually rescued a group of refugees in Thailand. The Thais were pushing these boats offshore. This one boat I happened on, it was tied behind a Thai gunboat, thirty-four men, women, and children, mostly women and children. The Thais were getting ready to cut it loose. They were forcing the refugees back out to sea. And a lot of refugees were dying out there. At any rate, I benighted myself, I convinced the local governor that I had the authority of the United States and he let them ashore.[36]

Harpold's bold move was reported soon after in the *New York Times* with righteous approval by Henry Kamm, and later in the *Washington Post*, where Jack Anderson picked up the story as Harpold was preparing his congressional testimony.[37] Both pieces corroborate Harpold's memory precisely. Harpold also claims that his trip inspired CBS investigator Ed Bradley to take his camera crew to a refugee camp in the Pacific, which produced a hauntingly effective report.[38] While it isn't clear whether

Harpold specifically propelled Bradley to that undeniably persuasive documentary, Harpold's work, magnified by journalists Kamm and Anderson, joined the activism and media coverage responsible for the tide of public opinion moving Congress toward the Refugee Act of 1980. As one of many actors increasingly outraged at the refugees' plight and lobbying American policymakers to broaden the nation's welcome, Harpold's individual contribution was neither necessary nor sufficient to turn that tide, but it was a significant piece, one of the several that worked together to change the United States' course.

Yet Harpold's shining public service, accomplished at great risk to himself and with the most spotless intentions, also worked against his own genuine hopes for peace and justice. His work in 1978 and his memory of it in 2011 reveal the classic outlines of the refugee narrative in the service of liberal empire. Scholars in critical ethnic studies have thoroughly critiqued this narrative, which circulates in both popular and academic arenas. Yến Lê Espiritu, in her astute critique of the corpus of scholarly work on Vietnamese refugees, the "most studied arrival cohort in U.S. immigration history," details the treatment of migrants as "objects of rescue," passive and desperate. The work she reviews brackets the US role in creating the conditions causing the barrage of death and dislocation in southeast Asia, hailing America instead only as capacious savior, celebrating the refugees' adjustment to their new home. The figure of the "good refugee" in particular comes into focus for Espiritu as anchor of the attempt to refigure the Vietnam War in memory as a "good war": necessary, moral, and successful. This logic extends into the present, where it carries water for legacy policies, justifying, for example, US intervention in the Middle East.[39]

The figure of the refugee in US popular and public spheres functions as a vigorous ideological laborer on behalf of liberal war and empire, as Mimi Nguyen has demonstrated in her answer to Espiritu's call for a "critical refugee studies." The "gift" refugees are supposed to have received and the insuperable debt they apparently owe is highlighted in the public personas of former refugees whose stories particularly fascinate US audiences; that gift, Nguyen argues, reinforces ideas of universal humanism that underpin imperial projects. This is not an ideal to protect, she charges, upsetting vast reservoirs of liberal assumption, for it justifies imperial violence: this notion of the gift "instrumentalizes an idea of human freedom as a universal value, and intensifies an administrative and bureaucratic legality as its rational order to reinforce a politics of war, terror, and occupation."[40]

In light of this critique, Harpold's work can be read more subtly. He makes no gesture to US responsibility for the events that provoked the displacement, but offers congratulations for its stepping in where other countries have proven unwilling or unable—and in this case, tellingly, other Asian countries. The portrayal of the callousness of Thai officials is particularly revealing in its Orientalist overtones, framing an uncivilized failure to value human life. In the overall narrative, including events upon his return and the final decision by Congress, there is the thread of the goodness of the US public, who do the right thing once full information is disclosed to them, and of Harpold himself as the gallant hero, self-designated as deserving of monarchic recognition ("knighted" clearly intended within the spoonerist slip of the tongue, "benighted"), an unrivaled revelation of the *feeling* of sovereignty.[41]

Harpold certainly nourished the principles of liberal war, including its celebration of heroic savior figures. Yet this critique in no way implies that Harpold was anything but genuine in his intentions. Indeed, in speaking of the trip over thirty years later, Harpold was audibly moved, and his emotion echoes the broader wash of affect evident in the *Newsletter*'s pages. It would be too cynical to attribute this sentiment to a calculated attempt to construct an anticommunist alibi, and too naive to conclude that the refugees' plight was simply moving to its readers' tender hearts (although it was). Instead it is clear that Harpold and his fellows felt themselves in some ways deeply *like* the refugees they sought to love, know, befriend, help, and save.

This empathy, emanating from bitterness, watered the roots of a right-wing populism whose political effects have been terribly harmful to the United States and the world. I am arguing that we must understand ex-OPS thoughts and feelings not out of some insipid curtsey to a universal humanity but because such an understanding provides better ground from which to work against this toxic politics.

Harpold's tale of woe and salvation was commonplace in the pages of the *Public Safety Newsletter*, which overflowed with stories of escape, privation, and rescue. The tales confirm Espiritu and Nguyen's insights into the narrative function of the figure of the refugee, substantiating the virtue of the democracy that welcomed him or her and the universality and value of the concept of freedom itself.[42] The *Newsletter* circulated these stories, first with specifics, and then over and over again, until their actual details no longer even required rehearsal.

"At the time we were completing the preparation of this issue of the NEWS-LETTER," the editors wrote in May 1975, "we received several letters and phone calls from former colleagues who expressed concern with and over the Vietnam refugee situation."[43] The *Newsletter* thus let its readers hear about refugees through frequent personal updates. These regular dispatches immersed the reader in an affective undertow of nostalgia, fear, and hope, under the factual veneer of news of Southeast Asian counterparts who had survived and surfaced in the United States. The editors were grateful to learn that "Mr. Minh Ngo Dac, formerly in the Administrative Office, P.S.D. Saigon, is still in New York City although he is considering relocating to either San Francisco or Houston."[44] Ex-OPS wrote in to report that a former interpreter was working for Met Life in Tulsa, that a counterpart and his family had moved and were "involved in on-the-job training which will lead to managing a convenience store," that they had "heard from Peng, ... She and her husband escaped from Viet Nam by boat to Hong Kong in May. . . . They hoped to leave for the States before the end of November."[45]

A fairly standard pattern soon began to emerge in the refugee stories the *Newsletter* related. They told of former counterparts escaping terrible abuse and privations, sounded outrage and sympathy, and resolved to continue to contribute. One writer worried about a former friend, "former Province Police Chief of Tuyen-Duc," who was "in a 're-education' center near Hanoi." He told of his efforts, in vain so far, to help the man, and vowed ongoing commitment to his rescue.[46] Another gave a more detailed, harrowing story of a former counterpart "in prison because of his association with the U.S. AID program," and who, finally released, made his way with his family by boat. "Twice, during the crossing, he writes, their boat was stopped by pirates and they lost everything they had."[47] The letter writer asked for contributions, showing himself to be part of both the campaign to secure this family's asylum and the financial support it was receiving in the United States.

An unusually detailed account came from a man named Tien M. Truong, resettled in New Jersey. He sent a long, thorough, and profoundly sad account of the hardships of his escape and his precarious financial and health situation in its wake, suggesting that he had assimilated the utility of casting his woes in the narrative structure that would best secure the resources he and his family surely needed. Hopeful new arrivals quickly learned to frame their tales in these terms.[48] In the issue following the one in which the editors reproduced this tale in full, a North American ex-OPS reader thanked the PSN. "The account of Truong's adventures is a classic," he agreed. "Have you tried to give it publication in a newspaper? It deserves wider dissemination."[49]

It was apt to describe Truong's saga as a classic, for this was precisely the rote tale, composed of predictable stock pieces, then saturating the mainstream US news media. By its next issue, in June 1980, the *Newsletter* no longer even needed to specify its details. A former PSD on a road trip reported that he had visited a new arrival. Although he was glad to report that her "ten sisters and one brother and her mother and father are now all in this country," in Oklahoma City, it had not been easy along the way: "Her story of how she got here and then how the rest of the family got here just last July is not only a thriller but tugs at the heart-strings," he relayed, not bothering to list particulars.[50] The outlines of this tragedy of Greek proportions were well known, and the narrative form fairly constant: threat or fact of imprisonment, unwilling flight, dangers and privations, luck and courage, hardscrabble arrival. They contained, as well, the tacit notice of OPS's courageous service, sometimes rising to the surface in narratives of rescue.[51]

Escape narratives, like notices of sponsorship or other forms of refugee relief, all sounded a congratulatory note to the receiving nation and to its values, for which it stands, with liberty, and so on. Refugees were portrayed as heroic survivors of desperate odds only while they were still overseas; once they arrived in the United States, the *Newsletter* conveyed, they were enveloped in a safety net of helpful agencies and individuals. Escape narratives were therefore also narratives of rescue, in which OPS cast itself—as a collective and via its individual former members—as agent of salvation.

These stories of connections, intimate friendships, and ongoing collaborations painted a rosy picture of both OPS agents and their new compatriots. So did the reports of the refugees' progress, which the *Newsletter* listed in its relentlessly upbeat tone. People wrote that their sponsored family members or friends were "making a fantastic adjustment to life in the U.S. All are gainfully employed or in high school and college," were "happily and successfully adjusting to Big H," "have adjusted to live in the U.S.," were "doing well in Dallas," "also doing well," "all 3 have done extremely well here. We're very proud of them."[52]

These formulaic reports often contained an element of praise of successful refugees for the independence of their success. One report noted a refugee had "worked for my brother for a while and then went out on his own and is doing quite well," and that another, "always independent, refused all help to start out and is also doing quite well for himself."[53] A former Cambodian police chief whom ex-OPS had sponsored had moved on to California, while his brother-in-law "remained in Ocala and is doing well and completely on his own." The editors praised this news: "We share your feelings, JACK, that this is what should happen to all Southeast Asia refugees."[54] Refusing help and making it alone—the core of a right-wing populism associated with Reagan-style attacks on "big government"—was clearly the gold standard for refugee accomplishment.

Notices of successful adaptation invoked the "classic" refugee tale, what Espiritu, in the case of Vietnamese refugees specifically, calls the "desperate-turned-successful" narrative, rehearsing both the terrible nature of the conditions people fled and the wonders of the land of opportunity that received them. It overlooks, of course, the massive state structures erected to transport and receive the refugees and organize the vast networks of sponsors who softened their landing. As Espiritu argues, the tale helps justify US militarism and works to produce a sense of American identity, both in contradistinction to Southeast Asia and as benefactors to the refugees.[55] It also fed the "model minority" success story, by the 1970s the dominant stereotype associated with Asian Americans, which was a cornerstone of Cold War US liberalism and attendant antiblack racism.[56]

The structural resonance that lies coiled around the base of the *Newsletter*'s heart-tugging refugee stories is not exactly empathy, does not necessarily indicate racial tolerance, and should not send us searching for other progressive attitudes on the former police trainers' behalf. Nor does it diminish the aptness of Epiritu's and Nguyen's critiques. It does, however, offer tantalizing suggestions regarding the mutability of racial identifications and the failure of the concept of the state to align its constituent elements.

LABORS OF LOVE

The sense of identity produced among ex-OPS had a unique tinge. It ended up including the refugees both socially and professionally. While OPS officers interacted with Southeast Asian people abroad and at home in ways that very much warrant Epiritu's and Nguyen's critique, reinforcing narratives of refugee vulnerability, need, and adjustment, and entirely in favor of US intervention, mourning its curtailment in Vietnam, and their own agency's demise, they also stitched together a social field that offers a distinct set of insights about right-wing imperial nationalism and the identificatory possibilities of violence workers under its sway. These collaborators imagined themselves into a genuine community of pro-police, anticommunist imperial nationalists, leaping tall buildings of race and citizenship with a single bound. This imagination rested on the work they did together abroad, long before any refugee question surfaced. Idiosyncratically, employees of OPS were deeply involved with people from the nations in which OPS had served.

Public Safety agents came into unusually close contact with citizens of the host country because of the nature of their work. While US foreign service workers are notorious for residing in insular expatriate neighborhoods, Public Safety agents were different. They were dispersed across the nations they targeted, living in smaller towns with few US or other foreign residents, and many developed social as well as working relationships with local police officers and their support staff and families (figure 6.3). Back in the larger cities, OPS offices employed many nationals of the host country as secretaries, translators, or in other roles (figures 6.4 and 6.5). So OPS employees and host nationals were intimately engaged, sometimes literally. Romantic relationships index some of the profound feelings of connection and affiliation OPS officers felt toward the people with whom—and for whom, they deeply believed—they worked abroad.

A surprisingly large number of (ex-)OPS employees married women from the countries of their assignments. Vietnam in particular was home for many ex-OPS wives, including Ly, Binh, Anh, and Nga.[57] Many marriages between former Public Safety agents and foreign women began during the agents' work abroad, where there were ample opportunities for eligible partners to meet.[58] In other cases, where the couple met isn't obvious but the woman's nationality is clear, as when one couple reported visiting the wife's family in Saigon or when a wife's family arrived at a refugee camp in need of sponsorship.[59] Some notices of marriage didn't specify, but foreign origin seems likely from a name, such as Ling, Nguyen, and Amorn.[60] The women's last names were never given, reflecting the practices of the day regarding marriage and identity.

The vast majority of such couples—every case I found, though my method does not approach exhaustive coverage—involved Asian women and non-Asian men, mostly Anglo-surnamed (with the exception of a few Latinos). This was even true when the Asian spouse was the OPS employee

FIG 6.3 A Vietnam tour of duty, shared in the *Newsletter* in 2012, with the following text:

"During one of my tours in VN I was assigned to Kien Hoa Province where I inherited Tran Kim THIET interpreter, NPFF advisor Talamine, and Chief PHUC. I attached a photo with PHUC, do you recognize him, Jim? Bob Weidner PSD/MRIV."

"I hope Jim does, but sure enough that's Bob second from right.—Ed."

SOURCE: *PSN* 162 (APR. 2012), 2. PHOTOGRAPH SUBMITTED TO THE *NEWSLETTER* BY BOB WEIDNER.

FIG 6.4 OPS advisors in Vietnam, including Vietnamese counterparts. SOURCE: *PSN* 171 (MAR. 2016), 2. PHOTOGRAPH COURTESY OF CHARLIE VANN.

FIG 6.5 OPS advisors in Vietnam, including Vietnamese counterparts. SOURCE: *PSN* 171 (MAR. 2016), 2. PHOTOGRAPH COURTESY OF CHARLIE VANN.

and the North American was not.[61] Also, tellingly, I found no instance in which a female OPS employee (of any race) married an Asian man. Some OPS women announced marriages, usually to other foreign service workers, but always to Anglo-surnamed husbands.[62] So while the bias of these marriages toward Asian women with Euro-American men may reflect the preponderance of men among the workers on the US side, there were some eligible Euro-American women; gender imbalance does not fully explain it.

As abundant work in critical ethnic and gender studies has diagnosed, Asian bodies are resolutely feminized in US gender conventions, rendered exotic and attractive in uneven index of their subordination in global power networks.[63] OPS employees rehearsed that subordination daily in their foreign offices in relation to Asian secretaries, drivers, and translators in the field, where they directed and instructed (the misleadingly egalitarian term "counterpart" notwithstanding); back in the United States, where their foreign former colleagues were shunted into the profoundly vulnerable status of refugee; and, in later years, in the *Newsletter*, where foreign counterparts were often included unnamed (figure 6.6).[64] This is not a problem for normative heterosexuality: subordination feeds positively into gender conventions of feminine frailty. No wonder OPS men found the women in and from Southeast Asia so beguiling.

In an illustrative instance of the exoticist feminine ideal many ex-OPS officers projected onto Asian women, one man wrote from Taipei in 1979 that "since [his] days in Vietnam" he had wanted to "marry a beautiful 21-year old Oriental girl." Someone had obliged to individuate this generic role, confirmed a newspaper clipping of the wedding. "Her name is Vicky," he beamed, "Chinese father, Korean mother, and she is in the public relations field at the Taipei Hilton Hotel."[65] This pride at "Vicky's" employment shows, in a countervailing direction, that former Public Safety agents valued their wives' educational and occupational success. As the women's movement simmered in the background, another wrote that he was "proud of wife Anh who is working on the last of her Associate's Degree." A third boasted that his new wife had been a nurse in Vietnam and was about to "graduate with a degree in Obstetric Nursing from Loma Linda University." Still another reported joyously that he had married a woman from Hong Kong who had just finished a PhD in Molecular Biology. Yet commitments to a traditional marital modes remained alongside this willingness to celebrate

FIG 6.6 "Jack Sanders Remembered." Fatigue-dressed man never identified. SOURCE: *PSN* 154 (APR. 3, 2009): 1. PHOTOGRAPH SUBMITTED TO THE *NEWSLETTER* BY BOB HILDEBRAND.

the professional accomplishments of wives; this man made sure to observe parenthetically, with a tellingly pointed "of course," that she had taken his name.[66]

Exoticization and other projections do not rule out the possibility of genuine love and connection between people who share potent experiences despite great differences. But love, itself a cipher for a dense knot of affective and psychic projections, neither explains nor overshadows these complex associations.[67] Mired in racialized global interrelations and consonantly fraught gender norms, the romantic bonds of marriage (and surely sex, though sex was not allowed to rear its uncouth head in the *Newsletter*'s genteel pages) constitute an iteration of the "tense and tender ties" of lived global power relations, what Ann Stoler calls "the intimacies of empire."[68] Marriage does not erase the social differences between the parties to it but often relies on them for its affective satisfactions. That is, gendered hierarchies texturized with hierarchies of race and nation can be all the more attractive.

Understanding this gives us a better sense of how to approach the platonic relationships of sponsorship and other aid, for heterosexual romance is like—akin to—other relationships with refugees in that all involve intimacy, hierarchy, and projection.

Indeed, sponsorship often sprang directly from marital connections, when North American men were called upon to help the families of their foreign-born wives. The man married to Anh wrote in mid-1975 that he and his wife had eight refugees "under their wing" and were "involved in food-clothing-shelter and schooling."[69] A letter from him two years later sounded, the *Newsletter* editors joked, "as though he was running a one man refugee station," and Anh's parents were "still in Saigon," suggesting more to come.[70] Ly and her husband were watching out for her family in Phan Rang, they reported in July 1977, and were "hopeful."[71] Another couple was "looking after their family and ten of Nga's refugee relatives" by early 1976.[72] Another man begged off serving on a proposed committee because "the arrival of our Cambodian family has brought a heavy drain on my time." "Thanks Jack," the editors responded, admonishing folks to back off asking him for service; "we understand your position."[73]

The other frequent source of sponsorship involved relationships between former counterparts. The *Newsletter* was particularly keen to assist in connecting counterparts to each other. In an early issue, an ex-OPS agent working in Washington offered his help: "If someone wishes to sponsor a former VN National Policeman but do [sic] not know the name they should write to . . . ."[74] The *Newsletter* frequently shared information that could lead to helping counterparts, as when it published a request for help locating the former director of the Vietnamese National Police, or the query regarding the former chief at Binh Long from a man who had traveled to Camp Pendleton several times already "to try to locate some former counterparts. He was not successful but since that time has located [the] Chief of Police at Binh Tuy. He is now in Hawaii."[75]

Plenty of ex-OPS did manage to help people with whom they had been formally associated abroad. They sponsored the "former Lao Police Chief of Narcotics Bureau, [brought] to the United States along with his family" of nine; eight Vietnamese "friends and former employees"; and the former "Chief of Police of Phnom Penh" and his brother-in-law, whom the sponsors called our "Cambodian family."[76] One former OPS agent had sponsored some ten people, largely former OPS employees, including "three secretaries and their husbands and our No. 1. Interpreter, Long I and his kids."[77] Again, the *Newsletter* was much more than a passive vehicle for these engagements. The logic of the connection between US police and Southeast Asian former police may already have been abundantly obvious to former Public Safety staff, but the *Newsletter*'s commitment to action on that assumption further strengthened the link in practice.

Through these connections, ex-OPS stitched a transnational social field cemented by their shared yet asymmetric experiences of exile. For the former Public Safety employees, both North American and Southeast Asian, weren't just interested in helping each other and being helped. Their relations were not purely instrumental. They exchanged visits, met for meals, and invited each other to parties. Together, they remade a social world in the aftermath of their several exiles.

Visits and encounters earned frequent mention in the *Newsletter*. In addition to the Vietnamese guests at the fiftieth wedding anniversary and other visits noted already, one man "had the Manila Police Chief [and another former counterpart] . . . as dinner guests at his home in November. Real fine, George," editorialized the typesetter. "Anyone else enjoyed the company of our overseas colleagues?"[78] They had. Two others had dinner with "their former counterpart" who had been "Director of the VN Marine Police." The *Newsletter* reminded readers that this person now lived in San Diego and would "undoubtedly . . . like to hear from any former OPS people with whom he worked."[79] Dorothy Jacobson expressed "pleasure to be reunited with Mrs. Tuyet (Dinh Thi Mong Tuyet), long-time employee of PSD-Saigon. She and her husband, Toan, made it out in the exodus of those fleeing the communists, and settled first in Ft Worth. . . . We had a tearful and joyous reunion."[80]

Counterparts from places other than mainland Southeast Asia who had not become refugees appeared as well, via regular, jovial updates, but with a more attenuated sense of connection. "Bangkok hands will be happy to learn of the whereabouts of PHENPHAN, one of our front-office girls," who had married an ambassadorial staffer, the editors expected, and reported on OPS trainees in Zaire: "All of the old OPS counterparts are going strong—so reports Chuck—from Kinshasa where he is still with the Office of the Presidence de la Republique. Chuck says that General Singa, Gendarmerie

Dir., saved the day for Zaire in Shaba and is now a 'hero of the first water.'"
General Singa asked after his former Public Safety friends, as did "Gen
Babia, now the senior man in the Defense Department."[81]

At a luncheon in Dallas in 1979, a regular gathering of former Public
Safety hands held every year during the meeting of the International Association of Chiefs of Police (IACP), former OPS dined with Varney Dempster,
a Liberian former counterpart, who provided updates on six other Liberian officials who had also worked with OPS. Former OPS director Lauren
Goin commented that the attendees at the event included two Vietnamese refugees and several current police officials from Guam and Bolivia as
well as Liberia. "We did indeed leave a considerable legacy of leadership in
the various countries that we helped," Goin concluded.[82] Goin yearned to
believe—probably did believe—that OPS had been effective and productive. Dempster, unfortunately, was a poor vessel for such beliefs given his
abysmal human rights record, and the fact that the luncheon preceded by
months the coup after which he was murdered, likely alongside some of the
other Liberian officials also in attendance in Dallas.[83] Refugees were far better psychic investments. They represented a perfect mix of evidence that
OPS had been deeply needed and wrongly terminated, every fugitive body
further "proof" of communist strength and brutality.

No wonder these relationships were so attractive—to all involved. While
the voices of Vietnamese and other relocated OPS personnel are sparse in
the *Newsletter*'s pages, they are not absent. Migrants reached out to their
US American peers, too, and again, not only for material assistance. They
also seem to have felt a commonality and worked to feed that feeling in
themselves and others. Hia Thai asked to join the PSN mailing list, as "she
knows so many of the PSD group"; Nguyen Ngoc Cam sent season's greet-
ings and his Houston address; and the interpreter nicknamed "Long 1" was
in touch with quite a few of his former colleagues.[84] Even decades later, the
letter writer Truong (now calling himself "Mike T. Truong"), continued
to feel that his family belonged in the *Newsletter*, he showed, by sending
a photograph of himself and his son arriving at an Indonesian island in
1975 sure that other readers would share his pride at having survived such
desperate circumstances (figure 6.7).

A former OPS employee referred to as Madame Binh (full name never
provided) was among the most active socialites. A secretary to PSD Saigon,
she had moved to Texas. By 1977, she had been in contact with at least four
former OPS, and was, the *Newsletter* promised, eager "to hear from others."

She visited ex-OPS, attended an OPS luncheon in Dallas, and traveled to Washington, DC, for an OPS wedding, where she saw several other people from the OPS community.[85] Binh was a powerful engine of connection between former OPS employees of both nationalities, giving news of new migrants' arrivals and encouraging them to put themselves on the *Newsletter* mailing list.[86] When she connected with other Vietnamese former OPS office workers, Binh was sure the US American former OPS workers would want to know details.[87] She was equally sure that readers would want to know about her new life: that she worked at the American Heart Association, was proud of a new granddaughter, and "had another car accident in Nov. but not as bad as the one in 1976."[88] This was a genuine personal relationship, or at least one imagined as such by the writer, editors, and some readers.

One remarkable case allows for a glimpse of something less innocuous to emerge from these anodyne accounts of social engagements. A former OPS employee wrote to the *Newsletter* that he had "lunch recently with VTN [yes, VTN] Police General Loan," a former counterpart running a restaurant.[89] Al Turner also lunched with Loan, who "owned a pizzeria in Virginia. We used to go down there and drink and talk," Turner remembered. He had met Loan when he was promoted to Saigon; his counterpart there, Major Tru, was "the #1 right arm of General [Nguyen Ngoc] Loan [Chief of National Police]." Loan, Turner informed me, was "the person pictured in the famous picture shooting a VC."[90]

Andrew Friedman recounts the controversy precipitated when the press discovered that Loan, running his pizza parlor in Burke, Virginia, was indeed the shooter in Eddie Adams's world-famous photograph from 1968 of a flak-jacketed soldier executing a man in handcuffs at close range.

The INS initiated deportation procedures, bringing charges of war crimes, which Loan beat with the help of "an army of defenders."[91] Perhaps this number included ex-OPS.

With acrid wit, Turner remembered Loan as a "hell of a nice guy. He was as vicious as they come. That was the type of place it was. Interesting times."[92] Despite the sarcasm audible in Turner's "hell of a nice guy," Turner *did* think Loan was a nice guy—enough to visit for "drink and talk," at least. Ambivalence seems to have gripped Turner in retrospect, perhaps producing the double reminder of context, both place and time ("the type of place. . . . Interesting times"), which we might read as a plea for understanding how he had found himself breaking bread with such a person. Loan's presence reminds us that what violence workers shared and what knit them together had to do with having collaborated in massively destructive events such as the US imperial interventions of the Cold War period.

I am not interested here in detailing the sins OPS may have committed, enabled, or excused. Other critics have covered that ground. My point is that however accurate the accusations against them, they felt themselves to be victims rather than perpetrators, and that such a feeling matters. It has pulled people into unexpected alliances (ex-OPS and refugees, workers and millionaires) that became influential political currents, in the 1980s channeled by Reagan, and brought again to the surface via Trump. Simple accusations of wrongdoing cast no light on these dynamics. Observers seeking to understand the history of the US punitive turn must understand people affectively, particularly when there have been such tremendous consequences from their pain.

For not only did North Americans working abroad bring the tactics and mindsets of counterinsurgency back to US policing, reinforcing the domestic carceral state.[93] Nor does the story end with the pro-punishment populism nurtured by the anguish of exile. In one final wrinkle of this increasingly strange tale, some ex-OPS managed to restage their collaborations after the fall. Some refugees who had been OPS counterparts in South Vietnam found jobs in the field of policing, often thanks to North American former Public Safety personnel who helped them look for work. They fortified the texture of carcerality by integrating pieces—people—formed abroad, when the former proxy agents of empire were transplanted to US soil.

In an astonishing twist, some refugees came full circle through watery or-
deals of statelessness all the way back into the bosom of the US state, finding
jobs in violence work, once again the colleagues of US police.

Sometimes it was former Public Safety personnel who found the migrants
this work. The ex-ops working as chief of police of Bladensburg, Maryland, hired the man who had been "a PSD Saigon Interpreter/Translator up
to 1966" as a dispatcher for his department.[94] J. B. Carnahan's driver from
Vietnam lived with him and his family in Alaska for a time; Carnahan
helped the man get work in his police department as a bailiff custodian.[95]
While churches were the more common institutional refugee sponsors, one
ex-ops wrote that he had tapped another potential body: his police department. He was "encouraging the local Police Department to sponsor one
or two NP [National Police (Vietnam)] refugees."[96] This surprising notice
of police involvement in refugee relief is actually a fairly logical extension of
their service charge, showing that police work can expand in whatever direction its era demands. If the department did do as suggested, that certainly would have facilitated police work for qualified candidates.

In other cases people found such labor without ex-ops help, or else the
assistance was not clear. An ops "friend and former counterpart, Pham
Cong Thanh," the *Newsletter* informed, was "doing well in Dallas, where
he works for the city in a security position. He is now shooting in local
police combat matches."[97] A later mention emphasized the continuity in
this man's positions: "Major Thanh was assigned to a training school as a
firearms instructor in Saigon. He is now doing about the same thing for
the Dallas Police Department."[98] Another former counterpart had settled
in Page, Arizona, working "for the city as a dispatcher, truck driver and
inspector for both the police and fire departments."[99]

Nor did the *Newsletter* limit itself to celebrating such work for counterparts, proper; one counterpart's *brother*, it reported, had found work
"walking the beat enforcing parking regulations in Arlington."[100] The ops
"family" was willing to extend fictive kinship along bloodlines. Police work
was also not the only cause for notice; private security work was equally
pleasing to note, as in the former Lao police chief of the narcotics bureau,
sponsored by ex-ops, who was by late 1977 "working as a security guard for
the H-Pilot Coal plant in Ashland," or the former NP captain who had secured a post "in the administration end of a large Security Patrol Company

in Bakersfield, CA."[101] The imagined community extended its shelter well over the strict borders of *police*.

This solidarity between North American and Southeast Asian former and current violence workers was not an expression of racial tolerance, and the broad resentment ex-OPS expressed at government bodies from Congress to the CIA to OPS itself did not compromise their thoroughgoing US nationalism. The ethnocentric conservatism of this antistate position continued unruffled, as summarized in Andy Best's unequivocal statement, "I believe very strongly that the American system is far superior to anything that was ever put together on this planet and I have tremendous positive thoughts about how much better it's going to get. I'm sorry that I'm not working 50 hours a week in law enforcement because of my age and this sort of thing, but I still have tremendous support for what's going on, for what's wrong and what needs to be improved."[102] Similar statements were expressed throughout the *Newsletter*'s pages across the years. Other patterns, such as frequent mention of Christian churches and god, and the many ex-OPS strongly engaged with the National Rifle Association, suggest the texture of their beliefs.[103]

The paradox in this politics sheds light on the conservative surge of the 1980s, particularly when placed in relation to the celebration of independence noted in the refugee stories. The antigovernment sentiment suffusing the Vietnam-era left had its echo, as scholars have extensively explored, in the antigovernment neoconservative Reagan right.[104] For this significant political bloc, dependence on government largesse was a capital sin (pun intended), emblematized in the viciously disparaged trope of the "welfare queen." The era saw the cuts in government benefits and the disintegration of the social safety net, alongside the tax and regulative bounty for corporations that have amplified US inequality in the last forty years. The figure of the independent refugee is the antiwelfare queen, a quintessential evocation of the model-minority stereotype as alibi for retributive antiblack social policy.[105] Recycling the ever-ready frontier myth of pioneer independence and its urban heir, the "self-made" man, the independent refugee signaled the impending mania for "small government"—small in every way but punitive capacity, as Gilmore and Gilmore have written of the "antistate state."[106]

Former OPS agents were unlike other conservative Americans—especially other veterans of the Vietnam conflict—in their pro-Vietnamese views and actions. Their experiences in OPS had bestowed upon them the ability to differentiate southern ally from northern communist, and to identify with the former. But they were a part of the national trend in their nationalist, pro-law enforcement positions, as in their feelings of betrayal and disappointment after the US defeat and withdrawal from the war.

Public Safety alums shared with a larger conservative current a tragic sense of collective injury, an unresolved, melancholic loss. Their specific case helps to refract the larger structure of feeling in which they formulated their scattershot antielitism. Sara Ahmed has beautifully analyzed right-wing nationalism in the United Kingdom as a product of felt harm; as she puts it, "hate generates its object as a defense against injury."[107] In the United States, this insight helps explain why small-government campaigners endorsed one avenue of government activity, the punitive. Here lies another reason to reject the notion that this conservatism emerged as racist backlash against "liberal excesses" or strategic mistakes by the civil rights movement.[108]

This contextualization also helps locate the rise of right-wing conservatism in the transnational sphere of empire in which it belongs. While many astute readers have pointed out the raw racism feeding this cohort, the view of transnational solidarities with nonwhite agents of empire outside the United States refines our sense of its formation. Recognizing that the roots of the punishment paradigm lie in the disaffections of exile underlines the tragic lost opportunity for coalition building in the service of a genuinely just antielitism.

CONCLUSION

OPS officers had not come home alone. In their wake a host of remnant colonial subjects traveled too, weaving their distinct filaments into the fabric of the US state. All the former OPS employees, gringo and foreign-born, were part of the endeavor we refer to with the shorthand "police"—violence workers—the heart of the concept of the state. They internalized that commonality profoundly enough to reproduce it after exile without the mediation of a colonial client state. Their collaborations were undeniably laden with the psychic burdens of racial prejudice, geopolitical hierarchy, and projection across an abyss of collateral differences. Nonetheless, friendship and collegiality between Southeast Asian migrants and gung-ho Yankee cops were vigorously cultivated on both sides, and the resulting relations were genuinely intimate.

Nationals of the US neocolonies Vietnam, Laos, and Cambodia leaned on backgrounds of OPS collaboration to navigate their devastating dislocations. Once proxy agents of US global power in colonial outposts, they installed themselves in the bosom of its national territory. Some were even employed by a police organization, some small branch of that state. While most of these were not gun-carrying, uniformed officers, as dispatchers or drivers they were nonetheless pieces of the police apparatus then busily involved in suppressing domestic dissent, the US territorial complement of the forces they had battled to subdue across the seas. They integrated a political subculture we rarely imagine as interracial, transnational, or anti-state. Their travels reveal a transnational geography of state activity, a map of the coloniality of power (re)constituted via spatial redistribution.[109]

In a brilliantly apt coinage, Andrew Friedman calls anticommunist Vietnamese in northern Virginia "repatriates of empire" to emphasize the continuity between imperial landscapes abroad and at home retraced by the refugees' movements.[110] Friedman is writing about people in the specific landscape anchored by CIA headquarters and the bucolic neighborhoods where the agency's busy bees spent leisurely nights. But anticommunist Southeast Asian refugees anywhere in the United States performed this beneficent deed: they coconstituted a projected space of empire, a salve for the wounds inflicted by those dread liberals in Congress. Refugees conferred a tinge of imperial continuity on the locations of their stateside encounters. And those who found work as police picked up unfinished collaborations as if their shared project might yet be accomplished.

The relationships this chapter has displayed show that in the wake of the fall of Saigon and the unavoidable fact of the US failure in that war, surrounded by antiwar and countercultural voices, and betrayed (they thought) by Congress's termination of their program, former OPS employees felt great solidarity with others who had also been forced to evacuate. They felt unwelcome and alienated from their government, too. Vietnamese and other Southeast Asian exiles, particularly police officers, and even more specifically individual police officers with whom OPS had worked, felt nobler to them—and made them feel nobler—than many of their fellow US citizens. In other words, ex-OPS officers felt that they too shouldered the burdens of exile.

We expect to find the pain of exile in refugees, of course, and perhaps in antiwar or other dissident groups who disagree with their governments or suffer state oppression, and maybe even in returning soldiers in whom it can be medicalized as "PTSD."[111] But in this chapter we have seen it in people who could lay claim to the most intimate of relations with the state. As discussed in previous portions of this book, police are theoretically coextensive to the state, a personification of that ostensibly definitional monopoly on legitimate violence. Yet they too throbbed with the harmonics of nostalgia, disappointment, and bitterness.

With ex-OPS personnel as our entrée, we learn more about the right-wing populism of this period, seeing its relation to a refugee structure of feeling. In the agony of exile afflicting North American subjects at the apex of US imperial power are truths regarding the notion of nation in the abstract: how easily the concord of nation is shattered, thanks to the sly seductions of the infinitely variable, always-toxic concept of "home." How nationalism is invariably made up of transnational pieces, in this case as an identification that remained deeply nationalist even as it leapt territorial lines.[112] How badly we need to reject any notion of natural coherence between nation and state. The recognition that police, quintessential avatars of state power, could feel alienation from their state is acid to the supposed tensile integrity of the nation-state. Its logic is ruptured by the understanding that *police* could identify with foreigners more intensely than their fellow citizens. The state is inadequate to contain even those social formations that most profoundly imagined themselves in state systems.

The former Public Safety agents, US- and foreign-born, stretched a transnational, anticommunist sense of *being police* well beyond racial or national bounds. If there is a feeling of paradox here, it reflects primarily the inadequacy of our terms for these objects.

A structure of feeling can point to submerged historical narratives, untapped potential, loose threads. Locating an "actively lived structure of feeling," as Raymond Williams acolytes write, allows us "to retrace the lines from the past to the present, pursuing alternate but suppressed narratives—the 'consciousness of aspirations and possibilities'—in order to differently understand the present" and explore "cul-de-sacs where unrealized possibilities were stranded."[113] Loose threads in the recent past are particularly urgent, for we yet twist and yearn in the shared currents of their possibilities. The recent past is strewn with these raw nerve endings, janglingly susceptible to the unrealized, to what could have been, to the ways we—for this past is in no way another country—have affected each other, and might yet move in concert.

The structure of feeling this chapter reveals is laden with the anguish of the *unheimlich*, the unsettled.[114] In it we see how the pain of empire afflicts the imperial center, starkly outlined on the minor figures who do the piece-work of the state. In the tensions afflicting violence workers we recognize yet another of the infinite ways in which the state is not a seamless mono-lith but splintered, riven. Breakable.

Reckoning with Police Lethality

We live in a profoundly violent world. The police killings in the United States that have appeared to be epidemic since Ferguson are the tip of the iceberg. Below the visible surface are the wrenching injustices of poverty and inequality, brutal prison systems, and the displacement and dispossession in places mined for human and natural resources or torn apart by war. The fact that so many people in the world are on the move—perhaps more so than at any point since the flows of New World colonization—is a sign of the stress inflicted on a huge number of creatures, human and other, and on our planet.[1]

Worlds of suffering, as Mary Louise Pratt has written: "vast zones of exclusion inhabited by millions of socially organized people who are and know themselves to be utterly dispensable to the global order of production and consumption. . . . A rapid immiseration, ecological devastation, and a destruction of lifeways unprecedented in human history."[2]

Across the disciplines and around far-flung corners of the globe, people have tried to describe life subject to this level of violence, or the mode of governance that produces it. Étienne Balibar suggests we have passed into "a world of the banality of objective cruelty which goes beyond the reproduction of structures."[3] Bertrand Ogilvie's *homme jetable*, or disposable man; the Argentine and then Latin American *población chatarra*, or junk people; Agamben's *homo sacer*, a "sacred man" living in conditions of "bare life"; Biehl's "social abandonment"; and Mbembe's necropolitics are all attempts to describe such conditions.[4] This series of coinages wrestles to comprehend the infliction of war, poverty, and disenfranchisement on a vast scale. Pratt's "impression," she writes, is that this is unique, "that such a situation has not existed before now, certainly not on this planetary scale."

It isn't that our era features the most violent conditions humans have ever inflicted. There is no constant line of upward growth. State-market violence during the massive dispossessions of the enclosure period in early modern Europe, for example, or the early years of colonial genocide and the slave trade, were likely moments as devastatingly lethal in their misery as the necropolitical 2000s.[5] But from the late middle of the twentieth century to our day, it seems that the world as a whole has become more violent.

Perhaps such a bald claim is impossible to prove. Would any data set be adequate to the empirical confirmation that violence overall has grown? Moreover, as the introduction wondered, what do we even mean by "violence?" How could we render the infinite and irresolvable types of dispossession into math? In the objection that a global surge in violence could not be quantified, I find reason to explore it all the more. The mania with data-driven research distorts critical inquiry.[6] A claim that cannot be verified with numbers, in contrast, must be scrutinized, pondered, contemplated. It is good for thinking. This final section of the book takes up this challenge, contemplating contemporary violence by observing what I see as two key constitutive dynamics. One is that inequality has grown. The other is that repressive technology has "improved." This conclusion walks through the paired, metalevel argument that the one-two punch of rising inequality and technological innovation has extended sanctioned killing fields in our day, thanks to what Pratt describes as the "particularly grotesque and systematic peculiarities of the reorganizing of the world by neoliberalism."[7]

Neoliberal capitalism, that market-worshipping economic approach inflicted on the world beginning in the 1970s, has concentrated economic power in the hands of ever smaller numbers of people while relentlessly immiserating everyone else. Neoliberalism exacerbated a global rise in inequality ongoing since the early nineteenth century. Researchers for UNICEF note that "global income inequality rose steadily from 1820 to 2002," accelerating after the 1970s. By now, alas, "we inhabit a planet in which the top quintile controls more than 80 percent of global income contrasted by a paltry percentage point for those at the bottom." Ours is a world, they write, "deeply corroded by income disparities."[8]

Because the United States appropriated so much more than its fair share of the world's wealth, the trend looks slightly different here: a period of relatively greater equality in the early Cold War preceded the rise of inequality. "America in the 1950s and 1960s was more egalitarian than it had been in more than a century," Robert Putnam has observed. "By the end of the twentieth century the gap between rich and poor in the United States had been increasing for nearly three decades, the longest sustained increase in inequality for at least a century."[9] Nor can we hope that the poor improved their lot in life, too, just less so than the rich, for this period saw a rise in real and tangible poverty. Gilmore reminds us of the impact of US federal government and financial institutions' decisions in the early 1970s. "The 1973 wage freeze was prelude to a twenty-five-year decline in ordinary people's real purchasing power, made instantly harsh as workers tried to buy necessities at inflated prices with devalued greenbacks," and conditions for the US poor further deteriorated amid the massive unemployment and displacement that followed.[10]

At this point, nobody contests these figures. So thoroughly have critics captured the debate over rich-poor gaps that even the smug field of economics has been forced to concede that capitalism is not on its way to enriching us all. With data-laden tables and an astonishing lack of engagement with Marx, Thomas Piketty's *Capital in the Twentieth Century* refuted the bullish notion that capitalism eventually levels off economic inequality (the Kuznets curve).[11] Instead, the arc we see (when we see any arc at all) is the "spectacular U-shape evolution" Emmanuel Saez and Gabriel Zucman trace from earlier inequality to the "substantial democratization" of the Great Depression through the 1970s, and back up to the tremendous levels of wealth disparity we see today.[12] Capitalism's gloves are off; no longer can analysts counsel patience so that trickle-down or the Kuznets curve can go to work. Instead "the class violence that is capitalism" is backlit for all to see.[13]

People subject to these forms of violence react decisively. The more they experience its ravages, the more they attempt to change the conditions of their lives. They opt out of poorly paid or wageless labor, create informal economies, migrate to sites of greater opportunity, and otherwise secede from state-market capture. Subsequently, in soulless escalation, they meet violence in its simplest, most immediate forms: guns, walls, borders, cages.

In other words, the more unequal are social relations, the more violence is required to preserve social hierarchies, and a cycle of exacerbated inequality and correspondingly greater violence can ensue as elites attempt to keep other people from leaving or revolting.[14]

In this viciously circular relationship, the more people are subject to state-market violence, the more their attempts to escape and thrive exacerbate the exercise of violence. All the more, researchers have shown, they inflict violence—"the fruit of poverty"—upon each other.[15] All the more, therefore, must violence workers ply their trades. Alexis de Tocqueville understood, two hundred years ago, that "the manners of society become more humane and gentle, in proportion as men become more equal and alike."[16] Jeffrey Reiman published the first edition of his incisive *The Rich Get Richer and the Poor Get Prison* (now in its tenth revision) in 1979; his insight that rising inequality is accompanied by prison growth is still indispensable.[17] Heidi Rimke recalls the real bottom line: capital destabilizes, requiring police.[18]

This is precisely what has happened over the last forty years in the United States, as this book has observed. As neoliberalism exacerbated inequality, police-inflected violence expanded and intensified.[19] Police forces mushroomed, budgets spreading like stains, and their fatal impact followed suit. How much, how badly? As with violence overall, police violence is somewhere between difficult and impossible to quantify. How should we think about police violence in a way that allows us to appreciate its magnitude?

Since Michael Brown's murder, a series of determined activist projects have attempted to address the question. Websites including "Killed by Police," "Fatal Encounters," "Mapping Police Violence," and the *Guardian*'s highly respected "The Counted" cross-reference news reports, crowd-sourced data, their own reporting, and official statistics such as those collected by the Bureau of Justice Statistics (BJS) or the FBI, suggesting the magnitude of police killings. They confirm the profound racism of police killings, the higher rate of such killings in the United States as opposed to other countries, the high percentage of all homicides committed by police, and the high likelihood that unarmed people will perish at the hands of police.[20] Impressive as these efforts are, they are very recent, counting deaths at most over the last four or five years.

Little help is available from the authorities. Despite government mania with statistical tracking in other arenas, official figures on police use of deadly force are unwieldy at best. The Justice Department began counting "justifiable homicides" by police only in 1963, but too few police departments contributed for the figures to hold up to comparison with the next stage of reporting. From 1968 to 1975, they counted "justifiable homicides" (the victims categorically defined as "felons") but never *un*justified police killings, allowing any deaths determined to be unlawful to be folded into the broader statistics for murder. As BJS statisticians explained in 2001: "one statistic that is impossible to obtain . . . (. . . from any currently existing database) is the number of murders by police. . . . Nothing in the database distinguishes murders by police officers from murders committed by others. Consequently the annual number of nonjustifiable homicides by police in the United States is unknown."[21] In 2000, BJS began to report deaths in custody, a new category that includes deaths in jails and prisons.[22] A component of deaths in custody, "arrest-related deaths" began to be counted in 2003, including homicides, suicides, accidents, death by natural causes, and causes "unknown," all again reported by police—and, participation in the report project was voluntary, at least until 2009.[23]

Government data collectors have been far more attentive when police are victims rather than perpetrators. Cases in which police are injured or killed in action are ideologically productive and so a great engine of spectacle hums around them, working to elevate police deaths to the level of political argument (the "Blue Lives Matter" retort). Recall, from this book's introduction, that the number of police killed on the job is far lower than casualties in agriculture or industry. Policing is simply not that dangerous of an occupation. More to the point, police deaths are infinitesimal in relation to the damage police inflict even if you restrict the equation to police homicides rather than the cumulative and intertangled lethalities of violence work.

That, however, would be a mistake. To see homicides as the primary category of police-inflicted harm is to misunderstand that damage dramatically. Police murder is only the most spectacular way police cause premature death, not the most common, certainly not the most insidious. In the period this book covers, police conferred lethality through a series of direct and indirect channels, many widened by LEAA-funded technology in "weaponry, communications systems, surveillance techniques, and intelligence operations," as chapter 1 noted.[24] One simple change involved the shift from revolvers to semiautomatic weapons.[25] Another was the SWAT team, whose contribution to police-inflicted death is sobering. SWAT teams sow death in the force they levy and the reactions they provoke, as sleeping citizens fumble to protect themselves against masked intruders who look more like burglars than the law. They have lowered the bar for warrants for no-knock entries, and their carelessness in ensuring that informants have provided a genuine suspect or even the right address is well documented, as are the copycat home invasions they enable by villains not in state employ. In 1972, there were a few hundred of these violently intrusive drug raids annually in the United States; by the early 1980s, that number had jumped to 3,000 annually. By 1996, it was up to 30,000 a year, and by 2001, the number was 40,000. SWAT-style units are now deployed not for the situations people cited to justify their creation, hostage taking and police standoffs, but simply to serve warrants, or even just to patrol. As Radley Balko and Diane Weber have shown, these developments have made US police vastly more lethal in action.[26]

More windingly fatal are technologies such as communications and surveillance systems. Yet data-gathering capacities bequeathed to police by OPS and other counterinsurgency practitioners were no neutral observational tools. Armored vehicles may be dramatic, Gilmore and Gilmore note, but "what matters more in terms of police legitimacy and power are more subtle objects such as standard-issue handguns, or out-of-sight capacities such as computerized profiling."[27] As Kirsten Weld argues regarding such systems in Guatemala (organized with the help of OPS), "the most lethal tools sent to Guatemala's police by the United States were not guns, munitions or helicopters but file cards and filing cabinets," enabling and justifying the most murderous policies of the US-backed dictatorship.[28] In the related context of the United States, these same OPS-inspired, LEAA-bequeathed systems, "along with training from federal officials, led to considerably higher rates of crime reporting from police agencies to the FBI for inclusion in its annual crime reports," those all-powerful alibis for tough-on-crime policymaking, as Mark Mauer observed.[29]

Perhaps most important in sheer numbers of people profoundly affected, are police contributions to incarceration. As we now know thanks to historical debunking of the "rising crime" myth, prison populations began to rise in the 1970s as legislators passed laws extending, even doubling, jail and prison sentences. Over the decade beginning in the late 1960s, global currents of anticommunist paranoia flowed home to mix with the United States' long histories of antiblack and procapital policing, conflating the offenses of crime and dissent, and seeding public support for vicious containment. The federal government reinstated the death penalty, felon disfranchisement, and the chain gang; created new federal sentencing guidelines that included extensions of capital crimes; and launched the drug war. As the federal level widened the net and tightened the noose, many states passed even harsher measures, launching the life-shortening, penury-inducing destitution of hyperincarceration.[30]

Prisons can be built and laws passed, but without the lever of police, no bodies will find themselves in cages. Enabled by legislation and armed by the counterinsurgency-era LEAA, police were ready when the bait of crack cocaine hit the streets. Drug offenses increased arrests eleven times between 1980 and 2001, while the probability that arrest would result in imprisonment more than doubled, and the number of people incarcerated for nonviolent offenses and violent crimes both tripled even as violent crime sunk to historic lows.[31] In the 1980s, an arrested person's chance of doing prison time soared, and sentence severity and sentence time served both increased, so the effect of "doubling the number of police officers . . . tripled the number of people in prison and jail."[32]

When our reckoning extends to the prison system that arrests feed, the slow death that is prison (though it is not always slow) changes the calculus of police lethality exponentially. The truly incriminating numbers are not those related to deaths in custody, but to custody, period. In a striking attempt to measure the public health impact of mass incarceration, epidemiologist Ernest Drucker considers the 7.3 million people in prison, on parole, or on probation, another 14 million arrested and held in jails, and their families, including 25 million children "exposed" to the disease by having a parent removed to a prison cell. Calculating prison's damage in the public health units of "years of life lost"—a definition notably compatible with Gilmore's understanding of violence—Drucker finds the Rockefeller drug laws three times worse than the World Trade Center attack, and drug incarcerations at least as bad as the ravages of AIDS.[33]

Even this calculus, however, underestimates police lethality. Yes: even recognizing the vast misery of the United States' obscene prison system as the handiwork of police still fails to appreciate the full police quota of contemporary violence. For not only are police essential to the overall lethality of the criminal justice system, but myths about police work function to justify all aspects of state-market violence, including war abroad and poverty at home. The alibi "police" provide for the state-market to go about its deadly business—as if the state were purely political and the market autonomous therefrom, as if civilian forces operated to contain only the dangerous at home and militaries expressed the benign state's political will abroad, as if nation-states were contained by their borders into well-bounded corporate bodies, interacting in tidy, well-regulated choreographies—this alibi ramifies across the planet, justifying dispossession through environmental destruction, the displacements of war, the violent suppression of unruly economies, brutal border control, and coercive spatial concentrations from ghettos to refugee camps. All of these, together with "domestic" criminal justice systems, represented out front by police, mesh to ensure the preservation of neoliberalism's inequities. This is the fruit of the labor that is violence work.

Somehow we must grasp this vast and banal terror. Police forces have grown in tandem with the private security industry, military capacity, academic fields of criminology, prison systems, and more, adding new technologies and methods across the interlinked fields of policing, security, war, academe, and prison to make range of violence work stunningly, intolerably lethal.

If it is true that inequality and technological development are at the base of this growth, the solutions are fairly clear. Technological development goes only in one direction; the part of lethality that reflects new tech cannot be undone. It is just as well, to avoid any temptation of technological determinism, and in any case, some new technologies pull in the other direction, such as cell phone videos of police abuse or the social media worlds in which they circulate and can galvanize protest. The violence-feeding factor that is within our control is inequality.

We can mitigate this violence only by making the world more fair. The task of resource redistribution is urgent. Racialized class inequalities must be addressed directly: policing cannot be split off and reformed in isolation from the economic order it serves. As Robert Reiner concludes from his long study of the history of police politics, "Democratic policing can be approximated to only in a context of social, not just liberal—and certainly not neo-liberal—democracy."[34] This is not to suggest that protestors should leave off their attempts to critique the police and focus *instead* on resource redistribution. On the contrary, police are all the more important targets of protest from this perspective, because policing's pretensions to legitimacy are so vital to the control function it performs. Policing enjoys widespread public opinion that its violence is legitimate because of its status as a carefully circumscribed, locally controlled and accountable, limited, public, civilian project dedicated not to the interests of capital nor the control of political opposition but simply to the containment of "crime."

Under contemporary conditions, governments need this legitimacy. They cannot rely on naked shows of force, for the conceits of democracy require at least some modicum of consent (though some would argue that this, too, is diminishing in our world of viciously enforced misery).[35] The capitalist state has had to negotiate this dilemma from its earliest historical moment; it conceded universal suffrage in a compromise with the rising classes of early industrial capitalism. It has had to secure consent, or, as Gramsci understood, to disguise its coercions as consensual.[36] As the still-unsurpassed work of the Birmingham school of cultural studies, *Policing the Crisis*, observed, in democracies, as class divisions widen and the working class grows in size, the law must maintain its appearance of legitimacy.[37] Police accomplish that, as long as people fail to protest their normal, quotidian, unexceptional work.

All this points to a sobering clinch: inasmuch as protests against police militarization or incidental police racism grant the categories that sustain the fiction of a benevolent state, autonomous from the market, they reinforce the damage they hope to curtail. Terrible power conceals itself behind the consequential myths of the criminal justice system, beginning with "crime" but extending immediately to those myths that posit police violence as exceptional: "police militarization," "paramilitarism," "police racism," "racial profiling," "excessive use of force," "police brutality," "police state," "police privatization," and, underlying all of these, "state" and "market" as autonomous realms. Today, appeals to respect the democratic tradition of police find resonance in policies to widen the net and reinforce the mechanisms of repression.

In working for justice at the hands of police, then, let us not imagine that police circulate in narrow ambits, nor that the history of US policing is anything but a thoroughly transnational story. Let us not protest police militarization nor decry police privatization. The police have not militarized or privatized, for they have always already been military and private in essence. They have simply grown more deadly, as have formally military and private security forces as well, in tandem with rising inequality and thanks to technological change. There lies a worthy target of critique: the lethal capacity of state-market violence inflicted at home *and* abroad. Instead of protesting this or that minor fragment of police practice, let us think *through* police to this broader context, and aim there, to short-circuit the transnational exchange upon which this mortal containment relies. A wealth of activist protests against "free trade," from Beijing to the Zapatistas to Seattle, and against oppressive state power, from Tahrir Square to Occupy and Black Lives Matter, as well as a watershed of wonderful intellectual work pulling against the legitimacy of state violence, suggests that the moment is ripe for this new angle of approach.[38]

Understanding that the uniformed municipal, civilian, public police are only ever one part of a broader violence apparatus is essential to understanding power. This book has spotlit a narrow sliver of the carceral state-market assemblage in order to gesture more widely to the United States' grossly expanded will to punish, persecute, and impoverish beginning in the mid–Cold War. In Cold War police forces' multiple border crossings we can see that police are not a force of good deployed against "crime" but channels for the distribution of state-market violence racially, spatially, and in the interests of capital—and often against the interests of the people channeling this power, who can be equally disempowered by its applications. Through the carefully circumscribed notion of *police*, violence is visited upon those who might disrupt aggregations of capital and privilege, and explained away to the watching world with the fictions of its democratic restraint.

A P P E N D I X

INTERVIEWS

"Ned Antonik." August 27, 2011. Pseudonym.

Andrew Best, Jr. November 15, 2010. No pseudonym.

Richard Burton. July 24, 2012. No pseudonym. Interview not used.

Jan Carnahan. July 11, 2012. No pseudonym.

"Midge Good." January 30, 2012. Pseudonym. Interview not used.

Morris Grodsky. October 27, 2010; November 1, 2010; November 8, 2010; November 21, 2010. No pseudonym.

Michael Harpold. September 7, 2011. No pseudonym.

Al Turner. May 18, 2011; May 25, 2011. No pseudonym.

ABBREVIATIONS

AID (or USAID)   United States Agency for International Development

BioReg   *Biographic Register*

CRC   City Records Collection, Los Angeles, CA

FSL   *Foreign Service List*

GPO   Government Publishing Office

IACP   International Association of Chiefs of Police

IAPA   Inter-American Police Academy

IMBPC   Index to the Minutes of the Board of Police Commissioners (Los Angeles)

IPA   International Police Academy

IPS   Internal Defense and Public Safety

MBPC   Minutes of the Board of Police Commissioners (Los Angeles)

NARA   United States National Archives and Records Administration, College Park

NOBLE   National Organization of Black Law Enforcement Executives

NYT   *New York Times*

OPS   Office of Public Safety

PSN   *Public Safety Newsletter*

SOA   School of the Americas

NOTES

Epigraph: Reiner, *Politics of the Police*, xiii.

INTRODUCTION

1　This phrasing relies on Gilmore, *Golden Gulag*, 28.
2　Feagin and Hahn, *Ghetto Revolts*; Murakawa, *First Civil Right*, 72; J. T. Camp, *Incarcerating the Crisis*, 12.
3　Takagi, "Garrison State."
4　Committee Against Police Abuse pamphlet, 1975, Box 1, Folder 12, "Police Brutality, 1975–1994," Frank I. Sanchez collection, # MSS612BC, Center for Southwest Research Activist manuscript collections, University of New Mexico, Albuquerque.
5　Skolnick and Fyfe, *Above the Law*, 77.
6　NOBLE, "NOBLE: An Overview," 3.
7　Hinds, "Police Use of Force"; E. J. Escobar, "Bloody Christmas"; M. S. Johnson, *Street Justice*; C. Agee, *Streets of San Francisco*; Kelley, "Thug Nation"; Murakawa, *First Civil Right*; Maguire and King, "Trends in the Policing Industry"; Uchida, "Development of the American Police."
8　Harring et al., "Management of Police Killings."
9　Platt, "Obama's Task Force on Policing."
10　Takagi, "LEAA's Research Solicitation," 58; Platt, "Obama's Task Force on Policing."
11　Walker, "Between Two Worlds," 24; Brown, *Working the Street*.
12　C. Agee, *Streets of San Francisco*; Balko, *Overkill*, 11; Center for Research on Criminal Justice, *Iron Fist*; Gilmore and Gilmore, "Beyond Bratton," 182–83; Greene and Mastrofski, *Community Policing*; Hansford, "Community Policing Reconsidered"; Harcourt, *Illusion of Order*, 46–47; Herbert, *Citizens, Cops, and Power*; Mitchell, Attoh, and Staeheli, "Broken Windows"; Moraff, "Community Policing"; Skogan, "Community's Role in Community Policing."
13　Wilkerson, "Emmet Till and Tamir Rice"; J. Feldman, "Roland Fryer Is Wrong"; LaCapria, "Harvard Study"; Balko, "Why It's Impossible"; Drucker, *Plague of Prisons*; Harris and Curtis, *Millennium Breach*. See also the discussion of police lethality in this book's conclusion.

14 Cohen, "Punitive City"; two excellent analyses of the process of turning good countercarceral intentions into net-widening policies are Schept, *Progressive Punishment*, and Story, "Prison in the City."

15 Camp and Heatherton, "We Charge Genocide"; "Chicago BLM Activist"; Gilmore and Gilmore, "Beyond Bratton"; Hasson, "Black Lives Matter Attorney"; Herzing, "Big Dreams and Bold Steps"; Kaba, "Summer Heat"; Martin, "Policing Is a Dirty Job"; M. D. Smith, "In Order to End Police."

16 Wagner, *Disturbing the Police*, 48.

17 Banton, *Policeman in the Community*; E. J. Watts, "Police in Atlanta"; E. J. Watts, "Police Priorities"; Rubenstein, *City Police*; Carte and Carte, *Police Reform*; Center for Research on Criminal Justice, *Iron Fist*; Walker, *Critical History*; Fogelson, *Big-City Police*; Miller, *Cops and Bobbies*; Richardson, *New York Police*; Monkkonen, *Police in Urban America*; D. Johnson, *American Law Enforcement*; Harring, *Policing a Class Society*. In Britain the models are even older: as late as 1991, a collection of historical essays on colonial policing in the British empire could still organize itself in relation to a classic published in 1952; see Anderson and Killingray, *Policing the Empire*.

18 Dulaney, *Black Police in America*; Appier, *Policing Women*; E. J. Escobar, *Race, Police*; E. J. Escobar, "Bloody Christmas"; Burt, "Tony Rios and Bloody Christmas"; Pagán, *Murder at the Sleepy Lagoon*; Bolton Jr. and Feagin, *Black in Blue*; Wolcott, *Cops and Kids*; Kitaeff, *Jews in Blue*; Moore, *Black Rage in New Orleans*.

19 Canaday, *Straight State*, 5; Balogh, "State of the State," 458; Sewell, *Logics of History*, 3–6; Arno Mayer, interviewed in Grandin and Joseph, *Century of Revolution*, 419, 11; see Kramer, "Power and Connection," for a marvelous discussion of historians' denial of US empire, a key part of the avoidance of the state. The history of the police I pursue in this book is a transnational, imperial history along the lines Kramer encourages.

20 Balogh, "State of the State." A well-taken exception is the school of "everyday state formation," which follows nonelites back to the state, positing state formation as a quotidian process guided by elites and nonelites in conversation. See Joseph and Nugent, *Everyday Forms of State Formation*; Wolfe, *Everyday Nation-State*; Auyero, *Patients of the State*. The dearth of histories of the police power in the US is also due to federalism and the legal fiction of the ostensible allocation of police power to the states. This has deterred scholars (not only historians) from investigations into the police power broadly since the earliest years of the twentieth century. As Dubber puts it, "The history of the federal police power in the United States . . . has been the history of its denial." Dubber, "New Police Science," 121. See also Tomlins, "Necessities of State."

21 Shearing, "Unrecognized Origins of the New Policing," 219; Johnston, *Rebirth of Private Policing*, 117. Note that Dubber and Valverde, "Introduction," 2, praise those legal historians who have revived the subject of police, including Pasquale Pasquino, Nikolas Rose, Mitchell Dean, William Novak, and Chris Tomlins.

22 Neocleous, *Fabrication of Social Order*, ix. A similar complaint is P. K. Manning, "Theorizing Policing." These complaints come from a critical site within the social sciences, particularly a field calling itself "the new police science," which works to recover police as a "predisciplinary object of study" and mode of governance, bringing together the multiple meanings of police and critical threads of police scholarship across the silos of discipline: Neocleous, *Fabrication of Social Order* (quotations in this footnote are from this source, xiii–xiv); Neocleous, *Critique of Security*; Tilly, "War Making and State Making"; Tilly, *Coercion, Capital, and European States*; Wolfe, *Everyday Nation-State*; Tullis, "Vietnam at Home"; Dubber and Valverde, *New Police Science*, esp. Neocleous, "Theoretical Foundations" and Dubber, "New Police Science"; Dubber and Valverde, *Police and the Liberal State*; Dubber, *Police Power*. This powerful and sophisticated work understands the extensive reach of police work, contains the critique of "militarization," and is dubious of "police brutality" and the separation of police from war. *Violence Work* is in great debt to the vision elaborated in this field, and hopes to direct it toward the vernacular conception of police prevailing in the fields of history and criminal justice as well as in popular parlance, by translating that vision into a more narrative, empirical frame.

23 Hall et al., *Policing the Crisis*, 38.

24 Center for Research on Criminal Justice, *Iron Fist*; Harring, *Policing a Class Society*; Harring, "Development of the Police Institution," criticizing the notion of crime as the cause in books by Roger Lane, James Richardson, and Sam Bass Warner, Jr., specifically; Reiner, *Politics of the Police*; Williams and Murphy, "Evolving Strategy of Police"; Walker, "Broken"; Strecher, "Revising the Histories"; Chambliss, "Policing the Ghetto Underclass"; Eck and Maguire, "Have Changes in Policing"; Harcourt, *Illusion of Order*; K. Williams, *Our Enemies in Blue*.

25 Schrader, "American Streets, Foreign Territory"; Schrader, *Policing Revolution*; Heatherton and Camp, *Policing the Planet*, especially essays by Hansford and Vitale; Vitale, *City of Disorder*; Vitale, "Rise of Command and Control Protest Policing"; Vitale, "Policing Protests in New York City"; Vitale, "Safer Cities Initiative"; Wall, "For the Very Existence of Civilization"; Wall, "On the Secret of the Drone"; Wall, "Unmanning the Police Manhunt."

26 Berger, *Captive Nation*; Blue, *Doing Time in the Great Depression*; M. Brown, *Culture of Punishment*; Cacho, *Social Death*; Camp, *Incarcerating the Crisis*; Chávez-García, *States of Delinquency*; Davis, *Are Prisons Obsolete?*; Dayan, *Law Is a White Dog*; Gilmore, *Golden Gulag*; Haley, *No Mercy Here*; Hames-Garcia, *Fugitive Thought*; Hernández, *City of Inmates*; Hernandez, *Migra!*; James, *Resisting State Violence*; James, *Warfare in the American Homeland*; Kunzel, *Criminal Intimacy*; Lichtenstein, *Twice the Work of Free Labor*; Loyd, *Health Rights Are Civil Rights*; Loyd, Mitchelson, and Burridge, *Beyond Walls and Cages*; McArdle and Erzen, *Zero Tolerance*; Meiners, *For the Children?*; Murakawa, *First Civil Right*; Paik, *Rightlessness*; Rhodes, *Total Confinement*; Rodriguez, *Forced Passages*; Schept, *Progressive Punishment*; Schrader, *American Streets, Foreign Territory*; Sentas, *Traces of Terror*; Shabazz, *Spatializing Blackness*; Story, *Prison in Twelve*

Landscapes; Tilton, *Dangerous or Endangered?*; Vargas, *Never Meant to Survive*; Wagner, *Disturbing the Peace*; Washington, "Prisons as a Part of American Studies"; C. Woods, *Development Arrested*; Zilberg, *Space of Detention*.

27 Most zealous in support of this fable is George Kelling, source of the notorious "broken windows" theory of zero-tolerance policing (Kelling, "Broken Windows"); he recounts his version of police history in Kelling and Moore, "Evolving Strategy of Policing"; a summary of this simplistic history is Uchida, "Development of the American Police." While less yoked to the veneration of police than these works, academic histories are implicated in some of their narrative lines; see, for example, Fogelson, *Big-City Police*; Monkkonen, *Police in Urban America*; Walker, *Critical History*; G. Woods, *Police in Los Angeles*.

28 Gramsci, *Selections from the Prison Notebooks*; Crehan, *Gramsci's Common Sense*; Camp, *Incarcerating the Crisis*, 16; Rothstein and Inouye, "Visual Games and the Unseeing of Race," 304.

29 Bittner, "Florence Nightingale."

30 Bureau of Labor Statistics (BLS) statistics show the highest fatality rates per 100,000 workers for agriculture, followed by transportation and mining. Most police deaths occurred in transportation accidents; BLS, "All Charts," 14, 20. See also Fleetwood, "Police Work."

31 Critical Resistance, "Common Sense"; Neocleous, *Critique of Security*; Neocleous and Rigakos, *Anti-Security*.

32 Hall et al., *Policing the Crisis*; Kappeler, Blumberg, and Potter, *Mythology of Crime and Criminal Justice*; Lynch and Michalowski, "Radical Concept of Crime"; J. I. Ross, *Cutting the Edge*; Punch, *Dirty Business*, 1; C. P. Wilson, *Cop Knowledge*; Papke, *Framing the Criminal*.

33 Reiner, *Politics of the Police*, 19.

34 Spitzer and Scull, "Privatization and Capitalist Development," 24.

35 Neocleous, *Fabrication of Social Order*, 92–93, and citing, in addition to Reiner and Spitzer and Scull, Banton, *Policeman in the Community*, 2, 7, 127; Bottomley and Coleman, "Criminal Statistics"; Bittner, "Police on Skid-Row"; Bayley, "What Do the Police Do?," 31–33; Ericson, *Reproducing Order*, 5–6, 206; and Ericson and Haggerty, *Policing the Risk Society*, 19.

36 "Dallas PD Chief Suggests Change."

37 Or, as Julilly Kohler-Hausmann argues in "Guns and Butter," it has built the carceral state on the structure bequeathed by the welfare state and in accordance with its already-existing logics of blame and punishment; see also Hinton, *From the War on Poverty*.

38 Cohen, "Punitive City," 353; Dean, "Military Intervention as 'Police' Action?" 194; Dubber, *Police Power*, xi; Monkkonen, "Cop History." On police discretion, see Brown, *Working the Street*.

39 Benjamin, "Critique of Violence," 243.

40 Agamben, "From the State of Control."

41 Foucault, "Omnes et Singulatum," 248; the second quotation is Turquet de Mayenne, in 1611.

42 Neocleous, "Theoretical Foundations," 19–20; Hartman, *Scenes*, 243n17.

43 Wagner, *Disturbing the Peace*, 5–7.

44 Tomlins, "Framing the Fragments," 267.

45 Blackstone, *Commentaries on the Laws of England*, 162, cited in Dubber, *Police Power*, xii, 49.

46 Bittner, "Capacity to Use Force."

47 L. Farmer, "Jurisprudence of Security," 146.

48 Agamben, "From the State of Control."

49 Seri, "All the People Necessary," 250.

50 Tomlins, "Necessities of State," 47, 48; emphasis in source.

51 Andreas, *Border Games*, 5; Huggins, *Political Policing*, 4; the profoundly political nature of policing is also superbly analyzed in Hall et al., *Policing the Crisis*.

52 Dubber, *Police Power*, 201. Note that by "state," Dubber here means one of the fifty.

53 Tilly, "War Making and State Making," 171.

54 Datta, "Security and the Void," 223.

55 Gilmore, "Fatal Couplings," 16.

56 Bittner, "Capacity to Use Force."

57 Huggins, Haritos-Fatouros, and Zimbardo, *Violence Workers*, 1; see also Cancelli, *Histórias de Violência*; this version is closer to the concept of "violence specialists" as developed by Tilly; see Auyero, *Patients of the State*, 44–45, citing Tilly, *Politics of Collective Violence*, 35.

58 As evidenced in the extensive academic literature on violence, including Agamben, *Homo Sacer*; Biehl, "Vita"; Mbembe, "Necropolitics"; Arendt, "Reflections on Violence"; Arendt, *On Violence*; Balibar, "Violence, Ideality and Cruelty"; Benjamin, "Critique of Violence"; Das, "Act of Witnessing"; Das, *Life and Words*; Dayan, "Legal Terrors"; Derrida, "Force of Law"; A. Feldman, *Formations of Violence*; Hartman, *Scenes*; Huggins, Haritos-Fatouros, and Zimbardo, *Violence Workers*; Judy, "Provisional Note"; Lawrence and Karim, "General Introduction"; Ogilvie, "Violence et representation"; Schinkel, *Aspects of Violence*; Taussig, *Shamanism, Colonialism, and the Wild Man*; Tilly, *Politics of Collective Violence*.

59 The classic formulation is Galtung, "Violence, Peace, and Peace Research"; see also Høivik, "Demography of Structural Violence"; Loyd, "Microscopic Insurgent"; a beautiful application is P. Farmer, "Anthropology of Structural Violence."

60 Gilmore, "Fatal Couplings," 16.

61 Gilmore, *Golden Gulag*, 28.

62 For insight on the ways private citizens are unknowingly conscripted into violence work—through the refusal to regulate gun ownership, for example, or the deliberate formation of gangs by prison officials through segregation and unfair distribution of "privileges," I thank Brackette Williams, personal communications, summer 2016; Mirpuri, "Radical Violence," adds mass shooters to this list; see also Rusche and Kirchheimer, *Punishment and Social Structure*;

White, "Concept of 'Less Eligibility'"; Buerger and Mazerolle, "Third-Party Policing"; Maguire and King, "Trends in the Policing Industry," 29.

63 I think it is misguided to admit a monopoly of legitimate violence only when official state agents commit, rather than authorize it, as Brian Wagner does in arguing that during slavery the state did not hold such a monopoly, as masters punished at their discretion (*Disturbing the Peace*, 7). I find it more compelling to think of the state as holding "singular control over who may commit violence, how, and to what end," as Gilmore and Gilmore write in "Restating the Obvious," 143–44.

64 Neocleous, *Fabrication of Social Order*, xi, 118; Seri, "All the People Necessary," 250.

65 Barthes, *Mythologies*.

66 This is evident in police expert Paul Chevigny's remark that policing is "almost totally local," offered in passing with no argumentative effort; Chevigny, "Foreword," viii.

67 The state has other limiting lines, as does "police"; one common one is civil society. The state/civil society dichotomy is a related but different framework. This is the first in a series of ways in which the terms discussed here slip among confusingly close sets of meanings, exchanging one set of border concepts for another. The next, noted in chapter 2, is that of civilian vs. sworn police; the third, in chapter 3, the use of "private sphere" to mean not the business world but the household. I note these in passing and invite others to interpret.

68 Deleuze, "Eight Years Later," 177. This is actually not so far from Poulantzas, who pointed out that the state is made up of multiple apparatuses or institutions, some of which are ideological (showing his debts to Althusser), such as the school, the church, or the family, and some of which are more nakedly repressive (police, army, and so on). The repressive ones are more unified and easier to see as such, but Poulantzas cautions that one must not neglect the others, for all are foundational to the whole; Poulantzas, "Problem of the Capitalist State," 77; see also Murakawa and Beckett, "Mapping the Shadow Carceral State." Abrams, too, emphasized the internal heterogeneity of the state in a way that is consistent with the notion of assemblage; Abrams, "Notes." Other scholars of police power have also found assemblage to be intellectually productive. Foucault speaks of "two great assemblages" in discussing police and war, "a military-diplomatic apparatus, on the one hand, and the apparatus of police . . . on the other"; Neocleous, *War Power, Police Power*, 12. See also Bachmann, Bell and Holmqvist, *War, Police, and Assemblages of Intervention*, which invites readers to consider using assemblage to explore the police-military-service bodies that fight, support, and clean up contemporary conflicts. Drawing on Deleuze and Guattari's *1000 Plateaus*, they define an assemblage as "a grouping of heterogeneous elements that, at some point, displays a kind of collective synergy and consistency" (Bachmann, Bell and Holmqvist, *War, Police*, 3–4). As they usefully elaborate, the grouping is ad hoc, subject to reorganization and transformation, with no central organizing power. It is not

a structure with formal, enduring totality but a network whose relations are never fully contained, and whose elements retain an independent existence. Increasingly, critical ethnic studies scholars suggest we conceive of race itself as an assemblage: Saldanha, *Psychedelic White*; Singh, "Whiteness of Police"; Puar, "I Would Rather Be a Cyborg"; Weheliye, *Habeas Viscus*.

69 Taussig, *Magic of the State*.

70 Polanyi, *Great Transformation*, 60; see also Graeber, *Debt*.

71 Jenkins, "Calibrating the Capitalist State."

72 E.g., Marx and Engels, *Communist Manifesto*, 37: "The executive of the modern state is nothing but a committee for managing the common affairs of the whole bourgeoisie." Poulantzas suggested that the state functions as glue, "the factor of cohesion" holding a given society together and helping it reproduce its unequal relations, "the domination of one class over the others." Poulantzas, "Problem of the Capitalist State," 73; see also "Preliminaries to the Study of Hegemony in the State," *Poulantzas Reader*, 79–80.

73 Hall, "State in Question," 23.

74 Gramsci in Hall et al., *Policing the Crisis*, 203–6; Jessop, *State Theory*, 339. See also Hall, "State in Question"; Jenkins, "Calibrating the Capitalist State"; Gerber, "Corporatism and State Theory." Meanwhile, a post-Marxist instrumentalism proposed a reinvigorated engagement with the people and institutions who make up the state, the better to see it as an internally complex tangle of agents and subjects; Evans, Rueschemeyer, and Skocpol, *Bringing the State Back In*; Skocpol, "Bringing the State Back In"; Calavita, *Inside the State*. Foucauldians tend to find the Skocpol-inspired literature flat, charging that it overemphasizes institutions; it is also explicitly anti-Marxist in inspiration, and unsurprisingly, Marxists see themselves caricatured in it, as Bob Jessop complains in *State Theory*. Timothy Mitchell charges attempts to "bring the state back in" with reducing the state "to a subjective system of decision making" and calls Skocpol's argument specifically a "voluntarist, ideological explanation" (Mitchell, "Limits of the State," 77, 86) and "institutionalist" (Mitchell, "Society, Economy, and the State Effect," 170). All in all scholars have demonstrated a veritable if irregular "obsession" with the state; Valverde, "Police, Sovereignty, and Law," 15. See also Skocpol, "Political Response to Capitalist Crisis." Jessop tracked a related arc of scholarly neglect of the state and then a reembrace in the 1970s; Jessop, *State Theory*, 338; so did Keller, "(Jerry-) Building a New American State," 248.

75 Abrams, "Notes." See also Trouillot, "Anthropology of the State."

76 W. Brown, *States of Injury*, 174–75; Gilmore and Gilmore, "Restating the Obvious," 143; J. Ferguson, *Anti-Politics Machine*, 273.

77 Mitchell, "Society, Economy," 169–70; Mitchell, "Limits of the State."

78 Mitchell, *Carbon Democracy*, 9.

79 Mitchell, *Carbon Democracy*, 11.

80 Graeber, *Debt*; Novak, "Myth of the 'Weak' American State"; Harvey, *Brief History of Neoliberalism*.

81 Foucault, Michel. "Society Must Be Defended," 255.

82 Mitchell adds a formidable arrow to the arsenal arrayed against neoliberalism's claims with his argument that there *was no* notion of "the economy" as a noun, not to mention a nationally bounded noun, prior to the 1930s. "The economy," he charges, placing it in scare quotes, was invented as an autonomous realm in the 1930s, as handmaid to development economics. Mitchell helps to show how the notion of "the state" (along with the other ostensibly noneconomic realm of "the household") served as the constitutive outer edge of the notion of "the economy," fixing them all to the real; Mitchell, "Fixing the Economy." The idea of the state is productive on behalf of other structures as well, such as global inequality. As Beth Baker-Cristales reasons, the idea of the state is a bulwark of the myths underlying international law, especially the notion that all states come to a global bargaining table as equals. (She also makes the wonderful point that it is odd that the state is widely believed to be old, while globalization is seen as new, since the two emerged together in the modern era); Baker-Cristales, "Magical Pursuits."

83 Abrams, "Notes," 63.

84 Martin, "Introduction," 12.

85 Gilmore and Gilmore, "Restating the Obvious," 146; see also Harcourt, "Occupy Wall Street."

86 Jung, "Solidarity, Liberalism, History."

87 Kelley, "Introduction," 7.

88 Chen, "Limit Point of Capitalist Equality."

89 Skinner, "State."

90 Da Silva, *Global Idea of Race*; Wynter, "Unsettling the Coloniality"; Vargas, *Never Meant to Survive*; Wilderson, *Incognegro*; Hua, *Trafficking Women's Human Rights*; Singh, *Black Is a Country*; Rodriguez, *Forced Passages*; Hames-Garcia, *Fugitive Thought*; Ngai, *Impossible Subjects*.

91 On the constitutive role of policing in creating race, see Sentas, *Traces of Terror*; Wagner, *Disturbing the Peace*; Hall et al., *Policing the Crisis*; Childs, *Slaves of the State*.

92 Hartman, *Scenes*, 199.

93 Da Silva, *Global Idea of Race*; Gilmore, *Golden Gulag*, 28; Vargas, *Never Meant to Survive*; James, *Resisting State Violence*, 46; Rodríguez, *Suspended Apocalypse*.

94 Clastres, *Society against the State*; Scott, *Art of Not Being Governed*; Biondi, *Sharing this Walk*.

95 Berlant, *Cruel Optimism*; Lepselter, *Resonance of Unseen Things*; Moreton, *To Serve God and Wal-Mart*; Melossi, "Gazette of Morality and the Social Whip."

96 Cacho, *Social Death*, 17; emphasis in source; Foreman, *Locking Up Our Own*.

97 Cacho, *Social Death*; Paik, *Rightlessness*; Hong, *Ruptures of American Capital*; Reddy, *Freedom with Violence*; R. A. Ferguson, *Aberrations in Black*; Coulthard, *Red Skin, White Masks*; Dayan, *Law Is a White Dog*; Berger, *Captive Nation*; Randall Williams, *Divided World*. For a view of the state as ir-

redeemable as a result of its gendered, racialized, class nature, see W. Brown, "Finding the Man in the State."

98 My sense of this process is of a practical, stepwise practice dedicated to encouraging the irruptions of commons that already exist all around us, rejecting "reformist reforms" or "carceral humanism" (which "casts the jailers as caring social service providers," in James Kilgore's explanation) in favor of abolitionist reforms focused on building the structures that can sustain a stateless, cageless world; Harney and Moten, *Undercommons*; Kilgore, "Repackaging Mass Incarceration"; Davis, *Are Prisons Obsolete?*; Ben-Moshe, "Tension between Abolition and Reform"; Gilmore, *Golden Gulag*; Shabazz, *Spatializing Blackness*, esp. the epilogue, "Fertile Ground."

99 J. T. Camp, *Incarcerating the Crisis*; Hinton, *From the War on Poverty*; Murakawa, *First Civil Right*.

CHAPTER 1. THE OFFICE OF PUBLIC SAFETY, THE LEAA, AND US POLICE

1 National Advisory Commission on Civil Disorders, "Kerner Commission Transcripts and Agenda of Hearings," part 5, reel 3, frame 310.

2 Prashad, *Darker Nations*; A. Escobar, *Encountering Development*, chap. 2; N. Smith, "Satanic Geographies of Globalization"; Gregg, *Inside Out, Outside In*.

3 Rostow, *Stages of Economic Growth*. Even radical thinkers subscribed to the core of this orthodoxy, an arc of heroic transformation leaving ethnic particularism behind for a "mature" embrace of national fulfillment; Saldaña-Portillo, *Revolutionary Imagination*. On the anthropology of development, see also Pathy, "Anthropology and the Third World."

4 McClintock, *Instruments of Statecraft*, 11–16; Klare and Kornbluh, *Low-Intensity Warfare*; Schrader, "American Streets, Foreign Territory."

5 Steinberg, "Asian Bastion Tugs at U.S. Ties"; this just two months after the term's first mention in a major US newspaper, "General, 43, Heads Guerrilla Force." "Sprawling" in Kalyvas, "Paradox of Terrorism in Civil War," 129; Kalyvas also lists some of the institutional authors of these books, semiofficial think tanks such as the Special Operations Research Office (SORO), the Counterinsurgency Information Analysis Center, and the Center for Research in Social Systems; Lobe also notes the "endless stream of books" on counterinsurgency published between 1955 and 1968; Lobe, "U.S. Police Assistance," 38. See also Tullis, "Vietnam at Home"; Schrader, "American Streets, Foreign Territory"; Schrader, "Local Policing Meets Global Counterinsurgency"; McClintock, *Instruments of Statecraft*, 11–16; Klare and Kornbluh, *Low-Intensity Warfare*; Ahern, *Vietnam Declassified*; Ucko, *New Counterinsurgency Era*. Several authors argue that forces long before that were practicing counterinsurgency, but not under that name nor in a way that would generate institutional

memory: McCoy, *Policing America's Empire*, 17; Cable, *Conflict of Myths*, 66–67, 96; even Klare and Kornbluh note that the United States had essentially practiced counterinsurgency against guerrillas in the Philippines, in the United States against Native Americans, and in Nicaragua in the 1930s.

6 Huggins, "U.S.-Supported State Terror"; Huggins, *Political Policing*; Black, *United States Penetration of Brazil*; Klare et al., *Supplying Repression*; Lefever, *U.S. Public Safety Assistance*; Lobe, "U.S. Police Assistance"; Kuzmarov, *Modernizing Repression*. On the development focus of counterinsurgency, see also Colby and Dennett, *Thy Will Be Done*, xvi; B. Simpson, "Indonesia's 'Accelerated Modernization.'" Police assistance programs had a much longer tail, as officials reminded Kennedy in a 1962 memo: "The US Government has in fact been engaged in providing police-type advice, assistance and training for many years. Our aid to the Philippine Constabulary dates back several decades. During World War II we began assisting the Iranian Gendarmerie, a program which also continues to this date. [censored portion] Then pursuant to NSC Action 1290-d in 1954 the US embarked on a much broader effort to strengthen the internal security capabilities of friendly nations, under what later became the Overseas Internal Security Program (OISP)." "Memorandum for the President. Subject: Report of the Committee on Police Assistance Programs," July 22, 1962, 9, Folder "IPS 1 General Policy Guidelines—Background (OPS Policy Papers) FY 62–72, Folder 2," AID A-1 Entry 18 ("Office of Public Safety, Office of the Director, Numerical File 1956–74"), RG 286, NARA. Accusations that OPS was purely a CIA cover include Colby and Dennett, *Thy Will Be Done*, 422, 398, citing Marchetti and Marks, *CIA and the Cult of Intelligence*, 123. Slightly more attenuated links are described in Agee, *Inside the Company*, 63, and throughout the historical work on OPS: Huggins, *Political Policing*; Langguth, *Hidden Terrors*; Klare and Kornbluh, *Low-Intensity Warfare*, esp. 10, 32; Lobe, "U.S. Police Assistance"; McClintock, *Instruments of Statecraft*, 188–96. OPS officers were quite sanguine about these connections, even open, as when Bill Parriott wrote that he had been invited to attend a reunion of CIA friends who had been in Saigon with him in 1962–65 and named eight specific people with no sense of any risk in disclosing their identities; PSN 17 (July 1978): 2.

7 The *felt* continuity between OPS and its predecessors is evident in the sharing of photographs of pre-OPS police advisors to Greece and Iran in the PSN in January 2010, and December 2005, respectively (see figures 1 and 2). Clearly the men who sent in these photos roughly fifty years later understood their pre-OPS and OPS work as continuous—rightfully so, given that the mission, the work, and even the people were substantially the same.

8 Office of Public Safety, "Agency for International Development, Office of Public Safety, A.I.D. Assistance to Civil Security Forces," March 26, 1973, 1, Folder "OPS HANDOUT–AID Assistance to Civil Security Forces," AID A-1 Entry 21 ("Office of Public Safety, Office of the Director, General Records, 1959–74"), RG 286, NARA, counts its achievements since 1954 when OPS's predecessor began under the ICA; it claims fifty-two countries assisted, over 7,519 police

officers trained in the United States, and "thousands" abroad. Scholarly counts include B. Simpson, "Indonesia's 'Accelerated Modernization'"; Klare, *Supplying Repression*, 23; Kuzmarov, *Modernizing Repression*; Lobe, "U.S. Police Assistance"; Black, *United States Penetration of Brazil*; Huggins, *Political Policing*, 189–91; Klare and Kornbluh, *Low-Intensity Warfare*, esp. Maechling Jr., "Counterinsurgency"; Nadelmann, *Cops across Borders*, 118–19; McCoy, "Torture in the Crucible of Counterinsurgency"; McSherry, *Predatory States*; see also Goin, preface to Saenz, OPS *Story*, xxiv; Thompson, "U.S. Agency 'Waylays' Communist Subversion"; Langguth, *Hidden Terrors*, 301; US House of Representatives Committee on Appropriations, *Foreign Assistance Appropriations for 1973*; US Senate, *Hearings before the Committee on Foreign Relations*.

Note that this simple count excludes OPS's predecessors, as well as the work OPS enabled to be carried out under the auspices of the Department of Defense. The GAO count of funds devoted to police assistance in its phase-out report on the Vietnam program, to illustrate, counted "USAID Funding" beginning in FY 1955, even though USAID did not exist institutionally until 1961, finding a total of over $153 million for the period 1955–74, and counting DOD expenditures, a total of $235,145,000—for the single nation of Vietnam; Comptroller General of the United States, "Phaseout of U.S. Assistance to Vietnam," 43.

9 US Senate, *Hearings before the Committee on Foreign Relations*; US Senate Committee on Foreign Relations, *United States Policies and Programs in Brazil*; US House of Representatives, *Hearings before the Committee on Standards of Official Conduct*; US House of Representatives Committee on Appropriations, *Foreign Assistance Appropriations for 1973*.

10 Grodsky, for example, went on to work for ICITAP, and told me in our interview that he was one of several; on ICITAP, see the Justice Department's description on its website, accessed July 25, 2016, https://www.justice.gov /criminal-icitap/about-icitap. For contemporary iterations of this aid, see McLeod, "Exporting U.S. Criminal Justice."

11 Nor do they see it as vindication.

12 Feagin and Hahn, *Ghetto Revolts*, 99; K. Ross, *May '68 and Its Afterlives*; Artières and Zancarini-Fournel, *68: Une histoire collective*; Prince, "Global Revolt of 1968 and Northern Ireland"; Gerd and Kenney, *Transnational Moments of Change*; Fink, Gassert, and Junker, *1968: World Transformed*; Frazier and Cohen, *Gender and Sexuality in 1968*; McClintock, *Instruments of Statecraft*.

13 "Report of the Interdepartmental Technical Subcommittee on Police Advisory Assistance Programs," June 11, 1962, 5, Folder "IPS History References," AID A-1 Entry 21 ("Office of Public Safety, Office of the Director, General Records, 1959–74"), RG 286, NARA.

14 "Report of the Interdepartmental Technical Subcommittee on Police Advisory Assistance Programs," June 11, 1962, 40, Folder "IPS History References," AID A-1 Entry 21 ("Office of Public Safety, Office of the Director, General Records, 1959–74"), RG 286, NARA.

15 Goldstein, *Poverty in Common*.

16 Like comparative frames in so many contexts (though not all), the suggestion of parallelism allows for the erasure of interconnection: Gregg, *Inside Out, Outside In*; Seigel, "Beyond Compare"; Stoler, "Tense and Tender Ties"; Weheliye, *Habeas Viscus*.

17 "Report of the Interdepartmental Technical Subcommittee on Police Advisory Assistance Programs," June 11, 1962, 5, Folder "IPS History References," AID A-1 Entry 21 ("Office of Public Safety, Office of the Director, General Records, 1959–74"), RG 286, NARA; emphasis mine.

18 Tullis, "Vietnam at Home," 14, 24.

19 Kohler-Hausmann, "Militarizing the Police," 48; Tullis, "Vietnam at Home," 102.

20 Tullis, "Vietnam at Home," 105.

21 Light, *From Warfare to Welfare*, 1.

22 Tullis, "Vietnam at Home," 24.

23 E. J. Escobar, "Dialectics of Repression," 1496; see also J. T. Camp, *Incarcerating the Crisis*, 41 (on James Baldwin's comparison of Black Panthers to Viet Cong); Kohler-Hausmann, "Militarizing the Police"; Goldstein, *Poverty in Common*; Tullis, "Vietnam at Home," 110; Dudziak, *Cold War Civil Rights*; Plummer, *Rising Wind*; Singh, *Black Is a Country*; Gaines, *American Africans in Ghana*. Nor was the comparison made only about these two places, the United States and Vietnam, or in one direction, likening foreign locales to the United States: it traveled anew, as when the US ambassador in Beirut characterized the "flavor" of violence in 1975 to the commercial sector there with the slogan associated with Watts: "Burn, baby, burn." Telegram Beirut 14158, Godley to State, November 13, 1975.

24 David Stockman, *Triumph of Politics*, 153–54, cited in Beckett, *Making Crime Pay*, 53.

25 A vestigial secrecy still limits understanding of the Cold War, particularly when the practices in question resonate with the present too closely for official comfort; the close relationship between OPS and the CIA, whose records are obviously less porous than some, exacerbates this for OPS, as does the closed nature of many police department archives and personnel files, often encased in legal prohibitions and stonewalling in practice. Police officers hired on short-term contracts are hard to trace. A. J. Langguth calls the hiring of the LAPD officers a "secret operation," citing an interview with Bryon Engle; Langguth, *Hidden Terrors*, 126. Engle did not provide Langguth with the officers' names, nor did he suggest that he had in his possession any document that could elaborate on their consultancy. Electronic personal communications with Langguth, February 2009. OPS didn't just hire police for short terms; it hired many categories of workers in this way, including employees in management, advertising, and accounting: Folder "Personnel—American. Contractors—1960/July 1962," USAID Entry UD-WW 400 ("Unclassified 'Brazil SUBJ/PROJ 56–73"), RG 286-75-162, NARA. Occasionally OPS hired police officers *as* management consultants, as in 1956 when OPS asked a consultant for the Los Angeles County Sheriff's Office, Fred Fimbres, to co-author a "Pre-Program Survey"; "Guatemala Program History," date unclear,

Folder "Country Fact (Hot) Book," AID A-1 Entry 21 ("Office of Public Safety, Office of the Director, General Records, 1959–74"), RG 286, NARA.

26 Los Angeles City Records Collection (CRC), Los Angeles, CA, Index to the Minutes of the Board of Police Commissioners (hereafter IMBPC) 5–16–62 [detailing item] #15; IMBPC 5–31–62 # 11; IMBPC 5–31–62 # 20; IMBPC 7–11–62, #11; IMBPC 8-8-62, #16.

27 IMBPC 9/4/63, #13; IMBPC 9/11/63, #10; IMBPC 9/18/63, #27 "Public Safety Program Venezuela—Caracas Leaves—Special."

28 Minutes of the Board of Police Commissioners (MBPC), December 18, 1963, 198, CRC. The letter thanks "Enrique Hernandez"; my research in the USAID records suggests this officer's first name was Robert; it is quite possible that USAID administrator David E. Bell simply mistook his employee's name.

29 Saenz, OPS Story; on the San Antonio TDYs: Briefing memo for the administrator, "Special Report on Venezuelan Terrorism for Special Group (C.I.) Agenda, Sept. 17, 1964, and the Public Safety Program," Folder "8 G Venezuela (Program) Subversive Organizations," AID A-1 Entry 21 ("Office of Public Safety, Office of the Director, General Records, 1959–74"), RG 286, NARA. On the LAPD in the Dominican Republic, see Saenz, OPS Story, 432.

30 IMBPC 2 December 1964, #4-I, labels: "Chief Parker, William H.," "India," "Dept. of State," "Agency for International Development," "Leave, Special," "Simon, Richard—Deputy Chief."

31 IMBPC September 27, 1971, 4-M, labeled "Leave (Special)," "Anti-Sniper Training," "Quantico, Virginia," "Sniper," "Training," "Federal Bureau of Investigation"; IMBPC April 12, 1971, 4-J, labeled "Leave (Special)," "Hale, Donald H. (Criminalist)," "Washington, D.C.," "Training," "Defense, Department of"; IMBPC July 22, 1970, 4-E, labels: "Leave, Special," "Training," "Special Weapons and Tactics," "Camp Pendleton, Calif."; IMBPC May 28, 1969, 5-C, "Leave, Special," "Training," "Spec Weapons and Tactics Section," "United States Marine Corps," "Camp Pendlelton"; IMBPC May 22, 1968 #4-D; IMBPC February 8, 1971, 4-B, "Leave, Special," "Camp Pendleton," "Training Day," "Metropolitan Division."

32 IMBPC May 16, 1962 #15; IMBPC May 31, 1962 # 11; IMBPC May 31, 1962 # 20.

33 "Officer Retires, Goes to Viet war"; Yaro, "Retired Officers Going to Saigon"; "Law Officers Planning Visit to Mexico"; all in *Scrapbook for 1966* PD-82–15, CRC.

34 Thompson, "U.S. Agency 'Waylays' Communist Subversion."

35 Seigel, "Beyond Compare."

36 S. W. Guth and B. L. Quick, *Termination Phase-Out Study, Public Safety Project, Venezuela*, April 1974, Folder "Venezuela—1," AID A-1 Entry 19 ("Office of Public Safety, Office of the Director, Program Surveys and Evaluations, 1959–74"), RG 286, NARA. Luna is listed as a PSA in this document although he seems to have served only this three-month period.

37 *BioReg* 1974, 219; Langguth, *Hidden Terrors*, 267. A "Richard Martinez" from Albuquerque also turns up in some of the left whistle-blowing exposés of CIA activities, but the details of his life are slightly different. In these accounts, he is a whistle blower himself, disgusted with the work he was asked to do and

willing to talk about it to reporters. See Blum, *CIA, Forgotten History*, 187; Kwitny, *Endless Enemies*, 348–52; Sklar, *Washington's War on Nicaragua*, 66; Poelchau, *Whitepaper Whitewash*, 47–51.

38 Texas Senate Hispanic Research Council, "Senator Gregory Luna"; no author, "Gregory Luna"; Luna's involvement in MALDEF makes him a wonderfully complex figure deserving of future research.

39 Huggins, *Political Policing*, 66.

40 Colby and Dennett, *Thy Will*, photo caption btw 560–61; they date his work there to February 1962; I have not been able to confirm the date.

41 Kohler-Hausmann, "Militarizing the Police"; Ackerman, "Bad Lieutenant"; Ackerman, "Chicago Police."

42 Best, *Bad Cop—No Doughnut*, 175–76; Arpaio's own website, SheriffJoe.com, reportedly confirmed his DEA experience, claiming he was stationed in Argentina and Turkey in addition to Mexico, but the website is not maintained.

43 Lynch, *Sunbelt Justice*; see also Abramsky, *American Furies*.

44 Light, *From Warfare to Welfare*; see also Tullis, "Vietnam at Home," 105–16.

45 Flamm, *Law and Order*, 6; 113–19; Seigel, "Nelson Rockefeller in Latin America."

46 E. J. Escobar, "Dialectics of Repression," 1494. Escobar dates this citation to sometime around 1967; Murakawa, "Origins of the Carceral Crisis," 388–423; Kohler-Hausmann, *Getting Tough*; Weaver, "Frontlash."

47 Flamm, *Law and Order*; Gilmore, "Globalization and U.S. Prison Growth"; Murakawa, "The Racial Antecedents to Federal Sentencing Guidelines"; Murakawa, *First Civil Right*; J. T. Camp, *Incarcerating the Crisis*.

48 J. T. Camp, *Incarcerating the Crisis*. As the eventual reforms were often ones police departments were already moving to embrace, urban unrest should be understood as the long-awaited disaster along the lines presented in Klein, *Shock Doctrine*. On US counterinsurgency policing in the context of the Islamophobic war on terror, see Kundnani, *Muslims Are Coming*. I also anticipate that Singh, *Exceptional Empire*, will shed useful light on the expansion of US policing as an effect of US imperial engagements globally.

49 Related commissions in this period included the National Commission on Reform of Federal Criminal Laws, 1966–71, and the National Commission on the Causes and Prevention of Violence, formed in 1968 after King's and Robert Kennedy's deaths; "Records of Temporary Committees, Commissions, and Boards (Record Group 220)," National Archives and Records Administration, *Guide to Federal Records*; on the 1968 commission, see Lewis L. Gould, "Introduction" to Lester, *Records of the National Commission on Violence*, v–x. Key predecessors included Eisenhower's Commission on Government Security, 1955–1957, and the President's Committee to Study the United States Military Assistance Program (the Draper Committee) of 1958–59; Kennedy's Committee on Juvenile Delinquency and Youth Crime, established in 1961 to help HEW implement the ten-million-dollar grant-in-aid program of the same name, discussed briefly in Feeley and Sarat, *Policy Dilemma*, 40; and as precursor to OLEA and LEAA in Murakawa, *First Civil Right*.

50 Kerner heard, for example, from the Research Analysis Corporation, a private military-research firm with extensive Army contracts, which offered its expertise in riot management based on techniques they had explored for the Pentagon; Tullis, "Vietnam at Home," 107–8 (see also 25–28); National Advisory Commission on Civil Disorders, "Kerner Commission Transcripts and Agenda of Hearings," part 5, reel 3, frame 310; NARMIC, Police on the Homefront, esp. Webb, "Back Home"; and Klare, "Bringing It Back." On the Katzenbach Commission, see Conley, 1967 President's Crime Commission Report, esp. Walker, "Between Two Worlds." OPS testimony to the Katzenbach Commission is noted in Institute for Defense Analyses, Task Force Report—Science and Technology, 139. On the importance of both, see also Murakawa, First Civil Right; Hinton, From the War on Poverty.

51 On Johnson's angry response to the Kerner Commission report's denunciation of white racism and his feeling that the report failed to admire his administration's accomplishments in social and racial justice, see Dallek, Flawed Giant, 515–17.

52 Feeley and Sarat, Policy Dilemma; on the "master plan," see 4; on the OLEA's role in strengthening policy lobby power, raising concern over crime, and legitimizing the idea of federal support for local and state law enforcement, see 36. See also Beckett, Making Crime Pay, 91; Weaver, "Frontlash"; Murakawa, First Civil Right, esp. chap. 3; Hinton, From the War on Poverty.

53 Varon, "Reexamination," 1306–7; Clynch, "Spending of Law Enforcement Assistance Administration"; C. H., "Law Enforcement Assistance Administration"; Feeley and Sarat, Policy Dilemma. The LEAA's predecessor organization also gave the bulk of its funds to police departments—two-thirds, according to Tullis, "Vietnam at Home," 149n42, citing DOJ, Third Annual Report to the President and the Congress on the Activities Under the Law Enforcement Assistance Act of 1965, 4.

54 Budget amounts from LEAA, Eleventh Annual Report of the LEAA Fiscal Year 1979, 97; "27-fold" from Raymond Eve, book review in Social Forces 55, no. 2 (December 1976): 559–60. See also McDonald, Finn, and Hoffman, ASP CJ Report; Cronin, Cronin, and Milakovich, U.S. v. Crime in the Streets; Diegelman, "Federal Financial Assistance for Crime Control"; DiIulio, Smith, and Saiger, "Federal Role in Crime Control"; Heymann and Moore, "Federal Role in Dealing with Violent Street Crime"; Navasky and Paster, Background Paper for Law Enforcement; Richman, "Violent Crime Federalism"; "mammoth" from Weaver, "Frontlash," 262. Murakawa points out that federal funding for police continued after the end of the LEAA in 1982, citing several funding programs in First Civil Right, 230n6.

55 Murakawa, First Civil Right.

56 Grodsky interview.

57 PSN 8 (Jan. 1976), 8; PSN 18 (Oct. 1978), 5; PSN 20 (May 1979), 4; PSN 25 (April 1980), 1; PSN 14 (July 1977), 3; PSN 16 (Mar. 1977), 1; PSN 19 (Feb. 1979), 3.

58 PSN 10 (July 1976), 2; PSN 15 (Dec. 1977), 1.

59 PSN 25 (Apr. 1980), 3.

60 *PSN* 14 (July 1977), 1.

61 *PSN* 7 (Nov. 1975), 2; *PSN* 8 (Jan. 1976), 7.

62 *PSN* 11 (Oct. 1976), 1.

63 *PSN* 3 (Feb. 1975), 7; *PSN* 8 (Jan. 1976), 8; *PSN* 18 (Oct. 1978), 5.

64 *PSN* 8 (Jan. 1976), 1.

65 *PSN* 12 (Dec. 1976), 1; *PSN* 20 (May 1979), 4.

66 Grodsky interview.

67 *PSN* 7 (Nov 1975), 2; *PSN* 21 (July 1979), 1; *PSN* 6 (Sept. 1975), 1; *PSN* 8 (Jan. 1976), 7; *PSN* 3 (Feb. 1975), 2; *PSN* 12 (Dec. 1976), 3; *PSN* 3 (Feb. 1975), 2; *PSN* 8 (Jan. 1976), 6; *PSN* 3 (Feb. 1975), 6; *PSN* 8 (Jan. 1976), 6.

68 *PSN* 21 (July 1979), 2; see also Quinney, *Critique of Legal Order*; Gibson, *Warrior Dreams*; Kohler-Hausmann, "Militarizing the Police"; Belew, *Bring the War Home*; Klare, "Bringing It Back," 72.

69 *PSN* 16 (Mar. 1977), 3; *PSN* 8 (Jan. 1976), 7; *PSN* 3 (Feb. 1975), 3; *PSN* 8 (Jan. 1976), 6.

70 *PSN* 20 (May 1979), 1; *PSN* 6 (Sept. 1975), 5; *PSN* 3 (Feb. 1975), 2; *PSN* 6 (Sept. 1975), 4; *PSN* 8 (Jan. 1976), 6; *PSN* 11 (Oct. 1976), 2.

71 Feeley and Sarat, *Policy Dilemma*; C. H., "Law Enforcement Assistance Administration"; Cronin, Cronin, and Milakovich, *U.S. v. Crime in the Streets*; Diegelman, "Federal Financial Assistance"; Heymann and Moore, "Dealing with Violent Street Crime"; Navasky, *Background Paper for Law Enforcement*; Richman, "Violent Crime Federalism"; Carey, *Law and Disorder*; Silver, *Crime Control Establishment*; Walker, "Between Two Worlds." These numbers are flawed, of course, as per Gilmore, *Golden Gulag*; Blumstein, *Crime Drop in America*; Weaver, "Frontlash" (which also includes an excellent challenge to UCR numbers); Murakawa, "Origins of the Carceral Crisis"; Murakawa and Beckett, "Penology of Racial Innocence."

72 US FBI, *Uniform Crime Reports*, 1963–1980, annually. On the difficulty of counting even the uniformed public police, see Maguire and King, "Trends in the Policing Industry"; Maguire et al., "Counting Cops"; and the conclusion to this book, note 16.

73 US Department of Justice, Law Enforcement Assistance Administration, *Trends in Expenditure and Employment Data for the Criminal Justice System, 1971–1974*, 11, 8.

74 Harring, Platt, Speiglman, and Takagi claim that thanks to the LEAA, the number of police doubled and their budgets grew four to five times in size; "Management of Police Killings," 41. It is actually quite difficult to count the hugely dispersed and diverse police forces across the United States. At least three agencies over the late twentieth century have collected statistical data on police employment, none of them in quite the same way and each with considerable idiosyncrasy; see Maguire and King, "Trends in the Policing Industry" ("Due to data-quality issues in counting cops, no reliable national data exist that can be used to track changes in police size in the United States over time," 24) and Maguire, Snipes, Uchida, and Townsend, "Counting Cops," an excellent discussion of the history of police censuses since the 1960s, the multiple orga-

nizations that count them, and their errors. Federal spending is the trend that is possible to count. For those trends, William Stuntz uses Bureau of Justice Statistics, which show a 148 percent rise in overall, inflation-adjusted police spending, 1972–2001, a 298 percent rise in spending on "criminal adjudication," and a 455 percent rise in spending on corrections, alongside an overall increase in government spending of 90 percent, all in inflation-adjusted dollars; Stuntz, "Political Constitution of Criminal Justice," 783–84n10, 784n11, 784n12. When the LEAA closed its doors, other agencies continued to supply federal funds to state and local police, including, as Murakawa notes: the Edward Byrne Memorial State and Local Law Enforcement Assistance Formula Grant Program, created in 1988; the Community-Oriented Policing Services Program, created in 1994, and the Local Law Enforcement Block Grants Program, launched in 1996; Murakawa, *First Civil Right*, 230n6.

75 Walker, "Between Two Worlds," 26; Center for Research on Criminal Justice, *Iron Fist*; on this federalization, see also Heymann and Moore, "Violent Street Crime"; Navasky, *Background Paper for Law Enforcement*; Marion, *Federal Government and Criminal Justice*.

76 Battles, *Calling All Cars*; Webb, "Back Home," 13.

77 LEAA's own material recognized this complaint, as in United States Department of Justice, Office of Justice Programs, *LEAA/OJP Retrospective*; see also Gapay, "Beyond Dick Tracy"; Herbers, "Conflicts Beset U.S. Anticrime Agency"; Otten, "Curbing Crime."

78 Klare, "Bringing It Back," 66–73.

79 Tullis, "Vietnam at Home," 134.

80 O'Toole, *Private Sector*, 169–70; on helicopters, see Los Angeles County Sheriff's Department and Guthrie, *Project Sky Knight* (note that this project began under the OLEA); see also Mitchell, *Carbon Democracy*; on 157 he notes that in the late 1960s, when projections of Vietnam war spending decreased, arms manufacturers sought foreign government buyers.

81 Tullis, "Vietnam at Home," 135, 141–44.

82 Tullis, "Vietnam at Home," 133–35, 145–50. Here Tullis notes that only 15 percent of funds were allowed to go to nonprofits or city agencies, explicitly to foreclose social programs. Riot-control programs had clear priority, signaled by a procedure for expediting such requests and the fact that not a single one was denied, even from "the bucolic states of Vermont, Utah, and Iowa, none of which had been deeply troubled by racial violence" (150). Expenditures on riot equipment by US police departments rose from $1 million in 1967 to $22 million two years later (151). Gilmore and Gilmore date helicopters in LA to a decade earlier: "Beyond Bratton," 177–78, citing Mike Davis, *City of Quartz*. On helicopters in Albuquerque, see Anthony "City Police Dept."

83 Feigenbaum, "100 Years of Tear Gas."

84 IMBPC 5-22-68 #4-D on SWAT team training at Camp Pendleton; Remer, "SWAT"; Tullis, "Vietnam at Home," 161; see also Churchill and Vander Wall, *COINTELPRO Papers*, xxxv (suggests the first SWAT team formed in Austin, Texas,

in 1963, and subsequently in Los Angeles under future police chief Darryl Gates); also Kraska and Kappeler, "Militarizing American Police," 6.

85 Balko, *Overkill*; NARMIC, *Police on the Homefront*; Tullis, "Vietnam at Home."

86 The IDA, a Cold War body founded in 1947, was a civilian, nonprofit think tank funded and fueled by federal government and military funds and research priorities, closely tied to universities, though these ties suffered after campus antiwar demonstrations; Walker, "Between Two Worlds"; Institute for Defense Analyses, "IDA's History and Mission"; Greenberg, "IDA."

87 Institute for Defense Analyses, *Task Force Report*, 68–79.

88 Naughton, "US to Tighten Surveillance of Radicals," cited in Webb, "Back Home," 12–13, also citing Stout, "Crime Control Test Near," and Klare, "Police Build National Apparatus."

89 O'Toole, *Private Sector*; Donner, *Protectors of Privilege*, 79–81, 362; D. Smith, "Upsurge of Police Repression," 49; Cardenas, "S.A. Police Organize 1st Intelligence Squad"; New Mexico State Police, *New Mexico State Police Annual Report, 1971*, 19.

90 Donner, *Protectors of Privilege*, 77.

91 Raymond Eve, reviewing Quinney, *Critique of Legal Order* in *Social Forces* 55, no. 2 (December 1976): 559–60.

92 Weaver, "Frontlash," 243; Dubber, "New Police Science"; Bernstein, *Greatest Menace*.

93 Dubber, *Police Power*, 191.

94 Marion, *Federal Government and Criminal Justice*, 3. For excellent critiques of the organized crime hype in Canada, with reflections on its imitations of US equivalents, see Naylor, "From Cold War to Crime War"; Naylor, "Mafias, Myths, and Markets"; Naylor, *Wages of Crime*.

95 Reich, *Life of Nelson A. Rockefeller*, 741; Seigel, "Nelson Rockefeller in Latin America."

96 LEIU, "History, Purpose, and Operations"; O'Toole, *Private Sector*, 127–33 (notes that for the first twenty years of its life, the LEIU existed in secret, 128); Donner, *Protectors of Privilege*, 67–81, 362; D. Smith, "Upsurge of Police Repression," 49; *Challenge of Crime in a Free Society*; *Kerner Report*; on further domestic intelligence efforts via COINTELPRO see Churchill and Vander Wall, *COINTELPRO Papers*; Glick, "Preface"; Halperin et al., *Lawless State*; McCoy, "Mission Myopia"; Grandin, *Empire's Workshop*.

97 Dubber, "New Police Science," 115. Karina Biondi also offers a useful challenge to the conceptualization of "organized crime" in *Sharing this Walk*, 97–98.

98 Glick, "Preface," xiv; Glick, *War at Home*; Tullis, "Vietnam at Home," chap. 5. Donner, *Protectors of Privilege*, epilogue, discusses both the movement to ban police surveillance in the mid-1970s and its revival in the 1980s.

99 Harring, Platt, Speiglman, and Takagi, "Management of Police Killings," 41.

100 Hinds, "Police Use of Excessive and Deadly Force"; Takagi, "Death by Police Intervention," 9.

101 Murakawa, *First Civil Right*. See also the wonderful critique of liberal counterinsurgency and its legacy in detention policy and practice today in Khalili, *Time in the Shadows*.

102 McCoy, *Policing America's Empire*; Schrader, "Policing Empire"; Kramer, "Power and Connection."

CHAPTER 2. CIVILIAN OR MILITARY?
DISTINCTION BY DESIGN

1 Smith to Jessup, September 10, 1964, Folder "Rio Grande do Sul—In and Out Corresp," USAID Entry UD-WW 400 ("Unclassified Brazil SUBJ/PROJ 56–73"), RG 286–75–162, NARA.

2 Department of State, *Biographic Register* (Washington, DC: GPO, 1968), 470. The state in which Smith worked is not specified in this source, nor have I been able to identify it.

3 Neocleous, "War as Peace"; Loyd, "Microscopic Insugent."

4 Wood, "Rebel Capability," 606n6; Rone, "Problems in Teaching Human Rights," 394. The distinction is further muddled by the wonderfully ironic distinction made *within* police departments between "sworn" or uniformed and "civilian" employees, and the whole question of the "civil" arena, as in civil society (which clearly excludes public police) or civil rights.

5 Kraska, "Militarization and Policing"; see also Kraska and Kappeler, "Militarizing American Police," 2.

6 See Samuel Huntington's classic presentation of clean separation, *Soldier and the State*; Demarest, "Overlap of Military," or Hill, Beger, and Zanetti, "Plugging the Security Gap." The exception proves the rule, as in Scobell and Hammitt, "Goons, Gunmen, and Gendarmerie."

7 Lobe, "U.S. Police Assistance," 17, citing Jeffries, *Colonial Police*, 30–31; Holmes, *Theodore Roosevelt and World Order*, 58–59; Bittner, *Functions of the Police in Modern Society*; Andreas and Price, "From War Fighting to Crime Fighting," 35; McClintock, *Instruments of Statecraft*, 30; Klare and Kornbluh, *Low-Intensity Warfare*; Skolnick and Fyfe, *Above the Law*, 116–17; Dunn, *Militarization of the U.S.-Mexico Border*, 12–13; Lutz, "Making War at Home"; Bittner, *Functions of the Police in Modern Society*, especially chap. 8, "Quasi-Military Organization of the Police," 52–62; J. V. Wilson, "Alternatives to Military Rank Titles," 16–17, 82; Smith and Ostrom, "Effects of Training," 30 (64 percent of 712 police officers interviewed believed military models of organization were appropriate for police departments). A beautifully context-specific analysis of militar*ism* in relation to prison growth and the carceral state is Ruth Wilson Gilmore's indispensable "Globalization and U.S. Prison Growth." On the paramilitary character of policing in British colonial settings, see Anderson and Killingray, *Policing the Empire*, and *Policing and Decolonization*, which note that paramilitary

characteristics intensified as police forces faced independence movements. Paramilitary elements were not absent in earlier moments, however; the sense these essays give is of a range of conventionally-defined military and civilian characteristics within any given police force. On militarization and fears about it in earlier periods, see Koistinen, "Toward a Warfare State"; Sherry, *In the Shadow of War*; Rohde, *Armed with Expertise*. On contemporary crossings, Nadelmann, "Cops Across Borders"; Huggins, *Political Policing*; Dunn, *Militarization of the U.S.-Mexico Border*; Global Policy Forum, "Private Military and Security Companies (PMSCs)"; Hill, Beger, and Zanetti, "Plugging the Security Gap or Springing a Leak." Crossing the military-civilian barrier also pulled violence workers over international boundaries, as Unterman documents in *Uncle Sam's Policemen*.

8 Kraska and Kappeler, "Militarizing American Police." See also Enloe, *Police, Military, and Ethnicity*; Bittner, "Quasi-Military Organization"; Jefferson, *Case against Paramilitary Policing*; Green, *Enemy Without*.

9 Giddens, *Nation-State and Violence*, 192, 327; see also Maechling, "Counterinsurgency," 31. Agreeing, Thomas Lobe sees police-military roles as existing along a "spectrum," with divisions ultimately unclear; Lobe, "Police Assistance," 34. On the development of this distinction in the classical era of constitution making, see John Gillis's introduction to his edited *Militarization of the Western World*; Gillis suggests that the distinction has decreasing salience in the contemporary world (2). See also Neocleous, *War Power, Police Power*.

10 Huggins, *Political Policing*, 4, xi.

11 Kraska, "Militarization and Policing," 503. Kraska is not denying the difference, just the notion that it is absolute. He maps it onto an evidently subjective continuum. In earlier work, he defends the militarization of the police as an "advance" in surveillance capability and greater rationalization of social control; Kraska, "Militarizing Criminal Justice."

12 Gramsci, *Selections from the Prison Notebooks*; see discussion in introduction above notes 28–29.

13 Khalili, *Time in the Shadows*.

14 Dudziak, *Cold War Civil Rights*; Borstelmann, *Cold War and the Color Line*; Von Eschen, *Race against Empire*; Singh, *Black Is a Country*. Nonintervention was occasionally written into treaties or laws such as the Geneva Accords or the Morse Amendment to the Mutual Securities Act, both of which the United States also tried to circumvent. When the Geneva Agreements prohibited a US military presence in newly independent Laos, for example, the United States set up "a military assistance program, a 'Programs Evaluation Office' (PEO)" in 1955, "staffed by nominal civilians: military personnel who had 'retired' or were put on reserve status for the duration of their stint"; McClintock, *Instruments of Statecraft*, 132; see also M. B. Young, *Vietnam Wars*, 41–42; on the Morse Amendment, see Colby and Dennett, *Thy Will Be Done*, 349.

15 US Department of State, Agency for International Development, "Setting Goals for a Hemisphere, Address at the White House; before Latin American

diplomats, Members of Congress, and their wives; March 13, 1961," *President Kennedy Speaks on the Alliance for Progress: Addresses and Remarks—The First Year* (Washington, DC, 1962), 1–2, Folder "IPS 1 General Policy Guidelines. Background," AID A-1 Entry 18 ("Office of Public Safety, Office of the Director, Numerical File 1956–74"), RG 286, NARA. On Kennedy's radical language, see Saldaña-Portillo, *Revolutionary Imagination in the Americas.*

16 "Statement by Assistant Secretary Edwin M. Martin before the Latin American Subcommittee of the House Foreign Affairs Committee on the Subject of Communist Subversion in the Hemisphere, February 18, 1963," 32, 50, Folder "IPS 1 General Policy Guidelines. Background," AID A-1 Entry 18 (Office of Public Safety, Office of the Director, Numerical File 1956–74), RG 286, NARA.

17 Atanasoski, *Difference Incorporated*; Callincos, "Ideology of Humanitarian Intervention"; Fassin, *Humanitarian Reason.*

18 Barnett, *Empire of Humanity*; Haskell, "Capitalism"; Skinner and Lester, "Humanitarianism and Empire"; Bricmont, *Humanitarian Imperialism*; Chomsky, "Humanitarian Imperialism"; Duffield, "Governing the Borderlands." See also A. Escobar, *Encountering Development*; J. Ferguson, *Anti-Politics Machine.*

19 "Congressional Testimony of [USAID] Administrator [Fowler] Hamilton," *AID Digest*, May, 1962, 36–37; clipping in Folder "IPS 1 General Policy Guidelines. Background," AID A-1 Entry 18 ("Office of Public Safety, Office of the Director, Numerical File 1956–74"), RG 286, NARA.

20 National Security Action Memorandum 206, December 4, 1962, 2, cited in Lobe, "U.S. Police Assistance," 46 footnote; emphasis Lobe's or memorandum authors.'

21 "Department of Defense Participation in Support of Foreign 'Police' Forces," [n.d., 1962], 2; Folder "IPS History References," AID A-1 Entry 21 (Office of Public Safety, Office of the Director, General Records, 1959–74), RG 286, NARA.

22 "Department of Defense Participation in Support of Foreign 'Police' Forces," n.d. [1962, suggest surrounding documents—*au*], 1, Folder "IPS History References," AID A-1 Entry 21 (Office of Public Safety, Office of the Director, General Records, 1959–74), RG 286, NARA.

23 This decision included a warning that AID "must greatly strengthen its capabilities to manage police programs if the objective is to be achieved"; "Memorandum for the President," July 20, 1962, Folder "IPS History References," AID A-1 Entry 21 (Office of Public Safety, Office of the Director, General Records, 1959–74), RG 286, NARA.

24 "Report of the Interdepartmental Technical Subcommittee on Police Advisory Assistance Programs," June 11, 1962, Folder "IPS History References," AID A-1 Entry 21 ("Office of Public Safety, Office of the Director, General Records, 1959–74"), RG 286, NARA. NARA Records of the Technical Services Division are in RG 286.3.5.

25 "Memorandum for the President. Subject: Report of the Committee on Police Assistance Programs," July 22, 1962, 20, Folder "IPS 1 General Policy Guidelines—Background (OPS Policy Papers) FY 62–72, Folder 2," AID A-1

Entry 18 ("Office of Public Safety, Office of the Director, Numerical File 1956–74"), RG 286, NARA.

26 Memorandum for the President, "Report of the Committee on Police Assistance Programs," 6–7, July 22, 1962, Folder "IPS 1 General Policy Guidelines— Background (OPS Policy Papers) FY 62–72, Folder 2," AID A-1 Entry 18 (Office of Public Safety, Office of the Director, Numerical File 1956–74), RG 286, NARA. This committee consisted of Byron Engle, CIA, chairing, Lt. Col. David R. Dingeman, Department of Defense, H. Lynn Edwards, Department of Justice, and Edward C. Kennelly, AID.

27 "Statement of Mr. Joseph J. Wolf, Special Assistant for Internal Defense, AID, before the Subcommittee on Inter-American Affairs, House Foreign Affairs Committee on Castro-Communist Subversion in the Western Hemisphere, March 4, 1963," Folder "IPS 1 General Policy Guidelines. Background," AID A-1 Entry 18 ("Office of Public Safety, Office of the Director, Numerical File 1956–74"), RG 286, NARA.

28 Bartlett Harvey, "1963–67 Foreign Assistance Program Review," draft distributed May 16, 1962, Section: "BOB [Bureau of the Budget] Spring Preview Exercise; Major Issues for MAP [Military Assistance Program] FY 63–67," 7, Folder "IPS 1 General Policy Guidelines. Background," AID A-1 Entry 18 ("Office of Public Safety, Office of the Director, Numerical File 1956–74"), RG 286, NARA.

29 Airgram, "AID/W" to "AID TO CIRCULAR XA 507, Public Safety Programs," December 14, 1965, 2, Folder "IPS 1 General Policy Guidelines—Background (OPS Policy Papers #3) Folder 3," AID A-1 Entry 18 (Office of Public Safety, Office of the Director, Numerical File 1956–74), RG 286, NARA.

30 "U.S. Overseas Internal Defense Policy Guidelines," 3rd draft [references adjacent in files suggest just prior to June 5—au], 1962, 20, 24, Folder "IPS 1 General Policy Guidelines. Background," AID A-1 Entry 18 (Office of Public Safety, Office of the Director, Numerical File 1956–74), RG 286, NARA. Comments on this draft recommended removing some of the less diplomatic language: Edward C. Kennelly to Mr. Martin M. Tank, "Comments Concerning State Paper 'Proposed Internal Defense Guidelines,'" June 5, 1962, Folder "IPS 1 General Policy Guidelines. Background," AID A-1 Entry 18 ("Office of Public Safety, Office of the Director, Numerical File 1956–74"), RG 286, NARA.

31 "U.S. Overseas Internal Defense Policy Guidelines," 3rd draft, 1962, 20, 24.

32 As Vijay Prashad posits, this was precisely the downfall of the great dream of the anti-imperial Third World; Prashad, *Darker Nations*.

33 "U.S. Overseas Internal Defense Policy Guidelines," 3rd draft, 1962, 31.

34 Memorandum for the President, "Report of the Committee on Police Assistance Programs," 6–7.

35 Earle G. Wheeler (Chairman, Joint Chiefs of Staff), "Memorandum for the Chairman, Special Group (CI)," October 23, 1965, Folder "IPS History References," AID A-1 Entry 21 (Office of Public Safety, Office of the Director, General Records, 1959–74), RG 286, NARA. See also "U.S. Overseas Internal

Defense Policy Guidelines," 3rd draft, 1962, 19: "The preventative aspect of US and indigenous capabilities cannot be overemphasized. It is far less costly to prevent subversion and insurgency than to defeat it after its appearance. The unfavorable arithmetic of previous counter-insurgent operations, where 10 to 15 soldiers have been required to cope successfully with each guerrilla, is something which every modernizing society should avoid."

36 Memorandum for the President, "Report of the Committee on Police Assistance Programs," 7.

37 Memorandum for the President, "Report of the Committee on Police Assistance Programs," 9–10.

38 Airgram, "Washington" to "AID TO CIRCULAR XA-113," re: "Joint State/AID Message for the Ambassador and Country Team," July 14, 1967, 3, n. 1, Folder "IPS 1 General Policy Guidelines—Background (OPS Policy Papers #3) Folder 3," AID A-1 Entry 18 (Office of Public Safety, Office of the Director, Numerical File 1956–74), RG 286, NARA. The echo is of the document cited above in note 22. See also acknowledgments that "civic action" was not confined to police: DEPTEL 91, Dhahran to Secretary of State, November 13, 1962, Folder "IPS 20–1 Civic Action," AID A-1 Entry 18 (Office of Public Safety, Office of the Director, Numerical File 1956–74) RG 286, NARA; Joseph J. Wolf, Deputy for Politico/Military Affairs, Memorandum, "Civic Action Meeting, July 15, 1963," July 9, 1963, Folder "IPS 20–1 Civic Action," AID A-1 Entry 18 (Office of Public Safety, Office of the Director, Numerical File 1956–74), RG 286, NARA; George L. Warren, Jr., "Chapter III, 'Special Programs,'" June 8, 1962, Folder "IPS 20–1 Civic Action," AID A-1 Entry 18 (Office of Public Safety, Office of the Director, Numerical File 1956–74), RG 286, NARA.

39 "Report of the Interdepartmental Technical Subcommittee on Police Advisory Assistance Programs," 29, Folder "IPS History References," AID A-1 Entry 21 ("Office of Public Safety, Office of the Director, General Records, 1959–74"), RG 286, NARA.

40 "OPS Personnel Data," Folder "IPS 21–6 Personnel and Staffing," AID A-1 Entry 18 (OPS, Office of the Director, Numerical File 1956–74), RG 286, NARA; Lobe, "Police Assistance for the Third World," esp. 56–61. OPS employees' state- or municipal-level police experience can also be tracked through US Department of State, *Foreign Service List* (Washington, DC: GPO, quarterly); Department of State, *Biographic Register* (Washington, DC: GPO, annually); and the *Public Safety Newsletter* (multiple locations: self-published), cited as *FSL*, *Bio-Reg*, and *PSN*, respectively. Insider Charles Maechling, Jr., claimed that OPS strained to hire "bona fide police specialists" as advisors in 1962 because it needed to purge police assistance's overclose association with the CIA; Maechling, "Counterinsurgency," 32. See also Saenz, OPS *Story*, 445.

41 "Report of the Interdepartmental Technical Subcommittee on Police Advisory Assistance Programs," June 11, 1962, 15, 17–21, 24, Folder "IPS History References," AID A-1 Entry 21 ("Office of Public Safety, Office of the Director, General Records, 1959–74"), RG 286, NARA.

42 "Report of the Interdepartmental Technical Subcommittee on Police Advisory Assistance Programs"; and Lobe, "Police Assistance," 60–61.

43 In a count of eighty-eight OPS employees in five Latin American countries for whom I could find trustworthy biographic information, at least fifty-eight had military experience, a ratio of two to one. They served in the army, air force, navy, marines, and two in the coast guard during World War II; FSL and *BioReg*.

44 Out of sixty-five public safety officials working in Brazil, Uruguay, and Venezuela between 1962 and 1969, only nine had backgrounds *without* civilian law enforcement work. FSL; *BioReg*. See also unattributed personnel files, "OPS Personnel Data," Folder "IPS 21–6 Personnel and Staffing," AID A-1 Entry 18 (OPS, Office of the Director, Numerical File 1956–74), RG 286, NARA; David B. Bell, "Memorandum for the Special Group (CI)," April 5, 1965, 5, Folder "IPS History References," AID A-1 Entry 21 (Office of Public Safety, Office of the Director, General Records, 1959–74), RG 286, NARA.

45 Lefever, *U.S. Public Safety Assistance*; Saenz, *OPS Story*.

46 Dunn, *Militarization of the U.S.-Mexico Border*, 21–22.

47 Lobe, "Police Assistance," 39; McClintock, *Instruments of Statecraft*, 400.

48 Maechling, "Counterinsurgency," 31; see also Klare and Kornbluh, *Low Intensity Warfare*, 19–22; Tullis, "Vietnam at Home."

49 Klare, "Interventionist Impulse," 57.

50 Black, *United States Penetration of Brazil*, 140. On the SOA, see Gill, *School of the Americas*.

51 Lobe, "Police Assistance," 62–63.

52 Saenz, *OPS Story*, 33–35, 43–46.

53 Bell, "Memorandum for the Special Group (CI)," 10; Saenz, *OPS Story*, 43–46.

54 Saenz, *OPS Story*, 444.

55 Klare and Kornbluh, *Low Intensity Warfare*, 19–22.

56 Saenz, *OPS Story*, 17, 41.

57 Grodsky interview.

58 Committee on Police Assistance Programs, "Memorandum for the President. Subject: Report of the Committee on Police Assistance Programs," July 22, 1962, 11, Folder "IPS 1 General Policy Guidelines—Background (OPS Policy Papers) FY 62–72, Folder 2," AID A-1 Entry 18 ("Office of Public Safety, Office of the Director, Numerical File 1956–74"), RG 286, NARA.

59 "Report of the Interdepartmental Technical Subcommittee on Police Advisory Assistance Programs," June 11, 1962, 5, Folder "IPS History References," AID A-1 Entry 21 ("Office of Public Safety, Office of the Director, General Records, 1959–74"), RG 286, NARA. An article in the *International Police Academy Review* focused condescendingly on one foreign police force (Uruguay's) that integrated women: Eduardo Molina Ferraro, "Feminine Police Corps," *International Police Academy Review* 1, no. 2 (April 1967): 6–7.

60 G. A. Hill (Rural Advisor PSD Sao Paulo) to [Frank] Jessup, June 1, 1965, "End of Tour Report," Folder "São Paulo—In and Out Correspondence," USAID Entry UD-WW 400 (Unclassified "Brazil SUBJ/PROJ 56–73"), RG 286-75-162, NARA.

61 George E. Miller to Frank A. Jessup, April 1, 1965, "Field visit, São Paulo—March 23, 1965 to March 31, 1965," Folder "Physical Security—Monthly and Trip / Rio de Janeiro," USAID Entry UD-WW 400 (Unclassified "Brazil SUBJ/PROJ 56-73"), RG 286-75-162, NARA.

62 Cited in Black, *United States Penetration of Brazil*, 152.

63 Folder "Santa Catarina—Month and Trip Reports"; Folder "Rio Grande do Sul—Monthly and Trip"; Folder "São Paulo—In and Out Correspondence"; all USAID Entry UD-WW 400 (Unclassified "Brazil SUBJ/PROJ 56-73"), RG 286-75-162, NARA.

64 [Dan] Mitrione to [Frank] Jessup, January 26, 1965, Folder "Rio de Janeiro—Monthly and Trip Report," USAID Entry UD-WW 400 (Unclassified "Brazil SUBJ/PROJ 56-73"), RG 286-75-162, NARA. Mitrione is the person killed by Tupamaro guerrillas in Uruguay, whose death, as portrayed in the film *State of Siege*, contributed to the demise of OPS.

65 "Shock troops" is given in English in the original, alongside Portuguese names for other troops; Mitrione to Walter P. Weyland (Deputy Chief, Public Safety Division), January 19, 1965, Folder "Rio de Janeiro—In and Out Correspondence," USAID Entry UD-WW 400 (Unclassified "Brazil SUBJ/PROJ 56-73"), RG 286-75-162, NARA.

66 J. Russell Prior (Public Safety Advisor—Brasilia) to Mr. Walter P. Weyland (Acting Chief, Public Safety Office), "Trip Report—Salvador—September 12-30, 1966," October 5, 1966, Folder "BAHIA—Monthly and Trip Reports FY 66 FY 67," USAID Entry UD-UP 33 (Unclassified USAID/Brazil. Office of the Public Safety Chief Advisor. Public Safety Area Offices. Subject Files 1957-1973), RG 286-75-150, now in P Entry 117, RG 286, NARA.

67 George E. Miller (P.S. Advisor, Physical Security, PSD/Brazil) THROUGH Mr. Frank A. Jessup (Chief, PSD/Brazil) to Bryon Engle (Dir., OPS/W), June, 15, 1965, "Completion of TDY Assignment—Guatemala," Folder "Physical Security—Correspondence—Rio de Janeiro," USAID Entry UD-WW 400 (Unclassified "Brazil SUBJ/PROJ 56-73"), RG 286-75-162, NARA.

The OPS role in the lethality of Guatemalan police and the direction of the Guatemalan military to police its own citizenry has been well documented; see Weld, *Paper Cadavers*; Grandin and Joseph, *Century of Revolution*; McClintock, *State Terror and Popular Resistance in Guatemala*; McClintock, *Instruments of Statecraft*, 400; Lobe, "U.S. Police Assistance," 39; Cullather, *Secret History*.

68 McClintock, *Instruments of Statecraft*, 400.

69 "Public Safety in Guatemala—A Useful Program," 1, Folder "IPS History of PS Program-Guatemala FY '70-72," AID A-1 Entry 18 (Office of Public Safety, Office of the Director, Numerical File 1956-74), RG 286, NARA. This report also attempted to defend OPS from charges of political policing by claiming that different policital regimes had supported it: "This project has been carried on for nearly ten years at the specific request of successive governments of varying political philosophies." Offered around 1972, the claim posits "variation" entirely

within the right-wing and military governments that followed the 1954 coup against democratically-elected Jacobo Árbenz.

70 *PSN* 3 (Feb. 1975), 5.

71 *PSN* 8 (Jan. 1976), 1, 7. The *Newsletter* simply reported that MacGregor retired from US Army STRATCOM in 1973, so there is some chance he served STRAT-COM during, that is, as an OPS officer, but I think the more likely sequence is from OPS to STRATCOM at some point before 1973. Many OPS employees left the agency before its termination. STRATCOM, or Strategic Communications Command, was a global unit created in 1962 (a Cuban Missile Crisis product) to succeed the US Army Communications Agency, and upgraded after a reorganization of all Army communications electronics in the mid-1960s. In charge of a huge combat-signal brigade in Vietnam after 1966, it lasted into the late 1970s, eventually directing all the Army's strategic and tactical communications, a vast mandate; see Sterling, "Strategic Communications Command (STRATCOM)," 430–31. The communications and intelligence emphases of counterinsurgency and of OPS converged in STRATCOM's core missions.

72 *PSN* 20 (May 1979), 5.

73 *PSN* 14 (July 1977), 2; on this district, see "U.S. Army Military District of Washington."

74 *PSN* 17 (July 1978), 3; *PSN* 8 (Jan. 1976), 6; *PSN* 20 (May 1979), 3; *PSN* 3 (Feb. 1975), 6; *PSN* 8 (Jan. 1976), 6.

75 Shea, "Transforming Military Diplomacy"; Ward, "Rethinking Foreign Area Officer Management."

76 DAO/AOSOP-P; deciphering of this acronym based on United States Mission to Vietnam, *Telephone Directory*, October 1974, 23; *PSN* 3 (Feb. 1975), 4. Kinney stayed with the DAO/AOSOP-P for some months more; the *Newsletter* claimed he was still there in its January 1976 issue, though it seems likely that information was out of date by that point; *PSN* 8 (Jan. 1976), 7.

77 *PSN* 3 (Feb. 1975), 6; *PSN* 8 (Jan. 1976), 6; both list him as "DAO/AOSOP-PS," another obsolete acronym referring to a subsection of the DAO in the Saigon Embassy, I surmise from the United States Mission to Vietnam, *Telephone Directory*, October 1974.

78 *PSN* 3 (Feb. 1975), 7; *PSN* 8 (Jan. 1976), 8.

79 *PSN* 5 (July 1975), 3; *PSN* 8 (Jan. 1976), 8.

80 *PSN* 10 (July 1976), 2; *PSN* 11 (Oct. 1976), 6.

81 *PSN* 3 (Feb. 1975), 7; *PSN* 6 (Sept. 1975), 3; *PSN* 8 (Jan. 1976), 1; *PSN* 8 (Jan. 1976), 8; PSN 10, 3; *PSN* 15 (Dec. 1977), 2; *PSN* 20 (May 1979), 4; *PSN* 26 (June 1980), 1.

82 *PSN* 14 (July 1977), 3.

83 After 1975, the CIA designated the *Biographical Register* as classified because it had become possible to track CIA agents by noting their disappearance from the *Register* prior to retirement. Echols is not, however, listed in Mader, *Who's Who in CIA*.

84 Saenz, OPS *Story*, 430; Kuzmarov, *Modernizing Repression*, 71, documents Echols's work in occupied Japan as well, identifying him as a lieutenant.

85 *PSN* 18 (Oct. 1978), 1; *PSN* 21 (July 1979), 2. The school at "North Island" may have been Australia's Swan Island, but the reference is obscure.

86 Eckert to Brown, July 8, 1970, "Background Information on the So-Called Death Squad," Folder [envelope] "Area Advisor/Brazil Reports FY 1970 IPS 1–2," USAID Entry UD-UP 33 (Unclassified "USAID/Brazil. Office of the Public Safety Chief Advisor. Public Safety Area Offices. Subject Files 1957–1973"), RG 286–75–150, now USAID P Entry 117, RG 286, NARA.

87 Herbert T. Jenkins, chief of police in Atlanta and a member of the Kerner Commission, treated this equation as obvious in a 1968 article for a police audience, declaring, "Crime and civil disorders have one thing in common—they are both a violation of the law"; Jenkins, "Commission Member Speaks," 35. On this phenomenon broadly, see Weaver, "Frontlash"; Murakawa, "Origins of the Carceral Crisis."

88 J. T. Camp, *Incarcerating the Crisis*; Nguyen, *Gift of Freedom*; Paik, *Rightlessness*; Randall Williams, *Divided World*.

89 International Police Academy, Training Division, "Prevention and Investigation of Contemporary Violence," n.d., 2, Folder "IPS 1 General Policy Guidelines—Background (OPS /Study) Folder 4," AID A-1 Entry 18 (Office of Public Safety, Office of the Director, Numerical File 1956–74), RG 286, NARA.

90 Simon, *Governing through Crime*; it also reveals the aptness of Neocleous's arguments in *War Power, Police Power*.

91 A history of the New York police written in 1880s described "the men who protect life and property, who keep in subjection the army of criminals. . . . The policeman, like the trusty sentinel, must go to his post and be prepared to meet all kinds of dangers; but not like the soldier in open battle, with his comrades and the noise and strife cheering him on. He has to encounter the hidden, and stealthy, and desperate foe." Augustine Costello, *Our Police Protectors* (New York, 1887), cited in *Iron Fist*, 18. Even the phrase "war on crime" is old; it has been used since at least the 1920s, if not before; see Gollomb, "War on Crime"; Coulter, "Jewish War on Crime," cited in Maller, "Juvenile Delinquency among the Jews in New York," especially 547n5; Kuhn, "International Cooperation in the Suppression of Crime" ("to the end that the war on crime may proceed, as Chief Justice Hughes has expressed it, 'on many fronts,'" 544); *People v. Les*, Michigan Supreme Court, cited in Inbau, "Scientific Evidence in Criminal Cases," discussing palm and fingerprints: "There is no reason why the police, in their unending war on crime, should be deprived of the use of well-tested scientific means as aids in the detection and apprehension of criminals," 516; E. W. Camp, "American Bar Association's Program," who writes, "What figures we have—and they are very inadequate—tend to show that in the war on crime we need the best police obtainable, and many more of them, equipped with the latest devices and all the newest gadgets," 217. Although Skolnick and Fyfe criticize what they call the "war model" of policing, they too note its age: it developed in 1829 when Robert Peel used a military organizational model and chose military commanders to head the new force;

Skolnick and Fyfe, *Above the Law*, 117. Nor can they resist the military metaphor themselves, even as they critique it: writing of how a centralized, military model affects police, they note that it weakens supervision and leadership on the "front lines of inner-city patrol units"; Skolnick and Fyfe, *Above the Law*, 124.

92 Lauren Goin, "Memorandum for the Administrator. Subject: Public Safety Activities," draft date February 26, 1974, 4, Folder "IPS 1 General Policy Guidelines—Background (OPS Program Assistance Reports/Study) Folder 4," AID A-1 Entry 18 (Office of Public Safety, Office of the Director, Numerical File 1956–74), RG 286, NARA.

93 Goin, Preface to Saenz, *OPS Story*, xxiv.

94 Grodsky interview.

95 Folder "IPS 11–1 Paramilitary," USAID Entry UD-UP 35 ("Unclassified 'USAID/ Brazil. Office of the Public Safety Chief Advisor. Subject Files Pertaining to the Public Safety Program, 1965–1972'"), RG 286–75–026, NARA; and Folder "IPS 11–2 Military Police," USAID Entry UD-UP 35 ("Unclassified 'USAID/Brazil. Office of the Public Safety Chief Advisor. Subject Files Pertaining to the Public Safety Program, 1965–1972'"), RG 286–75–026, NARA.

CHAPTER 3. "INDUSTRIAL SECURITY" IN ALASKA

Epigraph: Shearing, "Relation between Public and Private Policing," 410–11.

1 As with the confusion surrounding the term "civilian," this question is further muddled by the common use of "private" to mean the household or domestic sphere. If one prioritizes that definitional framework, the state and the market share a contradistinguished public sphere. I leave it to others to explore the ways this equally social distinction functions to challenge or reinforce the state-market divide, *e.g.*, is the domestic sphere meaningfully removed from the market?

2 Hall, "State in Question," 21–23.

3 Das and Verma, "Armed Police"; Stern, *Company-State*; Bernstein et al., *Iron Fist*; Fogelson, *Big City Police*; Miller, *Cops and Bobbies*; Harring, *Policing a Class Society*; Reiner, *Politics of the Police*; Hall et al., *Policing the Crisis*; Quinney, *Critique of Legal Order*; Jefferson, *Case against Paramilitary Policing*; Holloway, *Policing Rio de Janeiro*; C. Woods, *Development Arrested*; Neocleous, *Fabrication of Social Order*; Garland, *Culture of Control*; Websdale, *Policing the Poor*; Hernández, *Migra!*; McCrie, "Brief History of the Security Industry"; Kempa, "Public Policing"; Johnston, *Rebirth of Private Policing*.

4 Johnston, *Rebirth of Private Policing*, 215.

5 Johnston, *Rebirth of Private Policing*; O'Toole, *Private Sector*; Shearing, "Relation between Public and Private Policing"; Spitzer and Scull, "Privatization and Capitalist Development"; Weiss, "Cowboy Detectives"; McCrie, "Brief History of the Security Industry"; Kempa, "Public Policing, Private Security,"

esp. 88. This is another example of the ways the crossing of one border supposed to contain police often pulls them over another.

6 Coates, *Trans-Alaska Pipeline Controversy*, 171; Berry, *Alaska Pipeline*.

7 The Environmental Policy Act of 1969 required a statement on environmental impact for any federal action or legislation, with comments on those drafts by the EPA required by the 1970 amendments to the Clean Air Act; Kenworthy, "Ruckelshaus Asks a Delay," 1; Coates, *Trans-Alaska Pipeline Controversy*, 175, 217.

8 Conservationists have charged that the oil crisis of 1973 was artificially manufactured. See, for example, H. Manning, *Cry Crisis!*; for this analysis in a macro scale, see Klein, *Shock Doctrine*. Manning points out that Arab-produced oil was only 6 percent of the United States supply just prior to the embargo, and that conservation or increased imports from Canada could have covered the shortfall. Even "William F. Buckley, Jr. described the energy crisis as our having to get by with slightly more oil than we were using in 1970," Manning claimed, also noting that the crisis landed with pitch-perfect timing to divert attention from Watergate. H. Manning, *Cry Crisis!*, 30–31 (I have not been able to verify this Buckley citation). Whether the crisis was intentionally produced or not, it is clear that the feeling of crisis preceded the fall of 1973; that summer it was already palpable, as were shortages at gas stations, putting environmentalists on the defensive; Coates, *Trans-Alaska Pipeline Controversy*, 240–50. It is also undeniable that oil concerns exerted enormous political influence; in the case of Alaska, see LaRocca, *Alaska Agonistes*.

9 Malcolm, "Oil Pipeline Work Starts"; Dermot Cole, *Amazing Pipeline Stories*; Carnahan interview.

10 "Contract Awards."

11 "Amex Prices Take a Mixed Course."

12 Here I mean to gesture to the marvelous metaphor of the hydra as drawn out in Linebaugh and Rediker, *Many-Headed Hydra*, though this is a creature quite different from the resistant mass their imagery evokes.

13 Gilmore, *Golden Gulag*.

14 Cohen, *Folk Devils and Moral Panics*; Hall et al., *Policing the Crisis*.

15 Berry, *Alaska Pipeline*.

16 Berry, *Alaska Pipeline*, 17.

17 Berry, *Alaska Pipeline*, 23.

18 Hummel, "U.S. Military as Geographical Agent," 57–58.

19 Hummel, "U.S. Military as Geographical Agent," 58.

20 *PSN* 2 (Dec. 1974), 2 (Craft was there by 1974 at least, given this date); *PSN* 3 (Feb. 1975), 6. In January 1976, he recounted that he was still at it, aiming to pay off a ranch in Idaho; *PSN* 8 (Jan. 1976), 6.

21 Worthen joined up early; he was there by February 1975. *PSN* 3 (Feb. 1975), 3; on Gray, *PSN* 3 (Feb. 1975), 3.

22 *PSN* 3 (Feb. 1975), 5.

23 *BioReg '73*, 51; *PSN* 3 (Feb. 1975), 3; *PSN* 3 (Feb. 1975), 2.

24 *PSN* 11 (Oct. 1976), 2.

25 *BioReg '73*, 135; *PSN* 8 (Jan. 1976), 2.

26 *PSN* 10 (July 1976), 1.

27 Tilly, *Identities, Boundaries, and Social Ties*.

28 *PSN* 3 (Feb. 1975), 5; *PSN* 8 (Jan. 1976), 6; *PSN* 11 (Oct. 1976), 2.

29 *PSN* 3 (Feb. 1975), 5; *PSN* 10 (July 1976), 2.

30 Carnahan interview. Carnahan notes that construction work was well under way when he moved there in 1972, even ahead of the necessary approvals from Congress. The pipeline consortium was able to start significant chunks of the project regardless.

31 *PSN* 12 (Dec. 1976), 2; *BioReg '73*, 51; *PSN* 4 (May 1975), 5.

32 *PSN* 3 (Feb. 1975), 3; *PSN* 4 (May 1975), 5; *PSN* 8 (Jan. 1976), 6.

33 *BioReg '73*, 141; *PSN* 7 (Nov. 1975), 2; *PSN* 8 (Jan. 1976), 6.

34 *PSN* 10 (July 1976), 3.

35 *PSN* 12 (Dec. 1976), 2.

36 *BioReg '73*, 361.

37 *PSN* 12 (Dec. 1976), 2.

38 Berry, *Alaska Pipeline*, "arm" on 13, see also 17; Mitchell, "McJihad," 7; Stern, *Company-State*.

39 "Amex Prices Take a Mixed Course"; Malcolm, "Oil Pipeline Work Starts"; *PSN* 3 (Feb. 1975), 3.

40 Casey, *Alaska's Citizens*.

41 The Scandinavian corporation that bought Wackenhut in 2002 was Group 4 Falck; another merger in 2004 brought in Securicor under the name G4S. The Wackenhut Corporation officially changed its name to G4S Secure Solutions (USA), Inc., in 2010; G4S, "History."

42 GEO Group, "Historic Milestones."

43 O'Toole, *Private Sector*, 30–31; Weiss, "Cowboy Detectives"; Shearing, "Relation between Public and Private Policing." See also Unterman, *Uncle Sam's Policemen*, on overseas manhunts by the FBI and the Pinkerton Detective Agency around the turn to the twentieth century.

44 Stenning and Shearing, "Quiet Revolution"; Johnston, *Rebirth of Private Policing*.

45 Shearing, "Relation between Public and Private Policing"; see also Shearing and Stenning, "Modern Private Security"; Kakalik and Wildhorn, *Private Security in the United States*; O'Toole, *Private Sector*, chap. 3; Weiss, "Cowboy Detectives."

46 Stuart, "Billions for Protection," 119.

47 Kempa, "Public Policing, Private Security," 88.

48 Klare, "Rent-a-Cop," 487; cited in Spitzer and Scull, "Privatization and Capitalist Development," 19.

49 Weiss, "Cowboy Detectives," 7, citing O'Toole, *Private Sector*, n.p.

50 Montgomery, *Fall of the House of Labor*; O'Toole, *Private Sector*, 27; Smith and Morn, "History of Privatization in Criminal Justice," 9.

51 Weiss, "Cowboy Detectives," 7.

52 PSN, passim; chapter 4 will explain Section 607. They worked to portray this circumvention as legal: Matthew J. Harvey, Assistant Administrator for Legislative Affairs, to the Honorable James Abourezk, United States Senate, May 30, 1974, Folder "IPS 1 General Policy Guidelines—Background (Phase Out Study)—Folder 1," AID A-1 Entry 18 (Office of Public Safety, Office of the Director, Numerical File 1956–74), RG 286, NARA.

53 PSN 23 (Nov. 1979), 5.

54 Bryan L. Quick, Charles E. Sothan, and Arlen W. Jee, *Termination Phase-Out Study, Public Safety Project, Colombia*, April 1974, Attachment H, 47, AID A-1 Entry 19 ("Office of Public Safety, Office of the Director, Program Surveys and Evaluations, 1959–74"), RG 286, NARA; Clifton M. Monroe, *Study of the Industrial Security Operations of Empresa Colombiana de Petroleos (Ecopetrol)*, November 1969, AID A-1 Entry 19 ("Office of Public Safety, Office of the Director, Program Surveys and Evaluations, 1959–74"), RG 286, NARA; Elmer H. Adkins and George E. Miller, "Survey Report of the Surveillance and Protection, Saudi Arabian Oil Fields and Installations, for the Ministry of Interior, Kingdom of Saudi Arabia," December 1971, Folder "Public Safety-1," AID A-1 Entry 19 ("Office of Public Safety, Office of the Director, Program Surveys and Evaluations, 1959–74"), RG 286, NARA; George E. Miller "Completion of TDY Assignment—Guatemala," June 15, 1965, Folder "Physical Security—Correspondence—Rio de Janeiro," USAID Entry UD-WW 400, Unclassified "Brazil SUBJ/PROJ 56–73," RG 286-75–162, NARA.

55 Frank A. Jessup to Mr. Kent Lutey, "Protection of Vital Governmental Installations and Private Owned Industrial Facilities," September 13, 1965, Folder "Physical Security—Correspondence—Rio de Janeiro," USAID Entry UD-WW 400, Unclassified "Brazil SUBJ/PROJ 56–73," RG 286-75–162, NARA. Though one generally does not cite boxes in National Archive records, I do so here because there were, in this box, a large number of other files on industrial development projects: Box 4, "USAID/Brasilia, Division C&R, FY 63, Official Project Files (USOM)," USAID Entry UD-WW 400, Unclassified "Brazil SUBJ/PROJ 56–73," RG 286-75–162, NARA.

56 PSN 3 (Feb. 1975), 5; PSN 4 (May 1975), 7; PSN 9 (Mar. 1976), 1; PSN 19 (Feb. 1979), 6. Another such worker was Ronald Holko, mentioned in PSN 6 (Sept. 1975), 1; PSN 8 (Jan. 1976), 7; PSN 19 (Feb. 1979), 2.

57 PSN 16 (Mar. 1977), 3.

58 PSN 4 (May 1975), 8.

59 PSN 28 (Nov. 1980), 6; PSN 26 (June 1980), 1.

60 Weiss, "Cowboy Detectives," 7, citing O'Toole, *Private Sector*, n.p.

61 Carnahan interview.

62 The RAND Corporation report was published as Kakalik and Wildhorn, *Private Security in the United States*.

63 RAND's self-styled neutrality permeates its descriptions of its "nonpartisan" and "independent" analysis and the seminars it organizes such as "Politics

Aside," which advertises "Objective Analysis. Effective Solutions." But the "experts" it invites to populate its conferences and teach in its graduate school boast extensive government and armed forces service. See the RAND Corporation website pages "History and Mission" and "Politics Aside."

64 RAND emerged just after World War II out of an aircraft manufacturer, Douglas Aircraft Company, which built planes for the US Armed Forces. Douglas and RAND are both Cold War bodies, in great debt to the War for crucial federal contracts. See the RAND Corporation website, "History and Mission." RAND today operates in the ambiguous special category of "FFRDC," Federally Funded Research and Development Centers; elaboration of this status available via the National Science Foundation, "Technical Notes; Definitions."

65 Shearing, "Relation between Public and Private Policing," 410–11.

66 Stuart, "Billions for Protection."

67 This attempt to create regulation didn't go far; Kempa notes that regulation of private security is threadbare; Kempa, "Public Policing, Private Security," 98.

68 Shearing, "Relation between Public and Private Policing," 412–15.

69 Cunningham and Taylor, *Hallcrest Report*; Hallcrest still exists, advertising itself at hallcrestsystems.com.

70 The 1990 report is Cunningham, Strauchs, and Van Meter, *Private Security Trends (1970 to 2000), Hallcrest Report II* (Stoneham, MA: Butterworth-Heinemann, 1990); this report is summarized in Cunningham, Strauchs, and Van Meter, "Private Security: Patterns and Trends."

71 Cunningham, Strauchs, and Van Meter, "Private Security: Patterns and Trends," 2.

72 Charles B. DeWitt, "From the Director" in Cunningham, Strauchs, and Van Meter, "Private Security," 1.

73 Ennis, "Fear of Sabotage Spurs Industrial Security Drive." Burch argues that NAM prior to the 1930s was "predominately a spokesman for small and medium businesses," then "transformed during the early 1930s into an anti–New Deal vehicle dominated by big businesses"; P. H. Burch, "NAM as an Interest Group," cited in Skocpol, "Political Response to Capitalist Crisis," 168.

74 National Association of Manufacturers, *Bomb Threats to Industry*; Ennis, "Fear of Sabotage"; US Office of the Provost Marshal General, *Industrial Defense against Civil Disturbances, Bombings, Sabotage*.

75 US Federal Civil Defense Administration, *10 Steps to Industrial Survival*; US Business and Defense Services Administration, *Civil Defense Training for Business and Industry*.

76 Ennis, "Fear of Sabotage."

77 Pryor, "Invaders."

78 Riesel, "Vital Alaska Pipeline."

79 Anderson and Whitten, "Pipeline Sabotage Worries CIA."

80 Although by this time they judged the Trans-Alaska Pipeline to be better guarded than most: "Sabotage Called Oil Pipeline Peril."

81 Anderson and Whitten, "Oil Facilities Vulnerable to Attack."

82 Ponte, "Target: The Pipeline."

83 Ponte, "Target: The Pipeline."

84 Toni Morrison, "Romancing the Shadow," in *Playing in the Dark*, 33. Morrison writes, "These images of blinding whiteness seem to function as both antidote for and meditation on the shadow that is companion to this whiteness—a dark and abiding presence that moves the hearts and texts of American literature with fear and longing." Lest it seem I am reading too much into a simple news item, consider its author, Lowell Ponte, long-time right-wing radio commentator and journalist. In 1977, when he penned this article, his best-selling global warming send-up, *The Cooling*, had just been released. Ponte has never been overly concerned with fact or science, which makes his writing beautifully illustrative of the fears and fantasies entertained by a significant segment of the US collective imagination. Ponte pens fiction; Morrison's literary analysis applies.

85 J. T. Camp, *Incarcerating the Crisis*.

86 Watkins, *Dene Nation*; Berry, *Alaska Pipeline*.

87 A. Simpson, *Mohawk Interruptus*, comments brilliantly on this dynamic for the Mohawk nation.

88 LaRocca, *Alaska Agonistes*, xi.

89 Pryor, "Invaders."

90 Anderson and Whitten, "Pipeline Sabotage Worries CIA." The congressman may have been voicing critique of the pipeline, but it is confusing that Patton was willing to voice what in some ways was a criticism of his company. He may have been angling for some free security work from the feds, or hoping to curry favor with military men seeking to contain threats to their supremacy in the field of violence work. For a similar argument in the context of trade (security is impossible, given the vastness of the project), see Nordstrom, *Global Outlaws*.

91 Coates, *Trans-Alaska Pipeline Controversy*, 307; "Sabotage Blasts."

92 Exxon Valdez Oil Spill Trustee Council website, accessed 6/6/16, http://www.evostc.state.ak.us/%3FFA=facts.qa.

93 Coates, *Trans-Alaska Pipeline Controversy*, 307; "Suspect Charged."

94 Carnahan interview.

95 Indeed, it is a classic antipolitics machine; J. Ferguson, *Anti-Politics Machine*. On the productive work of moral panics for policing, see Hall et al., *Policing the Crisis*.

96 Huber, "Enforcing Scarcity," 817–18; Mitchell, *Carbon Democracy*; see also Gilmore, *Golden Gulag*. An interesting public discussion of surplus as problem is Grant and Billiter, "Glut of Alaska Oil."

97 Chaput, Braun, and Brown, "An Invitation to Entertain Fear," editors' preface to *Entertaining Fear*, vii–xiii; Chaput, "Introduction." As Chaput writes, discourses of fear "ensure the capitalist status quo" by refusing to notice it as context; Chaput, "Introduction," 2. See also C. Calhoun, "World of Emergencies"; Robin, *Fear: History of a Political Idea*; Schultz, *Fear Itself*.

98 M. Watts, "Tale of Two Gulfs"; Endicott, "Human Error."

99 Haycox, "Fetched Up"; M. Watts, "Tale of Two Gulfs." The frequent focus in the *Exxon Valdez* spill on the captain's intoxication is a good example of the ways individual details serve to obfuscate the statistical inevitability of such "accidents."

100 Pryor, "Invaders."

101 Pryor, "Invaders."

102 Carnahan interview.

103 *PSN* 3 (Feb. 1975), 4. Carnahan remembered it slightly differently in his interview.

104 Bukro, "Law's Iron Fist."

105 E.g., Abrams, "Notes."

106 Bourdieu, *Distinction*.

107 Carnahan interview.

108 *PSN* 13 (Mar. 1977), 3.

109 Neocleous, *Monstrous and the Dead*; Hobbes, *Hobbes's Leviathan*.

CHAPTER 4. CORPORATE STATES AND GOVERNMENT MARKETS

1 Stern, "U.S. Firm."

2 Weiss, writing in *PSN* 4 (May 1975), 4.

3 "Sanders Associates Inc. Fails to Get Saudi Job." Sanders explained that the Saudis considered the price of "the $400 million contract to build a highway patrol system" too high. The Saudi government invited Sanders to consult on the project instead; the company added that they did not know of any other companies negotiating for the contract.

4 Hanieh, *Capitalism and Class*, 57–58; Bsheer, "A Counter-Revolutionary State." Deep thanks to Rosie Bsheer for reshaping my understanding of the Saudi Arabian context.

5 Bsheer, "A Counter-Revolutionary State"; Wolfe-Hunnicutt, "End of the Concessionary Regime"; Hanieh, *Capitalism and Class*, 37–43.

6 DEPTEL 91, Dhahran to Secretary of State, November 13, 1962, Folder "IPS 20–1 Civic Action," AID A-1 Entry 18 (Office of Public Safety, Office of the Director, Numerical File 1956–74) RG 286, NARA; a two-year contract was signed in March 1968 and extended in April 1970; another was signed in 1971 (month unclear), and a third in April 1973, set to expire in March 1975, reveals "Public Safety Program, Saudi Arabia," probably part of an untitled briefing book on OPS Phase-Out, January 13, 1973, Folder "IPS 1 General Policy Guidelines—Background (OPS Program Assistance Reports/Study) Folder 4," AID A-1 Entry 18 (Office of Public Safety, Office of the Director, Numerical File 1956–74), RG 286, NARA.

7 Hanieh, *Capitalism and Class*, 44–45 (quote on 45). Timothy Mitchell reminds us that prior to nationalization, oil was sold in the currency used by the inter-

national company that produced it, not that of the source or destination country. Oil from Iran traded in British pounds, but the balance of the global oil trade was conducted in dollars. "In practice, what sustained the value of the dollar was that countries had to use the American currency to purchase the essential materials that formed the bulk of international trade, above all oil," Mitchell writes. Gold mattered, especially after the Bretton Woods Agreement fixed the dollar to it, but "the value of the dollar as the basis of international finance depended on the flow of oil." Mitchell, *Carbon Democracy*, 111.

8   Hanieh, *Capitalism and Class*, 36.

9   Hanieh, *Capitalism and Class*, 45.

10 The term "hinge years" is from Yergin, *Prize*, cited in Wolfe-Hunnicutt, "End of the Concessionary Regime," 209.

11 This is a carceral "spatial fix" in the most sophisticated meaning of "spatial" as an ideologically inflected, deeply social register of relationships in motion: Gilmore, *Golden Gulag*; Harvey, *Spaces of Capital*.

12 Mitchell, *Carbon Democracy*, esp. 154–60; Wolfe-Hunnicutt, "End of the Concessionary Regime," chap. 4.

13 Matthew J. Harvey, Assistant Administrator for Legislative Affairs, to the Honorable James Abourezk, United States Senate, May 30, 1974, Folder "IPS 1 General Policy Guidelines—Background (Phase Out Study)—Folder 1," AID A-1 Entry 18 ("Office of Public Safety, Office of the Director, Numerical File 1956–74"), RG 286, NARA; no author, "Office of Public Safety," May 22, 1974, Folder "IPS 1 General Policy Guidelines—Background (Phase Out Study)—Folder 1," AID A-1 Entry 18 ("Office of Public Safety, Office of the Director, Numerical File 1956–74"), RG 286, NARA. The full text of the Foreign Assistance Act is available at http://www.usaid.gov/sites/default/files/documents/1868/faa.pdf. Of the nine Public Safety staff members still listed at Saudi Arabia's Department of Technical Services in 1975, at least four (Alkassim, Ziegler, Campbell, and Wagner) would remain in Saudi Arabia in some capacity, as this chapter will detail; for the nine, see "Public Safety Program, Saudi Arabia," probably part of an untitled briefing book on OPS Phase-Out, January 13, 1973, Folder "IPS 1 General Policy Guidelines—Background (OPS Program Assistance Reports/Study) Folder 4," AID A-1 Entry 18 (Office of Public Safety, Office of the Director, Numerical File 1956–74), RG 286, NARA.

14 Untitled briefing book on OPS Phase-Out, January 13, 1973, 1, Folder "IPS 1 General Policy Guidelines—Background (OPS Program Assistance Reports/Study) Folder 4," AID A-1 Entry 18 (Office of Public Safety, Office of the Director, Numerical File 1956–74), RG 286, NARA.

15 Multiple documents, 1974, reporting Saudis' desires to increase US assistance and perform a large-scale survey, in Folder "Saudi Arabia IPS-13," USAID A1 Entry 30 (Public Safety, OPS Division; Africa, Near East, South America Branch; Subject Files, 1956–1972), RG 286, NARA.

16 *PSN* 4 (May 1975), 4.

17 *PSN* 4 (May 1975), 4.

18 Hardin had to be medevacked out (PSN 4 [May 1975], 6); he soon retired (PSN 6 [Sept. 1975], 1; PSN 8 [Jan. 1976], 7).

19 PSN 4 (May 1975), 1.

20 Four documents from the same folder: untitled briefing book on OPS Phase-Out, December 13, 1973; "Police Assistance in the Future—Potential Issues"; Goin, "Annex I," to Goin, "Memorandum for the Administrator. Subject: Public Safety Activities"; and "Alternative Approaches to Assisting Civil Police Forces Which Would Continue to Utilize Unique Assets"; ALL in Folder "IPS 1 General Policy Guidelines—Background (OPS Program Assistance Reports/ Study) Folder 4," AID A-1 Entry 18 (Office of Public Safety, Office of the Director, Numerical File 1956–74), RG 286, NARA.

21 Untitled briefing book on OPS Phase-Out, January 13, 1973, 2, Folder "IPS 1 General Policy Guidelines—Background (OPS Program Assistance Reports/ Study) Folder 4," AID A-1 Entry 18 (Office of Public Safety, Office of the Director, Numerical File 1956–74), RG 286, NARA; Goin, "Annex I," 1, to his "Memorandum for the Administrator. Subject: Public Safety Activities," draft date February 26, 1974, Folder "IPS 1 General Policy Guidelines—Background (OPS Program Assistance Reports/Study) Folder 4," AID A-1 Entry 18 (Office of Public Safety, Office of the Director, Numerical File 1956–74), RG 286, NARA.

22 Untitled briefing book on OPS Phase-Out, January 13, 1973, 2, Folder "IPS 1 General Policy Guidelines—Background (OPS Program Assistance Reports/ Study) Folder 4," AID A-1 Entry 18 (Office of Public Safety, Office of the Director, Numerical File 1956–74), RG 286, NARA.

23 Untitled briefing book on OPS Phase-Out, January 13, 1973, 5, Folder "IPS 1 General Policy Guidelines—Background (OPS Program Assistance Reports/ Study) Folder 4," AID A-1 Entry 18 (Office of Public Safety, Office of the Director, Numerical File 1956–74), RG 286, NARA.

24 An unabashedly open statement of the narcotics transfers was offered in PSN 4 (May 1975), 4: "Almost concurrently with the phasing out of OPS, the Agency's Office of International Narcotics Control was established in the Bureau of Services (AID/SER/INC). Mary Wampler, who for the past several years has been Special Assistant to the Administrator for narcotics matters (A/AID), is the new office director. The ex-OPS personnel who have been assigned to this continuing activity are: Cesar Bernal, Acting Deputy Director; Frank Craig; William Andrews; Elliott K. Chan; Rudy Hall; Paul Katz; Francis Perry, and Jim McCarthy. (McCarthy is extended to 30 June and will be terminated at that time [sic]. Providing the administrative assistance is Charlotte Hudlow and Ann Hess. This group will be augmented by several persons being transferred from the former A/AID office or elsewhere in AID." See also Huggins, "U.S.-Supported State Terror"; Huggins, Political Policing.

25 PSN 9 (Mar. 1976), 2, reported a UPI news release dated March 4 that "Iran formally terminated the services of the U.S. advisory mission to its state police," concluding a program of thirty-four years. I did not pursue this line of research; perhaps another scholar will be interested to detail the Iran thread.

26 Airgram, AmEmbassy JIDDA to Department of State, "Public Safety U-127 Report for August, 1971"; Ziegler was still there in 1973, according to "Public Safety Program, Saudi Arabia," probably part of an untitled briefing book on OPS Phase-Out, January 13, 1973, Folder "IPS 1 General Policy Guidelines—Background (OPS Program Assistance Reports/Study) Folder 4," AID A-1 Entry 18 (Office of Public Safety, Office of the Director, Numerical File 1956–74), RG 286, NARA. *PSN* 8 (Jan. 1976), 4, 8; *PSN* 11 (Oct. 1976), 6; *PSN* 12 (Dec. 1976), 2.

27 *PSN* 8 (Jan. 1976), 4 (quote); *PSN* 5 (July 1975), 2; *PSN* 6 (Sept. 1975), 5.

28 *PSN* 18 (Oct. 1978), 4.

29 GlobalSecurity.org, "Royal Saudi Naval Forces (RSNF) History."

30 *PSN* 8 (Jan. 1976), 4; *BioReg* '73, 4.

31 Goin, "Annex I," 1–2, to Goin, "Memorandum for the Administrator. Subject: Public Safety Activities," draft date February 26, 1974, Folder "IPS 1 General Policy Guidelines—Background (OPS Program Assistance Reports/Study) Folder 4," AID A-1 Entry 18 (Office of Public Safety, Office of the Director, Numerical File 1956–74), RG 286, NARA.

32 *PSN* 7 (Nov. 1975), 3; see also *PSN* 10 (July 1976), 2; *PSN* 12 (Dec. 1976), 1; *PSN* 14 (July 1977), 1; *PSN* 16 (Mar. 1977), 5.

33 Jeter Williamson, "Public Safety Project—Saudi Arabia" report, 1968 (author name revealed in a memo to Byron Engle also in this folder), Folder "Saudi Arabia IPS-1-3," USAID A1 Entry 30 (Public Safety, OPS Division; Africa, Near East, South America Branch; Subject Files, 1956–1972), RG 286, NARA; "Public Safety Program, Saudi Arabia," probably part of an untitled briefing book on OPS Phase-Out, January 13, 1973, monetary count on 3, Folder "IPS 1 General Policy Guidelines—Background (OPS Program Assistance Reports/Study) Folder 4," AID A-1 Entry 18 (Office of Public Safety, Office of the Director, Numerical File 1956–74), RG 286, NARA.

34 E. R. Bishop, Office of Public Safety, AID, "Report of Study of Saudi Arabian Public Security Forces, Riot Control, Capabilities and Requirements," January 1969, 7, Folder "Saudi Arabia-1" (2nd of 2, same title), AID A-1 Entry 19 ("Office of Public Safety, Office of the Director, Program Surveys and Evaluations, 1959–74"), RG 286, NARA.

35 Airgram 1973, "AmEmbassy JIDDA" to Department of State, "Public Safety U-127 Report for February 1973," 1, Folder "SAUDI ARABIA (monthly Reports—Sept. 1971 to July 1973)," AID A-1 Entry 21 ("Office of Public Safety, Office of the Director, General Records, 1959–74"), RG 286, NARA.

36 Airgram 1973, "AmEmbassy JIDDA" to Department of State, "Public Safety U-127 Report for July 1973," Folder "SAUDI ARABIA (monthly Reports—Sept. 1971 to July 1973)," AID A-1 Entry 21 ("Office of Public Safety, Office of the Director, General Records, 1959–74"), RG 286, NARA.

37 Goin, "Memorandum for the Administrator. Subject: Public Safety Activities," draft date February 26, 1974, 19, Folder "IPS 1 General Policy Guidelines—Background (OPS Program Assistance Reports/Study) Folder 4," AID A-1 Entry 18 (Office of Public Safety, Office of the Director, Numerical File 1956–74), RG 286, NARA.

38 *PSN* 8 (Jan. 1976), 4 (quote); *PSN* 5 (July 1975), 2; *PSN* 6 (Sept. 1975), 5.

39 A. Escobar, *Encountering Development*; J. Ferguson, *Anti-Politics Machine*.

40 Thanks to Mark Neocleous for pointing me to another relevant borrowing of the phrase "masters of all they surveyed" from William Cowper's eighteenth-century poetry: Burnett, *Masters of All They Surveyed*, an excellent work on European explorers and their colonizing mapmaking. The survey for OPS operated in much the way the map operated for Burnett's protagonists.

41 To give a sense, there were thirteen boxes of records of "Program Surveys and Evaluations, 1959–74" when I first consulted them at the National Archives: AID A-1 Entry 19 (Office of Public Safety, Office of the Director, Program Surveys and Evaluations, 1959–74), RG 286, NARA. On Saudi Arabian surveys specifically, a 1966 survey is in Folder "Kingdom of Saudi Arabia IPS-1-1"; one from 1971 is in Folder "Saudi Arabia IPS-1-2"; the 1969 survey of Frontier Force, Coast Guard and Ports is in "Kingdom of Saudi Arabia IPS-1-5"; all in USAID A1 Entry 30 ("Public Safety, OPS Division; Africa, Near East, South America Branch; Subject Files, 1956–1972"), RG 286, NARA; a 1969 survey is E. R. Bishop, Office of Public Safety, AID, "Report of Study of Saudi Arabian Public Security Forces, Riot Control, Capabilities and Requirements," January 1969, 7, Folder "Saudi Arabia-1" (2nd of 2, same title), AID A-1 Entry 19 ("Office of Public Safety, Office of the Director, Program Surveys and Evaluations, 1959–74"), RG 286, NARA; on the 1971 survey, see also Elmer H. Adkins, "Survey Report of the Surveillance and Protection, Saudi Arabian Oil Fields and Installations, for the Ministry of Interior, Kingdom of Saudi Arabia," December 1971, Folder "Public Safety-1," AID A-1 Entry 19 ("Office of Public Safety, Office of the Director, Program Surveys and Evaluations, 1959–74"), RG 286, NARA. After OPS, surveys continued to occupy ex-OPS agents such as Frank Walton, who went to work as a consultant for LECAR (Law Enforcement Consulting and Research) conducting "Police Department surveys, Building security studies and an organized crime study, etc.," the largest of which was "a seven-month study he conducted of Law Enforcement in Kuwait" (*PSN* 4 [May 1975], 8).

42 Seigel, "William Bratton in the Other LA."

43 *PSN* 4 (May 1975), 1.

44 *PSN* 4 (May 1975), 4.

45 Bordenkircher and Hatem, for example, went stateside to long careers in domestic law enforcement, Bordenkercher to run prisons, serving first as warden of the West Virginia Penitentiary and then of the Kentucky State Prison at Eddyville (*PSN* 3 [Feb. 1975], 6; *PSN* 4 [May 1975], 1; *PSN* 8 [Jan. 1976], 6; *PSN* 11 [Oct. 1976], 2), and Hatem in October 1976 to direct an LEAA/Bureau of Indian Affairs project with the Miccosukee tribe in Florida's Everglades National Park area (*PSN* 11 [Oct. 1976], 1), becoming, by the end of 1977, chief of the Miccosukee Tribal Police Force (*PSN* 15 [Dec. 1977], 3).

46 *PSN* 20 (May 1979), 2; Mayfield was "in Saudi, working with Mike Dobrichan" too (*PSN* 19 [Feb. 1979], 4), while Staley told lunch companions at an OPS gathering in April 1979 that he "had just returned from Saudi Arabia" (*PSN* 20

[May 1979], 1), likely meaning the same project. Alert readers may remember Staley from his picture in Alaska in figure 3.1.

47 *PSN* 18 (Oct. 1978), 3.

48 *PSN* 20 (May 1979), 2; *PSN* 24 (Jan. 1980), 2; *PSN* 26 (June 1980), 1.

49 *PSN* 20 (May 1979), 2; Goodchild was still there as per *PSN* 24 (Jan. 1980), 3; *PSN* 26 (June 1980), 1.

50 *PSN* 16 (Mar. 1977), 5; *PSN* 17 (July 1978), 6; *PSN* 20 (May 1979), 2; *PSN* 25 (Apr. 1980), 2; *PSN* 26 (June 1980), 1.

51 No author, "A.I.D.'s Office of Public Safety," no date, 6, 7, Folder "OPS HANDOUT— AID Assistance to Civil Security Forces," AID A-1 Entry 21 ("Office of Public Safety, Office of the Director, General Records, 1959–74"), RG 286, NARA.

52 Saenz, *OPS Story*, 427; *BioReg '73*, 156.

53 *BioReg '73*, 139.

54 *BioReg '73*, 160.

55 *BioReg '73*, 38.

56 *BioReg '73*, 225.

57 "John Clifford 'Jack' Zeigler," obituary, *Arizona Republic*, October 5, 2012, reprinted at *AZCentral.com*, accessed 6/28/14, http://www.legacy.com/obituaries /azcentral/obituary.aspx?pid=160273662. Note that Zeigler here is spelled Z-e-i, just as in *BioReg*; most citations in the *PSN* spell it Z-i-e, as do documents at the National Archive.

58 *BioReg '73*, 55.

59 The one was Alkassim, the electronics engineer; *BioReg '73*, 4. No *BioReg '73* entries for Moyers, Bishonden, Romero, Goodchild (perhaps because he was British), Gray (or Grey), Boyling, Young, or Sullivan; *BioReg* entries but no pre-AID info for Vukovich, Dobrichan, Bordenkircher (perhaps because he was too young, born in 1935), Wagner, Phippen, or Merseth.

60 *PSN* 27 (Sept. 1980), 4. In this same issue, Goodchild showed the mission evolving across the generations: he asked for help locating a position for his son, "ex-police, and in personnel administration combined with security and specializes in training security personnel for commercial and private purposes."

61 Vukovich had stayed in Saigon after OPS's termination to work for the Defense Attaché Office, a military post to US embassies involved primarily in intelligence gathering. He returned to the US, planning to retire (*PSN* 5 [July 1975], 3; *PSN* 8 [Jan. 1976], 8).

62 *PSN* 11 (Oct. 1976), 6; *PSN* 10 (July 1976), 2; *PSN* 11 (Oct. 1976), 4.

63 *PSN* 12 (Dec. 1976), 2. In between assignments Boyling lived with his wife Bo Linh in San Francisco (*PSN* 7 [Nov. 1975], 1; *PSN* 8 [Jan. 1976], 6, gives her name as Dinh, *PSN* 12 [Dec. 1976], 6). In late 1975, he gave an address care of Stanwick International on Kharg Island, Iran (*PSN* 12 [Dec. 1976], 2). Boyling seems to have retired by April 1980, reporting that he was back in the United States "doing some lazy fishing" (*PSN* 25 [Apr. 1980], 1).

64 *PSN* 17 (July 1978), 2; Saudi Aramco, "Berri Gas Plant."

65 *PSN* 3 (Feb. 1975), 3, 5; *PSN* 13 (Mar. 1977), 3.

66 PSN 16 (Mar. 1977), 2; PSN 24 (Jan. 1980), 2.

67 PSN 28 (Nov. 1980), 1.

68 PSN 16 (Mar. 1977), 3. Gordon and wife Peggy had started up an import-export business in Chiang Mai, Thailand, "specializing in tribal handicrafts and collectors' mineral specimens" (PSN 4 [May 1975], 4; PSN 11 [Oct. 1976], 6). It isn't clear what happened to that business, but by November 1979, Gordon had joined the Diablo Canyon (California) Nuclear Plant's security program on a part-time basis (PSN 27 [Sept. 1980], 2).

69 PSN 23 (Nov. 1979), 1.

70 PSN 12 (Dec. 1976), 2; PSN 26 (June 1980), 5; it is unclear whether Mary Kay was a former OPS employee herself.

71 PSN 8 (Jan. 1976), 4; PSN 12 (Dec. 1976), 1.

72 PSN 5 (July 1975), 2; it is unclear whether Fargo International here refers to the bank, the airport, or the New Zealand manufacturer; PSN 8 (Jan. 1976), 4, 6.

73 PSN 12 (Dec. 1976), 2. Jeter Williamson also paid Ziegler a visit, without telling the newsletter what he was doing otherwise; PSN 8 (Jan. 1976), 4.

74 This is another example of the imperial engagements of the "covert capital" as so beautifully set out in Friedman, *Covert Capital*, which I discuss further in chapter 6.

75 PSN 3 (Feb. 1975), 3; PSN 8 (Jan. 1976), 8; PSN 15 (Dec. 1977), 2.

76 PSN 19 (Feb. 1979), 3.

77 PSN 20 (May 1979), 2.

78 PSN 4 (May 1975), 4; PSN 7 (Nov. 1975), 1; PSN 8 (Jan. 1976), 8; PSN 9 (Mar. 1976), 3. In July 1976 Scott wrote that he "continues with his work as a consultant and is 'leasing more land in the southwest for exploration and oil development'" in Honduras (PSN 10 [July 1976], 1), where he stayed several more years (PSN 11 [Oct. 1976], 5; PSN 17 [July 1978], 6).

79 PSN 19 (Feb. 1979), 1.

80 PSN 4 (May 1975), 6; PSN 8 (Jan. 1976), 4; TAI stands for Tourgee and Associates, Incorporated. Completing that assignment, Powell relocated to Raleigh to work with Aerotron, "a manufacturer of 2 way radios—in the marketing end of the business," he explained (PSN 12 [Dec. 1976], 2). He continued part-time consulting into his retirement (PSN 25 [Apr. 1980], 1).

81 PSN 4 (May 1975), 8.

82 PSN 7 (Nov. 1975), 1; PSN 8 (Jan. 1976), 6; PSN 12 (Dec. 1976), 2.

83 PSN 17 (July 1978), 2.

84 Johnston, *Rebirth of Private Policing*, 114.

85 Holmes and Narver was founded in 1933, the same year as Aramco, and has collaborated on Aramco projects over the years (see, for example, Telemedia.com, "Telemedia International—Clients" list; "ADL Charges over 200 U.S. Firms"). It joined forces with four other companies to become AECOM Government Services, Inc., in 1990, and as such contracted support for the Multinational Force and Observers (Organization of the Multinational Force and Observers, http://www.mfo.org/support.php) and worked on Federal projects through the

Department of Defense, building secret facilities for the military (Haghhor, zoominfo profile). It was involved in the Nevada underground nuclear test facility in the 1950s and helped revamp the LAPD downtown facility in 2008 (Aecom, "What We Do: Government," and Aecom, "What We Do: Architecture"). It was accused of racial discrimination in 1992 (*Kimble v. Holmes and Narver Services Incorporated and E*) and contract fraud in 1988 (O'Dell, "Fallout from Probe").

86 For institutional history, see Saudi Aramco's website, www.saudiaramco.com; Aramco also produces prolific printed matter, including Lebkicher, *Aramco and World Oil*; various handbooks such as Lebkicher, Rentz, Steineke et al., *Aramco Handbook*; and *Saudi Aramco World* (Texas: Aramco Services Company), Aramco's bimonthly magazine. A devastating indictment of the company's segregated labor relations is Vitalis, *America's Kingdom*; see also Midnight Notes, *Midnight Oil*.

87 Elmer H. Adkins, "Survey Report of the Surveillance and Protection, Saudi Arabian Oil Fields and Installations, for the Ministry of Interior, Kingdom of Saudi Arabia," December 1971, 1, 5, 20, Folder "Public Safety-1," AID A-1 Entry 19 ("Office of Public Safety, Office of the Director, Program Surveys and Evaluations, 1959–74"), RG 286, NARA. This despite the fact that Aramco *did* have its own security force in previous years (Rosie Bsheer, personal communication, October 26, 2017). I do not know if the survey's notice was wilfull ignorance or if the security force had been, at this point, disbanded.

88 Adkins, "Survey Report."

89 O'Toole, *Private Sector*, 42.

90 *PSN* 26 (June 1980), 1.

91 Wolfe-Hunnicutt, "End of the Concessionary Regime."

92 Saudi Aramco, "Our Company."

93 Mitchell, "Limits of the State."

94 Davis, "Unlikely, but Boise Means Big Business"; Roscow, *800 Miles to Valdez*, 100; Baer and Wee, "URS Corp. Acquires Washington Group"; Feder, "Agee Leaving Morrison Knudsen."

95 Hartung, "Mercenaries, Inc.," 26–28.

96 Hartung, "Mercenaries, Inc.," 26–28.

97 Vitalis, *America's Kingdom*.

98 E. R. Bishop, Office of Public Safety, AID, "Report of Study of Saudi Arabian Public Security Forces, Riot Control, Capabilities and Requirements," January 1969, 2–4, Folder "Saudi Arabia-1" (2nd of 2, same title), AID A-1 Entry 19 ("Office of Public Safety, Office of the Director, Program Surveys and Evaluations, 1959–74"), RG 286, NARA.

99 The second comment is from a British diplomat; Hertog, *Princes, Brokers, and Bureaucrats*, 31, 90.

100 Here I aim to invoke Patricia Williams: "That life is complicated is a fact of great analytic importance," as discussed by Avery Gordon in *Ghostly Matters*, 3 and passim.

101 Hinton, *War on Poverty*; Murakawa, *First Civil Right*; Murakawa and Beck-ett, "Mapping the Shadow Carceral State"; Kohler-Hausmann, *Getting Tough*; Kohler-Hausmann, "Guns and Butter"; Sparrow, *Warfare State*.

102 Parker, "What Exactly Happened?"; Freeman, "Horror at Fallujah"; see also Gettleman, "Enraged Mob."

103 Murphy, "Cheney's Halliburton Ties Remain"; Krugman, "Patriots and Prof-its"; Marshall, "Lies We Are Told about Iraq"; "Our Opinion"; "Suspect Stays on the Job."

104 FAQ's for PBS Frontline, *Private Warriors*.

105 Greenwald, "Militarization of U.S. Police"; see also Goodman, "Cops or Sol-diers?"; Goodman, "Ferguson Crackdown"; Zeese and Flowers, "Ferguson Exposes the Reality."

CHAPTER 5. PROFESSORS FOR POLICE

1 Carnahan interview.

2 Editors, "Editorial: Berkeley's School of Criminology, 1950–1976"; Uchida, "Development of the American Police"; Carte and Carte, *Police Reform in the United States*; Skolnick and Fyfe, *Above the Law*, 174. Berkeley's closing in the 1970s makes it once again exceptional in that its school closed just as pro-grams across the nation were emerging.

3 Wakeman, *Spymaster*, 192–96; see also correspondence between Vollmer and Israel Castellanos, head of the Cuban Bureau of National Identity in the mid-1930s, in the August Vollmer Collection of the Bancroft Library at UC Berke-ley, cited in Bronfman, *Measures of Equality*, 130.

4 Harring, *Policing a Class Society*; Allinson, "Great LEEP Backward?"; LAPD online, "Los Angeles Police Academy."

5 Marion, *Federal Government and Criminal Justice*, 9–10.

6 In addition, the LEAA's predecessor in 1965, the OLEA, allocated $7.3 million a year for three years, with over $4 million going to police training. Griffin, *Study of Relationships*, 11; Chang and McKean, "Criminology, Delinquency, and Corrections."

7 Griffin, *Study of Relationships*, 11; IACP, *Directory*; LEAA, *Second Annual Re-port*, 54, latter two cited in Webb, "Back Home," 10.

8 Allinson, "Great LEEP Backward?," 14.

9 Givan et al., *Justice and Safety Education*, 34.

10 Walker, "Between Two Worlds"; see also Webb, "Back Home," 10.

11 Tullis, "Vietnam at Home," 109–10; Chang and McKean, "Criminology, Delin-quency, and Corrections," 211.

12 Chang and McKean, "Criminology, Delinquency, and Corrections," 212.

13 Tullis, "Vietnam at Home," 109–10; Greenberg, "IDA."

14 Klare, "Bringing It Back."

15 Rohde, "Gray Matters," 121.

16 Rohde, "Gray Matters," 121–22.

17 Ernst, *Forging a Fateful Alliance*, 4.

18 McCann, *PSN* 149 (Sept. 2007), 1; Lobe, "U.S. Police Assistance," 49; a report on a joint USAID/University of Kentucky project in 1972–73 and another joining Paraguay and Georgia Tech are in the folder "Reports," Box 4, USAID Entry UD-WW 428 ("Unclassified USAID/Caracas"), RG 286-74-155, NARA.

19 Ernst, *Forging a Fateful Alliance*, 63.

20 Ernst, *Forging a Fateful Alliance*, esp. 8–13; see also Lobe, "U.S. Police Assistance," 50.

21 Ernst, *Forging a Fateful Alliance*, xiv–xv.

22 Ernst, *Forging a Fateful Alliance*; see also Dressel, *College to University*; Scigliano and Fox, *Technical Assistance In Vietnam*; Smuckler, *University Turns to the World*.

23 Tullis, *Vietnam at Home*, 44; Lobe, "U.S. Police Assistance," 50; McClintock, *Instruments of Statecraft*, 188.

24 Ernst, *Forging a Fateful Alliance*, 73, 76.

25 A series of reports on OPS in Brazil for 1965–66 included MSU's project to improve audiovisual equipment and expertise in Brazil, including training audiovisual experts for work in schools, police departments, and elsewhere: Folder "INF—3.3 MSU Reports FY '64," USAID Entry UD-WW 400 ("Unclassified 'Brazil SUBJ/PROJ 56–73'"), RG 286-75-162, NARA.

26 *PSN* 24 (Jan. 1980), 1; Shields was not himself a PSA but a "friend of PSD," who "later went with IIS," the Institute for International Studies out of Yale, another academic foreign policy strategy school, on which, see Farish, *Contours of America's Cold War*, 25–28.

27 *PSN* 24 (Jan. 1980), 4.

28 *BioReg* 1966, 569.

29 *BioReg* 1967, 219.

30 *BioReg* 1973, 254.

31 *PSN* 18 (Oct. 1978), 5.

32 *PSN* 3 (Feb. 1975), 6; *PSN* 8 (Jan. 1976), 6; *PSN* 10 (July 1976), 1; no author, "Norman C. Colter, Obituary."

33 Turner interview.

34 Lt. Robert Posey of the Kentucky State Police took a sabbatical from service to get a master's at MSU, then returned to start the well-fated program at EKU, for example; Givan et al., *Justice and Safety Education*, 5. When the Federal Law Enforcement Training Center set up, moreover, it poached MSU's dean, as this chapter will discuss below.

35 Carnahan interview.

36 David B. Bell, "Memorandum for the Special Group (CI)," April 5, 1965, 10, 13, Folder "IPS History References," AID A-1 Entry 21 (Office of Public Safety, Office of the Director, General Records, 1959–74), RG 286, NARA.

37 Folders "Higher Education," "Professional Education," "Secondary," "University of Wisconsin," "Vocational Training," "Edu. General," "Elementary," "Higher

Education," "Library Operation," and repeats of all of these in USAID Entry UD-WW 428 ("Unclassified USAID/Caracas"), RG 286-74-155, NARA.

38 Payne to Brown, "Student Demonstration in Maceio 1–15–68," January 18, 1968, USAID Entry UD-UP 33 ("Unclassified 'USAID/Brazil. Office of the Public Safety Chief Advisor. Public Safety Area Offices. Subject Files 1957–1973'"), RG 286-75-150, NARA.

39 Airgram, "AID TO CIRCULAR/A 384, Public Safety Training, International Police Academy," May 22, 1974, Folder "IPS 1 General Policy Guidelines—Background (Phase Out Study)—Folder 1," AID A-1 Entry 18 ("Office of Public Safety, Office of the Director, Numerical File 1956–74"), RG 286, NARA.

40 No author, "Office of Public Safety, International Police Academy, June 1974," Folder "OPS HANDOUT—AID Assistance to Civil Security Forces," AID A-1 Entry 21 ("Office of Public Safety, Office of the Director, General Records, 1959–74"), RG 286, NARA.

41 *PSN* 6 (Sept. 1975), 4; *PSN* 8 (Jan. 1976), 6; *PSN* 25 (Apr. 1980), 4; *PSN* 5 (July 1975), 6; *PSN* 8 (Jan. 1976), 8; *PSN* 12 (Dec. 1976), 3; *PSN* 8 (Jan. 1976), 1; *PSN* 16 (Mar. 1977), 2; *PSN* 19 (Feb. 1979), 3; *PSN* 4 (May 1975), 6, 8; *PSN* 8 (Jan. 1976), 7; *PSN* 3 (Feb. 1975), 6; *PSN* 8 (Jan. 1976), 7; *PSN* 4 (May 1975), 4.

42 *PSN* 8 (Jan. 1976), 6; *PSN* 14 (July 1977), 2; *PSN* 25 (Apr. 1980), 6; *PSN* 14 (July 1977), 2; *PSN* 26 (June 1980), 2.

43 *PSN* 4 (May 1975), 3; *PSN* 8 (Jan. 1976), 2, 7; *PSN* 8 (Jan. 1976), 7; *PSN* 13 (Mar. 1977), 1; I wonder whether the listing of the second man as a professor might be an error, a repeat of the first's position—though the two did both work in Vietnam in 1968–69, so perhaps they had helped each other obtain similar posts, as ex-OPS so often did.

44 *PSN* 10 (July 1976), 2; *PSN* 18 (Oct. 1978), 2.

45 *PSN* 3 (Feb. 1975), 6; *PSN* 8 (Jan. 1976), 6; *PSN* 11 (Oct. 1976), 2.

46 *PSN* 5 (July 1975), 3; *PSN* 6 (Sept. 1975), 5; *PSN* 8 (Jan. 1976), 6. At the 1974 state Chiefs of Police Association, he met the former OPS agent then leading the police department in Abingdon, who later asked him for help finding a teaching job, as he had finished a degree in police science; *PSN* 3 (Feb. 1975), 2; *PSN* 5 (July 1975), 3; *PSN* 8 (Jan. 1976), 8; *PSN* 11 (Oct. 1976), 5; *PSN* 19 (Feb. 1979), 5.

47 *PSN* 3 (Feb. 1975), 5; *PSN* 7 (Nov. 1975), 3; *PSN* 8 (Jan. 1976), 3, 6; *PSN* 12 (Dec. 1976), 1.

48 *PSN* 3 (Feb. 1975), 3; *PSN* 8 (Jan. 1976), 6, 8; *PSN* 15 (Dec. 1977), 3; *PSN* 11 (Oct. 1976), 3.

49 *PSN* 23 (Nov. 1979), 1; *PSN* 16 (Mar. 1977), 3.

50 *PSN* 3 (Feb. 1975), 6; *PSN* 8 (Jan. 1976), 4, 6; *PSN* 11 (Oct. 1976), 2; *PSN* 16 (Mar. 1977), 1; *PSN* 19 (Feb. 1979), 6.

51 *PSN* 10 (July 1976), 3; *PSN* 19 (Feb. 1979), 4.

52 *PSN* 15 (Dec. 1977), 1.

53 *PSN* 3 (Feb. 1975), 7; *PSN* 8 (Jan. 1976), 8.

54 *PSN* 21 (July 1979), 3; Fiore and Boxall, "Local Elections."

55 *PSN* 7 (Nov. 1975), 1; *PSN* 11 (Oct. 1976), 3.

56 *PSN* 7 (Nov. 1975), 3; *PSN* 20 (May 1979), 3.

57 *PSN* 6 (Sept. 1975), 4; *PSN* 9 (Mar. 1976), 1; *PSN* 12 (Dec. 1976), 2; no author, "Dr. Harry Eugene Bruno."

58 *PSN* 149 (Sept. 2007), 1; *PSN* 3 (Feb. 1975), 7; *PSN* 4 (May 1975), 5; *PSN* 7 (Nov. 1975), 2; *PSN* 8 (Jan. 1976), 3; *PSN* 8 (Jan. 1976), 7.

59 *PSN* 3 (Feb. 1975), 4; *PSN* 6 (Sept. 1975), 2; *PSN* 8 (Jan. 1976), 7; *PSN* 10 (July 1976), 1; *PSN* 11 (Oct. 1976), 2; *PSN* 14 (July 1977), 1; *PSN* 15 (Dec. 1977), 2; Grodsky interview.

60 *PSN* 3 (Feb. 1975), 7; *PSN* 8 (Jan. 1976), 7; *PSN* 7 (Nov. 1975), 2. In addition, an Indiana University study entitled "Evaluating the Organization of Service Delivery: Police" hired a former OPS agent who was chief of police for the cities of San Fernando and Oxanard (both in California) and a doctoral student in Public Administration at USC; *PSN* 6 (Sept. 1975), 5; *PSN* 8 (Jan. 1976), 8.

61 *PSN* 11 (Oct. 1976), 1, 5.

62 *PSN* 25 (Apr. 1980), 3; Laughlin retired to Bloomfield, Indiana, as he revealed in his autobiography, *Gringo Cop*; *PSN* 5 (July 1975), 5.

63 *PSN* 3 (Feb. 1975), 6; *PSN* 8 (Jan. 1976), 7.

64 Saenz, OPS *Story*, 432.

65 *PSN* 25 (Apr. 1980), 1.

66 "Memorandum of Understanding" between "Indiana University, School of Public and Environmental Affairs, Bloomington, Indiana," and "Indiana Organized Crime Prevention Council, Indianapolis, Indiana," signed 9/28/78, 10/30/78, 10/26/78; Contract files, C256, Office of University Archives and Records Management, Indiana University, Bloomington. IU's Department of Police Administration, housed in the College of Arts and Sciences, was chaired from 1958 to 1987 by the inventor of the breathalyzer, according to the IU Archives' description of his papers; Jankowski, "Robert F. Borkenstein Papers."

67 "Memorandum of Understanding" between "Indiana University, School of Public and Environmental Affairs, Bloomington, Indiana," and "Indiana Organized Crime Prevention Council, Indianapolis, Indiana," signed 9/28/78, 10/30/78, 10/26/78; Contract files, C256, Office of University Archives and Records Management, Indiana University, Bloomington.

68 "Indiana University—Purdue University at Indianapolis Route Sheet for Research and Sponsored Program Support," dated 10/18/78, 10/23/78; Contract files, C256, Office of University Archives and Records Management, Indiana University, Bloomington.

69 "ICJPA Grant Amendment Request," dated 8/24/79, re: grant *PSN* 78C-E04-019-025. Subgrantee: Indiana Organized Crime Prevention Council; Project Title: IN Organized Crime Prevention Council; Contract files, C256, Office of University Archives and Records Management, Indiana University, Bloomington.

70 Turner interview. All subsequent citations in this section are Turner unless otherwise noted.

71 Turner interview; see also *PSN* 10 (July 1976), 3; *PSN* 17 (July 1978), 3. Turner was not the highest-level director of FLETC but inaugural director of the police training school; F. S. Calhoun, *Trainers*, 40.

72 Koerner, *Skies Belong to Us*.

73 Turner interview.

74 *PSN* 18 (Oct. 1978), 2. For more on Glen Boyce, *PSN* 9 (Mar. 1976), 2; *PSN* 10 (July 1976), 3; *PSN* 16 (Mar. 1977), 6; on Tori Groshong, *PSN* 10 (July 1976), 3; Jack Larrimore, *PSN* 10 (July 1976), 3; *PSN* 16 (Mar. 1977), 6.

75 Turner interview.

76 *PSN* 11 (Oct. 1976), 1.

77 Ernst, *Forging a Fateful Alliance*, 11–12; F. S. Calhoun, *Trainers*, 89; Brandstatter was also a former policeman, reports Calhoun.

78 *PSN* 3 (Feb. 1975), 3, 6; *PSN* 8 (Jan. 1976), 7; *PSN* 10 (July 1976), 2, 3; *PSN* 13 (Mar. 1977), 3; *PSN* 16 (Mar. 1977), 6.

79 *PSN* 3 (Feb. 1975), 7; *PSN* 8 (Jan. 1976), 8; *PSN* 10 (July 1976), 3; *PSN* 11 (Oct. 1976), 1.

80 *PSN* 7 (Nov. 1975), 2; *PSN* 8 (Jan. 1976), 6; *PSN* 11 (Oct. 1976), 3; *PSN* 12 (Dec. 1976), 1; *PSN* 13 (Mar. 1977), 3; *PSN* 16 (Mar. 1977), 6.

81 Grodsky interview.

82 *PSN* 8 (Jan. 1976), 1.

83 Grodsky interview.

84 Grodsky, *Home Boy's Odyssey*.

85 F. S. Calhoun, *Trainers*, 1; this wariness is repeated several times, e.g., 28.

86 F. S. Calhoun, *Trainers*, 2.

87 F. S. Calhoun, *Trainers*, 89.

88 F. S. Calhoun, *Trainers*, 113–14.

89 F. S. Calhoun, *Trainers*, 2.

90 McManus, *Police Training and Performance Study*, v–vi.

91 Smith and Ostrom, "Effects of Training and Education."

92 Walker, "Between Two Worlds"; Griffin, *Study of Relationships*.

93 Smith and Ostrom, "Effects of Training and Education."

94 Allinson, "Great LEEP Backward," 16, citing Sherman et al., *Quality of Police Education*.

95 Webb, "Back Home," 11.

96 Chang and McKean, "Criminology, Delinquency, and Corrections," 210.

97 Zahn, "Thoughts on the Future of Criminology."

98 Garland and Sparks, "Criminology, Social Theory," 191, 193; Chang and McKean, "Criminology, Delinquency, and Corrections"; on the field's interdisciplinarity, see also Zahn, "Thoughts on the Future."

99 Garland and Sparks, "Criminology, Social Theory," 201.

100 Zahn, "Thoughts on the Future."

101 Arnold, "Criminal Justice," 90.

102 Arnold, "Criminal Justice," 90.

103 Arnold, "Criminal Justice," 87; the field's lack of relevance is bemoaned by Garland and Sparks, "Criminology, Social Theory," 191; Zahn, "Thoughts on the Future."

104 Arnold, "Criminal Justice."

105 Farrell and Koch, "Criminal Justice, Sociology, and Academia"; Farrell and Thomas, "Sociology, Humanism."

106 Murakawa and Beckett, "Penology of Racial Innocence," 696; see also M. Brown, *Culture of Punishment.*

107 J. Young, *Criminological Imagination.*

108 Clear, "Policy and Evidence," 6.

109 Schept, Wall, and Brisman, "Building, Staffing, and Insulating," 2, 7. On the field's western or first world biases, see Cain, "Orientalism."

110 Webb, "Back Home," 17.

111 Flitcraft, "Winning Hearts and Minds," 22.

112 Flitcraft, "LEAA: Campus Cops' Hot Line," 25–27.

113 Boger and Orfield, *School Resegregation*; Orfield et al., *Dismantling Desegregation*; Bell, *Silent Covenants.*

114 Katz and Rose, *Public Education Under Siege*; Shelly, *Money, Mandates, and Local Control*; Erickson, *Class War.*

115 Guerrero, *Silence at Boalt Hall*; Fair, *Notes of a Racial Caste Baby*; Herring and Collins, "Retreat from Equal Opportunity?"

116 Meiners, "Ending the School-to-Prison Pipeline."

117 Morris points out this timing congruence in *Devil's Butcher Shop*, 45; see also Meiners, "Building an Abolition Democracy"; Coley and Barton, "Locked Up and Locked Out"; McGrew, *Education's Prisoners*; University of California Infocenter, "State Spending on Corrections and Education."

118 Blumenson and Nilsen, "How to Construct an Underclass"; see also Moreton, *To Serve God and Wal-Mart.*

CHAPTER 6. EXILES AT HOME

1 Chandola, "Who Are the Refugees?"; Desbarats, "Ethnic Differences in Adaptation"; Finnan, "Occupational Assimilation of Refugees"; Floriano, "Life in a Camp"; Kelly, *From Vietnam to America*; Haines, Rutherford, and Thomas, "Family and Community"; Heder, "Kampuchean-Vietnamese Conflict"; Huyck and Bouvier, "Demography of Refugees"; Kissman and Van Tran, "Life Satisfaction among the Indochinese Refugees"; Kurth, "America Must Do More"; Martin, "Vietnamese Students"; Montero, *Vietnamese Americans*; Mortland, "Transforming Refugees in Refugee Camps"; Osborne, "Indochinese Refugees"; Strand, "Employment Predictors among Indochinese Refugees"; Stuart-Fox, "Laos: The Vietnamese Connection"; Vo, *Viet Kieu in America*; Vo, *Vietnamese Boat People*; Chan, *Vietnamese American 1.5 Generation*; Wain, *Refused*; Zaharlick and Brainard, "Demographic Characteristics"; Zanetti, "Admission of Refugees."

2 Espiritu, "Toward a Critical Refugee Study"; Nguyen, *Gift of Freedom*; Tang, *Unsettled*. This framing was beautifully challenged when people fleeing Hurricane

Katrina were called refugees; see C. Woods, "In the Wake of Katrina"; Petrucci
and Head, "Hurricane Katrina's Lexical Storm"; Masquelier, "Why Katrina's
Victims Aren't Refugees."

3 Friedman, *Covert Capital*, 24, 26.

4 Stoler, *Haunted by Empire*; Stoler, "Tense and Tender Ties"; Lowe, *Intimacies of Four Continents*.

5 Williams developed the concept of the structure of feeling to get at the vital, intangible sphere in which the experience of the quality of life at a particular time and place is distilled. This angle of approach offers an opportunity to move away from "more formal concepts of 'world view' or 'ideology'" toward "affective elements of consciousness and relationships . . . social experience." Raymond Williams, *Marxism and Literature*, 132.

6 This is, for example, why Christopher Agee's excellent social history of the San Francisco police, *Streets of San Francisco*, objects to seeing the police as an arm of the state and in the service of capitalism: on the basis of local police failures to support specific City Hall agendas.

7 Another way to say this is that it is the wage that exploits even as it seems to reward.

8 Roediger, *Wages of Whiteness*; Guinier and Torres, *Miner's Canary* (coined "racial bribe" far before the term's better-known use in the popular book that suggests mass incarceration is a "new Jim Crow").

9 Here I am drawing on the astute discussion of projection, objectification, and identification in Lott, *Love and Theft*.

10 Andy Best, "Editorial," *PSN* 149 (Sept. 2007), 3.

11 Best interview.

12 Grodsky interview.

13 Carnahan interview.

14 Antonik interview.

15 *PSN* 6 (Sept. 1975), 2.

16 "Identity Withheld as Requested: The Turbulent Past," *PSN* 149 (Sept. 2007), 3.

17 Harpold interview.

18 *PSN* 23 (Nov. 1979), 2.

19 *PSN* 25 (Apr. 1980), 8. Bill Burgess showed that he was similarly intimidated, though without the political critique, when he wrote that some ex-OPS agents might not write to the *Newsletter* because "their lives, as in my case, have been rather bland in comparison to the adventures and travels of their old friends" (*PSN* 25 [Apr. 1980], 4).

20 Bordenkircher and Bordenkircher, *Tiger Cage*, 11.

21 Bordenkircher and Bordenkircher, *Tiger Cage*, 11, 13. Colby discusses Phoenix in his autobiography, *Honorable Men*.

22 McClintock, *Instruments of Statecraft*, 191–92.

23 McCann in *PSN* 149 (Sept. 2007), 1.

24 Harpold interview.

25 Antonik interview.

26 Antonik interview.

27 *PSN* 4 (May 1975), 5.

28 *PSN* 8 (Jan. 1976), 1.

29 *PSN* 8 (Jan. 1976), 8; *PSN* 5 (July 1975), 2; *PSN* 6 (Sept. 1975), 5. Other ex-OPS personnel at refugee camps included a man "assigned to the Inter-Agency Task Force at Ft. Chaffee," Arkansas (*PSN* 5 [July 1975], 2; *PSN* 6 [Sept. 1975], 6; *PSN* 8 [Jan. 1976], 3); a Security Officer at Fort Chaffee (*PSN* 5 [July 1975], 2; *PSN* 6 [Sept. 1975], 6; *PSN* 8 [Jan. 1976], 6); a functionary in the US fisheries program for Vietnamese refugees (*PSN* 10 [July 1976], 2), location not specified (on the fisheries program, see Starr, "Troubled Waters"); and a woman "named to the Governor's task Group on Resettlement of Indo-Chinese Refugees" (*PSN* 27 [Sept. 1980], 2), unclear whether as an honorary or a paid appointment, though either way, it likely functioned for her as professional activity.

30 *PSN* 4 (May 1975), 2.

31 *PSN* 4 (May 1975), 2; another man visited the Camp Pendleton Vietnamese refugees, presumably also to try to lend a hand (*PSN* 4 [May 1975], 3).

32 *PSN* 25 (Apr. 1980), 5.

33 *PSN* 4 (May 1975), 2–3.

34 *PSN* 7 (Nov. 1975), 3; the 47 and the 13 both mentioned in *PSN* 5 (July 1975), 2; another couple sponsored three people from Vietnam (*PSN* 20 [May 1979], 1).

35 *PSN* 25 (Apr. 1980), 3. Another notice of someone sponsoring two people named the assisted men, suggesting they were known to its readership; *PSN* 26 (June 1980), 1.

36 Harpold interview.

37 Kamm, "Irritation on Refugees Grows"; Anderson, "Asian Refugees' Fate."

38 Bradley, "Island."

39 Espiritu, "Toward a Critical Refugee Study."

40 Nguyen, *Gift of Freedom*, xi. Nguyen posits a continuity between colonialism and a postcolonial liberal order, drawing on Derrida and Foucault to understand how "structures of race and coloniality underpin modern concepts of human freedom and progress" (Nguyen, *Gift of Freedom*, 6, 14), joining the growing scholarly corpus denouncing regimes of racial death that includes Denise Ferreira da Silva, Lisa Marie Cacho, Giorgio Agamben, and Hortense Spillers.

41 Berlant, *Cruel Optimism*; Hoad, "Sovereign Feeling."

42 Espiritu, "Towards a Critical Refugee Study"; Nguyen, *Gift of Freedom*. For critiques of the concept of freedom and its ilk, see Silva, *Toward a Global Idea of Race*; Hua, *Trafficking Women's Human Rights*.

43 *PSN* 4 (May 1975), 1.

44 *PSN* 18 (Oct. 1978), 5.

45 *PSN* 8 (Jan. 1976), 4; *PSN* 14 (July 1977), 3; *PSN* 24 (Jan. 1980), 3. Another person sent in a clipping from the Columbus *Dispatch* on two Vietnamese refugees who had set up an auto repair shop in Columbus; one had been "a former chief of police in the southwest district of Saigon and the second, Thai Ngau

had been a deputy chief in the Saigon area" (PSN 16 [Mar. 1977], 2). The editors also reported that "former Director of [Vietnam's] National Police Training Tran Minh Cong [was] living and teaching school in Laguna Hills CA" (PSN 11 [Oct. 1976], 2).

46 PSN 19 (Feb. 1979), 5.

47 PSN 21 (July 1979), 1. See also the letter reporting the trials of Laotian former contacts, including "accounts of the tortures and privations" they experienced in their four years of incarceration; PSN 25 (Apr. 1980), 5.

48 PSN 24 (Jan. 1980), 5; Espiritu, "Towards a Critical Refugee Study," 425.

49 PSN 25 (Apr. 1980), 3.

50 PSN 26 (June 1980), 2.

51 One report of a successful refugee resettlement included the detail that the man "credits a former police advisor for saving his life by helping him into the US Embassy compound in those last hours"; PSN 11 (Oct. 1976), 2. Such explicit mentions of rescue were the tip of the iceberg of the larger structure of suggestion.

52 PSN 20 (May 1979), 4, PSN 27 (Sept. 1980), 2; PSN 17 (July 1978), 3; PSN 21 (July 1979), 3; PSN 26 (June 1980), 1; PSN 20 (May 1979), 1.

53 PSN 26 (June 1980), 1.

54 PSN 14 (July 1977), 2.

55 Espiritu, "Towards a Critical Refugee Study," 411.

56 Wu, *Color of Success*.

57 See marriages to Ly, PSN 14 (July 1977), 3; Binh, PSN 10 (July 1976), 3; Anh, PSN 13 (Mar. 1977), 1; Nga, PSN 8 (Jan. 1976), 2; PSN 19 (Feb. 1979), 3. I have also found instances of adoptive children, such as the two J. B. Carnahan and his wife adopted, one from Vietnam, and one from the Philippines (interview), or another Vietnamese adopted daughter, Tammy (PSN 23 [Nov. 1979], 1). One OPS employee's daughter worked for Eastern Airlines, and the *Newsletter* reported, "When she has extra time, Susan goes to Korea to bring back orphans for adoptive parents" (PSN 15 [Dec. 1977], 6). Carnahan also claimed in our interview that among OPS agents, "there were quite a few that adopted children." But these are too few to provide good fodder for generalized interpretation.

58 One man told the *Newsletter* that he had met and married his wife when he worked for AID, Saigon; the couple moved to Gaithersburg in 1975 (PSN 20 [May 1979], 5). Another "later married a girl that he met while working in Bangkok back in 1973" (PSN 23 [Nov. 1979], 5). When a third sent word in 1978 that he and his spouse had moved into a new home, he explained that she had returned with him to the United States four years earlier (PSN 17 [July 1978], 1).

59 PSN 6 (Sept. 1975), 4 (both cases).

60 Ling (PSN 13 [Mar. 1977], 4), Nguyen (PSN 19 [Feb. 1979], 4; while more common as a surname, Nguyen can be a first name too), and Amorn, whose husband promised she would prepare Thai food for visitors, confirming her background in an invitation to his former fellows to come pay them a visit (PSN 10 [July 1976], 2).

61 Such was the case of "PHENPHAN, one of our front-office girls" in Bangkok, as the *Newsletter* announced. "She is now Mrs. Stanley Nowak and as of last report . . . was living in New Delhi where her husband is with the U.S. Embassy" (*PSN* 14 [July 1977], 3).

62 As with Jerry Jelsch and director Byron Engle (*PSN* 2 [Dec. 1974], n.p.), two people who met working in Bangkok in 1972 (*PSN* 7 [Nov. 1975], 3; also mentioned in *PSN* 21 [July 1979], 2), another couple in which the man was a city government employee, though the woman may have been Asian-American (*PSN* 19 [Feb. 1979], 5). One couple married around 1970 in Saigon, *PSN* 24 (Jan. 1980), 1; another was mentioned as if their marriage were new, *PSN* 8 (Jan. 1976), 7. The one exception may be the marriage of an Anglo-surnamed woman to a man whose name sounds Filipino, *PSN* 4 (May 1975), 3.

63 Eng, *Racial Castration*; Han, "Being an Oriental"; Lye, *America's Asia*; Pycke and Johnson, "Asian American Women." See also Khoo, *Chinese Exotic*; Mohanty, "Under Western Eyes"; Hong and Ferguson, *Strange Affinities*.

64 All of these "rehearsals" provided ample instances of Bourdieu's conceptualization of habitus, social processes that create patterns of interaction, shaping expectations and assumptions, and of the performativity of social identities, particularly gender relations in larger fields of power as theorized by Judith Butler. See Bourdieu, *Distinction*; Butler, *Gender Trouble*; Butler, *Excitable Speech*.

65 *PSN* 24 (Jan. 1980), 8.

66 *PSN* 19 (Feb. 1979), 3; *PSN* 17 (July 1978), 1; *PSN* 25 (Apr. 1980), 4.

67 As Holland points out in *Erotic Life of Racism*, interracial intimacy need not mitigate against racism in the slightest, and can as easily buttress and feed the presumptions of prejudice. See also Hodes, *White Women, Black Men*; Hodes, *Sex, Love, Race*; Povinelli, *Empire of Love*.

68 Stoler, "Tense and Tender Ties"; see also Stoler, *Haunted by Empire*, esp. Lowe, "Intimacies of Four Continents."

69 *PSN* 5 (July 1975), 3

70 *PSN* 13 (Mar. 1977), 1.

71 *PSN* 14 (July 1977), 3.

72 *PSN* 8 (Jan. 1976), 2. A happy father sent news of his successful evacuation of his wife Binh's family to Los Angeles, along with word of their second child, and later reported that he and Binh had some of her family members with them in Kansas City; *PSN* 6 (Sept. 1975), 3; *PSN* 20 (May 1979), 4. When a Vietnamese family arrived at Elgin Air Force Base, the wife contacted her cousin, married to an ex-OPS (both women unnamed), who then sponsored the family; *PSN* 6 (Sept. 1975), 4.

73 *PSN* 6 (Sept. 1975), 1.

74 *PSN* 4 (May 1975), 1.

75 *PSN* 17 (July 1978), 2; *PSN* 17 (July 1978), 3.

76 *PSN* 15 (Dec. 1977), 2; *PSN* 7 (Nov. 1975), 2; *PSN* 8 (Jan. 1976), 7; *PSN* 14 (July 1977), 2.

77 *PSN* 25 (Apr. 1980), 3.

78 PSN 25 (Apr. 1980), 3; PSN 26 (June 1980), 2; PSN 2 (Dec. 1974), n.p.

79 PSN 17 (July 1978), 3. Other instances of social engagement include a family trip to the beach, included visiting OPS friends both Anglo-named and Vietnamese (PSN 8 [Jan. 1976], 3), or the case of Dudley Britton, who kept "close touch with a number of the relocated Vietnamese that were associated with us and who are now in the Texas area," wrote (Lauren) Jack Goin (PSN 23 [Nov. 1979], 3). Another ex-OPS had sought out a Vietnamese restaurant in Washington, DC, in a notably proprietary culinary gesture of nostalgia. He met the owner (I imagine him in the dining room expounding upon his relationship to the cuisine's country of origin), who turned out to have been a Lion's International District governor in Saigon, he reported (PSN 8 [Jan. 1976], 4).

80 PSN 27 (Sept. 1980), 2. Another ex-OPS wrote from Bangkok, "I see Col JOK, now retired. He often asks about Jim HARRINGON." PSN 23 (Nov. 1979), 5; also PSN 24 (Jan. 1980), 1.

81 PSN 14 (July 1977), 3; PSN 15 (Dec. 1977), 3. Another person wrote that he had recently visited former counterparts in Quito and Brunswick, including one who had become a colonel in charge of the National Police Intelligence Office, and a lieutenant colonel in command of the Police Training Academy there (PSN 16 [Mar. 1978], 6).

82 PSN 23 (Nov. 1979), 3, 4.

83 Dash, "Self-Confident Liberia"; "Sergeant Doe Ends Liberia's Long Changelessness"; "Voices from the Ranks." The coup was also mentioned in PSN 27 (Sept. 1980), 3. Whether the coup was US-backed I do not know, but US aid quintupled in the period after the coup, as Dash documents. See also Liebenow, Liberia; Sawyer, Effective Immediately, 55.

84 PSN 26 (June 1980), 2; PSN 19 (Feb. 1979), 6; on the "Number One interpreter in IV Corps, Tran Van Long," nicknamed "Long 1," see PSN 18 (Oct. 1978), 1; PSN 20 (May 1979), 3; PSN 23 (Nov. 1979), 1.

85 PSN 14 (July 1977), 1; PSN 15 (Dec. 1977), 2; PSN 17 (July 1978), 3; PSN 20 (May 1979), 2; PSN 23 (Nov. 1979), 1.

86 PSN 20 (May 1979), 2; PSN 24 (Jan. 1980), 1.

87 PSN 20 (May 1979), 2; PSN 23 (Nov. 1979), 1.

88 PSN 15 (Dec. 1977), 2; PSN 17 (July 1978), 3; PSN 19 (Feb. 1979), 4.

89 PSN 13 (Mar. 1977), 2; I do not understand the parenthetical.

90 Turner interview.

91 Friedman, Covert Capital, 196–98.

92 Turner interview.

93 Schrader, Policing Revolution.

94 PSN 8 (Jan. 1976), 3.

95 Carnahan interview.

96 PSN 6 (Sept. 1975), 4.

97 PSN 21 (July 1979), 3.

98 PSN 23 (Nov. 1979), 3.

99 PSN 7 (Nov. 1975), 1.

100 *PSN* 16 (Mar. 1977), 5.

101 *PSN* 15 (Dec. 1977), 2; *PSN* 6 (Sept. 1975), 3.

102 Best interview.

103 Joe Gregory was with the International Department of the NRA in Washington, DC (*PSN* 3 [Feb. 1975], 5, 6; *PSN* 8 [Jan. 1976], 7). Bob Joerg was a field representative for the NRA covering Georgia, Florida, and the Carolinas (*PSN* 4 [May 1975], 6; *PSN* 8 [Jan. 1976], 7). He "had a nice visit with Byron Engle at the National Police Combat Pistol Championship in Jackson, MS," the *Newsletter* shared (*PSN* 7 [Nov. 1975], 1). Byron Engle was deeply involved in gun affairs. He traveled a great deal, including safaris and other hunting trips. He served on the NRA Board of Directors (Saenz, *OPS Story*, 3, 120) as well as the Executive Committee and Legislative Committee, which he chaired (*PSN* 5 [July 1975], 3). He went to Indianapolis to attend the NRA annual meeting in 1976 (*PSN* 10 [July 1976], 1), where he saw Leonard Friesz, then "working as a consultant for Ruger" (*PSN* 5 [July 1975], 3). Friesz represented Ruger at the NRA's Indianapolis meeting (*PSN* 10 [July 1976], 1) and later was "running his own business and is reported to be doing well in arms and ammo" (*PSN* 12 [Dec. 1976], 4). Arthur Thurston, a banker in Shelbyville, Indiana, was also at that Indianapolis meeting (*PSN* 10 [July 1976], 1; *PSN* 11 [Oct. 1976], 5). Dudley Britton taught hunter safety at Claremore Junior College, "the site of the John Davis Gun Collection," the *Newsletter* reported; the Engles visited it and him. "Dudley will be spending a great deal of his time at the Pershing Range in Claremore College," the *Newsletter* promised, and relayed that Britton would welcome other ex-OPS as guests (*PSN* 8 [Jan. 1976], 4; *PSN* 19 [Feb. 1979], 6).

104 On the populism driving vindictive criminal justice policy, see Zimring, Hawkins, and Kamin, *Punishment and Democracy*; on the conservative politics growing out of racism grafted onto anti-government populism, see Lowndes, *From the New Deal to the New Right*; on this dynamic in the 1990s, see Windlesham, *Politics, Punishment, and Populism*; on anti-government populism reinforcing liberal (as opposed to radical) convention, see Datta, "Security and the Void"; on grassroots conservatism, see Gross, "From the Streets to the Courts"; on the continuity of the long tradition of vigilante groups in anti-government, right-wing populists, see O'Toole, *Private Sector*, 149; a good overview is Kazin, *Populist Persuasion*.

105 Kohler-Hausmann, *Getting Tough*. This despite many refugees' long-term need for "welfare," as Eric Tang details in his wonderful ethnography of Cambodian immigrants in New York, *Unsettled*. Tang analyzes the discursive utility of the poverty-stricken refugee in the hyperghetto, continually available for salvation.

106 Gilmore and Gilmore, "Restating the Obvious."

107 Ahmed, *Cultural Politics of Emotion*, 42.

108 Weaver, "Frontlash," 237; Singh, *Black Is a Country*.

109 Quijano, "Coloniality of Power."

110 Friedman, *Covert Capital*, 24 and *passim*. McGuire and Coutin, "Transnational Alienage and Foreignness," also theorizes this relationship.

111 Psychiatrists and other medical researchers have found and named in these refugees a feeling of "'exile shock,' an acute sense of powerlessness and insecurity," and have suggested that refugees had structures of trauma similar to those of veterans of the Vietnam War; Kissman and Van Tran, "Life Satisfaction," 29, citing Lamphier, "Refugee Resettlement Models in Action," and August and Gianola, "Symptoms of War Trauma."

112 Practitioners of transnational method and their predecessors in diaspora studies have long understood this; for one account of this tradition, see Seigel, "Beyond Compare."

113 Dickens, "Unarticulated Pre-emergence"; Gallagher and Greenblatt, *Practicing New Historicism*, 60.

114 Homi Bhabha called this the postmodern condition of exile, though he understood it as a malady besetting postcolonial figures; Bhabha, *Location of Culture*.

CONCLUSION

1 Adams, "Migration"; United Nations Population Fund, "Migration."

2 Pratt, "Planetary Longings."

3 Balibar, "Three Concepts of Politics," 24–25.

4 Ogilvie, "Violence et representation"; Judy, "Provisional Note on Formations of Planetary Violence"; Agamben, *Homo Sacer*; Biehl, "Vita"; Mbembe, "Necropolitics."

5 On the violence of New World colonialism, see Taussig, *Shamanism, Colonialism, and the Wild Man*; on that of the slave trade, see Hartman, *Scenes*.

6 Nowhere does it do so more severely than in criminology and the criminal justice system; see J. Young, *Criminological Imagination*; Fan, "Disciplining Criminal Justice"; Muhammad, *Condemnation of Blackness*; Jones, "Qualitative Inquiry"; Clear, "Policy and Evidence."

7 Pratt, "Planetary Longings."

8 Ortiz and Cummins, "Global Inequality," 20, 19; Ortiz and Cummins also note that income inequality was a taboo topic until the ILO (International Labor Organization) published a "pioneering report" in 2004 ("Global Inequality," 10). See also OECD, *Divided We Stand*; Svampa, *La sociedad excluyente*.

9 Putnam, *Bowling Alone*, 359. In support, Fogelson suggests that urban police were more repressive in the late 1920s-early 1930s than in the mid-1960s; Fogelson, *Big-City Police*, 247.

10 Gilmore, "Globalisation and US Prison Growth," 178; see also Bonica, McCarty, Poole, and Rosenthal, "Why Hasn't Democracy Slowed Rising Inequality?" and the *Economist* online, "Income inequality in America."

11 Piketty, *Capital in the Twenty-First Century*. Piketty famously disavowed having been influenced by Marx in Chotiner, "Thomas Piketty."

12 Saez and Zucman, "Exploding Wealth Inequality in the United States." Thanks to Rebecca Lave for leading me to Saez, and Thomas Jessen Adams for conversations on Piketty.

13 Rimke, "Security," 192.

14 Scott, *Art of Not Being Governed*; the Midnight Notes collective articulated this in contextualizing the 1990–91 Gulf War: Midnight Notes, *Midnight Oil*, viii.

15 Wilkinson, "Why Is Violence More Common?" Here we also should reflect on the allocation of blame and guilt in the liberal notion that "poverty causes crime" and that obscene alibi for the worst racist containment, "black-on-black crime," and recognize instead that poverty *is* state-market crime. Police kill more people because of semiautomatic weapons—not their own in this case, but those the state allows to circulate by refusing gun regulation and organizing extralegal economies, and then cites to justify the murder of their owners (recall Mirpuri, "Racial Violence"). "The fruit of poverty" is Enrique Dussel, interviewed in Hopkins, "Entrevista a Enrique Dussel."

16 Tocqueville, *Democracy in America*, 390.

17 Reiman, *Rich Get Richer and the Poor Get Prison*.

18 Rimke, "Security," 192.

19 Pemberton, "Deaths in Police Custody," traces increased fatalities among people in police custody in England and Wales in the twenty years prior to his study, attributing the rise to neoliberalism and its authoritarian state; see also Harring et al., "Management of Police Killings," 41; Hinds, "Police Use of Excessive and Deadly Force."

20 "Killed by Police"; Burghart, "Fatal Encounters"; "Mapping Police Violence"; "Counted." See also Krieger et al., "Trends in US Deaths Due to Legal Intervention among Black and White Men"; Erfani-Ghettani, "Defamation of Joy Gardner"; Burns and Crawford, *Policing and Violence*; Loftin et al., "Underreporting of justifiable homicides committed by police officers in the United States"; Pemberton, "Deaths in Police Custody"; Bier, "By the Numbers."

21 Brown and Langan, *Policing and Homicide*, 28.

22 Bureau of Justice Statistics, Deaths in Custody Reporting Program.

23 A. M. Burch, "Arrest-Related Deaths, 2003–2009."

24 Hinds, "Police Use of Excessive and Deadly Force"; Takagi, "Death by Police Intervention," 9.

25 National Committee on Criminal Justice, "Evolution and Development of Police Technology"; Cook, "Technology of Personal Violence."

26 Balko, *Overkill*; Weber, "Warrior Cops"; Balko, *Rise of the Warrior Cop*; a British equivalent is Jefferson, *Case against Paramilitary Policing*.

27 Gilmore and Gilmore, "Beyond Bratton," 176.

28 Weld, "How the US Institutionalized Surveillance."

29 Mauer, *Race to Incarcerate*, 49; Hall et al., *Policing the Crisis*.

30 Weaver, "Frontlash"; Abramsky, *American Furies*; Gilmore, *Golden Gulag*; Gottschalk, *Prison and the Gallows*; Gottschalk, *Caught*; Hinton, *From the War on Poverty to the War on Crime*; Murakawa, *First Civil Right*; Simon, *Governing through Crime*.

31 Drucker, *Plague of Prisons*, 93, citing Loury, *Race, Incarceration and American Values*, 7–8.

32 Chambliss, "Policing the Ghetto Underclass," quote on 192. As David Cole has pointed out, "sentence severity" is crucial: "From 1973 to 2003, the prison population increased every year, even though arrests for most crimes fell, because the average time served almost doubled." David Cole, "Punitive Damage."

33 Drucker, *Plague of Prisons*, chapter 6, "Orders of Magnitude"; see also Clear, *Imprisoning Communities*.

34 Reiner, *Politics of the Police*, 14; see also Neocleous, *Fabrication of Social Order* and Neocleous, *Administering Civil Society*.

35 Mbembe, "Necropolitics."

36 Hall, "State in Question," 9–11. Hall traces earlier social forms, including absolutist and feudal states, as well as stateless societies, in this excellent piece. On Gramsci, see Hall et al., *Policing the Crisis*, 203–6. A useful analysis of the production of state hegemony is Jenkins, "Calibrating the Capitalist State in the Neoliberal Era."

37 Hall et al., *Policing the Crisis*, 192–93.

38 In addition to the works in critical prison studies cited in note 27 of the introduction, these include Belew, *Bring the War Home*; Camp and Heatherton, *Policing the Planet*; K. P. Feldman, *Shadow over Palestine*; Goldstein, *Poverty in Common*; Gottschalk, *Caught*; Hinton, *From the War on Poverty to the War on Crime*; Kohler-Hausmann, *Getting Tough*; Kramer, "Power and Connection"; Kramer, *Blood of Government*; McCoy, *Policing America's Empire*; Muhammad, *Condemnation of Blackness*; Neocleous, *Administering Civil Society*; Neocleous, *Critique of Security*; Neocleous, *Fabrication of Social Order*; Neocleous, *War Power, Police Power*; Nguyen, *Gift of Freedom*; Singh, *Exceptional Empire*; Wall, "Unmanning the Police Manhunt"; B. Williams, *Classifying to Kill*; so much of this, obviously, is in a field long prepared by generations of activist groundwork.

Abrams, Philip. "Notes on the Difficulty of Studying the State." *Journal of Historical Sociology* 1, no. 1 (March [1977] 1988): 58–89.

Abramsky, Sasha. *American Furies: Crime, Punishment, and Vengeance in the Age of Mass Imprisonment*. Boston, MA: Beacon Press, 2007.

Ackerman, Spencer. "Bad Lieutenant: American Police Brutality, Exported from Chicago to Guantánamo." *Guardian* online. Accessed August 14, 2015. http://www.theguardian.com/us-news/2015/feb/18/american-police-brutality-chicago-guantanamo.

———. "How Chicago Police Condemned the Innocent: A Trail of Coerced Confessions." *Guardian* online. February 20, 2015. Accessed August 14, 2015. http://www.theguardian.com/us-news/2015/feb/19/chicago-police-richard-zuley-abuse-innocent-man.

Adams, Paul. "Migration: Are More People on the Move Than Ever Before?" BBC News, May 28, 2015. Accessed September 9, 2016. http://www.bbc.com/news/world-32912867.

Adeline Masquelier. "Why Katrina's Victims Aren't Refugees: Musings on a 'Dirty' Word." *American Anthropologist* 108, no. 4 (December 2006): 735–43.

"ADL Charges over 200 U.S. Firms, 25 Banks Waging Economic War against Israel Jointly with the Arabs." *Jewish Telegraphic Agency*, March 12, 1976. Accessed October 4, 2012. http://archive.jta.org/article/1976/03/12/2974774/adl-charges-over-200-us-firms-25-banks-waging-economic-war-against-israel-jointly-with-the-arabs.

Aecom. "What We Do: Government." Accessed October 6, 2012. http://www.aecom.com/What+We+Do/Government/Logistics,+Operations+and+Maintenance/_carousel/Nevada+Test+Site,+U.S.+Department+of+Energy.

———. "What We Do: Architecture." Accessed October 6, 2012. http://www.aecom.com/What+We+Do/Architecture/_projectsList/Los+Angeles+Police+Department+(LAPD)+Headquarters.

Agamben, Giorgio. "From the State of Control to a Praxis of Destituent Power." *Roar Magazine*, February 4, 2014. Accessed February 12, 2014. http://roarmag.org/2014/02/agamben-destituent-power-democracy.

———. *Homo Sacer: Sovereignty and Bare Life*. Translated by Daniel Heller-Roazen. Stanford, CA: Stanford University Press, 1998.

Agee, Christopher. *The Streets of San Francisco: Policing and the Creation of a Cosmopolitan Liberal Politics, 1950–1972*. Chicago: University of Chicago Press, 2014.

Agee, Philip. *Inside the Company: CIA Diary*. Harmondsworth, UK: Penguin, 1975.

Ahern, Thomas L., Jr. *Vietnam Declassified: The CIA and Counterinsurgency*. Lexington: University Press of Kentucky, 2010.

Ahmed. *The Cultural Politics of Emotion*. New York: Routledge, 2004.

Allinson, Richard. "A Great LEEP Backward?" *Change* 12, no. 1 (January 1980): 14–16.

"Amex Prices Take a Mixed Course." *New York Times*, September 7, 1974, 35.

Anderson, David M., and David Killingray, eds. *Policing and Decolonization: Politics, Nationalism, and the Police, 1917–65*. Manchester, UK: Manchester University Press, 1992.

———. *Policing the Empire: Government, Authority, and Control, 1830–1940*. Manchester, UK: Manchester University Press, 1991.

Anderson, Jack. "Asian Refugees' Fate Hinges on U.S." *Washington Post*, March 15, 1978, C27.

Anderson, Jack, and Les Whitten. "Oil Facilities Vulnerable to Attack." *Washington Post*, June 29, 1977, C17.

———. "Pipeline Sabotage Worries CIA." *Washington Post*, December 31, 1976, D15.

Andreas, Peter. *Border Games: Policing the U.S.-Mexico Divide*. 2nd ed. Ithaca, NY: Cornell University Press, 2009.

Andreas, Peter, and Richard Price. "From War Fighting to Crime Fighting: Transforming the American National Security State." *International Studies Review* 3, no. 3 (2001): 31–52.

Anthony, Chuck. "City Police Dept. Gets Grant for Helicopter." *Albuquerque Journal*, April 7, 1972, A-1 and A-6.

Appier, Janis. *Policing Women: The Sexual Politics of Law Enforcement and the LAPD*. Philadelphia, PA: Temple University Press, 1998.

Arendt, Hannah. *On Violence*. Orlando, FL: Harcourt Brace, [1969] 1970.

———. "Reflections on Violence." *New York Review of Books*, February 27, 1969. Accessed September 3, 2011. http://www.cooperativeindividualism.org/arendt-hanna_reflections-on-violence.html.

Arnold, William R. "Criminal Justice: Review of a Field." *Mid-American Review of Sociology* 6, no. 2 (winter 1981): 79–95.

Artières, Philippe, and Michelle Zancarini-Fournel. *68: Une histoire collective*. Paris: La Découverte, 2008.

"A Suspect Stays on the Job." *Los Angeles Times*, March 16, 2004, B12.

Atanasoski, Neda. *Humanitarian Violence: The U.S. Deployment of Diversity*. Minneapolis: University of Minnesota Press, 2013.

August, Lynn R., and Barbara A. Gianola. "Symptoms of War Trauma Induced Psychiatric Disorders: South Asian Refugees and Vietnam Veterans." In "Migration and Health," special issue, *International Migration Review* 21, no. 3 (autumn 1987): 820–32.

Auyero, Javier. *Patients of the State: The Politics of Waiting in Argentina*. Durham, NC: Duke University Press, 2012.

Bachmann, Jan, Colleen Bell, and Caroline Holmqvist, eds. *War, Police, and Assemblages of Intervention*. London: Routledge, 2015.

Baer, Justin, and Gillian Wee. "URS Corp. Acquires Washington Group." *Seattle Times*, May 29, 2007. Accessed June 17, 2014. http://seattletimes.com/html/businesstechnology/2003725375_washgroup29.html.

Baker-Cristales, Beth. "Magical Pursuits: Legitimacy and Representation in a Transnational Political Field." *American Anthropologist* 110, no. 3 (September 2008): 349–59.

Balibar, Étienne. "Three Concepts of Politics: Emancipation, Transformation, Civility." In *Politics and the Other Scene*, 1–39. New York: Verso, 2002.

———. "Violence, Ideality and Cruelty." In *Politics and the Other Scene*, 129–45. New York: Verso, 2002.

Balko, Radley. *Overkill: The Rise of Paramilitary Police Raids in America*. Washington, DC: Cato Institute, 2006.

———. *Rise of the Warrior Cop: The Militarization of America's Police Forces*. New York: PublicAffairs, 2013.

———. "Why It's Impossible to Calculate the Percentage of Police Shootings That Are Legitimate." *Washington Post*, July 14, 2016. Accessed August 27, 2016. https://www.washingtonpost.com/news/the-watch/wp/2016/07/14/why-its-impossible-to-calculate-the-percentage-of-police-shootings-that-are-legitimate/#.

Balogh, Brian. "The State of the State among Historians." *Social Science History* 27, no. 3 (2003): 455–63.

Banton, Michael. *The Policeman in the Community*. London: Tavistock, 1964.

Barnett, Michael N. *Empire of Humanity: A History of Humanitarianism*. Ithaca, NY: Cornell University Press, 2011.

Barthes, Roland. *Mythologies*. Paris: Éditions du Seuil, 1957.

Bass, Sandra. "Policing Space, Policing Race: Social Control Imperatives and Police Discretionary Decisions." *Social Justice* 28, no. 1 (spring 2001): 156–76.

Battles, Kathleen. *Calling All Cars: Radio Dragnets and the Technology of Policing*. Minneapolis: University of Minnesota Press, 2010.

Bayley, David. "What Do the Police Do?" In *Themes in Contemporary Policing*, edited by William Saulsbury, Joy Mott, and Tim Newburn, 29–41. London: Policy Studies Institute, 1996.

Beckett, Katherine. *Making Crime Pay: Law and Order in Contemporary American Politics*. New York: Oxford University Press, 1997.

Belew, Kathleen. *Bring the War Home: The White Power Movement and Paramilitary America*. Cambridge, MA: Harvard University Press, forthcoming.

Bell, Derrick. *Silent Covenants: Brown v. Board of Education and the Unfulfilled Hopes for Racial Reform*. New York: Oxford University Press, 2004.

Benjamin, Walter. "Critique of Violence." In *Selected Writings*, edited by Marcus Bullock and Michael W. Jennings, 1:236–52. Cambridge, MA: Belknap Press, 1996.

Ben-Moshe, Liat. "The Tension between Abolition and Reform." In *The End of Prisons: Reflections from the Decarceration Movement*, edited by Mechthild E. Nagel and Anthony J. Nocella II, 83–92. Amsterdam: Rodopi, 2013.

Berger, Daniel. *Captive Nation: Black Prison Organizing in the Civil Rights Era*. Chapel Hill: University of North Carolina Press, 2014.

Berlant, Lauren. *Cruel Optimism*. Durham, NC: Duke University Press, 2011.

Bernstein, Lee. *The Greatest Menace: Organized Crime in Cold War America*. Amherst: University of Massachusetts Press, 2002.

Berry, Mary Clay. *Alaska Pipeline: The Politics of Oil and Native Land Claims*. Bloomington: Indiana University Press, 1975.

Best, Andrew, Sr. *Bad Cop—No Doughnut*. N.p.: Andrew Best, 2011.

Bhabha, Homi. *The Location of Culture*. London: Routledge, 1994.

Biehl, João. "Vita: Life in a Zone of Social Abandonment." *Social Text* 68, vol. 19, no. 3 (fall 2001): 131–49.

Bier, Daniel. "By the Numbers: How Dangerous Is It to Be a Cop?" *Freeman*, August 19, 2014. Accessed October 14, 2015. http://fee.org/freeman/by-the-numbers-how-dangerous-is-it-to-be-a-cop/.

Biondi, Karina. *Sharing This Walk: An Ethnography of Prison Life and the PCC in Brazil*. Edited and translated by John F. Collins. Chapel Hill: University of North Carolina Press, 2016.

Bittner, Egon. "The Capacity to Use Force as the Core of the Police Role." In *The Functions of the Police in Modern Society*, 36–47. Chevy Chase, MD: National Institute of Mental Health, Center for Studies of Crime and Delinquency, 1970.

———. "Florence Nightingale in Pursuit of Willie Sutton: A Theory of the Police." In *The Potential for Reform of Criminal Justice*, edited by H. Jacob, 17–44. Beverly Hills, CA: Sage, 1974.

———. *The Functions of the Police in Modern Society*. Chevy Chase, MD: National Institute of Mental Health, 1970.

———. "The Police on Skid-Row: A Study of Peace Keeping." *American Sociological Review* 32, no. 5 (1967): 699–715.

———. "The Quasi-Military Organization of the Police." In *The Functions of the Police in Modern Society*, 52–62. Chevy Chase, MD: National Institute of Mental Health, Center for Studies of Crime and Delinquency, 1970.

Black, Jan. *United States Penetration of Brazil*. Philadelphia: University of Pennsylvania Press, 1977.

Blackstone, William. *Commentaries on the Laws of England*. Vol. 4, *Of Private Wrongs [cont.] Of Public Wrongs*. [Oxford: Clarendon Press, 1765–1769.] Buffalo, NY: W. S. Hein, 2002.

Blue, Ethan. *Doing Time in the Great Depression: Everyday Life in Texas and California Prisons*. New York: New York University Press, 2012.

Blum, William. *The CIA, A Forgotten History: U.S. Global Interventions since World War 2*. London: Zed Books, 1986.

Blumenson, Eric, and Eva S. Nilsen. "How to Construct an Underclass, *or* How the War on Drugs Became a War on Education." *Journal of Gender, Race and Justice* 6 (2002): 61–110.

Blumstein, Alfred. *The Crime Drop in America*. Rev. ed. New York: Cambridge University Press, 2006.

Boger, John Charles, and Gary Orfield. *School Resegregation: Must the South Turn Back?* Chapel Hill: University of North Carolina Press, 2005.

Bogess, Scott, and John Bound. "Did Criminal Activity Increase during the 1980's? Comparisons across Data Sources." Research Report no. 93–280, Population Studies Center, University of Michigan, Ann Arbor, 1993.

Bolton, Jr., Kenneth, and Joe R. Feagin. *Black in Blue: African-American Police Officers and Racism*. New York: Routledge, 2004.

Bonica, Adam, Nolan McCarty, Keith T. Poole, and Howard Rosenthal. "Why Hasn't Democracy Slowed Rising Inequality?" *Journal of Economic Perspectives* 27, no. 3. (summer 2013): 103–24.

Bordenkircher, D. E., and S. A. Bordenkircher. *Tiger Cage: An Untold Story*. Cameron, WV: Abbey, 1998.

Borstelmann, Thomas. *The Cold War and the Color Line: American Race Relations in the Global Arena*. Cambridge, MA: Harvard University Press, 2001.

Bottomley, A. Keith, and Clive A. Coleman. "Criminal Statistics: The Police Role in the Discovery and Detection of Crime." *International Journal of Criminology and Penology* 4 (1976): 33–58.

Bourdieu, Pierre. *Distinction: A Social Critique of the Judgment of Taste*. Translated by Richard Nice. Cambridge, MA: Harvard University Press, 1984.

Bradley, Ed. "The Island." CBS, *Sixty Minutes*, June 24, 1979. Accessed September 1, 2013. http://www.cbsnews.com/video/watch/?id=6777978n.

Bricmont, Jean. *Humanitarian Imperialism: Using Human Rights to Sell War*. Translated by Diana Johnstone. New York: Monthly Review Press, 2006.

Bronfman, Alejandra. *Measures of Equality: Social Science, Citizenship, and Race in Cuba, 1902–1940*. Chapel Hill: University of North Carolina Press, 2004.

Brown, Jodi M., and Patrick A. Langan (BJS statisticians). *Policing and Homicide, 1976–98: Justifiable Homicide by Police, Police Officers Murdered by Felons*. Washington, DC: US Department of Justice, Office of Justice Programs, March 2001, NCJ 180987.

Brown, Michael. *Working the Street: Police Discretion and the Dilemmas of Reform*. New York: Russell Sage Foundation, 1981.

Brown, Michelle. *The Culture of Punishment: Prison, Society, and Spectacle*. New York: New York University Press, 2009.

Brown, Wendy. "Finding the Man in the State." *Feminist Studies* 18, no. 1 (spring 1992): 7–34.

———. *States of Injury: Power and Freedom in Late Modernity*. Princeton, NJ: Princeton University Press, 1995.

Brownstein, H. *The Rise and Fall of a Violent Crime Wave: Crack Cocaine and the Social Construction of a Crime Problem.* New York: Harrow and Heston, 1996.

Bsheer, Rosie. "A Counter-Revolutionary State: Popular Movements and the Making of Saudi Arabia." *Past and Present* 238, issue 1 (Feb. 2018), 233–77.

Buerger, Michael, and Lorraine Green Mazerolle. "Third-Party Policing: A Theoretical Analysis of an Emerging Trend." *Justice Quarterly* 15, no. 2 (1998): 301–27.

Bukro, Casey. "How Law's Iron Fist Tamed Alaska's Oil Field." *Chicago Tribune*, February 20, 1977, 5.

Burch, Andrea M. (BJS statistician). "Arrest-Related Deaths, 2003–2009." *Bureau of Justice Statistics Statistical Tables*. Washington, DC: US Department of Justice, Office of Justice Programs, November 2011, NCJ 235385.

Burch, Philip H., Jr. "The NAM as an Interest Group." *Politics and Society* 4, no. 1 (fall 1973): 100–105.

Bureau of Justice Statistics. "Deaths in Custody Reporting Program." Bureau of Justice Statistics website. Accessed August 2, 2016. http://www.bjs.gov/index.cfm?ty=tp&tid=19.

Burghart, D. Brian. "Fatal Encounters." Weblog. Accessed March 13, 2017. http://www.fatalencounters.org.

Burnett, D. Graham. *Masters of All They Surveyed: Exploration, Geography, and a British El Dorado.* Chicago: University of Chicago Press, 2000.

Burns, Ronald G., and Charles E. Crawford, eds. *Policing and Violence.* Upper Saddle River, NJ: Prentice Hall, 2002.

Burt, Kenneth C. "Tony Rios and Bloody Christmas: A Turning Point between the Los Angeles Police Department and the Latino Community." *Western Legal History* 14 (summer/fall 2001): 159–92.

Butler, Judith. *Excitable Speech: A Politics of the Performative.* London: Routledge, 1997.

———. *Gender Trouble.* New York: Routledge, 1990.

C. H. "Law Enforcement Assistance Administration: Anticrime Agency Faces Criticism, Lowered Budget." *Science* 193, no. 4247 (July 2, 1976): 36–37.

Cable, Larry. *Conflict of Myths: The Development of American Counter-Insurgency Doctrine and the Vietnam War.* New York: New York University Press, 1986.

Cacho, Lisa Marie. *Social Death: Racialized Rightlessness and the Criminalization of the Unprotected.* New York: New York University Press, 2012.

Cain, Maureen. "Orientalism, Occidentalism and the Sociology of Crime." *British Journal of Criminology* 40, no. 2 (spring 2000): 239–60.

Calavita, Kitty. *Inside the State: The Bracero Program, Immigration, and the I. N. S.* New York: Routledge, 1992.

Calhoun, Craig. "A World of Emergencies." *Canadian Review of Sociology* 41, no. 4 (November 2004): 373–95.

Calhoun, Frederick S. *The Trainers: The Federal Law Enforcement Training Center and the Professionalization of Federal Law Enforcement.* Washington, DC: Government Printing Office, 1996.

Callincos, Alex. "The Ideology of Humanitarian Intervention." In *Masters of the Universe: NATO's Balkan Crusade*, edited by Tariq Ali, 175–89. London: Verso, 2000.

Camp, E. W. "The American Bar Association's Program with Respect to Criminal Law." *Annals of the American Academy of Political and Social Science* 175 (September 1934): 214–17.

Camp, Jordan T. *Incarcerating the Crisis: Freedom Struggles and the Rise of the Neoliberal State.* Berkeley: University of California Press, 2016.

Camp, Jordan T., and Christina Heatherton. "We Charge Genocide: An Interview with Breanna Champion, Page May, and Asha Rosa Ransby-Sporn." In Camp and Heatherton, *Policing the Planet*, 259–66.

———, eds. *Policing the Planet: Why the Policing Crisis Led to Black Lives Matter.* New York: Verso, 2016.

Canaday, Margot. *The Straight State: Sexuality and Citizenship in Twentieth-Century America.* Princeton, NJ: Princeton University Press, 2009.

Cancelli, Elizabeth. *Histórias de Violência, Crime e Lei no Brasil.* Brasília: Editora Universidade de Brasília, 2004.

Cardenas, Leo. "S. A. Police Organize 1st Intelligence Squad." *San Antonio Express,* July 16, 1964, n.p.

Carey, Sarah C. *Law and Disorder IV: A Review of the Federal Anti-Crime Program Created by Title I of the Omnibus Crime Control and Safe Streets Act of 1968.* Washington, DC: Center for National Security Studies, 1976.

Carte, Gene, and Elaine Carte. *Police Reform in the United States: The Era of August Vollmer, 1905–1932.* Berkeley: University of California Press, 1975.

Casey, Linda. *Alaska's Citizens Lock Out Private Prisons.* Helena, MT: National Institute on Money in State Politics, 2008. Accessed June 19, 2012. http://www.followthemoney.org/press/Reports/Alaskas_Citizens_Lock_Out_Private_Prisons.pdf.

Cassidy, Peter. "Operation Ghetto Storm: The Rise in Paramilitary Policing." *Covert Action Quarterly* 62 (fall 1997): 20–25.

Center for Research on Criminal Justice (Susie Bernstein, Lynn Cooper, Elliot Currie, John Frappier, Sidney Harring, Tony Platt, Pat Poyner, Gerda Ray, Richard Schauffler, Joy Scruggs, and Larry Trujillo). *The Iron Fist and the Velvet Glove: An Analysis of the U.S. Police.* Berkeley: Center for Research on Criminal Justice, 1975.

Chambliss, William J. "Policing the Ghetto Underclass: The Politics of Law and Law Enforcement." *Social Problems* 41, no. 2 (May 1994): 177–94.

Chan, Sucheng, ed. *The Vietnamese American 1.5 generation: Stories of War, Revolution, Flight, and New Beginnings.* Philadelphia, PA: Temple University Press, 2006.

Chandola, Harish. "Who Are the Refugees?" *Economic and Political Weekly* 10, no. 15 (April 12, 1975): 614–16.

Chang, Dae, and Jerome McKean. "Criminology, Delinquency, and Corrections." *International Review of Modern Sociology* 11, no. 1/2 (1981): 201–29.

Chaput, Catherine. "Introduction: Fear, Affective Energy, and the Political Economy of Global Capitalism." In Chaput, Braun, and Brown, *Entertaining Fear*, 1–28.

Chaput, Catherine, M. J. Braun, and Danika M. Brown, eds. *Entertaining Fear: Rhetoric and the Political Economy of Social Control.* New York: Peter Lang, 2010.

Chávez-García, Miroslava. *States of Delinquency: Race and Science in the Making of California's Juvenile Justice System*. Berkeley: University of California Press, 2012.

Chen, Chris. "The Limit Point of Capitalist Equality: Notes toward an Abolitionist Antiracism." *Endnotes* 3, September 2013. Accessed October 15, 2015. http://endnotes.org.uk/articles/22.

Chevigny, Paul. *Edge of the Knife: Police Violence in the Americas*. New York: New York University Press, 1995.

———. *Police Power: Police Abuses in New York City*. New York: Vintage, 1969.

"Chicago BLM Activist: 'We Need to Abolish the Police.'" *Fox News Insider*, July 12, 2016. Accessed September 6, 2016. http://insider.foxnews.com/2016/07/12/chicago-blm-activist-we-need-abolish-police.

Childs, Dennis. *Slaves of the State: Black Incarceration from the Chain Gang to the Penitentiary*. Minneapolis: University of Minnesota Press, 2015.

Chomsky, Noam. "Humanitarian Imperialism: The New Doctrine of Imperial Right." *Monthly Review* 60, no. 4 (September 2008). February 9, 2017. http://monthlyreview.org/2008/09/01/humanitarian-imperialism-the-new-doctrine-of-imperial-right/.

Chotiner, Isaac. "Thomas Piketty: I Don't Care for Marx." *New Republic*, May 5, 2014. Accessed January 31, 2016. https://newrepublic.com/article/117655/thomas-piketty-interview-economist-discusses-his-distaste-marx.

Churchill, Ward, and Jim Vander Wall. *The COINTELPRO Papers: Documents from the FBI's Secret Wars against Dissent in the United States*. 2nd ed. Cambridge, MA: South End Press, 2002 [1990].

Clastres, Pierre. *Society against the State: Essays in Political Anthropology*. Translated by Robert Hurley in collaboration with Abe Stein. New York: Zone Books, 1987.

Clear, Todd R. *Imprisoning Communities: How Mass Incarceration Makes Disadvantaged Neighborhoods Worse*. New York: Oxford University Press, 2007.

———. "Policy and Evidence: The Challenge to the American Society of Criminology: 2009 Presidential Address to the American Society of Criminology." *Criminology* 48, no. 1 (2010): 1–25.

Clynch, Edward J. "The Spending of Law Enforcement Assistance Administration Block Grants by the States: A Report." *Justice System Journal* 2, no. 2 (1976): 157–68.

Coates, Peter A. *The Trans-Alaska Pipeline Controversy*. Fairbanks: University of Alaska Press, 1991.

Cohen, Stanley. *Folk Devils and Moral Panics*. 3rd ed. London: Routledge, 2004.

———. "The Punitive City: Notes on the Dispersal of Social Control." *Contemporary Crises* 3/4 (1979): 339–63.

Colby, Gerard, and Charlotte Dennett. *Thy Will Be Done: The Conquest of the Amazon, Nelson Rockefeller and Evangelism in the Age of Oil*. New York: HarperCollins, 1995.

Colby, William Egan, and Peter Forbath. *Honorable Men: My Life in the CIA*. New York: Simon and Schuster, 1978.

Cole, David. "Punitive Damage." Review of *Inferno*, by Robert A. Ferguson. *New York Times Sunday Book Review*, May 16, 2014. Accessed May 21, 2014. http://www.nytimes.com/2014/05/18/books/review/inferno-by-robert-a-ferguson.html?_r=0.

Cole, Dermot. *Amazing Pipeline Stories*. Washington, DC: Epicenter Press, 1997.

Coley, Richard J., and Paul E. Barton. "Locked Up and Locked Out: An Educational Perspective on the U.S. Prison Population." Educational Testing Service, February 2006. Accessed October 12, 2015. www.ets.org/research/pic.

Comptroller General of the United States. "Phaseout of U.S. Assistance to Vietnam in Support of Police Organizations, Law Enforcement, and Public Safety Related Programs." February 1975.

Conley, John A., ed. *The 1967 President's Crime Commission Report: Its Impact 25 Years Later*. Highland Heights, KY: Academy of Criminal Justice Sciences, 1994.

"Contract Awards." *New York Times*, September 7, 1974, 40.

Cook, Philip J. "The Technology of Personal Violence." *Crime and Justice* 14 (1991): 1–71.

Cooper, Fred. *Colonialism in Question: Theory, Knowledge, History*. Berkeley: University of California Press, 2005.

Coulter, E. K. "The Jewish War on Crime." *Current Jewish Record*, November 1931.

Coulthard, Glen Sean. *Red Skin, White Masks: Rejecting the Colonial Politics of Recognition*. Minneapolis: University of Minnesota Press, 2014.

"The Counted: People Killed by Police in the US." Online database maintained by the *Guardian*. Accessed March 13, 2017. https://www.theguardian.com/us-news/ng-interactive/2015/jun/01/about-the-counted.

Crehan, Kate A. F. *Gramsci's Common Sense: Inequality and Its Narratives*. Durham, NC: Duke University Press, 2016.

Cronin, Thomas E., Tania Z. Cronin, and Michael E. Milakovich. *U.S. v. Crime in the Streets*. Bloomington: Indiana University Press, 1981.

Cullather, Nick. *Secret History: The CIA's Classified Account of Its Operations in Guatemala, 1952–54*. Stanford, CA: Stanford University Press, 1999.

Cunningham, William C., John J. Strauchs, and Clifford W. Van Meter. "Private Security: Patterns and Trends." National Institute of Justice *Research in Brief*. Washington, DC: Govt. Pubs. Dept., August 1991.

———. *Private Security Trends (1970 to 2000), The Hallcrest Report II*. Stoneham, MA: Butterworth-Heinemann, 1990.

Cunningham, William C., and Todd H. Taylor. *The Hallcrest Report: Private Security and Police in America*. Portland, OR: Chancellor, 1985.

"Dallas PD Chief Suggests Change of 'Give It to the Cops' Mentality." ABC News, July 11, 2016. Accessed August 25, 2016. http://abcnews.go.com/us/video/dallas-pd-chief-suggests-change-give-cops-mentality-40494668.

Dallek, Robert. *Flawed Giant: Lyndon Johnson and His Times, 1961–1973.* New York: Oxford University Press, 1998.

Das, Dilip D., and Arvind Verma. "The Armed Police in the British Colonial Tradition: The Indian Perspective." *Policing: An International Journal of Police Strategies and Management* 21, no. 2 (1998): 354–67.

Das, Veena. "The Act of Witnessing: Violence, Poisonous Knowledge, and Subjectivity." In *Violence and Subjectivity,* edited by Veena Das, Arthur Kleinman, Mamphela Ramphele, and Pamela Reynolds, 205–25. Berkeley: University of California Press, 2000.

———. *Life and Words: Violence and the Descent into the Ordinary.* Berkeley: University of California Press, 2007.

Dash, Leon. "A Self-Confident Liberia Emerges from 2-year 'Rule of the Gun.'" *Washington Post,* June 17, 1982, A30.

Datta, Ronjon Paul. "Security and the Void: Aleatory Materialism contra Governmentality." In *Anti-Security,* edited by Mark Neocleous and George S. Rigakos, 217–41. Ottawa: Red Quill Books, 2011.

Davis, Angela Y. *Are Prisons Obsolete?* New York: Seven Stories Press, 2003.

Davis, L. J. "Unlikely, but Boise Means Big Business." *New York Times Magazine,* June 11, 1989. Accessed June 17, 2014. http://www.nytimes.com/1989/06/11/magazine/unlikely-but-boise-means-big-business.html.

Dayan, Colin. *The Law Is a White Dog: How Legal Rituals Make and Unmake Persons.* Princeton, NJ: Princeton University Press, 2011.

———. "Legal Terrors." *Representations* 92 (fall 2005): 42–80.

Dean, Mitchell. "Military Intervention as 'Police' Action?" In *The New Police Science: The Police Power in Domestic and International Governance,* edited by Markus Dirk Dubber and Mariana Valverde, 185–206. Stanford, CA: Stanford University Press, 2006.

Deleuze, Gilles. "Eight Years Later: 1980 Interview." In *Two Regimes of Madness: Texts and Interviews, 1975–1995,* edited by David Lapoujade, translated by Ames Hodges and Mike Taormina, 176–80. New York: Semiotext(e), 2006.

Demarest, Geoffrey. "The Overlap of Military and Police in Latin America." US Army Foreign Military Studies Office, April 1995. Accessed January 30, 2014. http://fmso.leavenworth.army.mil/documents/milpolre.htm.

Derrida, Jacques. "Force of Law: The Mystical Foundation of Authority." In *Deconstruction and the Possibility of Justice,* edited by Drucilla Cornell, Michel Rosenfeld, and David Gray Carlson, 3–67. New York: Routledge, 1992.

Desbarats, Jacqueline. "Ethnic Differences in Adaptation: Sino-Vietnamese Refugees in the United States." *International Migration Review* 20, no. 2 (summer 1986): 405–27.

DeWitt, Charles B. "From the Director." In Cunningham, Strauchs, and Van Meter, "Private Security," 1.

Dickens, Josh. "Unarticulated Pre-emergence: Raymond Williams' 'Structures of Feeling.'" *Constellations,* no. 1, November 28, 2011. Accessed September 2,

2013. http://www2.warwick.ac.uk/fac/arts/english/constellations/structures _of_feeling.

Diegelman, Robert F. "Federal Financial Assistance for Crime Control: Lessons of the LEAA Experience." *Journal of Criminal Law and Criminology* 73 (1982): 994–1011.

DiIulio, John J. Jr., Steven K. Smith, and Aaron J. Saiger. "The Federal Role in Crime Control." In *Crime*, edited by James Q. Wilson and Joan Petersilia, 445–462. San Francisco, CA: Institute for Contemporary Studies, 1995.

Domanick, Joe. *To Protect and to Serve: The LAPD's Century of War in the City of Dreams*. New York: Pocket Books, 1994.

Donner, Frank. *Protectors of Privilege: Red Squads and Police Repression in Urban America*. Berkeley: University of California Press, 1990.

Dressel, Paul. *College to University: The Hannah Years at Michigan State, 1935–1969*. East Lansing: Michigan State University Press, 1987.

Drucker, Ernest. *A Plague of Prisons: The Epidemiology of Mass Incarceration in America*. New York: New Press, 2011.

Dubber, Markus Dirk. "The New Police Science and the Police Power Model of the Criminal Process." In *The New Police Science: The Police Power in Domestic and International Governance*, edited by Dubber and Valverde, 107–44. Stanford, CA: Stanford University Press, 2006.

———. *The Police Power: Patriarchy and the Foundations of American Government*. New York: Columbia University Press, 2005.

Dubber, Markus Dirk, and Mariana Valverde. "Introduction: Perspectives on the Power and Science of Police." In *The New Police Science*, edited by Dubber and Valverde, 1–16. Stanford, CA: Stanford University Press, 2006.

———, eds. *The New Police Science: The Police Power in Domestic and International Governance*. Stanford, CA: Stanford University Press, 2006.

Dudziak, Mary. *Cold War Civil Rights: Race and the Image of American Democracy*. Princeton, NJ: Princeton University Press, 2000.

Duffield, Mark. "Governing the Borderlands: Decoding the Power of Aid." *Disasters* 25, no. 4 (December 2001): 308–20.

Dulaney, W. Marvin. *Black Police in America*. Bloomington: Indiana University Press, 1996.

Dunn, Timothy. *The Militarization of the U.S.-Mexico Border, 1978–1992: Low Intensity Conflict Doctrine Comes Home*. Austin: CMAS Books, University of Texas at Austin, 1996.

Eck, John, and Edward Maguire. "Have Changes in Policing Reduced Violent Crime? An Assessment of the Evidence." In *The Crime Drop in America*, revised, edited by Alfred Blumstein, 207–65. New York: Cambridge University Press, 2006.

Economist. "Income Inequality in America: The 99 Percent." *Economist* online, October 26, 2011. Accessed May 27, 2014. http://www.economist.com/blogs /dailychart/2011/10/income-inequality-america.

Editors. "Editorial: Berkeley's School of Criminology, 1950–1976." *Crime and Social Justice* 6 (fall/winter 1976): 1–3. Accessed July 26, 2015. https://www.social justicejournal.org/SJEdits/06Edit-1.html.

Eng, David L. *Racial Castration: Managing Masculinity in Asian America*. Durham, NC: Duke University Press, 2001.

Enloe, Cynthia H. *Police, Military, and Ethnicity: Foundations of State Power*. New Brunswick, NJ: Transaction Books, 1980.

Endicott, William. "Human Error Suspected in Pipeline Blast." *Los Angeles Times*, July 10, 1977, A1.

Ennis, Thomas W. "Fear of Sabotage Spurs Industrial Security Drive." *New York Times*, October 2, 1970, 20.

Erfani-Ghettani, Ryan. "The Defamation of Joy Gardner: Press, Police and Black Deaths in Custody." *Race and Class* 56, no. 3 (January 1, 2015): 102–12.

Erickson, Megan. *Class War: The Privatization of Childhood*. Brooklyn, NY: Verso, 2015.

Ericson, Richard V. *Reproducing Order: A Study of Police Patrolwork*. Toronto: University of Toronto Press, 1982.

Ericson, Richard V., and Kevin D. Haggerty. *Policing the Risk Society*. Oxford: Clarendon Press, 1997.

Ernst, John. *Forging a Fateful Alliance: Michigan State University and the Vietnam War*. East Lansing: Michigan State University Press, 1998.

Escobar, Arturo. *Encountering Development: The Making and Unmaking of the Third World*. Princeton, NJ: Princeton University Press, 1995.

Escobar, Edward J. "Bloody Christmas and the Irony of Police Professionalism: The Los Angeles Police Department, Mexican Americans, and Police Reform in the 1950s." *Pacific Historical Review* 72, no. 2 (May 2003): 171–99.

———. "The Dialectics of Repression: The Los Angeles Police Department and the Chicano Movement, 1968–1971." *Journal of American History* 79, no. 4 (March 1993): 1483–514.

———. *Race, Police, and the Making of a Political Identity: Mexican Americans and the Los Angeles Police Department, 1900–1945*. Berkeley: University of California Press, 1999.

Espiritu, Yén Lê. "Toward a Critical Refugee Study: The Vietnamese Refugee Subject in US Scholarship." *Journal of Vietnamese Studies* 1, nos. 1–2 (2006): 410–33.

Evans, Peter, Dietrich Rueschemeyer, and Theda Skocpol, eds. *Bringing the State Back In*. Cambridge: Cambridge University Press, 1985.

Eve, Raymond. Review of Quinney, *Critique of Legal Order*. In *Social Forces* 55, no. 2 (December 1976): 559–60.

Fair, Bryan K. *Notes of a Racial Caste Baby: Color Blindness and the End of Affirmative Action*. New York: New York University Press, 1997.

Fan, Mary De Ming. "Disciplining Criminal Justice: The Peril amid the Promise of Numbers." *Yale Law and Policy Review* 26, no. 1 (fall 2007): 1–74.

Farish, Matthew. *The Contours of America's Cold War*. Minneapolis: University of Minnesota Press, 2010.

Farmer, Lindsay. "The Jurisprudence of Security: The Police Power and the Criminal Law." In *The New Police Science: The Police Power in Domestic and International Governance*, edited by Markus Dirk Dubber and Mariana Valverde, 145–67. Stanford, CA: Stanford University Press, 2006.

Farmer, Paul. "An Anthropology of Structural Violence." *Current Anthropology* 45, no. 3 (June 2004): 305–17.

Farrell, William, and Charles Thomas. "Sociology, Humanism and Criminal Justice Education." *Michigan Sociological Review* 11 (fall 1997): 97–108.

Farrell, William, and Larry Koch. "Criminal Justice, Sociology, and Academia." *American Sociologist* 26, no. 1. Special issue, *Sociology, Law, and Ethics* (spring 1995): 52–61.

Fassin, Didier. *Humanitarian Reason: A Moral History of the Present*. Berkeley: University of California Press, 2011.

Feagin, Joe R., and Harlan Hahn. *Ghetto Revolts: The Politics of Violence in American Cities*. New York: Macmillan, 1973.

Feder, Barnaby J. "Agee Leaving Morrison Knudsen." *New York Times*, February 2, 1995. Accessed June 17, 2014. http://www.nytimes.com/1995/02/02/business /agee-leaving-morrison-knudsen.html.

Feeley, Malcolm, and Austin Sarat. *The Policy Dilemma: Federal Crime Policy and the Law Enforcement Assistance Administration, 1968–1978*. Minneapolis: University of Minnesota Press, 1980.

Feigenbaum, Anna. "100 Years of Tear Gas." *The Atlantic*, August 16, 2014. Accessed May 22, 2016. http://www.theatlantic.com/international/archive/2014/08/100 -years-of-tear-gas/378632/.

Feldman, Allen. *Formations of Violence: The Narrative of the Body and Political Terror in Northern Ireland*. Chicago: University of Chicago Press, 1991.

Feldman, Justin. "Roland Fryer Is Wrong: There Is Racial Bias in Shootings by Police." Scholar.Harvard.edu blogpost, July 12, 2016. Accessed August 27, 2016. http://scholar.harvard.edu/jfeldman/blog/roland-fryer-wrong-there-racial -bias-shootings-police#.V4emZ_RJMmQ.facebook.

Feldman, Keith P. *A Shadow over Palestine: The Imperial Life of Race in America*. Minneapolis: University of Minnesota Press, 2015.

Ferguson, James. *Anti-Politics Machine: Development, Depoliticization, and Bureaucratic Power in Lesotho*. Minneapolis: University of Minnesota Press, 1994.

Ferguson, Roderick A. *Aberrations in Black: Toward a Queer of Color Critique*. Minneapolis: University of Minnesota Press, 2004.

Fink, Carole, Philipp Gassert, and Detlef Junker. *1968: The World Transformed*. Cambridge: Cambridge University Press, 1998.

Fiore, Faye, and Bettina Boxall. "Local Elections Long Beach City Council." *Los Angeles Times*, May 31, 1990. Accessed June 27, 2015. http://articles.latimes.com /1990-05-31/news/hl-748_1_long-beach.

Flamm, Michael W. *Law and Order: Street Crime, Civil Unrest, and the Crisis of Liberalism in the 1960s*. New York: Columbia University Press, 2005.

Fleetwood, Blake. "Police Work Isn't as Dangerous as You May Think." *Huffington Post* January 15, 2015. Accessed October 14, 2015. http://www.huffingtonpost .com/blake-fleetwood/how-dangerous-is-police-w_b_6373798.html.

Flitcraft, Ann. "LEAA: Campus Cops' Hot Line." NARMIC, *Police on the Homefront*, 25–27.

———. "Winning Hearts and Minds." NARMIC, *Police on the Homefront*, 21–24.

Floriano, Carol Milardo. "Life in a Camp." *American Journal of Nursing* 80, no. 11 (November 1980): 2027–30.

Fogelson, Robert M. *Big-City Police*. Cambridge, MA: Harvard University Press, 1977.

Forman, James, Jr. *Locking Up Our Own: Crime and Punishment in Black America*. New York: Farrar, Straus and Giroux, 2017.

Foucault, Michel. "Omnes et Singulatum: Towards a Criticism of Political Reason." In *Essential Works of Foucault (1954–1984)*, edited by James D. Faubion, 3:298–325. London: Allen Lane, 2001.

———. "Society Must Be Defended," *Lectures at the College de France, 1975–1976*, edited by Mauro Bertani and Alessandro Fontana. Translated by David Macey. NY: Picador, 2003.

Frazier, Lessie Jo, and Deborah Cohen, eds. *Gender and Sexuality in 1968: Transformative Politics in the Cultural Imagination*. New York: Palgrave Macmillan, 2009.

Freeman, Colin. "Horror at Fallujah." SFGate (*San Francisco Chronicle* online), April 1, 2004. Accessed October 17, 2014. http://www.sfgate.com/news/article /Horror-at-Fallujah-savage-attack-Bodies-2772639.php.

Friedman, Andrew. *Covert Capital: Landscapes of Denial and the Making of Empire in the Suburbs of Northern Virginia*. Berkeley: University of California Press, 2013.

Gaines, Kevin. 2006. *American Africans in Ghana: Black Expatriates and the Civil Rights Era*. Chapel Hill: University of North Carolina Press.

Gallagher, Catherine, and Stephen Greenblatt. *Practicing New Historicism*. Chicago: University of Chicago Press, 2000.

Galtung, Johann. "Violence, Peace, and Peace Research." *Journal of Peace Research* 6, no. 3 (1969): 167–91.

Gapay, Les. "Beyond Dick Tracy: Police Go Space-Age in Big Cities and Small, to Dismay of Critics." *Wall Street Journal*, August 9, 1971, 1, 21.

Garland, David. *The Culture of Control: Crime and Social Order in Contemporary Society*. Chicago: University of Chicago Press, 2001.

Garland, David, and Richard Sparks. "Criminology, Social Theory, and the Challenge of Our Times." *British Journal of Criminology* 40, no. 2 (spring 2000): 189–204.

"General, 43, Heads Guerrilla Force." *New York Times*, January 25, 1962, 16.

GEO Group. "Historic Milestones." The GEO Group. Accessed June 27, 2012. http:// www.geogroup.com/about_us/history.html.

Gerber, Larry G. "Corporatism and State Theory: A Review Essay for Historians." *Social Science History* 19, no. 3 (fall 1995): 313–32.

Gerd, Rainer Horn, and Padraic Kenney. *Transnational Moments of Change: Europe, 1945, 1968, 1989*. Lanham, MD: Rowman and Littlefield, 2004.

Gettleman, Jeffrey. "Enraged Mob in Falluja Kills 4 American Contractors." *New York Times*, March 31, 2004. Accessed October 17, 2014. http://www.nytimes.com/2004/03/31/international/worldspecial/31cnd-iraq.html.

Geyer, Michael. "The Militarization of Europe, 1914–1945." In *The Militarization of the Western World*, edited by John R. Gillis, 65–102. New Brunswick, NJ: Rutgers University Press, 1989.

G4S. "History." G4S corporate website. Accessed June 27, 2012. http://www.g4s.us/en-us/Who%20we%20are/History/.

Gibson, James. *Warrior Dreams: Paramilitary Culture in Post-Vietnam America.* New York: Hill and Wang, 1994.

Giddens, Anthony. *A Contemporary Critique of Historical Materialism.* Vol. 2, *The Nation-State and Violence.* Berkeley: University of California Press, 1981.

Gill, Lesley. *The School of the Americas: Military Training and Political Violence in the Americas.* Durham, NC: Duke University Press, 2004.

Gillis, John, ed. *The Militarization of the Western World.* New Brunswick, NJ: Rutgers University Press, 1989.

Gilmore, Ruth Wilson. "Fatal Couplings of Power and Violence: Notes on Racism and Geography." *Professional Geographer* 54, no. 1 (2002): 15–24.

———. "Globalization and U.S. Prison Growth: From Military Keynesianism to Post-Keynesian Militarism." *Race and Class* 40, no. 2/3 (October 1998): 171–88.

———. *Golden Gulag: Prisons, Surplus, Crisis, and Opposition in Globalizing California.* Berkeley: University of California Press, 2007.

Gilmore, Ruth Wilson, and Craig Gilmore. "Beyond Bratton." In Camp and Heatherton, *Policing the Planet,* 173–99.

———. "Restating the Obvious." In *Indefensible Space: The Architecture of the National Insecurity State,* edited by Michael Sorkin, 141–62. New York: Routledge, 2008.

Givan, Richard, and Cynthia Miller, with Gary Cordner, Bruce Wolford, James McClanahan, and Rhonda Smith, eds. *Justice and Safety Education at Eastern Kentucky University: "A Historical Perspective."* Richmond, KY: College of Justice and Safety, EKU [ca. 2002].

Glick, Brian. "Preface" to Ward Churchill and Jim Vander Wall, *The COINTELPRO Papers: Documents from the FBI's Secret Wars against Dissent in the United States,* x–xvi. 2nd ed. Cambridge, MA: South End Press, [1990] 2002.

———. *War at Home: Covert Action against U.S. Activists and What We Can Do about It.* Boston, MA: South End Press, 1989.

Global Policy Forum. "Private Military and Security Companies (PMSCs)." GlobalPolicy.org. Accessed September 11, 2015. https://www.globalpolicy.org/pmscs.html.

GlobalSecurity.org. "Royal Saudi Naval Forces (RSNF) History." *GlobalSecurity.org.* Accessed January 10, 2015. http://www.globalsecurity.org/military/world/gulf/rsnf-history.htm.

Goldstein, Alyosha. *Poverty in Common: The Politics of Community Action during the American Century.* Durham, NC: Duke University Press, 2012.

Gollomb, Joseph. "The War on Crime." *The American Journal of Police Science* 2, no. 3 (May–June 1931): 262–67. Reprinted from *Vanity Fair*, July 1931.

Goodman, Amy. "Cops or Soldiers? Pentagon, DHS Helped Arm Police in Ferguson with Equipment Used in War." *Democracy Now*, August 15, 2014. Accessed October 17, 2014. http://www.democracynow.org/2014/8/15/cops_or_soldiers _pentagon_dhs_helped.

———. "Ferguson Crackdown Sparks Review of Police Militarization that Mainly Targets Communities of Color." *Democracy Now*, August 29, 2014. Accessed October 17, 2014. http://www.democracynow.org/2014/8/29/ferguson _crackdown_sparks_review_of_police.

Gottschalk, Marie. *Caught: The Prison State and the Lockdown of American Politics.* Princeton, NJ: Princeton University Press, 2015.

———. *The Prison and the Gallows: The Politics of Mass Incarceration in America.* Cambridge: Cambridge University Press, 2006.

Gould, Lewis L. "Introduction" to *Records of the National Commission on Violence,* edited by Robert E. Lester, v–x. Microfilmed reels from the Johnson presidential library. Bethesda, MD: LexisNexis, n.d.

Gramsci, Antonio. *Selections from the Prison Notebooks of Antonio Gramsci.* Edited and translated by Quintin Hoare and Geoffrey Nowell Smith. New York: International Publishers, 1971.

Grandin, Greg. *Empire's Workshop: Latin America, the United States, and the Rise of the New Imperialism.* New York: Metropolitan Books, 2006.

Grandin, Greg, and Gilbert M. Joseph, eds. *A Century of Revolution: Insurgent and Counterinsurgent Violence during Latin America's Long Cold War.* Durham, NC: Duke University Press, 2010.

Grant, Linda, and Bill Billiter. "Glut of Alaska Oil Presents U.S. Dilemma." *Los Angeles Times*, April 15, 1979, A1.

Green, Penny. *The Enemy Without: Policing, Class Consciousness and the Miners' Strike.* Buckingham, UK: Open University Press, 1990.

Greenberg, D. S. "IDA: University-Sponsored Center Hit Hard by Assaults on Campus." *Science* 160, no. 3829 (May 17, 1968): 744–48.

Greene, Jack R., and Stephen D. Mastrofski, eds. *Community Policing: Rhetoric or Reality.* New York: Praeger, 1988.

Greenwald, Glenn. "The Militarization of U.S. Police: Finally Dragged into the Light by the Horrors of Ferguson." *Intercept*, August 14, 2014. Accessed October 17, 2014. https://firstlook.org/theintercept/2014/08/14/militarization-u-s -police-dragged-light-horrors-ferguson/.

Gregg, Robert. *Inside Out, Outside In: Essays in Comparative History.* New York: St. Martin's, 2000.

"Gregory Luna." Texas State Cemetery records online. Accessed 21 April 2009. http:// www.cemetery.state.tx.us/pub/user_form.asp?step=1&pers_id=6570.

Griffin, Gerald R. *A Study of Relationships between Level of College Education and Police Patrolmen's Performance.* Saratoga, CA: Century Twenty One, 1980.

Grodsky, Morris. *The Home Boy's Odyssey: The Saga of the Journey from Orphan Boy to Criminalist*. Bloomington, IN: First Books, 2004.

Gross, Ariela. "From the Streets to the Courts: Doing Grassroots History of Race, Law and Conservatism in the United States." Paper presented at Indiana University, April 2013.

Guerrero, Andrea. *Silence at Boalt Hall: The Dismantling of Affirmative Action*. Berkeley: University of California Press, 2002.

Guinier, Lani, and Gerald Torres. *The Miner's Canary: Enlisting Race, Resisting Power, Transforming Democracy*. Cambridge, MA: Harvard University Press, 2003.

Haghhor, Bashir. Zoominfo profile. Accessed October 4, 2012. http://www.zoominfo .com/#!search/profile/person?personId=1174437125&targetid=profile.

Hagopian, Patrick. *The Vietnam War in American Memory: Veterans, Memorials, and the Politics of Healing*. Amherst: University of Massachusetts Press, 2009.

Haines, David, Dorothy Rutherford, and Patrick Thomas. "Family and Community among Vietnamese Refugees." In "Refugees Today," special issue, *International Migration Review* 15, no. 1/2 (spring–summer 1981): 310–19.

Haley, Sarah. *No Mercy Here: Gender, Punishment, and the Making of Jim Crow Modernity*. Chapel Hill: University of North Carolina Press, 2016.

Hall, Stuart. "The State in Question." In *The Idea of the Modern State*, edited by Gregor McClellan, David Held, and Stuart Hall, 1–28. Milton Keynes: The Open University Press, 1984.

Hall, Stuart, with Chas Critcher, Tony Jefferson, John Clarke, and Brian Roberts. *Policing the Crisis: Mugging, the State, and Law and Order*. New York: Holmes and Meier, 1978.

Halperin, Morton, Jerry Berman, Robert Borosage, and Christine Marwick. *The Lawless State: The Crimes of the U.S. Intelligence Agencies*. New York: Penguin, 1976.

Hames-Garcia, Michael. *Fugitive Thought: Prison Movements, Race, and the Meaning of Justice*. Minneapolis: University of Minnesota Press, 2004.

Han, Chong-Suk. "Being an Oriental, I Could Never Be Completely a Man: Gay Asian Men and the Intersection of Race, Gender, Sexuality, and Class." *Race, Gender and Class* 13, no. 3/4 (2006): 82–97.

Hanieh, Adam. *Capitalism and Class in the Gulf Arab States*. New York: Palgrave Macmillan, 2011.

Hansford, Justin. "Community Policing Reconsidered: From Ferguson to Baltimore." In Camp and Heatherton, *Policing the Planet*, 215–25.

Harcourt, Bernard. *Illusion of Order: The False Promise of Broken Windows Policing*. Cambridge, MA: Harvard University Press, 2001.

———. "Occupy Wall Street's 'Political Disobedience.'" *New York Times*, October 13, 2011. Accessed March 26, 2012. http://opinionator.blogs.nytimes.com /2011/10/13/occupy-wall-streets-political-disobedience.

Harney, Stefano, and Fred Moten. *The Undercommons: Fugitive Planning and Black Study*. New York: Minor Compositions, 2013.

Harring, Sidney L. *Policing a Class Society: The Experience of American Cities, 1865–1915*. New Brunswick, NJ: Rutgers University Press, 1983.

———. "The Development of the Police Institution in the United States." *Crime and Social Justice* 5 (spring–summer 1976): 54–59.

Harring, Sidney L., Tony Platt, Richard Speiglman, and Paul Takagi. "The Management of Police Killings." *Crime and Social Justice* 8 (fall–winter 1977): 34–43.

Harris, Fred, and Lynn Curtis. *The Millennium Breach: Richer, Poorer, Racially Apart.* 2nd ed. Washington, DC: Milton S. Eisenhower Foundation and The Corporation for What Works, 1998. Accessed December 6, 2013. http://www.eisenhowerfoundation.org/docs/millennium.pdf.

"Dr. Harry Eugene Bruno." Obituary. *Bartlesville Examiner-Enterprise,* January 7, 2014. Accessed June 27, 2015. http://www.legacy.com/obituaries/examiner-enterprise/obituary-print.aspx?n=harry-eugene-bruno&pid=168940220.

Hartman, Saidiya. *Scenes of Subjection: Terror, Slavery, and Self-Making in Nineteenth-Century America.* New York: Oxford University Press, 1997.

Hartung, William D. "Mercenaries, Inc.: How a U.S. Company Props Up the House of Saud." *Progressive* (April 1996): 26–28.

Harvey, David. *A Brief History of Neoliberalism.* New York: Oxford University Press, 2005.

———. *Spaces of Capital: Towards a Critical Geography.* New York: Routledge, 2001.

Haskell, Thomas L. "Capitalism and the Origins of the Humanitarian Sensibility, Part 1." *American Historical Review* 90, no. 2 (April 1985): 339–61.

Hasson, Peter. "Black Lives Matter Attorney: Dismantle and Abolish the Police." *Daily Caller,* July 11, 2016. Accessed September 6, 2016. http://dailycaller.com/2016/07/11/black-lives-matter-attorney-dismantle-and-abolish-the-police/#ixzz4JUc5YbVo.

Hattori, Tomohisa. "Reconceptualizing Foreign Aid." *Review of International Political Economy* 8, no. 4 (winter 2001): 633–60.

Haycox, Stephen. "'Fetched Up': Unlearned Lessons from the *Exxon Valdez.*" *Journal of American History* (June 2012): 219–28.

Heder, Stephen P. "The Kampuchean-Vietnamese Conflict." *Southeast Asian Affairs* (1979): 157–86.

Herbers, John. "Conflicts Beset U.S. Anticrime Agency." *New York Times,* December 28, 1970, 1, 36.

Herbert, Steven K. *Citizens, Cops, and Power: Recognizing the Limits of Community.* Chicago: University of Chicago Press, 2006.

Hernández, Kelly Lytle. *City of Inmates: Conquest, Rebellion, and the Rise of Human Caging in Los Angeles, 1771–1965.* Chapel Hill: UNC Press, 2017.

———. *Migra! A History of the U.S. Border Patrol.* Berkeley: University of California Press, 2010.

Herring, Cedric, and Sharon M. Collins. "Retreat from Equal Opportunity? The Case of Affirmative Action." In *The Bubbling Cauldron: Race, Ethnicity, and the Urban Crisis,* edited by Michael Peter Smith and Joe R. Feagin, 163–81. Minneapolis: University of Minnesota Press, 1995.

Hertog, Steffen. *Princes, Brokers, and Bureaucrats: Oil and the State in Saudi Arabia.* Ithaca, NY: Cornell University Press, 2010.

Herzing, Rachel. "Big Dreams and Bold Steps toward a Police-Free Future." Truthout.com. September 16, 2015. Accessed July 8, 2016. http://www.truth -out.org/opinion/item/32813-big-dreams-and-bold-steps-toward-a-police -free-future.

Heymann, Philip B., and Mark H. Moore. "The Federal Role in Dealing with Violent Street Crime: Principles, Questions, and Cautions." *Annals of the American Academy of Political and Social Science* 543 (January 1996): 103–15.

Hill, Stephen, Randall Beger, and John Zanetti. "Plugging the Security Gap or Springing a Leak: Questioning the Rise of Paramilitary Policing in US Domestic and Foreign Policy." *Democracy and Security* 3 (2007): 301–21.

Hinds, Lennox S. "The Police Use of Excessive and Deadly Force: Racial Implications." In *A Community Concern: Police Use of Deadly Force*, compiled by Robert N. Brenner. Washington, DC: Department of Justice, Law Enforcement Assistance Administration, National Institute of Law Enforcement and Criminal Justice, 1979, 7–11.

Hinton, Elizabeth. *From the War on Poverty to the War on Crime: The Making of Mass Incarceration in America*. Cambridge, MA: Harvard University Press, 2016.

———. "'A War within Our Own Boundaries': Lyndon Johnson's Great Society and the Rise of the Carceral State." *Journal of American History* (June 2015): 100–112.

Hoad, Neville. "Sovereign Feeling: HIV/AIDS, The Right to Sexual Orientation, Dignity and the South African Constitution." *UCLA Journal of International Law and Foreign Affairs* 18, no. 123 (2013): 124–58.

Hobbes, Thomas. *Hobbes's Leviathan*. Oxford: Clarendon Press, [1651] 1965.

Hodes, Martha, ed. *Sex, Love, Race: Crossing Boundaries in North American History*. New York: New York University Press, 1999.

———. *White Women, Black Men: Illicit Sex in the Nineteenth-Century South*. New Haven, CT: Yale University Press, 1999.

Høivik, Tord. "The Demography of Structural Violence." *Journal of Peace Research* 14, no. 1 (1977): 59–73.

Holland, Sharon Patricia. *The Erotic Life of Racism*. Durham, NC: Duke University Press, 2012.

Holloway, Thomas H. *Policing Rio de Janeiro: Repression and Resistance in a Nineteenth-Century City*. Stanford, CA: Stanford University Press, 1993.

Holmes, James R. *Theodore Roosevelt and World Order: Police Power in International Relations*. Washington, DC: Potomac Books, 2006.

Hong, Grace Kyungwon. *The Ruptures of American Capital: Women of Color Feminism and the Culture of Immigrant Labor*. Minneapolis: University of Minnesota Press, 2006.

Hong, Grace Kyungwon, and Roderick A. Ferguson, eds. *Strange Affinities: The Gender and Sexual Politics of Comparative Racialization*. Durham, NC: Duke University Press, 2011.

Hopkins, Alicia. "Entrevista a Enrique Dussel 'La violence es fruto de la pobreza.'" *Filosofía*, August 13, 2011. Accessed September 7, 2011. http://www.filosofia.mx /index.php/perse/archivos/la_violencia_es_fruto_de_la_pobreza.

Hua, Julietta. *Trafficking Women's Human Rights*. Minneapolis: University of Minnesota Press, 2011.

Huber, Matthew T. "Enforcing Scarcity: Oil, Violence, and the Making of the Market." *Annals of the Association of American Geographers* 101, no. 4 (2011): 816–26.

Huggins, Martha K. *Political Policing: The United States and Latin America*. Durham, NC: Duke University Press, 1998.

———. "U.S.-Supported State Terror: A History of Police Training in Latin America." In "Contragate and Counter Terrorism: A Global Perspective," special issue, *Crime and Social Justice* 27/28 (1987): 149–71.

Huggins, Martha K., Mika Haritos-Fatouros, and Philip G. Zimbardo. *Violence Workers: Police Torturers and Murderers Reconstruct Brazilian Atrocities*. Berkeley: University of California Press, 2002.

Hummel, Laurel J. "The U.S. Military as Geographical Agent: The Case of Cold War Alaska." *Geographical Review* 95, no. 1 (January 2005): 47–72.

Huntington, Samuel. *The Soldier and the State: The Theory and Politics of Civil-Military Relations*. Cambridge, MA: Belknap Press, 1957.

Huyck, Earl E., and Leon F. Bouvier. "The Demography of Refugees." *Annals of the American Academy of Political and Social Science* 476 (May 1983): 39–61.

IACP. *Directory: Law Enforcement Education 1970*. Washington, DC: IACP, 1970.

Inbau, Fred E. "Scientific Evidence in Criminal Cases." *Journal of Criminal Law and Criminology* 25, no. 3 (September–October 1934): 500–516.

Institute for Defense Analyses. "IDA's History and Mission." Webpage of the Institute for Defense Analyses. Accessed May 18, 2014. https://www.ida.org/aboutus/studiesandanalysiscenter.php.

———. *Task Force Report: Science and Technology*. Washington, DC: Government Printing Office, 1967.

James, Joy. *Resisting State Violence: Racialism, Gender, and Race in U.S. Culture*. Minneapolis: University of Minnesota Press, 1996.

———, ed. *Warfare in the American Homeland: Policing and Prison in a Penal Democracy*. Durham, NC: Duke University Press, 2007.

Jankowski, Amy L. "Robert F. Borkenstein Papers, 1928–2002, bulk 1940–2002: A Guide to His Papers at the Indiana University Archives." *Archives Online at Indiana University*. http://webapp1.dlib.indiana.edu/findingaids/view?doc.view=entire_text&docId=InU-Ar-VAC0762.

Jefferson, Tony. *The Case against Paramilitary Policing*. Buckingham, UK: Open University Press, 1990.

Jeffries, Charles. *The Colonial Police*. London: Max Parish, 1952.

Jenkins, Colin. "Calibrating the Capitalist State in the Neoliberal Era: Equilibrium, Superstructure, and the Pull Towards a Corporate-Fascistic Model." *Hampton Institute: A Working-Class Think Tank*, February 4, 2014. Accessed October 15, 2015. http://www.hamptoninstitution.org/calibrating-capitalism-in-the-neoliberal-era.html.

Jenkins, Herbert T. "A Commission Member Speaks." *Police Chief* (May 1968): 35+.

Jessop, Bob. *State Theory: Putting the Capitalist State in Its Place*. Cambridge, MA: Polity Press, 1990.

"John Clifford 'Jack' Zeigler." Obituary. *Arizona Republic*, October 5, 2012. Reprinted at AZCentral.com. Accessed June 28, 2014. http://www.legacy.com/obituaries /azcentral/obituary.aspx?pid=160273662.

Johnson, David. *American Law Enforcement: A History*. St. Louis, MO: Forum Press, 1981.

Johnson, Marilynn S. *Street Justice: A History of Police Violence in New York City*. Boston, MA: Beacon Press, 2003.

Johnston, Les. *The Rebirth of Private Policing*. London: Routledge, 1992.

Jones, Michelle. "Qualitative Inquiry." Unpublished paper shared with the author, summer 2016.

Joseph, Gilbert M., and Daniel Nugent, eds. *Everyday Forms of State Formation: Revolution and the Negotiation of Rule in Modern Mexico*. Durham, NC: Duke University Press, 1994.

Judy, Ronald. "Provisional Note on Formations of Planetary Violence." *boundary 2* 33, no. 3 (fall 2006): 141–50.

Jung, Moon-Ho. "Solidarity, Liberalism, History." *American Quarterly* 68, no. 2 (June 2016): 257–61.

Kaba, Mariame. "Summer Heat." *New Inquiry* June 6, 2015. Accessed September 6, 2016. http://thenewinquiry.com/essays/summer-heat/.

Kakalik, James S., and Sorrel Wildhorn. *Private Security in the United States*, 5 vols. (The RAND Corporation Report). Washington, DC: US Department of Justice, National Institute of Law Enforcement and Criminal Justice, Law Enforcement Assistance Administration, 1972.

Kalyvas, Stathis N. "The Paradox of Terrorism in Civil War." *Journal of Ethics* 8, no. 1 (2004): 97–138.

Kamm, Henry. "The Irritation on Refugees Grows." *New York Times*, January 25, 1978, A4.

Kappeler, Victor E., Mark Blumberg, and Gary W. Potter. *The Mythology of Crime and Criminal Justice*. Prospect Heights, IL: Waveland Press, 1993.

Karsten, Peter. "Militarization and Rationalization in the United States, 1870–1914." In *The Militarization of the Western World*, edited by John R. Gillis, 30–44. New Brunswick, NJ: Rutgers University Press, 1989.

Katz, Michael B., and Mike Rose, eds. *Public Education Under Siege*. Philadelphia: University of Pennsylvania Press, 2013.

Kazin, Michael. *The Populist Persuasion: An American History*. New York: Basic Books, 1995.

Keller, Morton. "(Jerry-)Building a New American State." *Reviews in American History* 11, no. 2 (June 1983): 248–52.

Kelley, Robin D. G. "Introduction." In *Race, Capitalism, Justice: A Boston Review*, edited by Walter Johnson with Robin D. G. Kelley, 5–8. Cambridge, MA: Boston Review, 2017.

———. "Thug Nation: On State Violence and Disposability." In Camp and Heatherton, *Policing the Planet*, 15–33.

Kelling, George L., and Mark Moore. "The Evolving Strategy of Policing." In *The Police and Society: Touchstone Readings*, edited by Victor Kappeler, 3–27. 2nd ed. Prospect Heights, IL: Waveland Press, [1988] 1999.

Kelly, Gail Paradise. *From Vietnam to America: A Chronicle of the Vietnamese Immigration to the United States*. Boulder, CO: Westview Press, 1977.

Kempa, Michael. "Public Policing, Private Security, Pacifying Populations." In *Anti-Security*, edited by Mark Neocleous and George S. Rigakos, 85–105. Ottawa, Canada: Red Quill Press, 2001.

Kenworthy, E. W. "Ruckelshaus Asks a Delay On Alaska Pipeline Permit." *New York Times*, March 15, 1971, 1.

Khalili, Laleh. *Time in the Shadows: Confinement in Counterinsurgencies*. Stanford, CA: Stanford University Press, 2013.

Khoo, Olivia. *The Chinese Exotic: Modern Diasporic Femininity*. Hong Kong: Hong Kong University Press, 2007.

Kilgore, James. "Repackaging Mass Incarceration." *Prison Legal News*, November 2014, 36. Accessed May 6, 2017. https://www.prisonlegalnews.org/news/2014/nov/8/repackaging-mass-incarceration/.

"Killed by Police." Website. Accessed March 13, 2017. http://killedbypolice.net.

Kimble v. Holmes and Narver Services Incorporated and E. 995 F2d 1063. Accessed October 4, 2012. http://judicialview.com/Court-Cases/Civil_Rights/Kimble-v.-Holmes-and-Narver-Services-Incorporated-and-E/12/476734.

Kissman, Kris, and Thanh Van Tran. "Life Satisfaction among the Indochinese Refugees." *International Review of Modern Sociology* 19, no. 1 (spring 1989): 27–35.

Kitaeff, Jack. *Jews in Blue: The Jewish American Experience in Law Enforcement*. Youngstown, NY: Cambria Press, 2006.

Klare, Michael T. "Bringing It Back: Planning for the City." In NARMIC, *Police on the Homefront*, 66–73.

———. "The Interventionist Impulse: US Military Doctrine for Low-Intensity Warfare." In *Low-Intensity Warfare: Counterinsurgency, Proinsurgency, and Antiterrorism in the Eighties*, edited by Michael T. Klare and Peter Kornbluh, 49–79. New York: Pantheon Books, 1988.

———. "Police Build National Apparatus." *Guardian*, February 21, 1970, 5.

———. "Rent-a-Cop: The Boom in Private Police." *Nation* 221 (November 1975): 487.

Klare, Michael T., and Cynthia Arnson. *Supplying Repression: U.S. Support for Authoritarian Regimes Abroad*. Washington, DC: Institute for Policy Studies, [1977] 1981.

Klare, Michael T., and Peter Kornbluh, eds. *Low-Intensity Warfare: Counterinsurgency, Proinsurgency, and Antiterrorism in the Eighties*. New York: Pantheon Books, 1988.

Klein, Naomi. *The Shock Doctrine: The Rise of Disaster Capitalism*. New York: Metropolitan Books / Henry Holt, 2007.

Koerner, Brendan I. *The Skies Belong to Us: Love and Terror in the Golden Age of Hijacking*. New York: Crown, 2013.

Kohler-Hausmann, Julilly. *Getting Tough: Welfare and Imprisonment in 1970s America*. Princeton, NJ: Princeton University Press, 2017.

———. "Guns and Butter: The Welfare State, the Carceral State, and the Politics of Exclusion in the Postwar United States." *Journal of American History* 102, no. 1 (June 2015): 87–99.

———. "Militarizing the Police: Officer Jon Burge, Torture, and War in the 'Urban Jungle.'" In *Challenging the Prison-Industrial Complex: Activism, Arts, and Educational Alternatives*, edited by Stephen John Hartnett, 43–71. Champaign: University of Illinois Press, 2011.

Koistinen, Paul. "Toward a Warfare State: Militarization in America during the Period of the World Wars." In *The Militarization of the Western World*, edited by John R. Gillis, 47–64. New Brunswick, NJ: Rutgers University Press, 1989.

Kopel, David, and Paul Blackman. "Can Soldiers Be Peace Officers? The Waco Disaster and the Militarization of American Law Enforcement Period." *Akron Law Review* 30 (1997): 619–59.

Kramer, Paul A. *The Blood of Government: Race, Empire, the United States, and the Philippines*. Chapel Hill: University of North Carolina Press, 2006.

———. "Power and Connection: Imperial Histories of the United States in the World." *American Historical Review* 116, no. 5 (2011): 1348–91.

Kraska, Peter B. "Enjoying Militarism: Political/Personal Dilemmas in Studying U.S. Police Paramilitary Units." *Justice Quarterly* 13 (1996): 405–30.

———. "Militarization and Policing—Its Relevance to 21st Century Police." *Policing* 1, no. 4 (2007): 501–13.

———. "Militarizing Criminal Justice: Exploring the Possibilities." *Journal of Political and Military Sociology* 27, no. 2 (winter 1999): 205–15.

———, ed. *Militarizing the American Criminal Justice System: The Changing Roles of the Armed Forces and the Police*. Boston, MA: Northeastern University Press, 2001.

Kraska, Peter B., and Victor E. Kappeler. "Militarizing American Police: The Rise and Normalization of Paramilitary Units." *Social Problems* 44, no. 1 (1997): 1–18.

Krieger, Nancy, Mathew V. Kiang, Jarvis T. Chen, and Pamela D. Waterman. "Trends in US Deaths Due to Legal Intervention Among Black and White Men, Age 15–34 Years, by County Income Level: 1960–2010." *Harvard Public Health Review* 3 (January 2015): 1–5. Accessed October 13, 2015. http://harvardpublichealthreview.org/190/.

Krugman, Paul. "Patriots and Profits." *New York Times*, December 16, 2003, A35.

Kuhn, Arthur. "International Cooperation in the Suppression of Crime." *American Journal of International Law* 28, no. 3 (July 1934): 541–44.

Kundnani, Arun. *The Muslims Are Coming: Islamophobia, Extremism, and the Domestic War on Terror*. New York: Verso Books, 2014.

Kunzel, Regina. *Criminal Intimacy: Prison and the Uneven History of Modern American Sexuality*. Chicago: University of Chicago Press, 2008.

Kurth, James R. "America Must Do More." *Foreign Policy* 36 (autumn 1979): 12–19.

Kuzmarov, Jeremy. *Modernizing Repression: Police Training and Nation Building in the American Century.* Amherst: University of Massachusetts Press, 2012.

Kwitny, Jonathan. 1984. *Endless Enemies: The Making of an Unfriendly World.* New York: Congdon & Weed / St. Martin's Press.

LaCapria, Kim. "A 'Harvard Study' Doesn't Disprove Racial Bias in Officer-Involved Shootings." *Snopes.com.* July 15, 2016. Accessed August 27, 2016. http://www.snopes.com/2016/07/15/harvard-study-officer-involved-shootings/.

Lamphier, C. M. "Refugee Resettlement Models in Action." *International Migration* 17 (spring 1983): 4–33.

Langguth, A. J. *Hidden Terrors: the Truth about U.S. Police Operations in Latin America.* New York: Pantheon, 1978.

LAPD Online. "The Los Angeles Police Academy." Accessed July 27, 2015. http://www.lapdonline.org/history_of_the_lapd/content_basic_view/1134.

LaRocca, Joe. *Alaska Agonistes: The Age of Petroleum. (How Big Oil Bought Alaska).* North East: Rare Books, Ink, 2003.

Laughlin, David L. *Gringo Cop.* New York: Carlton Press, 1975.

"Law Officers Planning Visit to Mexico." *Valley News,* April 28, 1966, n.p. or 22-A-East.

Lawrence, Bruce B., and Aisha Karim. "General Introduction: Theorizing Violence in the Twenty-First Century." In *On Violence: A Reader,* edited by Lawrence and Karim, 1–15. Durham, NC: Duke University Press, 2007.

LEAA, *Eleventh Annual Report of the LEAA Fiscal Year 1979.* Washington, DC: Government Printing Office, 1980.

——. *Second Annual Report of the LEAA Fiscal Year 1970.* Washington, DC: Government Printing Office, 1970.

Lebkicher, Roy. *Aramco and World Oil.* New York: Russell Moore, 1952.

Lebkicher, Roy, George Rentz, Max Steineke, et al. *Aramco Handbook.* NH: Aramco, 1960.

Lefever, Ernest W. *U.S. Public Safety Assistance: An Assessment.* Washington, DC: Brookings Institution, 1973.

LEIU (Association of Law Enforcement Intelligence Units). "History, Purpose, and Operations." Subpage of Association website. Accessed June 29, 2012. http://leiu.org/node/2?q=node/1.

Lepselter, Susan. *The Resonance of Unseen Things: Poetics, Power, Captivity, and UFOs in the American Uncanny.* Ann Arbor: University of Michigan Press, 2016.

Lester, Robert E., ed. *Records of the National Commission on Violence.* Bethesda, MD: LexisNexis, n.d.

Lewis, Penny. *Hardhats, Hippies, and Hawks: The Vietnam Antiwar Movement as Myth and Memory.* Ithaca, NY: ILR Press, 2013.

Lichtenstein, Alexander C. *Twice the Work of Free Labor: The Political Economy of Convict Labor in the New South.* London: Verso, 1996.

Liebenow, J. Gus. *Liberia: The Quest for Democracy.* Bloomington: Indiana University Press, 1987.

Light, Jennifer. *From Warfare to Welfare: Defense Intellectuals and Urban Problems in Cold War America*. Baltimore, MD: Johns Hopkins University Press, 2003.

Linebaugh, Peter, and Marcus Rediker. *The Many-Headed Hydra: Sailors, Slaves, Commoners, and the Hidden History of the Revolutionary Atlantic*. Boston, MA: Beacon Press, 2000.

Lobe, Thomas D. "U.S. Police Assistance for the Third World." PhD diss., University of Michigan, 1975.

Loftin, C., B. Wiersema, D. McDowell, and A. Dobrin. "Underreporting of Justifiable Homicides Committed by Police Officers in the United States, 1976–1998." *American Journal of Public Health* 93, no. 7 (2003): 1117–21.

Los Angeles County Sheriff's Department and C. Robert Guthrie. *Project Sky Knight: A Demonstration in Aerial Surveillance and Crime Control*. Washington, DC: US Department of Justice, Office of Law Enforcement Assistance, 1968.

Lott, Eric. *Love and Theft: Blackface Minstrelsy and the American Working Class*. New York: Oxford University Press, 1993.

Loury, Glenn. *Race, Incarceration and American Values*. Cambridge, MA: MIT Press, 2008.

Lowe, Lisa. *The Intimacies of Four Continents*. Durham, NC: Duke University Press, 2015.

Lowndes, Joseph. *From the New Deal to the New Right: Race and the Southern Origins of Modern Conservatism*. New Haven, CT: Yale University Press, 2009.

Loyd, Jenna M. "'A Microscopic Insurgent': Militarization, Health, and Critical Geographies of Violence." *Annals of the Association of American Geographers* 99, no. 5 (2009): 863–73.

———. *Health Rights Are Civil Rights: Peace and Justice Activism in Los Angeles, 1963–1978*. Minneapolis: University of Minnesota Press, 2014.

Loyd, Jenna M., Matt Mitchelson, and Andrew Burridge, eds. *Beyond Walls and Cages: Prisons, Borders, and Global Crisis*. Athens: University of Georgia Press, 2012.

Lutz, Catherine. *Homefront: The Military City and the American Twentieth Century*. Boston, MA: Beacon Press, 2001.

———. "Making War at Home in the United States: Militarization and the Current Crisis." *American Anthropologist* 104, no. 3 (2002): 723–35.

Lye, Colleen. *America's Asia: Racial Form and American Literature, 1893–1945*. Princeton, NJ: Princeton University Press, 2004.

Lynch, Michael J., and Raymond Michalowski. "The Radical Concept of Crime." In *Primer in Radical Criminology: Critical Perspectives on Crime, Power and Identity*, 63–82. 4th ed. Monsey, NY: Criminal Justice Press Project, 2006.

Lynch, Mona. *Sunbelt Justice: Arizona and the Transformation of American Punishment*. Stanford, CA: Stanford University Press, 2010.

MacPherson, Myra. *Long Time Passing: Vietnam and the Haunted Generation*. Bloomington: Indiana University Press, 2001.

Mader, Julius. *Who's Who in CIA: A Biographical Reference Work on 3,000 Officers of the Civil and Military Branches of Secret Services of the USA in 120 Countries*. Berlin: Julius Mader, 1968.

Maechling, Charles Jr. "Counterinsurgency: The First Ordeal by Fire." In *Low-Intensity Warfare: Counterinsurgency, Proinsurgency, and Antiterrorism in the Eighties,* edited by Michael T. Klare and Peter Kornbluh, 21–48. New York: Pantheon Books, 1988.

Maguire, Edward R., J. B. Snipes, C. D. Uchida, and M. Townsend. "Counting Cops: Estimating the Number of Police Officers and Police Agencies in the United States." *Policing: An International Journal of Police Strategies and Management* 21, no. 1 (1998): 97–120.

Maguire, Edward R., and William R. King. "Trends in the Policing Industry." In "To Better Serve and Protect: Improving Police Practices," special issue, *Annals of the American Academy of Political and Social Science* 593 (May 2004): 15–41.

Malcolm, Andrew H. "Oil Pipeline Work Starts; 10,000 on Job in Alaska." *New York Times,* March 1975, 61.

Maller, Julius B. "Juvenile Delinquency among the Jews in New York." *Social Forces* 10, no. 4 (May 1932): 542–49.

Manning, Harvey. *Cry Crisis! Rehearsal in Alaska.* San Francisco, CA: Friends of the Earth, 1974.

Manning, Peter K. "Theorizing Policing: The Drama and Myth of Crime Control in the NYPD." *Theoretical Criminology* 5, no. 3 (2001): 315–44.

Mapping Police Violence. "Mapping Police Violence." Accessed September 6, 2016. http://mappingpoliceviolence.org.

Marchetti, Victor, and John D. Marks. *The CIA and the Cult of Intelligence.* New York: Knopf, 1974.

Marion, Nancy E. *Federal Government and Criminal Justice.* New York: Palgrave Macmillan, 2011.

Marshall, Victor. "The Lies We Are Told about Iraq." *Los Angeles Times,* January 5 2003, 2.

Martin, John. "Vietnamese Students and Their American Advisors." *Change* 8, no. 10 (November 1976): 11–14.

Martin, José. "Policing Is a Dirty Job, but Nobody's Gotta Do It: 6 Ideas for a Cop-Free World." *Rolling Stone,* December 16, 2014.

Marx, Karl, and Frederick Engels. *The Communist Manifesto: A Modern Edition.* New York: Verso, 2012.

Mauer, Marc. *Race to Incarcerate.* 2nd ed. New York: New Press/W. W. Norton, 2006.

Mbembe, Achille. "Necropolitics." Translated by Libby Meintjes. *Public Culture* 15, no. 1 (2003): 11–40.

McArdle, Andrea, and Tanya Erzen, eds. *Zero Tolerance: Quality of Life and the New Police Brutality in New York City.* New York: New York University Press, 2001.

McClintock, Michael. *The American Connection.* Vol. 2, *State Terror and Popular Resistance in Guatemala.* London: Zed Books, 1985.

———. *Instruments of Statecraft: U.S. Guerrilla Warfare, Counterinsurgency, and Counter-Terrorism, 1940–1990.* New York: Pantheon Books, 1992.

McCoy, Alfred W. "Mission Myopia: Narcotics as 'Fall Out' from the CIA's Covert Wars." In *National Insecurity: U.S. Intelligence After the Cold War,* edited by Craig R. Eisendrath, 118–48. Philadelphia, PA: Temple University Press, 2000.

————. *Policing America's Empire: The United States, the Philippines, and the Rise of the Surveillance State*. Madison: University of Wisconsin, 2009.

————. "Torture in the Crucible of Counterinsurgency." In *Iraq and the Lessons of Vietnam: Or, How Not to Learn from the Past*, edited by Marilyn B. Young and Lloyd C. Gardner, 230–62. New York: New Press, 2007.

McCrie, Robert D. "A Brief History of the Security Industry in the United States." In *Business and Crime Prevention*, edited by Mark Felson and Ronald V. Clarke, 197–218. Monsey, NY: Criminal Justice Press, 1997.

McCulloch, Jude. *Blue Army: Paramilitary Policing in Australia*. Carlton South, Victoria, Australia: Melbourne University Press, 2001.

McDonald, Douglas, Peter Finn, and Norman Hoffman. *ASP CJ Report (Overview of Criminal Justice in U.S. over Past Three Decades): Chapter for DOJ Strategic Plan 2000–2005*. Cambridge, MA: Abt Associates, 1999. Accessed October 13, 2015. http://www.abtassociates.com/reports/3871.pdf.

McEnaney, Laura. *Civil Defense Begins at Home: Militarization Meets Everyday Life in the Fifties*. Princeton, NJ: Princeton University Press, 2000.

McGrew, Ken. *Education's Prisoners: Schooling, the Political Economy, and the Prison Industrial Complex*. New York: Peter Lang, 2008.

McGuire, Connie, and Susan Bibler Coutin. "Transnational Alienage and Foreign-ness: Deportees and Foreign Service Officers in Central America." *Identities: Global Studies in Culture and Power* 20, no. 6 (2013): 689–704.

McLeod, Allegra M. "Exporting U.S. Criminal Justice." *Yale Law and Policy Review* 29, no. 1 (fall 2010): 83–164.

McManus, George P. *Police Training and Performance Study*. New York: New York City Police Department, 1977.

McSherry, J. Patrice. *Predatory States: Operation Condor and Covert War in Latin America*. Lanham, MD: Rowman and Littlefield, 2005.

Meiners, Erica R. "Building an Abolition Democracy; or, The Fight against Public Fear, Private Benefits, and Prison Expansion." In *Challenging the Prison-Industrial Complex: Activism, Arts, and Educational Alternatives*, edited by Stephen John Hartnett, 15–40. Urbana: University of Illinois Press, 2011.

————. "Ending the School-to-Prison Pipeline/Building Abolition Futures." *Urban Review* 43 (2011): 547–65.

————. *For the Children? Protecting Innocence in a Carceral State*. Minneapolis: University of Minnesota Press, 2016.

Melossi, Dario. "Gazette of Morality and the Social Whip: Punishment, Hegemony and the Case of the USA, 1970–92." *Social and Legal Studies* 2 (1993): 259–79.

Midnight Notes. *Midnight Oil: Work, Energy, War, 1973–1992*. Jamaica Plain, MA: Midnight Notes, 1992.

Miliband, Ralph. *The State in Capitalist Society*. New York: Basic Books, 1969.

Miller, Wilbur R. *Cops and Bobbies: Police Authority in New York and London, 1830–1870*. Chicago: University of Chicago Press, 1977.

Milton, Catherine, Jeanne Wahl Halleck, James Lardner, and Gary L. Albrecht. *Police Use of Deadly Force*. Washington, DC: Police Foundation, 1977.

Mirpuri, Anoop. "Radical Violence, Mass Shootings, and the U.S. Neoliberal State." *Critical Ethnic Studies* 2, no. 1 (spring 2016): 73–106.

Mitchell, Don, Kafui Attoh, and Lynn A. Staeheli. "'Broken Windows Is Not the Panacea': Common Sense, Good Sense, and Police Accountability in American Cities." In Camp and Heatherton, *Policing the Planet*, 237–57.

Mitchell, Timothy. *Carbon Democracy: Political Power in the Age of Oil*. London: Verso Books, 2011.

———. "Fixing the Economy." *Cultural Studies* 12, no. 1 (1998): 82–101.

———. "The Limits of the State: Beyond Statist Approaches and Their Critics." *American Political Science Review* 85, no. 1 (March 1991): 77–96.

———. "McJihad: Islam in the U.S. Global Order." *Social Text* 20, no. 4 (2002): 1–18.

———. "Society, Economy, and the State Effect." In *State/Culture: State-Formation after the Cultural Turn*, edited by George Steinmetz, 76–97. Ithaca, NY: Cornell University Press, 1999.

Mohanty, Chandra Talpade. "Under Western Eyes: Feminist Scholarship and Colonial Discourses." *Feminist Review* 30 (autumn 1988): 61–88.

Molina Ferraro, Eduardo. "Feminine Police Corps." *International Police Academy Review* 1, no. 2 (April 1967): 6–7.

Monkkonen, Eric H. "From Cop History to Social History: The Significance of the Police in American History." *Journal of Social History* 15, no. 4 (summer 1982): 575–91.

———. *Police in Urban America, 1860–1920*. Cambridge: Cambridge University Press, 1981.

Montero, Darrel. *Vietnamese Americans: Patterns of Resettlement and Socioeconomic Adaptation in the United States*. Boulder, CO: Westview Press, 1979.

Montgomery, David. *The Fall of the House of Labor: The Workplace, the State, and American Labor Activism, 1865–1925*. Cambridge: Cambridge University Press, 1987.

Moore, Leonard N. *Black Rage in New Orleans: Police Brutality and African American Activism from World War II to Hurricane Katrina*. Baton Rouge: Louisiana State University Press, 2010.

Moraff, Christopher. "Community Policing: Where Do We Go from Here?" *Crime Report* September 6, 2016.

Moreton, Bethany. *To Serve God and Wal-Mart: The Making of Christian Free Enterprise*. Cambridge, MA: Harvard University Press, 2009.

Morris, Roger. *The Devil's Butcher Shop: The New Mexico Prison Uprising*. New York: Franklin Watts, 1983.

Morrison, Toni. *Playing in the Dark: Whiteness and the Literary Imagination*. New York: Vintage Books, 1993.

Mortland, Carol A. "Transforming Refugees in Refugee Camps." *Urban Anthropology and Studies of Cultural Systems and World Economic Development* 16, no. 3/4 (fall–winter 1987): 375–404.

Muhammad, Khalil Gibran. *The Condemnation of Blackness: Race, Crime, and the Making of Modern Urban America*. Cambridge, MA: Harvard University Press, 2010.

Murakawa, Naomi. *The First Civil Right: How Liberals Built Prison America*. New York: Oxford University Press, 2014.

———. "The Origins of the Carceral Crisis." In *Race and American Political Development*, edited by Joseph Lowndes, Julie Novkov, and Dorian T. Warren, 234–55. New York: Routledge, 2008.

———. "The Racial Antecedents to Federal Sentencing Guidelines: How Congress Judged the Judges from *Brown* to *Booker*." *Roger Williams University Law Review* 11 (winter 2006): 473–94.

Murakawa, Naomi, and Katherine Beckett. "Mapping the Shadow Carceral State: Toward an Institutionally Capacious Approach to Punishment." *Theoretical Criminology* 16, no. 2 (2012): 221–44.

———. "The Penology of Racial Innocence: The Erasure of Racism in Study and Practice of Punishment." *Law and Society Review* 44 (September/December 2010): 695–730.

Murphy, Jarrett. "Cheney's Halliburton Ties Remain." *CBS News*, September 26, 2003. Accessed October 17, 2014. http://www.cbsnews.com/news/cheneys -halliburton-ties-remain/.

Nadelmann, Ethan Orram. *Cops Across Borders: The Internationalization of U.S. Criminal Law Enforcement*. University Park: Pennsylvania State University Press, 1993.

National Action / Research on the Military-Industrial Complex (NARMIC). *Police on the Homefront: They're Bringing It All Back*. Philadelphia, PA: NARMIC, 1971.

National Advisory Commission on Civil Disorders. "Kerner Commission Transcripts and Agenda of Hearings." July 29–November 9, 1967. In *Civil Rights during the Johnson Administration, 1963–1969, Microform: A Collection from the Holdings of the Lyndon Baines Johnson Library, Austin, Texas*, edited by Steven F. Lawson. Part 5. Frederick, MD: University Publications of America, 1987.

National Archives and Records Administration. *Guide to Federal Records*. Accessed December 2, 2013. http://www.archives.gov/research/guide-fed-records /groups/220.html#220.10.3.

National Association of Manufacturers. *Bomb Threats to Industry, Suggested Action to Protect Employees and Property*. Washington, DC: National Association of Manufacturers, 1971.

National Committee on Criminal Justice Technology. "The Evolution and Development of Police Technology." National Institute of Justice. Washington, DC: Seaskate, 1998. Accessed July 21, 2016. http://www.police-technology.net/id59 .html.

National Science Foundation. "Technical Notes; Definitions." Accessed November 20, 2012. http://www.nsf.gov/statistics/fedfunds/pubs/dst42/technote/perform.htm.

Naughton, James M. "U.S. to Tighten Surveillance of Radicals." *New York Times*, April 12, 1970, 1.

Navasky, Victor, with Darrell Paster. *Background Paper for Law Enforcement: The Federal Role*. Report of the Twentieth Century Fund Task Force on the Law Enforcement Asstistance Administration. New York: McGraw-Hill, 1976.

Naylor, R. T. "From Cold War to Crime War: The Search for a New 'National Security' Threat." *Transnational Organized Crime* 1, no. 4 (winter 1995): 37–56.

———. "Mafias, Myths, and Markets: The Theory and Practice of Enterprise Crime." *Transnational Organized Crime* 3, no. 3 (1997): 1–45.

———. *The Wages of Crime: Black Markets, Illegal Finance, and the Underground Economy*. Ithaca, NY: Cornell University Press, [2002] 2005.

Nelson, Jill, ed. *Police Brutality: An Anthology*. New York: W. W. Norton, 2000.

Neocleous, Mark. *Administering Civil Society: Towards a Theory of State Power*. New York: St. Martin's Press, 1996.

———. *Critique of Security*. Montreal, Canada: McGill-Queen's University Press, 2008.

———. *The Fabrication of Social Order: A Critical Theory of Police Power*. London: Pluto Press, 2000.

———. *The Monstrous and the Dead: Burke, Marx, Fascism*. Cardiff: University of Wales Press, 2005.

———. "Theoretical Foundations of the 'New Police Science.'" In *The New Police Science: The Police Power in Domestic and International Governance*, edited by Dubber and Valverde, 17–41. Stanford, CA: Stanford University Press, 2006.

———. "War as Peace, Peace as Pacification." *Radical Philosophy* 159 (January/February 2010): 8–17.

———. *War Power, Police Power*. Edinburgh, Scotland: Edinburgh University Press, 2014.

Neocleous, Mark, and George S. Rigakos, eds. *Anti-Security*. Ottawa, Canada: Red Quill Press, 2001.

New Mexico State Police. *New Mexico State Police Annual Report, 1971*. Santa Fe: New Mexico State Police, Planning and Research Division, 1972.

Ngai, Mae. *Impossible Subjects: Illegal Aliens and the Making of Modern America*. Princeton, NJ: Princeton University Press, 2004.

Nguyen, Mimi. *The Gift of Freedom: War, Debt, and Other Refugee Passages*. Durham, NC: Duke University Press, 2012.

NOBLE (National Organization of Black Law Enforcement Executives). "NOBLE: An Overview." In *A Community Concern: Police Use of Deadly Force*, compiled by Robert N. Brenner, 3–5. Washington, DC: Department of Justice, Law Enforcement Assistance Administration, National Institute of Law Enforcement and Criminal Justice, 1979.

Nordstrom, Carolyn. *Global Outlaws: Crime, Money, and Power in the Contemporary World*. Berkeley: University of California Press, 2007.

"Norman C. Colter, Obituary." CentralMaine.com. Accessed June 27, 2015. http://obituaries.centralmaine.com/obituaries/mainetoday-centralmaine/obituary.aspx?n=norman-c-colter&pid=160797250&.

Novak, William. "The Myth of the 'Weak' American State." *American Historical Review* (June 2008): 752–72.

———. *The People's Welfare: Law and Regulation in Nineteenth Century America.* Chapel Hill: University of North Carolina Press, 1996.

O'Dell, John. "Fallout from Probe Is Already Hitting Holmes and Narver." *Los Angeles Times*, July 15, 1988. Accessed October 6, 2012. http://articles.latimes.com /1988-07-15/business/fi-7297_1_holmes-narver.

OECD. *Divided We Stand: Why Inequality Keeps Rising.* OECD, 2011. Accesed May 27, 2014. www.oecd.org/els/social/inequality; http://www.oecd.org/social/soc /49499779.pdf.

"Officer Retires, Goes to Viet War." *Citizen-News*, January 6, 1966, n.p.

Ogilvie, Bertrand. "Violence et representation: La Production de l'homme jetable." *Lignes* 26 (October 1995): 113–42.

Orfield, Gary, Susan E. Eaton, and the Harvard Project on School Desegregation. *Dismantling Desegregation: The Quiet Reversal of Brown v. Board of Education.* New York: The New Press, 1996.

Organization of the Multinational Force and Observers. Accessed October 6, 2012. http://www.mfo.org/support.php.

Ortiz, Isabel, and Matthew Cummins. "Global Inequality: Beyond the Bottom Billion—A Rapid Review of Income Distribution in 141 Countries." UNICEF Working Paper, UNICEF, 2011. Accessed May 27, 2014. http://www.unicef.org /socialpolicy/index_58230.html.

Osborne, Milton. "The Indochinese Refugees: Cause and Effects." *International Affairs* 56, no. 1 (January 1980): 37–53.

O'Toole, George. *The Private Sector: Private Spies, Rent-a-Cops, and the Police-Industrial Complex.* New York: W. W. Norton, 1978.

Otten, Alan L. "Curbing Crime: The 'Safe Streets' Act Yields Scattered Gains against Lawlessness." *Wall Street Journal*, February 4, 1970, 1, 17.

"Our Opinion: Revoke Contracts with Halliburton." *York Daily Record*, February 15, 2004, 2.

Pagán, Eduardo Obregón. *Murder at the Sleepy Lagoon: Zoot Suits, Race, and Riot in Wartime L.A.* Chapel Hill: University of North Carolina Press, 2003.

Paik, A. Naomi. *Rightlessness: Testimony and Redress in U.S. Prison Camps since World War II.* Chapel Hill: University of North Carolina Press, 2016.

Papke, David R. *Framing the Criminal: Crime, Cultural Work, and the Loss of Critical Perspective, 1830–1900.* New York: Archon Books, 1987.

Parker, Laura. "What Exactly Happened That Day in Fallujah?" *USA Today*, June 11, 2007, 13A. Accessed October 17, 2014. http://usatoday30.usatoday.com /printedition/news/20070611/a_blackwater11.art.htm.

Pathy, Jaganath. "Anthropology and the Third World." *Economic and Political Weekly* 16, no. 14 (April 4, 1981): 623–27.

PBS Frontline. *Private Warriors.* Accessed October 17, 2014. http://www.pbs.org /wgbh/pages/frontline/shows/warriors/contractors/highrisk.html; FAQ's at http://www.pbs.org/wgbh/pages/frontline/shows/warriors/faqs/.

Pemberton, Simon. "Deaths in Police Custody: The 'Acceptable' Consequences of a 'Law and Order' Society?" *Outlines* 2 (2005): 23–42.

Petrucci, Peter R., and Michael Head. "Hurricane Katrina's Lexical Storm: The Use of 'Refugee' as a Label for American Citizens." *Australasian Journal of American Studies* 25, no. 2 (December 2006): 23–39.

Piketty, Thomas. *Capital in the Twenty-First Century*. Translated by Arthur Goldhammer. Cambridge, MA: Belknap Press of Harvard University Press, 2014.

Platt, Tony. "Obama's Task Force on Policing: Will It Be Different This Time?" *Social Justice* blog, February 28, 2015. Accessed September 6, 2016. http://www.socialjusticejournal.org/2015/02/.

Plummer, Brenda Gayle. *Rising Wind: Black Americans and U.S. Foreign Affairs, 1935–1960*. Chapel Hill: University of North Carolina Press, 1996.

Poelchau, Warner. *White Paper Whitewash: Interviews with Philip Agee on the CIA and El Salvador*. New York: Deep Cover Books, 1981.

Polanyi, Karl. *The Great Transformation: The Political and Economic Origins of Our Time*. Boston, MA: Beacon Press, [1944] 2001.

Ponte, Lowell. *The Cooling*. Englewood Cliffs, NJ: Prentice-Hall, 1976.

———. "Target: The Pipeline." *Chicago Tribune*, July 31, 1977, A1.

Poulantzas, Nicos. "Preliminaries to the Study of Hegemony in the State." In *The Poulantzas Reader: Marxism, Law, and the State*, edited by James Martin, 74–119. New York: Verso, 2008.

———. "The Problem of the Capitalist State." *New Left Review* 1, no. 58 (November/December 1969): 67–78.

Povinelli, Elizabeth A. *The Empire of Love: Toward a Theory of Intimacy, Genealogy, and Carnality*. Durham, NC: Duke University Press, 2006.

Prashad, Vijay. *The Darker Nations: A People's History of the Third World*. New York: New Press, 2007.

Pratt, Mary Louise. "Planetary Longings: Sitting in the Light of the Great Solar TV." In *World Writing: Poetics, Ethics, Globalization*, edited by Mary Gallagher, chapter 8. Toronto: University of Toronto Press, 2008.

Prince, Simon. "The Global Revolt of 1968 and Northern Ireland." *Historical Journal* 49, no. 3 (September 2006): 851–75.

Pryor, Larry. "The 'Invaders'—A Test for the Pipeline." *Los Angeles Times*, November 18, 1975, A1.

Puar, Jasbir K. "'I Would Rather Be a Cyborg Than a Goddess': Becoming-Intersectional in Assemblage Theory." *Philosophia* 2, no. 1 (2012): 49–66.

Punch, Maurice. *Dirty Business: Exploring Corporate Misconduct*. London: Sage, 1996.

Putnam, Robert D. *Bowling Alone: The Collapse and Revival of American Community*. New York: Simon and Schuster, 2000.

Pycke, Karen D., and Denise L. Johnson. "Asian American Women and Racialized Femininities: 'Doing' Gender across Cultural Worlds." *Gender and Society* 17, no. 1 (February 2003): 33–53.

Quijano, Anibal. "Coloniality of Power, Eurocentrism, and Latin America." *Nepantla: Views from the South* 1, no. 3 (2000): 533–80.

Quinney, Richard. *Critique of Legal Order: Crime Control in Capitalist Society*. Boston, MA: Little, Brown, 1974.

RAND Corporation. "History and Mission." Accessed November 20, 2012. http://www.rand.org/about/history.html.

———. "Politics Aside." Accessed November 20, 2012. http://www.rand.org/politicsaside.html.

Reddy, Chandan. *Freedom with Violence: Race, Sexuality, and the U.S. State.* Durham, NC: Duke University Press, 2011.

Reich, Cary. *The Life of Nelson A. Rockefeller: Worlds to Conquer, 1908–1958.* New York: Doubleday, 1996.

Reiman, Jeffrey H. *The Rich Get Richer and the Poor Get Prison: Ideology, Class, and Criminal Justice.* New York: Wiley, 1979.

Reiner, Robert. *The Politics of the Police.* 2nd ed. London: Harvester Wheatsheaf, 1992.

Remer, Larry. "SWAT: The Police Berets." *Nation,* May 24, 1975, 627.

Rhodes, Lorna A. *Total Confinement: Madness and Reason in the Maximum Security Prison.* Berkeley: University of California Press, 2004.

Richardson, James. *The New York Police: Colonial Times to 1901.* New York: Oxford University Press, 1978.

Richman, Daniel. "The Past, Present, and Future of Violent Crime Federalism." *Crime and Justice* 34, no. 1 (2006): 377–439.

Riesel, Victor. "Vital Alaska Pipeline Is Wide Open to Terrorist Attack." *Milwaukee Sentinel,* June 15, 1977, 14.

Rimke, Heidi. "Security: Resistance." In *Anti-Security,* edited by Mark Neocleous and George S. Rigakos, 191–215. Ottawa: Red Quill Books, 2011.

Robin, C. *Fear: The History of a Political Idea.* Oxford: Oxford University Press, 2004.

Robinson Finnan, Christine. "Occupational Assimilation of Refugees." *International Migration Review* 15, nos. 1/2, "Refugees Today" (spring–summer 1981): 292–309.

Rodriguez, Dylan. *Forced Passages: Imprisoned Radical Intellectuals and the U.S. Prison Regime.* Minneapolis: University of Minnesota Press, 2005.

———. *Suspended Apocalypse: White Supremacy, Genocide, and the Filipino Condition.* Minneapolis: University of Minnesota Press, 2009.

Roediger, David R. *The Wages of Whiteness: Race and the Making of the American Working Class.* New York: Verso, 1991.

Rohde, Joy. *Armed with Expertise: The Militarization of American Social Research during the Cold War.* Ithaca, NY: Cornell University Press, 2013.

———. "Gray Matters: Social Scientists, Military Patronage, and Democracy in the Cold War." *Journal of American History* (June 2009): 99–122.

Rone, Jemera. "Problems in Teaching Human Rights to Practitioners." *European Journal of Education* 29, no. 4 (1994): 391–97.

Roscow, James P. *800 Miles to Valdez: The Building of the Alaska Pipeline.* Englewood Cliffs, NJ: Prentice-Hall, 1977.

Ross, Jeffrey Ian, ed. *Cutting the Edge: Current Perspectives in Radical/Critical Criminology and Criminal Justice.* Westport, CT: Praeger, 1998.

Ross, Kristin. *May '68 and Its Afterlives.* Chicago: University of Chicago Press, 2002.

Rostow, Walt Whitman. *The Stages of Economic Growth: A Non-Communist Manifesto*. Cambridge: Cambridge University Press, 1960.

Rothstein, Bret L., and Karen M. Inouye. "Visual Games and the Unseeing of Race in the Late Nineteenth Century." *American Quarterly* 68, no. 2 (June 2016): 287–313.

Rousey, D. C. *Policing the Southern City: New Orleans, 1805–1889*. Baton Rouge: Louisiana State University Press, 1996.

Rubenstein, Jonathan. *City Police*. New York: Ballantine Books, 1974.

Rusche, Georg, and Otto Kirchheimer. *Punishment and Social Structure*. New York: Russell and Russell, [1939] 1968.

"Sabotage Blasts Fail to Halt Alaska Pipeline Oil Flow." *Los Angeles Times*, July 27, 1977, B1.

"Sabotage Called Oil Pipeline Peril: Contrast in Security." *New York Times*, September 2, 1979, 32.

Saenz, Adolph. *The OPS Story*. San Francisco, CA: Robert D. Reed, 2002.

Saez, Emmanuel, and Gabriel Zucman. "Exploding Wealth Inequality in the United States." *Washington Center for Equitable Growth*, October 20, 2014. Accessed May 30, 2015. http://equitablegrowth.org/research/exploding-wealth-inequality-united-states.

Saldaña-Portillo, Maria Josefina. *The Revolutionary Imagination in the Americas and the Age of Development*. Durham, NC: Duke University Press, 2003.

Saldanha, Arun. *Psychedelic White: Goa Trance and the Viscosity of Race*. Minneapolis: University of Minnesota Press, 2007.

"Sanders Associates Inc. Fails to Get Saudi Job," *Wall Street Journal*, August 16, 1978, 19.

Saudi Aramco. "Berri Gas Plant." Accessed June 21, 2014. http://www.saudiaramco.com/en/home/our-operations/gas/major-gas-processing-plants/berri-gas-plant.html#our-operations%257C%252Fen%252Fhome%252Four-operations%252Fgas%252Fmajor-gas-processing-plants%252Fberri-gas-plant.baseajax.html.

———. "Our Company." Accessed October 6, 2012. http://www.saudiaramco.com/en/home.html#our-company.

———. *Saudi Aramco World*. Magazine. Texas: Aramco Services. Accessed October 3, 2012. http://www.saudiaramcoworld.com/issue/201205/default.htm.

———. Website. Accessed October 6, 2012. http://www.saudiaramco.com/en/home.html.

Sawyer, Amos. *Effective Immediately: Dictatorship in Liberia, 1980–1986: A Personal Perspective*. Bremen, West Germany: Liberia Working Group, 1987.

Schept, Judah. *Progressive Punishment: Job Loss, Jail Growth, and the Neoliberal Logic of Carceral Expansion*. New York: New York University Press, 2015.

Schept, Judah, Tyler Wall, and Avi Brisman. "Building, Staffing, and Insulating: An Architecture of Criminological Complicity in the School-to-Prison Pipeline." *Social Justice* 41, no. 4 (2014): 96–115.

Schinkel, W. *Aspects of Violence: A Critical Theory*. Basingstoke, UK: Palgrave Macmillan, 2010.

Schrader, Stuart. *Policing Revolution: Cold War Counterinsurgency at Home and Abroad*. Berkeley: University of California Press, forthcoming.

———. "American Streets, Foreign Territory: How Counterinsurgent Knowledge Militarized Policing and Criminalized Color." PhD diss., New York University, 2014.

———. "Local Policing Meets Global Counterinsurgency: The 1964 Riots and the Transnational Frontlash." Paper presented at the American Studies Association Annual Meeting, Washington, DC, November 2013.

———. "Policing Empire." *Jacobin*, September 5, 2014. Accessed September 8, 2016. https://www.jacobinmag.com/2014/09/policing-empire/.

Schultz, Nancy L., ed. *Fear Itself: Enemies Real and Imagined in American Culture*. West Lafayette, IN: Purdue University Press, 1999.

Scigliano, Robert, and Guy H. Fox. *Technical Assistance in Vietnam: The Michigan State University Experience*. New York: Praeger, 1965.

Scobell, Andrew, and Brad Hammitt. "Goons, Gunmen, and Gendarmerie: Toward a Reconceptualization of Paramilitary Formations." *Journal of Political and Military Sociology* 26, no. 2 (winter 1998): 213–27.

Scott, James C. *The Art of Not Being Governed: An Anarchist History of Upland Southeast Asia*. New Haven, CT: Yale University Press, 2010.

Seigel, Micol. "Beyond Compare: Comparative Method after the Transnational Turn." *Radical History Review* 91 (winter 2005): 62–90.

———. "Nelson Rockefeller in Latin America: Global Currents of U.S. Prison Growth." *Comparative American Studies* 13, no. 3 (September 2015): 161–76.

———. "William Bratton in the Other LA." In *Beyond Walls and Cages: Bridging Immigrant Justice and Anti-Prison Organizing in the United States*, edited by Jenna Loyd, Matt Mitchelson, and Andrew Burridge, 115–25. Athens: University of Georgia Press, 2012.

Sentas, Victoria. *Traces of Terror: Counter-Terrorism Law, Policing, and Race*. Oxford: Oxford University Press, 2014.

"Sergeant Doe Ends Liberia's Long Changelessness." *Economist*, April 19, 1980, 37.

Seri, Guillermina. "All the People Necessary Will Die to Achieve Security." In *Anti-Security*, edited by Mark Neocleous and George S. Rigakos, 243–64. Ottawa: Red Quill Books, 2011.

Sewell, William H., Jr. *The Logics of History: Social Theory and Social Transformation*. Chicago: University of Chicago Press, 2005.

Shabazz, Rashad. *Spatializing Blackness: Architectures of Confinement and Black Masculinity in Chicago*. Urbana: University of Illinois Press, 2015.

Shea, Timothy. "Transforming Military Diplomacy." *Joint Forces Quarterly* 38 (2005): 48–52.

Shearing, Clifford D. "The Relation between Public and Private Policing." In *Modern Policing*, special issue of *Crime and Justice* 15 (1992): 399–434.

———. "The Unrecognized Origins of the New Policing: Linkages between Public and Private Policing." In *Business and Crime Prevention*, edited by Mark

Felson and Ronald Clarke, 219–30. Monsey, NY: Criminal Justice Press, 1997.

Shearing, Clifford, and Phillip Stenning. "Modern Private Security: Its Growth and Implications." In *Crime and Justice* 3 (1981): 193–245.

Shelly, Bryan. *Money, Mandates, and Local Control in American Public Education.* Ann Arbor: University of Michigan Press, 2011.

Sherman, Lawrence W., et al. *The Quality of Police Education in San Francisco.* San Francisco, CA: Jossey-Bass, 1978.

Sherry, Michael S. *In the Shadow of War: The United States since the 1930s.* New Haven, CT: Yale University Press, 1995.

Silliman, Jael, and Anannya Bhattacharjee, eds. *Policing the National Body: Race, Gender, and Criminalization in the United States.* Boston, MA: South End Press, 2002.

Silva, Denise Ferreira da. *Toward a Global Idea of Race.* Minneapolis: University of Minnesota Press, 2007.

Silver, Isidore. *The Crime Control Establishment.* Englewood Cliffs, NJ: Prentice Hall, 1974.

Simon, Jonathan. *Governing through Crime: How the War on Crime Transformed American Democracy and Created a Culture of Fear.* Oxford: Oxford University Press, 2007.

Simpson, Audra. *Mohawk Interruptus: Political Life across the Borders of Settler States.* Durham, NC: Duke University Press, 2014.

Simpson, Brad. "Indonesia's 'Accelerated Modernization' and the Global Discourse of Development, 1960–1975." *Diplomatic History* 33, no. 3 (2009): 467–86.

Singh, Nikhil Pal. *Black Is a Country: Race and the Unfinished Struggle for Democracy.* Cambridge, MA: Harvard University Press, 2004.

———. *Exceptional Empire: Race, War, and Sovereignty in U.S. Globalism.* Cambridge, MA: Harvard University Press, forthcoming.

———. "The Whiteness of Police." *American Quarterly* 66, no. 4 (December 2014): 1091–99.

Sinyangwe, Sam. "Mapping Police Violence." Online database. Accessed March 13, 2017. https://mappingpoliceviolence.org.

Skinner, Quentin. "The State." In *Political Innovation and Conceptual Change*, edited by Terrence Ball, James Farr, and Russell L. Hanson, 90–131. Cambridge: Cambridge University Press, 1988.

Skinner, Rob, and Alan Lester. "Humanitarianism and Empire: New Research Agendas." *Journal of Imperial and Commonwealth History* 40, no. 5 (2012): 729–47.

Sklar, Holly. *Washington's War on Nicaragua.* Boston, MA: South End Press, 1988.

Skocpol, Theda. "Bringing the State Back In: Retrospect and Prospect." *Scandinavian Political Studies* 31, no. 2 (2008): 109–24.

———. "Political Response to Capitalist Crisis: Neo-Marxist Theories of the State and the Case of the New Deal." *Politics and Society* 10 (1980): 155–201.

Skogan, Wesley G. "The Community's Role in Community Policing." *National Institute of Justice Journal* 231 (August 1996): 31–34.

Skolnick, Jerome H., and James J. Fyfe. *Above the Law: Police and the Excessive Use of Force.* New York: Free Press, 1993.

Smith, Beverley A., and Frank T. Morn. "The History of Privatization in Criminal Justice." In *Privatization in Criminal Justice: Past, Present, and Future,* edited by David Shichor and Michael J. Gilbert, 3–22. Cincinnati: Anderson Publishing, 2001.

Smith, Damu. "The Upsurge of Police Repression: An Analysis." *Black Scholar* 12, no. 1 (January/February 1981): 35–57.

Smith, Dennis C., and Elinor Ostrom. "The Effects of Training and Education on Police Attitudes and Performance: A Preliminary Analysis." Paper prepared for 1973 Annual Meeting of the Society for the Study of Social Problems. Bloomington: Indiana University, Department of Political Science, 1973.

Smith, Mychal Denzel. "In Order to End Police Brutality, We Need to End the Police." *Nation,* February 25, 2015. Accessed September 6, 2016. https://www.thenation.com/article/order-end-police-brutality-we-need-end-police/.

Smith, Neil. "The Satanic Geographies of Globalization: Uneven Development in the 1990s." *Public Culture* 10, no. 1 (1997): 169–89.

Smuckler, Ralph. *A University Turns to the World: A Personal History of the Michigan State University International Story.* East Lansing: Michigan State University Press, 2003.

Sparrow, James T. *Warfare State: World War II Americans and the Age of Big Government.* New York: Oxford University Press, 2011.

Spitzer, Steven, and Andrew Scull. "Privatization and Capitalist Development: The Case of the Private Police." *Social Problems* 25, no. 1 (1977): 18–29.

Starr, Paul. "Troubled Waters: Vietnamese Fisherfolk on America's Gulf Coast." "Refugees Today," special issue, *International Migration Review* 15, no. 1/2 (spring–summer 1981): 226–38.

Steinberg, Rafael. "Asian Bastion Tugs at U.S. Ties." *Washington Post,* March 18, 1962, E5.

Stenning, Phillip, and Clifford Shearing. "The Quiet Revolution: The Nature, Development, and General Legal Implications of Private Policing in Canada." *Criminal Law Quarterly* 22 (1980): 220–48.

Stern, Laurence. "U.S. Firm Eyes a Saudi Contract Barred to AID." *Washington Post,* November 2, 1975, 7.

Stern, Philip J. *The Company-State: Corporate Sovereignty and the Early Modern Foundation of the British Empire in India.* New York: Oxford University Press, 2011.

Sterling, Christopher H., ed. *Military Communications: From Ancient Times to the 21st Century.* Santa Barbara, CA: ABC-CLIO, 2008.

———. "Strategic Communications Command (STRATCOM)." In *Military Communications: From Ancient Times to the 21st Century,* edited by Christopher H. Sterling, 430. Santa Barbara, CA: ABC-CLIO, 2008.

Stoler, Ann Laura, ed. *Haunted by Empire: Geographies of Intimacy in North American History*. Durham, NC: Duke University Press, 2006.

———. "Tense and Tender Ties: The Politics of Comparison in North American History and (Post) Colonial Studies." *Journal of American History* 88, no. 3 (December 2001): 829–65.

Story, Brett. "The Prison in the City: Tracking the Neoliberal Life of the 'Million Dollar Block.'" *Theoretical Criminality* 20, no. 3 (August 2016): 257–76.

———, dir. *The Prison in Twelve Landscapes*. Toronto, Canada: Oh Ratface Films, 2016.

Stout, Jared. "Crime Control Test Near." *Washington Star*, July 4, 1970.

Strand, Paul J. "Employment Predictors among Indochinese Refugees." *International Migration Review* 18, no. 1 (spring 1984): 50–64.

Strecher, Victor. "Revising the Histories and Futures of Policing." *Police Forum* 1, no. 1 (1991): 1–9.

Stuart, Reginald. "Billions for Protection: Jittery Americans Rent or Buy Security Plans." *New York Times*, March 30, 1975, 119.

Stuart-Fox, Martin. "Laos: The Vietnamese Connection." *Southeast Asian Affairs* (1980): 191–209.

Stuntz, William J. "The Political Constitution of Criminal Justice." *Harvard Law Review* 119, no. 3 (January 2006): 780–851.

Sturken, Marita. *Tangled Memories: The Vietnam War, the AIDS Epidemic, and the Politics of Remembering*. Berkeley: University of California Press, 1997.

"Suspect Charged in 'Amateurish' Attempt to Blow Up Pipeline." *Washington Post*, July 28, 1977, A5.

Svampa, Maristella. *La sociedad excluyente: La Argentina bajo el signo del neoliberalismo*. Buenos Aires: Aguilar, Altea, Taurus, Alfaguara, 2005.

Takagi, Paul. "Death by Police Intervention." In *A Community Concern: Police Use of Deadly Force*, compiled by Robert N. Brenner, 7–11. Washington, DC: Department of Justice, Law Enforcement Assistance Administration, National Institute of Law Enforcement and Criminal Justice, 1979.

———. "A Garrison State in 'Democratic' Society." *Crime and Social Justice* 1 (spring–summer 1974): 27–33.

———. "LEAA's Research Solicitation: Police Use of Deadly Force." *Crime and Social Justice* 11 (spring–summer 1979): 51–59.

Tang, Eric. *Unsettled: Cambodian Refugees in the New York City Hyperghetto*. Philadelphia, PA: Temple University Press, 2015.

Taussig, Michael T. *Magic of the State*. New York: Routledge, 1997.

———. *Shamanism, Colonialism, and the Wild Man: A Study in Terror and Healing*. Chicago: University of Chicago Press, 1987.

Telemedia.com. "Telemedia International—Clients." List. Accessed October 4, 2012. http://www.telemediainc.com/tele/clients.html.

Texas Senate Hispanic Research Council. "Senator Gregory Luna." Texas Senate Hispanic Research Council online. Accessed 21 April 2009. http://www.tschrc.org/senluna.html.

Thompson, Robert. "U.S. Agency 'Waylays' Communist Subversion." *Los Angeles Times*, February 10, 1963, L1.

Tilly, Charles. *Coercion, Capital, and European States, AD 990–1990*. Cambridge: Basil Blackwell, 1990.

———. *Identities, Boundaries, and Social Ties*. Boulder, CO: Paradigm, 2005.

———. *The Politics of Collective Violence*. New York: Cambridge University Press, 2003.

———. "War Making and State Making as Organized Crime." In *Bringing the State Back In*, edited by Peter Evans, Dietrich Rueschemeyer, and Theda Skocpol, 169–86. Cambridge: Cambridge University Press, 1985.

Tilton, Jennifer. *Dangerous or Endangered? Race and the Politics of Youth in Urban America*. New York: New York University Press, 2010.

Tocqueville, Alexis de. *Democracy in America*. Translated by Henry Reeve. Boston, MA: J. Allyn, 1873.

Tomlins, Christopher. "Framing the Fragments: Police, Genealogies, Discourses, Locales, Principles." In *The New Police Science: The Police Power in Domestic and International Governance*, edited by Markus Dirk Dubber and Mariana Valverde, 248–94. Stanford, CA: Stanford University Press, 2006.

———. *Law, Labor, and Ideology in the Early American Republic*. Cambridge: Cambridge University Press, 1993.

———. "Necessities of State: Police, Sovereignty, and the Constitution." *Journal of Policy History* 20, no. 1 (2008): 47–63.

Trouillot, Michel-Rolph. "The Anthropology of the State in the Age of Globalization: Close Encounters of the Deceptive Kind." *Current Anthropology* 42, no. 1 (February 2001): 125–38.

Tullis, Tracy. "A Vietnam at Home: Policing the Ghettos in the Counterinsurgency Era." PhD diss., New York University, 1999.

Turse, Nick. *Kill Anything that Moves: The Real American War in Vietnam*. New York: Metropolitan Books/Henry Holt, 2013.

Uchida, Craig D. "The Development of the American Police: An Historical Overview." In *Critical Issues in Policing: Contemporary Readings*, edited by Roger G. Dunham and Geoffrey Alpert, 18–35. 2nd ed. Prospect Heights, IL: Waveland, 1993.

Ucko, David H. *The New Counterinsurgency Era: Transforming the U.S. Military for Modern Wars*. Washington, DC: Georgetown University Press, 2009.

United Nations Population Fund. "Migration." United Nations, 2015. Accessed September 9, 2016. http://www.unfpa.org/migration.

United States Army Military District of Washington. "About MDW." Accessed May 16, 2014. http://mdwhome.mdw.army.mil.

United States Business and Defense Services Administration. *Civil Defense Training for Business and Industry*. Washington, DC: Business and Defense Services Administration, US Department of Commerce in cooperation with the Office of Civil Defense, Department of Defense, Government Publishing Office, 1968.

United States Department of Defense, Office of the Assistant Secretary of Defense (Public Affairs). "Defense and Justice Departments Announce 'Troops to Cops' Program." News release, May 2, 1995. Accessed June 16, 2011. http://www .defense.gov/releases/release.aspx?releaseid=475.

United States Department of Justice. *Third Annual Report to the President and the Congress on the Activities Under the Law Enforcement Assistance Act of 1965*. April 1, 1968.

United States Department of Justice, Law Enforcement Assistance Administration. *Trends in Expenditure and Employment Data for the Criminal Justice System, 1971–1974*. Washington, DC: Government Printing Office, 1976.

United States Department of Justice, Office of Justice Programs. LEAA/OJP *Retrospective: 30 Years of Federal Support to State and Local Criminal Justice*. Washington, DC: US Department of Justice, July 11, 1996.

United States Department of State. *Biographic Register*. Washington, DC: Government Printing Office, annual.

United States Federal Bureau of Investigation, 1963–1980. *Uniform Crime Reports*. Washington, DC: Government Printing Office, annual.

United States Federal Civil Defense Administration. *10 Steps to Industrial Survival*. Washington, DC: Government Printing Office, 1956.

United States House of Representatives. 94th Cong., 2d sess. *Hearings before the Committee on Standards of Official Conduct, House of Representatives*, July–September. Washington, DC: Government Printing Office, 1976.

United States House of Representatives, Committee on Appropriations. *Foreign Assistance Appropriations for 1973, Hearings, 1972, Pt. II*. Washington, DC: Government Printing Office, 1973.

United States Office of the Provost Marshal General. *Industrial Defense against Civil Disturbances, Bombings, Sabotage*. Washington, DC: Government Printing Office, 1970, 1971.

United States President's Commission on Law Enforcement and Administration of Justice. *The Challenge of Crime in a Free Society: A Report*. Washington, DC: Government Printing Office, 1967.

United States Senate. 93d Cong., 1st sess. *Hearings before the Committee on Foreign Relations, Foreign Economic Assistance, June*. Washington, DC: Government Printing Office, 1973.

United States Senate, Committee on Foreign Relations. *United States Policies and Programs in Brazil: Hearings before the U.S. Senate Subcommittee on Western Hemisphere Affairs, 5 May*. Washington, DC: Government Printing Office, 1971.

University of California Infocenter. "State Spending on Corrections and Education." Accessed October 12, 2015. http://universityofcalifornia.edu/infocenter /california-expenditures-corrections-and-public-education, 2015.

Unterman, Katherine. *Uncle Sam's Policemen: The Pursuit of Fugitives across Borders*. Cambridge, MA: Harvard University Press, 2015.

Valverde, Mariana. "Police, Sovereignty, and Law: Foucaultian Reflections." In *Police and the Liberal State*, edited by Markus Dirk Dubber and Mariana Valverde, 15–32. Stanford, CA: Stanford University Press, 2008.

Vargas, João Costa. *Never Meant to Survive: Genocide and Utopias in Black Diaspora Communities*. Lanham, MD: Rowman and Littlefield, 2010.

Varon, Jay N. "A Reexamination of the Law Enforcement Assistance Administration." *Stanford Law Review* 27, no. 5 (May 1975): 1306–7.

Vitale, Alex S. *City of Disorder: How the Quality of Life Campaign Transformed New York Politics*. New York: New York University Press, 2008.

———. "The Rise of Command and Control Protest Policing in New York City." In *The New York City Police Department: The Impact of Its Policies and Practices*, edited by John Eterno and Eli Silverman, 163–182. Boca Raton, FL: CRC Press, 2014.

———. "Policing Protests in New York City." In *Urbanization, Policing, and Security: Global Perspectives*, edited by Gary Cordner, AnnMarie Cordner, and Dilip K. Das, 275–300. New York: Taylor and Francis, 2009.

———. "The Safer Cities Initiative and the Removal of the Homeless: Reducing Crime or Promoting Gentrification on LA's Skid Row?" *Criminology and Public Policy* 9, no. 4 (November 2010): 867–74.

Vitalis, Robert. *America's Kingdom: Mythmaking on the Saudi Oil Frontier*. Stanford, CA: Stanford University Press, 2007.

Vo, Nghia M., ed. *The Viet Kieu in America: Personal Accounts of Postwar Immigrants from Vietnam*. Jefferson, NC: McFarland, 2009.

———. *The Vietnamese Boat People, 1954 and 1975–1992*. Jefferson, NC: McFarland, 2006.

"Voices from the Ranks." *Economist*, May 24, 1980, 54.

Von Eschen, Penny. *Race against Empire: Black Americans and Anticolonialism, 1937–1957*. Ithaca, NY: Cornell University Press, 1997.

Wagner, Bryan. *Disturbing the Peace: Black Culture and the Police Power after Slavery*. Cambridge, MA: Harvard University Press, 2009.

Wain, Barry. *The Refused: The Agony of the Indochinese Refugees*. New York: Simon and Schuster, 1981.

Wakeman, Frederic E. *Spymaster: Dai Li and the Chinese Secret Service*. Berkeley: University of California Press, 2003.

Walker, Samuel. "Between Two Worlds: The President's Crime Commission and the Police, 1967–1992." In *The 1967 President's Crime Commission Report: Its Impact 25 Years Later*, edited by John A. Conley, 21–35. Highland Heights, KY: Academy of Criminal Justice Sciences, 1994.

———. "'Broken Windows' and Fractured History: The Use and Misuse of History in Recent Police Patrol Analysis." *Justice Quarterly* 1, no. 1 (1984): 75–90.

———. *A Critical History of Police Reform: The Emergence of Professionalization*. Lexington, MA: Lexington Books, 1977.

Wall, Tyler. "'For the Very Existence of Civilization': White Dogs, Black Threats, and Police Terror." Unpublished paper shared with the author.

———. "On the Secret of the Drone, or the Signature and Personality of Police." Unpublished paper presented at "Reconfiguring Global Space: The Geography, Politics, and Ethics of Drone Warfare." Indiana University Bloomington, July 14, 2015.

———. "Unmanning the Police Manhunt: Vertical Security as Pacification." *Socialist Studies* 9, no. 2 (winter 2013): 32–56.

Ward, William E. "Rethinking Foreign Area Officer Management." *Joint Forces Quarterly* 61 (2011): 47–52.

Washington, Mary Helen. "Prisons as a Part of American Studies." *American Studies Association Newsletter* (March 1999): 1, 8.

Watkins, Mel, ed. *Dene Nation, the Colony Within*. Toronto: University of Toronto Press, 1977.

Watts, Eugene J. "The Police in Atlanta, 1890–1905." *Journal of Southern History* 39, no. 2 (May 1973): 165–82.

———. "Police Priorities in Twentieth Century St. Louis." *Journal of Social History* 14, no. 4 (summer 1981): 649–73.

Watts, Michael. "The Tale of Two Gulfs: Life, Death, and Dispossession along Two Oil Frontiers." *American Quarterly* 64, no. 3 (September 2012): 437–67.

Weaver, Vesla Mae. "Frontlash: Race and the Development of Punitive Crime Policy." *Studies in American Political Development* 21 (fall 2007): 230–65.

Webb, Lee. "Back Home: The Campus Beat." In NARMIC, *Police on the Homefront*, 1–20.

Weber, Diane Cecilia. "Warrior Cops: The Ominous Growth of Paramilitarism in American Police Departments." CATO *Institute Briefing Paper 50*. Washington, DC: CATO Institute, 1999.

Websdale, Neil. *Policing the Poor: From Slave Plantation to Public Housing*. Boston, MA: Northeastern University Press, 2001.

Weheliye, Alexander G. *Habeas Viscus: Racializing Assemblages, Biopolitics, and Black Feminist Theories of the Human*. Durham, NC: Duke University Press, 2014.

Weiss, Robert P. "From Cowboy Detectives to Soldiers of Fortune: Private Security Contracting and Its Contradictions on the New Frontiers of Capitalist Expansion." *Social Justice* 34, no. 3/4 (2007–8): 1–19.

Weld, Kirsten. "How the US Institutionalized Surveillance." *Al Jazeera America*, May 24, 2014. Accessed May 26, 2014. http://america.aljazeera.com/opinions /2014/5/institutionalizingsurveillanceusnsaguatemalaarchive.html.

———. *Paper Cadavers: The Archives of Dictatorship in Guatemala*. Durham, NC: Duke University Press, 2014.

White, Ahmed. "The Concept of 'Less Eligibility' and the Social Function of Prison Violence in Class Society." *Buffalo Law Review* 56 (2008): 737–820.

Wilderson, Frank B. *Incognegro: A Memoir of Exile and Apartheid*. Boston, MA: South End Press, 2008.

Wilkerson, Isabel. "Emmet Till and Tamir Rice, Sons of the Great Migration." *New York Times Sunday Review*, February 14, 2016, SR4.

Wilkinson, Richard G. "Why Is Violence More Common Where Inequality Is Greater?" *Annals of the New York Academy of Science* 1036 (2004): 1–12.

Williams, Brackette. *Classifying to Kill Killers: A Cognitive Ethnography of the U.S. Post-*Furman *Death Penalty.* Forthcoming.

Williams, Hubert, and Patrick V. Murphy. "The Evolving Strategy of Police: A Minority View." In *The Police and Society: Touchstone Readings,* edited by Victor Kappeler, 29–52. 2nd ed. Prospect Heights, IL: Waveland Press, 1999.

Williams, Kristian. *Our Enemies in Blue: Police and Power in America.* Cambridge, MA: South End Press, 2007.

Williams, Randall. *The Divided World: Human Rights and Its Violence.* Minneapolis: University of Minnesota Press, 2010.

Williams, Raymond. *Marxism and Literature.* Oxford: Oxford University Press, 1977.

Wilson, Christopher P. *Cop Knowledge: Police Power and Cultural Narrative in Twentieth-Century America.* Chicago: University of Chicago Press, 2000.

Wilson, James Q., and George L. Kelling. "Broken Windows." *Atlantic Monthly,* March 1982. Accessed October 15, 2015. http://www.theatlantic.com/magazine/archive/1982/03/broken-windows/304465.

Wilson, Jerry V. "Alternatives to Military Rank Titles in Law Enforcement." *Police Chief* 41, no. 4 (April 1974): 16–17, 82.

Windlesham, Lord [David James George Hennessy]. *Politics, Punishment, and Populism.* New York: Oxford University Press, 1998.

Wolcott, David B. *Cops and Kids: Policing Juvenile Delinquency in Urban America, 1890–1940.* Columbus: Ohio State University Press, 2005.

Wolfe-Hunnicutt, Brandon. "The End of the Concessionary Regime: Oil and American Power in Iraq, 1958–1972." PhD diss., Stanford University, 2011.

Wolfe, Justin. *The Everyday Nation-State: Community and Ethnicity in Nineteenth-Century Nicaragua.* Lincoln: University of Nebraska Press, 2007.

Wood, Reed M. "Rebel Capability and Strategic Violence against Civilians." *Journal of Peace Research* 47, no. 5 (September 2010): 610–14.

Woods, Clyde, ed. "In the Wake of Katrina: New Paradigms and Social Visions," special issue of *American Quarterly,* 61, no. 3 (September 2009).

———. *Development Arrested: The Blues and Plantation Power in the Mississippi Delta.* New York: Verso, 1998.

Woods, Gerald. *The Police in Los Angeles: Reform and Professionalization.* New York: Garland, 1993.

Wright, Steve. "New Police Technologies: An Exploration of the Social Implications and Unforeseen Impacts of Some Recent Developments." *Journal of Peace Research* 15, no. 4 (1978): 305–22.

Wu, Ellen. *The Color of Success: Asian Americans and the Origins of the Model Minority.* Princeton, NJ: Princeton University Press, 2014.

Wynter, Sylvia. "Unsettling the Coloniality of Being/Power/Truth/Freedom: Towards the Human, after Man, Its Overrepresentation—An Argument." CR: *The New Centennial Review* 3, no. 3 (2003): 257–337.

Yaro, B. "Retired Officers Going to Saigon." *Los Angeles Times*, October 1, 1966, n.p.

Yergin, Daniel. *The Prize: The Epic Quest for Oil, Money, and Power*. New York: Simon and Schuster, 1991.

Young, Jock. *The Criminological Imagination*. Cambridge, MA: Polity Press, 2011.

Young, Marilyn B. "Korea: The Post-War War." *History Workshop Journal* 51 (spring 2001): 112–26.

———. "Now Playing: Vietnam." OAH *Magazine of History* 18, no. 5 (October 2004): 22–26.

———. *The Vietnam Wars: 1945–1990*. New York: HarperCollins, 1991.

Young, Marilyn B., and Lloyd C. Gardner, eds. *Iraq and the Lessons of Vietnam: Or, How Not to Learn From the Past*. New York: New Press, 2007.

Zaharlick, Amy, and Jean Brainard. "Demographic Characteristics, Ethnicity and the Resettlement of Southeast Asian Refugees in the United States." *Urban Anthropology and Studies of Cultural Systems and World Economic Development* 16, no. 3/4 (fall–winter 1987): 327–73.

Zahn, Margaret. "Thoughts on the Future of Criminology—The American Society of Criminology 1998 Presidential Address." *Criminology* 37, no. 1 (1999): 1–15.

Zanetti, Diana L. "Admission of Refugees under the Revised Immigration and Nationality Act." *In Defense of the Alien* 7 (1984): 145–50.

Zeese, Kevin, and Margaret Flowers. "Ferguson Exposes the Reality of Militarized, Racist Policing." *Truthout*, August 18, 2014. Accessed October 17, 2014. http://truth-out.org/news/item/25645-ferguson-exposes-the-reality-of-militarized-racist-policing.

Zilberg, Elana. *Space of Detention: The Making of a Transnational Gang Crisis between Los Angeles and San Salvador*. Durham, NC: Duke University Press, 2011.

Zimring, Franklin E., Gordon Hawkins, and Sam Kamin. *Punishment and Democracy: Three Strikes and You're Out in California*. New York: Oxford University Press, 2001.

INDEX

Note: References to illustrations and photographs appear in *italics*.

(*PSN*): academic and educational work of, 112, 131–34, 137–38 (*see also* Federal Law Enforcement Training Center); anticommunism of, 150, 163–64, 175–78; and CIA, 113, 149, 153; conservatism of, 174–75; employment after OPS, 68–70, 84–85, 150–51, 228n24 (*see also* specific fields); feelings of exile and alienation among, 148–56, 174–75, 176–78; intelligence work of, 69–70, 113; involvement with the NRA, 245n103; military service of, 68–69; nationalism of, 15, 147–49, 163–64, 174–78; perceptions of, 150–52, 153–56, *154*, *155*, 240n19; police work by, 43–44, 81; prison work of, 44, 81–82; relationships with host nationals, 163–72, 242n58, 242n60, 243n62; relationships with Southeast Asian refugees, 146–78, 224n79, 241n29, 242n57; security work by, 77, 78–82, 84–86, 110–12, 113–14 (*see also* Wackenhut Security Corporation); work in Alaska, 16, 78–82; work in Saudi Arabia, 105–7, 109–14
Exxon Valdez spill, 226n99

Faisal (Crown Prince, then King). *See* bin Abdulaziz, Faisal
FBI. *See* Federal Bureau of Investigation
fear: as justification for increased policing, 48–49, 184–85; moral panics (*see* moral panics); of organized crime (*see* crime: organized); of the Other, 38–39
Federal Bureau of Investigation (FBI), 75, 84, 88, 116, 124
Federal Law Enforcement Training Center (FLETC), 131, 137–39
feeling, structure of, 92, 146–78, 240n5
Ferguson, James, 18
Finn, Thomas (ex-OPS), 43
First Line of Defense, The (OPS training film), 64
FLETC. *See* Federal Law Enforcement Training Center
Flitcraft, Ann, 144
FOA. *See* Foreign Operations Administration
Força Pública (paramilitary force in Brazil), 66–67. *See also* Brazil
Ford Foundation, 125

Foreign Assistance Act, 30, 103, 104, 105, 131
foreign assistance programs, 27–28, 30, 33–51, 58–62, 202n6, 212n14. *See also* Office of Public Safety
Foreign Operations Administration (FOA), 128
Fort Davis, 61
Foucault, Michel, 4, 6, 8, 19, 145, 198n68
Fowler, Dave (ex-OPS), 113
Friedman, Andrew, 171–72, 176

Garland, David, 141
gender, 20, 166–68, 243n67
GEO Group, Incorporated, The. *See* Wackenhut Security Corporation
Georgia Tech, 128
Gibson, Guy (ex-OPS), 80–81
Giddens, Anthony, 53
Gilmore, Ruth Wilson, 10, 11, 181
Gilmore, Ruth Wilson, and Craig Gilmore, 18, 19
Glen, Hill, 66
Goin, Lauren "Jack" (director of OPS), 71, 103, 104–7, 111
Goodchild, Arthur (ex-OPS), 110, 231n60
Gorham, Frank (ex-OPS), 81
Gramsci, Antonio, 5–6. *See also* "common sense"
Gray, Glenn (ex-OPS), 80, 98, 112
Greig, David (ex-OPS), 129
Grodsky, Morris (ex-OPS), 41–42, 65, 137–38, 150
Groshong, Tori (ex-OPS), 137
Guatemala, 68, 184, 217n67, 217n69
Guth, Stanley (ex-OPS), 133

Hall, Stuart, 74
Hallcrest Report, 87
Hallcrest Systems, 87
Halliburton, 119
Hardin, Herbert (ex-OPS), 104, 111
Harpold, Mike (exOPS), 151–52, *154*, 157–59
Hartman, Saidiya, 21
Hartung, William, 117
Hatem, Roy (ex-OPS), 43, 103–4, 230n45
helicopters, 46
Herrmann, William W. (ex-OPS), 44
Hertog, Steffen, 117–18
hijacking, 136

Holmes and Narver, 114, 115, 232n85
homicides, police. *See* police: killings by
Huff, Charlie (ex-OPS), 44
Huggins, Martha, 10–11, 53–54, 105
humanitarianism, 55–56

IACP. *See* International Association of
Chiefs of Police
IAPA. *See* Inter-American Police Academy
ICA. *See* International Cooperation
Administration
ICITAP. *See* International Criminal Investi-
gative Training Assistance Program
IDA. *See* Institute for Defense Analyses
incarceration, 19, 184–86. *See also* prison
system, US
Indiana, 133–34
Indiana University, 128, 133–34, 237n60
inequality, 22, 180–82, 185–88
Institute for Defense Analyses (IDA),
125–26, 210n86
Inter-American Police Academy (IAPA),
28, 61, 63, 64. *See also* Fort Davis; Inter-
national Police Academy
Internal Security Act of 1950, 88–89
International Association of Chiefs of
Police (IACP), 2, 28, 43. *See also Police
Chief* magazine
International Cooperation Administration
(ICA), 28. *See also* counterinsurgency
International Criminal Investigative Train-
ing Assistance Program (ICITAP), 30
International Police Academy (IPA), 15,
28, 68–69
IPA. *See* International Police Academy

Janson, Lowell (ex-OPS), 81
Jeffers, Frank (ex-OPS), 151
Jessup, Frank (ex-OPS), 133
Jew, Chester (ex-OPS), 137
Johnston, Les, 74
Joint Commission on Economic Coopera-
tion, 104–5

Kappeler, Victor, 53
Katzenbach, Nicholas, 40. *See also*
Katzenbach Commission
Katzenbach Commission, 39–40, 48
Kelley, Robin, 20

Kelling, George, 196n27
Kempa, Michael, 75
Kennedy, John F., 55
Kennedy, Robert, 35
Kenney, John (ex-OPS), 132–33
Kerner, Otto, 25. *See also* Kerner
Commission
Kerner Commission, 25, 26, 39–40, 48,
207n51
King Khalid Military City, 110, 114
Kirker, Bill (ex-OPS), 152
Klare, Michael, 63
Kraska, Peter, 53, 54

LAPD. *See* Los Angeles Police Department
LaRocca, Joe, 92
Larrimore, Jack (ex-OPS), 137
Laughlin, David (ex-OPS), 133
Law Enforcement Assistance Act of 1965,
40
Law Enforcement Assistance Administra-
tion (LEAA), 26, 40–50, 86, 87, 124–25,
134, 183
Law Enforcement Education Program
(LEEP), 124–25. *See also* Law Enforce-
ment Assistance Administration;
police: education and training of
LEAA. *See* Law Enforcement Assistance
Administration
LEEP. *See* Law Enforcement Education
Program
legitimacy. *See* police: legitimacy of
LEIU. *See* Association of Law Enforcement
Intelligence Units
lethality. *See* police: lethality of
Lewis, Jim (ex-OPS), 110, 111, 133, 134
Lingo, Joseph (ex-OPS), 133
Loan, [Nguyễn Ngọc], 171–72
Lochner v. New York (1905), 10
Lockhart, Wayne (ex-OPS), 112
London Metropolitan Police, 5
Looney, Margie and Morrie (ex-OPS),
152–53
Los Angeles Board of Police Commission-
ers, 35–36
Los Angeles Police Department (LAPD),
34–36, 38–39, 46–47, 204n25, 232n85
Lowe, Robert C. (ex-OPS), 42
Luna, Gregory (ex-OPS), 36–37

protest. *See also* riots and civil unrest: anti-war protests, 33–34; linked to riots and crime, 38–39; outside the US, 28, 101, 117, 131; over university involvement in violence work, 126, 128, 131; against police misconduct, 2–3, 186–87; technologies used to suppress, 45–47

PSN. *See Public Safety Newsletter*

public, 73–74. *See also* police: as public not private; state

Public Safety Newsletter (PSN), 30–33, *31*, *32*; discussion of refugees in, 156–57, 160, 161–63, 173–74, 241n45, 243n61, 244n81; role in reconnecting OPS and former counterparts, 168–69

Public Safety Service, Inc., 106

Putnam, Robert, 181

race and racism, 1–3, 20, 21, 38–39, 142–43, 174

racial capitalism, 19–22

RAND Corporation, 73, 86, 87, 223n63, 224n64

Redemption (historical period), 1–2

Refugee Act of 1980, 159

refugee assistance, 146–78, 241n29, 243n72

refugees: employment of, 173–74, 241n45, 243n61, 244n81; narratives about, 146–47, 158–60, 174, 242n51; relationships with ex-OPS employees, 163–72, 244n79 (*see also* ex-OPS employees); relationship to US state and empire, 176; violence work of, 172, 173–74

Reiman, Jeffrey, 182

Reynolds, Robert (ex-OPS), 43, 129

Rimke, Heidi, 182

riots and civil unrest. *See also* Katzenbach Commission; Kerner Commission: domestic disturbances compared to Third World, 33–40, 204n23; responses to, 33–34, 45–47, 48, 101, 209n82; studies of (*see* criminal justice); viewed as coequal with crime, 38–39, 219n87

Rodriguez, John (ex-OPS), 69

Rogers, Richard (ex-OPS), 137

Rohde, Joy, 126

Ryan, George W., 116. *See also* Arabian-American Oil Company

Ryan, Jack, 116

Sabol, Paul (ex-OPS), 69

Saenz, Adolf (ex-OPS), 64–65

Safe Streets Act, 124

Sam Houston State College, 112, 132

Sanders Associates, 99, 100, 226n3

ibn Saud, Abdulaziz (King), 101

Saudi Arabia, 99–110, 114, 117–18

scale. *See* police: as local and domestic

School of the Americas (SOA), 63

Scott, Monroe (ex-OPS), 113, 232n78

SEARCH. *See* System for Electronic Analysis and Retrieval of Criminal Histories

Section 607, 103, 104, 105. *See also* Foreign Assistance Act

security (myth of), 6–7

security companies. *See also* Pinkerton National Detective Agency; Wackenhut Security Corporation; William J. Burns International Detective Agency: acting as military, 75, 119; continuing OPS work after termination, 106–7; ex-OPS employees employed by, 77, 78–82, 84–86, 110–12, 113–14; refugees hired by, 173–74

security industry, 77–78, 83–84, 85, 87, 88–96, 224n67

Severson, Phil (ex-OPS), 44

Smith, Adam, 17

Smith, Stanford C. (ex-OPS), 52

SORO. *See* Special Operations Research Office

Sothan, Charles (ex-OPS), 81–82

sovereignty, 91–92

Sparks, Richard, 141

Special Group for Counterinsurgency, 59. *See also* counterinsurgency

Special Operations Research Office (SORO), 126

Spier, Del (ex-OPS), 113

sponsorship. *See* refugee assistance

Staley, Tom (ex-OPS), 79, 230n46

state: as assemblage, 198n68; as entwined with market, 75, 100, 114, 118–19, 125–27, 200n82 (*see also* market; state-market); as incoherent, 118; theorization of, 14–20, 96; violence of, 21–23, 52–54, 180–82

state effects, 18–19, 116

state-market, 19–23, 74–75, 100, 180–82, 185–88

State of Siege (film), 30, 134

STRATCOM. *See* Strategic Communications Command
Strategic Communications Command (STRATCOM), 218n71
structure of feeling, 92, 146–78, 240n5
surveillance systems, 183, 184
SWAT teams, 47, 183–84
System for Electronic Analysis and Retrieval of Criminal Histories (SEARCH), 47

Task Force Report: Science and Technology (1967), 47
tear gas, 46, 47
"technical" (as alibi for police operations), 27, 57, 63, 72, 100, 105, 107
technology: as answer to police misconduct, 2; as foreign aid, 99–100, 128; as increasing police lethality, 45–51, 180, 183–84 (*see also* police: lethality of); role of LEAA in funding (*see* Law Enforcement Assistance Administration)
territoriality, 12–15, 91–92, 176–77. *See also* nationalism; state
terrorism, 85, 89–91, 92–93
Third World: domestic disturbances compared to, 33–40, 204n23
Tiger Cage: An Untold Story, 153
Tilly, Charles, 10
Trainers, The, 139. *See also* Federal Law Enforcement Training Center
Trans Alaska Pipeline System, 76–77, 80, 89–94, 222n30
Treasury Law Enforcement Training School, 135–36
Truong, Michael T. *See* Truong, Tien M.
Truong, Tien M. (refugee, ex-OPS), 161–62, 170, *171*
Tullis, Tracy, 34, 209n82
Turner, Al (ex-OPS), 129, 135–37, 171–72, 238n71

United States Operations Missions (USOM), 129
universities, 112, 123, 126, 128, 131–34, 143–45. *See also* criminal justice education; police: education and training of; specific institutions

University of California at Berkeley: police academy of, 123, 234n2
University of Houston, 112, 132
University of Kentucky, 128
University of Southern California (USC), 128, 132–33
urban unrest. *See* riots and civil unrest
USAID. *See* Agency for International Development
USC. *See* University of Southern California
USOM. *See* United States Operations Missions

Vietnam, 30, 65, 128–29, 146–78
Vietnam War, 34, 38–39
Vinnell Corporation, 69, 112, 114, 117, 120
violence, 11, 179–82, 185–88, 199n63
violence work, 9–12, 22, 45–47, 49–50, 52–54, 96, 120, 123
violence workers, 9–15, 34–38, 120, 126–27, 137–39, 148–49, 175–78
Vollmer, August, 123–24
Vukovich, Paul (ex-OPS), 69, 111–12, 231n61

Wackenhut Security Corporation, 16, 77, 80, 82–83, 84–85, 86, 222n41
Wagner, Bryan, 3
Wagner, Gunther (ex-OPS), 110, 113
Walker, Samuel, 125
Walters, Glenn (ex-OPS), 113
Walton, Frank (ex-OPS), 114, 129
Weatherwax, Bob (ex-OPS), 129
Weber, Max, 10
Weiss, John (ex-OPS), 103
Weld, Kirsten, 184
Whalen, Walter (ex-OPS), 133
William J. Burns International Detective Agency, 74–75
Williams, Gerald (ex-OPS), 81
Williams, Raymond, 147, 240n5
women, 164–68, 216n59, 243n62, 243n72

Yarborough, William P., 37
Young, Gordon (ex-OPS), 112, 232n68
Young, Jock, 143

Ziegler, John (ex-OPS), 112–13